Paradigms Regained

Pluralism and the Practice of Criticism

James L. Battersby

D0081742

upp

University of Pennsylvania Press   Philadelphia

Copyright © 1991 by James L. Battersby
All rights reserved
Printed in the United States of America

Library of Congress Cataloging-in-Publication Data

Battersby, James L.
    Paradigms regained : pluralism and the practice of criticism / James L. Battersby.
        p.   cm.
    Includes bibliographical references and index.
    ISBN 0-8122-3127-9
    1. Criticism. 2. Pragmatism. 3. Pluralism. I. Title.
PN81.B384   1991
801'.95—dc   91-18260
                                                                                      CIP

PN
81
B384
1991

FLORIDA STATE
UNIVERSITY LIBRARIES

JUL 22 1992

TALLAHASSEE, FLORIDA

for
LISA

Contents

Acknowledgments ix

Preface xi

Introduction: The Theory Market in a World Without a
Gold Standard 1

Part One: Problem Setting and Pluralism

1. Putting Pluralism on the Map 21
2. Map States and State Maps 40

Part Two: References, Meanings, Worlds

3. Eclecticism, or Worlds in Collision 57
4. Stable Worlds in Different Space-Times 63
5. Worlds Unacceptable, Irrelevant, or
Incommensurable 79
6. Incommensurable Worlds 119
7. Paradox Undone: Meaning, Reference, and Cognitive
Sameness 132

Part Three: Ad Hoc Categories and Textual Interests

8. Interpretation All the Way Down 161

9. Meaning and Available Scenarios   169

10. From Readers to Writers, Interpretation to Making   182

11. Human "Nature" and Language "Universals"   197

12. Intentions, Interests, Preferences, Choices   209

Part Four: Worlds Well Founded and Worlds Well Lost

13. Making Mistakes, Making Amends, Making Do   233

14. Conclusion: Worlds Without End   247

Notes   267

Bibliography   285

Index   299

Acknowledgments

At every stage in the making of this book I have been the beneficiary of wise counsel and generous assistance. And however well or ill-disposed my benefactors may be to public acknowledgment of their contribution—whether admonitory, cautionary, instigatory, editorial, or administrative—to the product before you, it is now my pleasant task to name names, to identify my witting and unwitting accomplices and confederates. To them every reader is indebted, for without their persistent efforts this work would have been at once more corpulent and less fit for public trials. If this text still pants and sweats occasionally, the incorrigibility of the recruit, not the regimen of the drill instructors, is to be faulted. Without further ceremony, then, I proceed to my "without whoms."

To the Trustees of the Ohio State University, the members of the Research Committees of the Graduate School and the College of Humanities (and especially to the Dean of the College, Michael Riley), I am, in the language of understatement, more than a little grateful for the invaluable gifts of financial assistance and released time from teaching. My colleagues, Mark Conroy and Walter Davis, gave the fledgling manuscript just what it needed, just at the moment of need: tough reading and strong encouragement. Also, when the text required special care and attention—when, that is, index, bibliography, and final copy had to be just right, just now, and somewhere else no later than yesterday—I was fortunate to have the remarkably intelligent and wonderfully efficient assistance of Natalie Tyler (who served ably as reader and critic as well as bibliographer extraordinaire), David Sims, and Gareth Euridge. Also, I have been especially fortunate in finding at the University of Pennsylvania Press editors who were boundless in their patience, generosity, and kindness, and who in innumerable ways made smooth what was rugged in my argument and prose, most notably Jerome Singerman and Alison Anderson.

I am also deeply indebted to William E. Cain and Ralph Rader, who by timely provision of careful reading, good advice, and friendly but unsparing criticism did much to sharpen my thought and gladden my heart. Beyond hope of repaying, I am indebted to three colleagues, the very three Plato encountered when he emerged from the cave of shadows, David Riede, James Phelan, and Lisa Kiser, each of whom read every word in every version of this work and forced me by gentle and rough persuasion to think again and again about this and that and countless other things. I cannot convince myself that I have always met their challenges and objections, but I shall make it my study now and in the future to deserve their care. Finally, there is the first of the "without whoms," the last named colleague above, to whom this book is dedicated; the professional work of this good woman, this scholar-critic, is literally the matter of legends (as every medievalist will testify), and my gratitude to her will not find remission from daily exercise, whilst this machine is to him.

Preface

When this book first took spade in hand, it had in view only a little groundclearing in the field of critical theory and, subsequently, some practical farming of the interpretive kind. But groundclearing in the rocky terrain of theory proved to be a more extensive and arduous employment than anticipated, and thus the labors and rewards of practical activity have been largely deferred. Less tropologically, this book can best be described as a reclamation project, an effort at once to recover for daily use much of what has been discarded as outmoded or worthless by current critical theory, especially by Marxist, Freudian, Lacanian, Bakhtinian, Foucauldian, deconstructive, New Historicist, or, in a word, poststructuralist theory, *and* to restore, if not to primacy at least to legitimacy, much in humanistic inquiry that has been rejected as oppressively and viciously reactionary (i.e., sexist, racist, or classist) by many current theorists. Generally speaking, the aim throughout has been to emphasize the importance and to defend the philosophical respectability of *phronēsis* (practical reasoning and knowledge) and *technē* (productive ability and knowledge) which have consistently been devalued (at best) by many modern theorists, who have made the valorization of theoretical knowledge (*epistēmē*) their business.

Despite their many differences, modern theorists by and large share the view that there is no mind- or discourse-independent world of things that authorizes or validates our claims and against which our assertions must be squared. And as the world (reality) goes, so goes the text as the bearer of stable, determinate meaning to which our interpretive statements must be adjusted and against which our opinions must be tested for accuracy and appropriateness. The prevailing doctrine, then, is that once meaning goes immanent, once, that is "things" and "thoughts"—and all that follows in their wake (facts, values, concepts, etc.)—go inside conceptual schemes, inside the language by which they are constituted what they are, then objectivity, determinate meaning, truth, justification, valid interpretation, and so on must be given up. Concomitantly with the loss of these goes the loss of authors, stable texts, and standards of value, since they are all nothing but precipitates of *always already* in place categories and systems of meaning that are themselves caught up in the endless deferral and supplementation of meaning characteristic of *language as such*. Most theorists are also united in their belief that disagreement with these principal articles of faith necessarily entails commitment, however inadvertent, to some form of naive realism, essentialism, or foundationalism.

The issues raised and the commonplaces problematized by the literary theorists are, of course, nothing other than locally differentiated avatars of more general and pervasive concerns of modern philosophy, both Continental and Anglo-American. If, broadly speaking, we have on the Continental side a preoccupation *either* with the endless deferral of meaning, the loss of stability in signifier and signified, and the emergence of the *other* to undermine or subvert what is affirmed on the surface (what is logocentrically asserted) *or* with the determination of the speaking and the spoken, the writing and the written by social, political, cultural, ideological conditions, we have on the Anglo-American side a concentration of attention on either the *incommensurability* of languages (theories, conceptual schemes), the view that each language is unique and, thus, not translatable into any other language, or the *inderterminancy of meaning*, the view that there are just too many statements (theories, meanings) that are compatible with the data. In the philosophical debates, as in those strictly focused on literary theory, the chief and disesteemed antagonists are objectivity, stability of reference across conceptual differences, and interpretation or translation.

Against the grain of much of the accepted wisdom this book rubs energetically, especially in its various attempts to demonstrate that in a world deprived of a (mind-independent) Foundation or a (discourse-independent) Transcendental Signified, it is still possible to talk usefully and intelligently about stable references and meanings across theoretical differences or conceptual schemes, about determinate meaning in and objective value judgment of literary and other works, about better and worse conceptual schemes or interpretations, and about much else currently under proscription. In place of the skepticism of deconstruction and the radical relativism of a host of critics (e.g., Barbara Herrnstein Smith, Stanley Fish, and many New Historicists), this text makes a case for a philosophically defensible pluralism (i.e., a relativism with muscles, with defeasibility criteria), a pluralism entirely compatible with what Hilary Putnam calls "internal realism" and Nelson Goodman "constructionalism." Briefly, this text works within a pluralist tradition of philosophical pragmatism. By extending, revising, and eliciting support from recent studies in the philosophy of mind (Putnam, Goodman, et al.), interpretation and mental representation (Davidson, Scheffler, et al.), and category formation (Lakoff, Johnson, Fillmore, et al.), this book seeks to show that notwithstanding revolutionary claims—there is nothing outside the text; everything is ideological; there are no texts or authors, but only a mosaic of signs; and so on—nothing in recent literary theory (in either its hermeneutic or its cultural/historical mode) has rendered obsolete, invalid, or second-rate inquiries into authors, interpretation, intentionality, determinate meaning, objective value judgments, and much else traditionally valued in Western criticism.

One important consequence of the elaboration and defense of the pragmatic, pluralist alternative to current opinion that can appropriately be mentioned here is a new understanding of interpretation and of the verification procedures of interpretive practice. In short, the arguments in support of intentionality and of stable reference and meaning across conceptual systems lead ineluctably to the substantiation of the rejected notion that the texts we confront, literary and otherwise, are already systems of meaning and justification when we confront them. The text is already a version or interpretation when we meet it. It is not a tablet on which we are free to write our scripture or on which successive dominant ideologies have *always already* imposed meanings, but, instead, a system of preregistered intentional satisfactions, a system answerable to its own justification or satisfaction conditions.

If the argument is tendentious in the meliorative or neutral sense of the term, so too is the style or manner of presentation. The occasional playfulness of the style seeks throughout to engage and please the good nature rather than to require the indulgence of the reader. Moreover, and more important, much of the sylistic exuberance is part of a deliberate if surreptitious strategy, making its own independent contribution to the assault on many contemporary practices.

Many theorists today comment repeatedly on the breakdown of distinctions among "kinds" of writing, insisting, for example, that the various traditional branches of inquiry—philosophy, history, psychology, literature—all reduce to literature or rhetoric (since all are "fictive" and "figural"), and that though all writing is caught up in the "play" of signification, some writing is especially valuable for its "jouissance," its energetic tropological enthusiasm. On the other hand, a depressing amount of this liberating talk of the literary status of theoretical writing is transported in the most turgid, obscurantist, convoluted, and impenetrable prose vehicle imaginable. In fact some polemicists, like Fredric Jameson and other Marxists or New Historicists, attempt to make a political virtue of obfuscation and stylistic infelicity by claiming that clear, perspicuous, accessible prose is a tool of oppression. Clarity is thus to intellectual discourse what the bayonet is to diplomacy or colonialism to native populations.

What I have attempted to show is that one can express complex arguments in clear, perspicuous, and lively prose without becoming a right-wing intellectual or an ideological reactionary, and that one can write metaphorically rich theoretical "literature" without subscribing to some hateful social program. Although I have no illusions about the literary *merit* of this book, I also have doubts about its *literary* qualities. The text is laced quite unparsimoniously with figural and rhetorical devices, recurrent metaphors and image patterns, and topical refrains and leitmotifs. Moreover, the biographical-personal and Rhode Island-centered nature of many of these recurrences works persistently, I think, to make this very much an author-conspicuous and author-driven book. The words, phrases, and ideas to which I turn again and again contribute quietly and unobtrusively to the points I make clearly and loudly in the text about meaning, reference, and intentionality and about how coming to an understanding of language in use requires the learning of a practice; readers learn *my practice* and the peculiar projectible properties of my discourse while reading, thus confirming inadvertently on their own pulses what I am arguing for openly.

With two caveats, this brief prefatory and preparatory essay can be concluded. First, the reader should recognize that while this book regularly supports its arguments with evidence taken from literary texts (including works written by, among many others, Dickinson, Shakespeare, Samuel Johnson, Wordsworth, Mark Akenside, Henry James), it most frequently draws on homely, "everyday" materials, on short, simple open-faced narratives, and on "chestnut" cases to illustrate its theoretical points. (This appeal to deceptively simple, easily grasped yet inherently rich examples and illustrative cases is very much in the philosophical tradition that this book aspires to follow— one thinks immediately perhaps of Totally Omniscient Jones; of the rabbit-duck; of *gavagai*, the jungle term translatable as, among numerous other things, "rabbit" or "undetached rabbit part"; of Twin Earth water; etc.) The virtue of these simple, reader-friendly examples is that they are not weighted down with accumulated controversy and thus can be considered in terms of the theoretical issues they raise and apart from factional interests. Of course, the burden is on those who disagree with the positions advanced in the book to show that what applies to these minimalist, everyday cases does not apply in exactly the same way to the more sophisticated literary cases or texts. Second, it is essential that the reader recognize that the pluralism, or "internal realism," for which this text attempts to provide an intellectual justification is not itself a practice; it is a position on practices. Although it makes possible many practices (indeed, all right, good, and true practices), it is not itself a particular practice. Thus this "theoretical" essay necessarily avoids extended exercises in practical criticism or analysis. To perform this or that exercise in such criticism would be to run the risk of confusing practice and principle and of appearing to recommend, in fact, to endorse a particular practice. What pluralism, following Putnam, steadfastly affirms is that "no theory or description is right for all purposes" or, correlatively, that many theories or descriptions are right under various circumstances of justification.

Introduction:
The Theory Market in a World
Without a Gold Standard

In certain academic circles—let us call them the hermeneutic circles or the humanities—it is a truth almost universally acknowledged that one can no longer be seriously engaged in literary study (or philosophy, law, history, cultural studies, and so on) without "doing theory" or without showing that whatever one is doing is sanctioned by or, at a minimum, not incompatible with or proscribed by *theory*. By the phrase "doing theory" we mean not the articulation of some particular intellectual position or the exercise of some particular critical practice but the expression of fealty in some form or other to a complex knot of beliefs and assumptions best characterized perhaps by its stark difference from the knot of discredited beliefs and assumptions informing *humanism*. At any rate, whatever humanism is or entails is anathema to theory.

And, of course, even those who reject theory, in the sense of turning away from approaches that consider language apart from "concrete social formations" or consider discourse apart from its historical (social, cultural, political, and, hence, ideological) dimensions—as deconstructionists, for example, tend to do—take certain "truths" of theory to be self-evident or established beyond the possibility of doubt. These critics—various Marxists, feminists, Foucauldians, New Historicists, and others—do theory even as they reject one kind of theorizing within the space opened up by *theory*. In brief, whatever may have been the case a few short years ago, when Walter Jackson Bate, M. H. Abrams, and others were talking about a crisis in criticism, evidently under the supposition that it could be averted or overcome, the consensus today is that everything worth doing rests in one way or another on the secure insights into language (or discourse) provided by structuralist and poststructuralist thought. Further, it is also generally assumed today that such insights have rendered most "traditional" interests or inquiries uninteresting, obsolete, inadmissible, or impossible. Those—like Bate, Abrams, Wayne Booth, E. D. Hirsch, and others—who fail to subscribe to these insights or who occasionally let their subscriptions lapse (occasional conformists) are guilty, it seems, of endorsing or backsliding into positivism, into some form of foundationalism, essentialism, or naive realism.

This long essay attempts to clear some space for projects and assumptions presumably "discredited" by much in structuralist and poststructuralist theory without at the same time falling victim to positivism or foundationalism. The way this essay finds is pluralism. By this designation, however, we are referring not to the undiscriminating, club-joining, gladhanding, hail-fellow-well-met pluralism of general acquaintance; not to the melting pot, transactional analysis, I'm-O.K.-you're-O.K., anything goes pluralism of common indulgence; not to the knee-callused orisant at the ecumenical altar, the Will Rogerian, intellectual unitarian who never met a scheme, theory, approach he didn't like, the softminded, tolerant fellow of "liberal democracy." We are referring, rather, to what for convenience—and in an effort to differentiate it from its obsequious and nonconsanguineous namesake—might be called "philosophical pluralism," a kind of pluralism worth knowing, one capable of discrimination and selection, of making better and worse determinations and good and bad, right and wrong judgments, of applying standards of acceptability to disputed cases. The pluralism that has our interest, in short, is one capable of objectivity; this pluralism is indistinguishable, finally, from—or at least compatible with—what Hilary Putnam has called "internal realism" and Nelson Goodman "constructionalism."[1]

At the outset it is important to recognize that this essay has as its primary aims the description and justification of a kind of pluralism that is for the most part a stranger to the residents of theory (as well as to all those for whom the term is equivalent to unquestioning, undiscriminating, all-embracing tolerance). Consequently, alternative "isms" or approaches are discussed only broadly and in passing for purposes of contrast, distinction, or illustration (though Mikhail Bakhtin's "ideologemes" and selected aspects of New Criticism, "interpretive community-ism," deconstruction, and historicism are examined in some detail). Nevertheless, in developing the positive case I have given emphasis to those elements of pluralism that speak directly to what the theorists have, as the saying goes, *put into question.* In general, however, I have not keyed my discussions to particular arguments in the theoretical literature (except when it would be ungenerous or impossible to avoid such keying) and have assumed in the reader sufficient familiarity with the current critical scene to recognize when and how my case applies to or challenges specific alternative views. More broadly, I have assumed throughout this essay that anything inconsistent or incompatible with the pluralism outlined here, even though not explicitly dealt with in the essay, is theoretically or practically deficient in one or another respect. In other words, to the extent that any critical approach or any aspect of that approach offends a stated or implied principle or value of pluralism, it is to that extent (but only to that extent) rejected (implicitly) as intellectually unacceptable. For example, much in contemporary poststructuralist theory exemplifies or slouches toward monism or "anything goes" relativism and is, thus, just that much offensive to the pluralism-worth-knowing.

By developing the positive case, especially those parts of it running counter to the prevailing views, I have been able to avoid being engaged in a series of negative analyses and, I hope, to elude the charge of unrepresentative and unfair selection, of talking, for example, about this critic but not that one, about the early but not the late work of this or that critic, about the shorter but not the longer pieces, and so on. Even so, I have everywhere concentrated on matters central to current debate, frequently putting questions to what others have "put into question" and regularly examining their *authority* for doing so in a world in which, as they persistently and rightly maintain, meaning and reference have gone immanent, in a world in which meaning and reference, objects and values are grounded, not in some transcendent order of things, but in some particular order of immanence, some particular conceptual scheme. Operating in the background of this essay and governing to a large extent its topics, then, are the issues on which theory has spoken authoritatively in the voice of either denunciation or affirmation, in a mood of either joy or terror.

From the perspective of pluralism, theory has accomplished much. On balance, however, despite its talk about "free play" (as in the "free play of the signifier"), its willingness to join together the most heterogeneous views (those, for example, of Freud, Marx, Jacques Derrida, Michel Foucault, and others) in the most amazing olios, and its general inability to supply any principled grounds for excluding any view whatsoever (to enunciate any principles of defeasibility, to recognize any constraints on, for example, interpretive liberty), as long as that view was free of even the slightest taint of "positivism" or "essentialism," theory has tended rather to narrow than to open inquiry, to retard than to promote critical diversity. And it has done so for the most part in two ways.

First, it has limited concern, generally speaking, to *language* or "discourse-centered" matters (i.e., to matters of sign and code relations or to discursive practices made possible by ruling elites from epoch to epoch, the practices allegedly governing what it is possible to say in any particular field at some given point in history, the rules and procedures speaking and spoken by the political or ideological unconscious of the era and manifest in quite the same form in all its diverse artifacts and cultural products, however apparently various their surface features).

Second, it has ruled out of court all "unsponsored" inquiries (inquiries, for example, into intentionality, determinate meaning, or interpretation) on the ground that they are wittingly or unwittingly committed to metaphysical foundations, are in the grip of or under the spell of one or another logocentric delusion.

Full justification of these claims cannot be provided here, of course, but something can be done by way of illustration. For example, it is not uninstructive to observe J. Hillis Miller equating theory with "an orientation toward language *as such*" [emphasis added]. According to this view, theory makes possible, indeed inevitable, "deconstructive rhetorical reading," makes possible, that is, "real reading," which is a "recognition of the way the rhetorical or tropological dimension of language undermines straightforward grammatical and logical meaning," as well as "an attempt, no doubt an impossible attempt, to confront what language itself has *always already* erased or forgotten, namely, the performative or positional power of language as inscription over what we catachrestically call the material."[2] This latter attempt to get at "things" or what the Marxist might call the "materiality," at real, historical, social, material conditions is impossible—*always already*, as these critics are fond of saying, always and permanently impossible—because the "materiality" is always, necessarily, mediated by language. Or, as Miller would have it, language *erases* what it names by standing in its place. Of course, in this deconstructive, rhetorical scheme, the name or signifier, along with its signified or meaning, refuses to stay in place. It floats and shifts, because language in this scheme *just is* a system of differential relations, of differences, traces, and supplements without center or anchor.

Similarly, something can undoubtedly be learned about the peculiar proclivities of theory from the following description of its operational agility, one which exhibits not only its customary maneuvers but its ability to find a mattress for some odd bedfellows, to combine, for example, structuralism and deconstruction, Saussure, Foucault, and Derrida, referentiality and nonreferentiality, the historical and the nonhistorical. To expose the "invisible apparatus" of English studies (or anything else for that matter), "we can proceed in what is now [1985] a *classic* structuralist/deconstructive mode of analysis. First we will locate *the binary oppositions* which organize the flow of value and power in our institution; then we will proceed to criticize or *undo* the *invidious* structure of those oppositions."[3] This description perhaps presents the warrior of theory dwindled to a beau, the solemn ceremony echoed in a harlequinade, the butterfly reduced to a windup toy, but it displays in clear epitome the underlying structure of countless dark and dense essays in the allegorical mode favored by theory, as one cultural product after another succumbs to one or another brilliantly inventive variation on the tediously iterative routine of predictable, mechanical analysis.

That there is much "reading" and "analysis" of the kind highlighted here going on today can be attributed undoubtedly to the widespread—virtually universal (in the universe that concerns us)—belief that only such reading as is either informed by or consonant with structuralist and poststructuralist insights into language (and, hence, into meaning and reference) can be intellectually justified. Even postmodern Marxists, Freudians, and New Historicists—even those, that is, with something of a vested interest in extralinguistic "facts" and "conditions"—have learned to read their words in "textual" terms, to reinterpret their interests in textual terms. And even those critics[4] whose real interests have taken them to what they embarrassedly recognize as "traditional" areas of concern have felt obliged to trick their productions out in modish linguistic garb or to buzz the sanctioned words at regular intervals in their humble, unsophisticated statements. Looking over the program of a recent Modern Language Association meeting, J. Hillis Miller observes that "even papers that were in fact old-fashioned *positivistic* literary history were dressed up . . . [to] sound theoretical."[5]

What Miller detects in the program is, of course, a general tendency variously manifested in literary (and other) studies today. It has come to pass that every critic *must* "do theory"; thus every critic needs to give every project, if not a poststructuralist slant, at least a poststructuralist ambience or vocabulary, while at the same time avoiding any locution that carries the slightest hint of what Miller, in a broad sweep, calls "positivism" and is elsewhere called "essentialism," "foundationalism," or "naive realism." The manifestations of this tendency cannot have gone unnoticed by anyone who has watched graduate students struggling to find dissertation topics or to make their yeomanly projects "theoretical," scanned the tables of contents of even the most "traditional," philological journals over the last few years, interviewed recent Ph.D.'s for assistant professorships, or witnessed colleagues on the verge of writing or submitting an essay for publication attempting to chart the rising and falling stock of now one and now another poststructuralism (as commodity traders in theory deal frantically and aggressively in "ism" futures, now selling Derrida low and now buying Bakhtin or Foucault or some hybrid "New Historicism" high).

Despite here and there some play with crude essentialist assumptions in the backwaters and on the sandlots of criticism, the poststructuralist game is really the only intellectual game in town, it seems. Only its views, we are repeatedly assured, "have legs." Obviously we cannot here track down all the common assumptions of theory in their manifoldly diverse representations in a vast array of specific writings, disentangle the perplexities of relation among distinct views, or delineate clearly the contradictions and disputes within the ranks of belief. Still, we can provide a fair, if somewhat crude, outline sketch of the bundle of beliefs or "truths" upon which the faith of theory depends.

Caveat lector—the reader should note that in presenting this bundle I, like the theorists whose beliefs I aim to describe, am not very fussy about consistency or greatly concerned about coherence, comprehensiveness, or contradiction. I am interested in what some theorists might call the *habitus* or the *archive* or the *political unconscious*, in what we talk with, not what we talk about, or in what we speak from, what precedes and speaks us, as the theorists might say. The reader who is made uncomfortable by the following sketch of theory at large is invited to revise and refine the sketch so that it conforms to his/her particular congeries of beliefs and operational principles and then to consider only so much of the following long essay in defense of pluralism as conflicts with his/her conception of things. If no conflict emerges, then the reader is either a closet pluralist, a pluralist in spite of himself, a *very* determined reader, one capable of adjusting all remarks to the dimensions of his conceptual bed, or a card-carrying member of "anything goes" relativism, the largest union in theory.

In brutal brevity, then, we would register the following as among the "truths" held to be self-evident by theory.

1. There is no unmediated vision, and, thus, no direct perception of things as they are in themselves. Such things as can be noted and discussed are contaminated through and through and from the beginning with *textuality*, that is, with our categories and signs. Consequently, we can have no objective knowledge of the world and no absolute truths.

2. Theories of knowing customarily provide some account of the relationship of *words, thoughts,* and *things*; and the principal logocen-

tric or foundationalist view is that truth entails a felicitous correspondence of our words to our thoughts and of our words and thoughts
to the mind- and discourse-independent things of the world. It is
with this world that what we say must be squared, or, perhaps more
clearly and forcefully put, this world is the maker good and true of
our assertions. Now, in *theory*, the "things" of the traditional "words-
thoughts-things" correspondence model are displaced or bracketed.
In effect, the traditional model is discarded and replaced by a "sign-
signifier/signified" model, in which linguistic elements achieve meaning not as a result of their reference (and correspondence) to existent
things, but as a result of their relations to other elements in a (sign)
system. In these systems no element is ever simply present. Each element depends for its meaning on its place in the system. There are
no positives, no positive presences, but only such presences as the
abstract relations of the system make possible (simply put, "tap" is
impossible, indeed inconceivable apart from the "top," "tip," "tag,"
"tan" system of differential relations). What counts, then, is the *langue*
(the rules and procedures governing structural systems), not the *pa-
role* (the individual utterance or writing), since the particular expressions are but local manifestations of systemic possibilities, are the
effects of rule-governed possibilities.

With such insights come, among other things, the dropping of
many scales from the eyes and the demystification of literature. For
if meaning (as well as reference) is the consequence of such relations,
then clearly the source and origin of meaning (to the extent that we
can speak of the source and origin at all) is no longer the author, but
the system of rules and procedures through which he operates or,
more properly put, which operates through him (the system itself is
without origin; it and each and every one of its elements are always
already prior to our recognition or mentioning; the origin is at the
end of an infinite regress). As Jonathan Culler, summing up the
structuralist enterprise, has noted: "although the human sciences begin by making man the object of knowledge, these disciplines find, as
their work advances, that the text is dissolved as its various functions
are ascribed to impersonal systems which operate through it."[6] And
as the author goes, so goes the reader, who becomes simply another
site of already-in-place textuality, because . . . .

3. Everything "knowable" and "discussable" is, as we have inti-
mated above, "already written," is without an origin or center. The
reader is no more empowered than the writer to "authorize" or delimit meanings. What is distinguished or identified is already part of
a system of differences (otherwise, it would not be noted or distinguishable). As Derrida informs us, "there never has been anything

but writing; there have never been anything but supplements, substitutive significations which could only come forth in a chain of differential references, the 'real' supervening, and being added only while taking a meaning from a trace and from an invocation of the supplement, etc."[7]

4. Texts go the way of authors and readers. Reading—or interpretation—becomes a rhetorical, allegorical, tropological, figural enterprise, because at bottom language is essentially figurative rather than referential, with one term or idea always implicated in or standing in for some other term or idea. Further, all reading is misreading, the attempt of one set of terms to stand for or stand in for another set (every text is a palimpsest, and every reading adds a layer to what is always already highly stratified). Moreover, those readings are best that act in complicity with the text's own deconstructive tendencies to be the cankerworm of its own rose, its tendencies to undermine or undo its own assertions.

5. On the other hand, or collaterally, although there is no center or origin, no grounding for reference, no extralinguistic, mind- or discourse-independent validator of our saying and writing, and, thus, no hope of achieving objective knowledge, and no way to establish— that is, prove—by some impartial tests or standards the validity of this as opposed to that view, *although all this is so*, it is nevertheless and also true that *what counts* as "true," "good," "natural," and "right" is determined by the changing interests of power elites from period to period. We cannot—it is here assumed—give up the historical dimension of discourse (as some deconstructionists seem inclined to do), while we are dispensing with authors, readers, and texts, inasmuch as when discourse is absorbed into the vast ether of language or allowed to whirl uncontrollably in the vortex of the abyss, we lose not only the discernible differences in social practices from epoch to epoch, but our means of accounting for their emergence and dissolution in changing ideological commitments and structures. What is spoken and what is speakable derives, we can be assured, from the always already written, always already in place constraints and the rules of the dominant ideology.

Every ideology is, as Fredric Jameson declares, a "strategy of containment," designed to master "revolution" and to suppress the contradictions necessarily implicated in its discourse (necessarily, of course, because of the nature of language *as such*), the contradictions that, if realized and foregrounded, would release revolutionary energies and lead to the emergence of a new ideology, which would newly define "truth," "freedom," the "natural," etc. The dialectic of history is a *discursive* dialectic, and discourse is "dialectical" because history/language is differential/antithetical; in every "positive" or "present" element of history/language there lurks the *other*, the different, usually antithetical other. (I here close the analogical space between discourse and history. History is dialectical, discourse differential; history is like discourse and discourse like history in that both disclose or are underwritten by the same mechanisms, the same binary features and operations.) And if Jameson—and others—send history to the school of Discourse, Jacques Lacan—and others—see to it that Freud matriculates at the selfsame academy, so that subjectivity can learn something about the instability of signification and the importance of the "other."

Further, notwithstanding the variety and degrees of complexity and sophistication of the discourses of an epoch, no discourse is privileged over any other discourse. There are no standards, no objective tests, no agreed-upon criteria in which adjudication can be grounded. Moreover, in some versions in which the notion of a ruling political/cultural unconscious figures prominently, we cannot in either speaking or understanding transcend the "historical" conditions of our own era, cannot transcend the immediate, local determinants of our speaking and thinking. The limits of consciousness are coterminous with the boundaries of our "archive." The past, along with everything else, is always filtered through our "archive," and thus meaning and understanding are always dependent upon and reflective of the historical and archival status of the interpreter. In short, the only past or the only text that we can know is the one constituted by the interests and categories of our epoch.

6. Switching from macropolitical communities to what have been called "interpretive communities," we find analogous formations and conditions. Reading (within a discipline) can occur only because, as Stanley Fish claims, "a set of interpretive assumptions is always in force."[8] The properties of texts—their "facts," references, meanings, values, etc.—are determined by readers rather than by authors. But readers are themselves precipitates of already existing categories and conceptual principles, for the "thoughts an individual can think and the mental operations he can perform have their source in some or other interpretive community. . . . It is interpretive communities, rather than either the text or the reader, that produce meanings and are responsible for the emergence of formal features."[9] In determining the facts, emphases, and values of the text, along with consciousness itself (its categories of thought and principles of inference), the "interpretive community" necessarily determines the "reasonable" as well, determines, that is, what counts as a good question and as a satisfactory answer. In short, the "reasonable" is itself something

internal to the interpretive system or discursive practice. Consequently, one community cannot *prove* its case to another community, demonstrate to another community the superior explanatory power of its view (of course, in extremis, one community cannot speak to, understand, or even acknowledge another community).

As a result, demonstration yields to persuasion, and persuasion is simply another name for power; in the "small world" of literary studies, as in the larger world of the political unconscious, might makes right. Persuasion reduces to power, the smile to the shove, when the parties to the debate cannot agree on the "facts," on what counts as evidence or proof, or on when the issues have been joined, mooted, or resolved. In general, however, many communities are recognized, though none, alas, can be chosen, that is chosen *over* another. None can be privileged relative to others, since any ground of preference would either presuppose the normative authority of the categories of one community or depend upon some agreed-upon, criterial value that was neither internal nor partial to any particular community.

7. In conclusion, the structuralist reader initially sought nothing so much as objective, "scientific" mastery over all texts by gaining access to the inner and deep operational imperatives of sign systems, the rules and procedures of systems considered apart from personal, local, historic, or "parolic" distractions. Here is postmodern theory in its "positivistic moment," when it was engaged in the production of something analogous to what was elsewhere called "logical positivism" or "set theory." In the movement to poststructuralist times, however, this structuralist reader has learned that such mastery is impossible; that readers and texts are mighty opposites engaged in interminable contests in which meaning and readability are always leaving traces while remaining just beyond reach; that texts and readers are equally intertextual, are equally sites of the already written, or crossroads where many already-in-place texts and voices meet; that there is no mastering what one is mastered by (the political or historical/cultural unconscious or, simply, the slip-slidingness or "un*present*-ability" of language itself); and that no master (or asserted or announced meaning) can escape having his (or its) oppressive and repressive practices undone by the suppressed, marginalized, but nevertheless potent slave within the impersonal system.

In rough form, then, such is the composite sketch of theory. To those undertaking a career in literary studies (or, more properly, cultural or discourse studies) today, these beliefs and assumptions (in some combination or other and with allowance made here and there for some addition, subtraction, and substitution) are fundamental conditions of existence. They are, so to speak, the center and origin of most inquiries and the underlying presuppositions of most essays, of those at any rate aspiring to or not wishing to incur the wrath of theory. Language, signs, discourse, and discursive formations and operations have taken center stage, leaving no roles or only bit parts for authors (as makers of artistic structures), readers (as interpreters or translators of authorially determined prior meanings), interpretation, determinate meaning, and clear, unequivocal reference. The new scripts of theory have no parts for intentionality, plot (as a system of morally determinate actions of central importance to the structure and effect of particular kinds of works), character (as the ethical ground of individual behavior), or for much else traditionally discussed and valued in literary (and other) studies. If present at all, superfluous lag such veterans on the stage of modern discussion.[10]

To many, if not to all modern theorists, the view appears to be that if there is no gold standard (no Transcendental Signified, no independently existing maker good and true of our assertions), no solid gold (real things) in some (metaphysical) Fort Knox to back up our paper (linguistic or merely verbal) negotiations, then no *scrip(t)* is better, more valuable, or more negotiable than any other scrip(t), and we can print as much of any kind of scrip(t) as we want and exchange one kind with another at will and ad infinitum. And some latter day American deconstructionists, along with many others, seem to think that once the gold standard is abandoned, there can be no constraints on spending, nor any "real" sense in which a "buck" is a "buck." Indeed, some critics seem at times to be so lost in theory as to be incapable of perceiving either the trees or the forest, the worms or the can, of finding and recognizing either a bounded entity or a bounded meaning. In the kaleidoscope of textuality (or ideology) all forms are transforms, all resolutions moments in the unending process of dissolution or revolution.

But, of course, like the rest of us, most of theory's adherents have developed survival skills and thus are capable of getting along reasonably well from day to day in the mundane world of "ordinary" experience. Most are reasonable enough human beings. They, for the most part, have not taken leave of their senses. They navigate the straits of ordinary reference and meaning with ease, manage, like the rest of us, to understand in no uncertain terms, as first this and then that discourse-occasion arises, which logocentric system is currently in place (can distinguish, for instance, "baseball bat" talk from "vampire bat" talk); they find trees and forests and open cans full of worms with as much skill as the inveterate and unregenerate essentialist. They would no sooner refuse to offer an (overstuffed) chair to an aged grandmother than would a believer in ultimate physics, despite the fact that grandmothers and chairs are dissolved in the differentiality and textuality of the theorist and the wave phenomena of the physicist. Like others, they find their way to their offices, which, like the rest of us, they open with dependable keys and in which they proceed deliberately and intentionally to write on their word processors the most reference-demolishing or politically incendiary things.

Difficulties arise for these critics when they start taking some of their attention-grabbing, promotional slogans—such as there is nothing outside the text ("il n'y a pas de hors texte"); readers, not authors produce texts; everything is ideological; there is no meaning or understanding except that produced within and by the "archive"; texts are produced by other texts; all texts undo or undermine what they affirm, and so on—not only quite seriously but also as definitively and generally "true." They also run into trouble when they suppose that any defense of such proscribed topics or such thoroughly discredited notions as objective knowledge, determinate meaning, the sharing of references and concepts across conceptual schemes and frameworks, and so on must rest on Foundationalist grounds, on belief in metaphysical foundations.

Having with good reason given up on Correspondence, on the possibility of grounding or fixing reference in any ultimate or absolute sense, these critics have tended to assume that they must also give up on most of what they had previously known about reference and meaning in their quotidian dealings with things and theses, at least while they are doing theory. They have tended to assume, further, that consequent upon the demise of the Transcendental Signified all is changed, changed utterly. Everywhere we look we find critics within the grip of theory passing from the ostensible stability to the actual instability of reference, from the surface to the deep, the manifest to the latent meaning, from the apparent, surface, or outer to the real, deep, or inner structure, from the grammatical or logical assertion to its grammatological, rhetorical, or tropological undoing or subversion. As a consequence of linguistic or ideological analysis, apparent certainties, stabilities, objectivities are seen for what they are, that is, epiphenomena of linguistic frolicking or effects of the will to power. In most of these discussions we have a form of reductionism, with the surface, manifest, outer being made good or true by the deep, latent, inner. In these schemes of analysis the suppressed, repressed, hidden, or "not said" is the quiet but powerful, the silent but significant partner. The real importance of the deeply privileged, inner, silent *other* depends on and is determined by some prior analysis of and special access to what really counts in the hierarchical weighting and significance of things, prior analysis, usually of what language, in its broad semiological sense, *just is* or what culture, in this or that epoch, *just is.*

Of course, the pluralist—the philosophical pluralist—has also given up on a metaphysical Foundation, on Correspondence, naive realism, and the Transcendental Signified, but he has done so without abandoning in the process most of what was available to him prior to his tergiversation. For the pluralist, specific, determinate reference is not contingent upon the endorsement or financial backing of some mind-independent reality. Indeed, meanings, references, facts, things, values, standards of justification, truth, rightness, wrongness, and so on emerge expediently and together, all at once, as we make from the conceptual materials available to us first this and then that conceptual scheme or system. In short, when the Foundation is dropped, everything stays in place; everything stays pretty much the same. We continue to do pretty much as we had been doing. We make and understand a variety of conceptual systems, finding our references and justification conditions, our criteria of rightness and wrongness, as we go along, as we participate in this or that practice. The chair we referred to yesterday is the chair we refer to today if (and only so long as) it remains functional for our present purposes within the same system of interest which endowed it with functionality yesterday. Authors write texts that retain through time their capacity to satisfy the justification conditions they previously satisfied and were initially constructed to satisfy.

For the pluralist, there are many true, right, and good (as well as, of course, many false, wrong, and bad) worlds, versions, or texts and, thus, many true, right, and good reference relations, foundations, or correspondences. What there is not, of course, for the pluralist is *one true* foundation, one reference relation which just is *the* reference relation, or one order of *truth.* In this view, a text is already a version, already an interpretation and a system of justification when we meet it.

We, of course, may make the text over in our own image, make it over in almost any image that pleases or interests us. We may create the text we do not find (may even insist that all texts are made, not found). But the pluralist differentiates himself from virtually all theorists in his official, on-the-job ability to *make* (i.e., interpret) texts that he does not in his personal and private capacity find appealing, agreeable, or even "true," to interpret texts that satisfy interests he does not share, to understand (internal) satisfactions at the level of what can only be called the text's interests, however noisome or strikingly new those interests may be to the pluralist personally. It is the burden of much of this essay, at any rate, to make good on these claims concerning the independence and knowability of the text's interests. Moreover, we assume that, except in the most trivial sense, these interests cannot be shaped or determined in their *particularity* or in their *specific meaning and emphasis* by any already in place categories of meaning or inference in the culture, or by the nature of language *as such*.

In this essay, the case for philosophical pluralism is made in conjunction with the cases for stability of reference and determinacy of meaning within conceptual schemes; for objective value judgments; for the persistence of references and concepts across theories, across theoretical differences; for the adjudication of disputes by appeal to shared methodological criteria, to standards shared, for example, across interpretive paradigms; and for much else. To a large extent, then, the essay makes its way forward by pushing against the resistance offered first by this and then by that belief or assumption of theory. The pluralism advocated here finds a clearing for itself only by opening up a way through the various modes in which theory is exhibited: the modes, for example, of *monism* (as evinced in some of the reductionist views of New Historicism), *eclecticism* (everywhere manifest in criticism today), *skepticism* (as in some forms of deconstruction), and *relativism* (as in interpretive communityism and in all those approaches that, while decrying total relativism and what Miller has called the "permissive pluralism" that says "anything goes," reject any constraints on interpretive ingenuity or fail to specify any principles of defeasibility that would put limits of tolerance or acceptability on interpretive activity or the play of the signifier).

This essay begins with an attempt to differentiate the pluralism worth knowing from the "isms" already on site with which it is usually confused (and which often take its name), namely, *eclecticism* and *relativism*.[11] We note, among other things, that eclecticism fails (as an "ism," that is) by trying to fit many worlds into one world, to make materials belonging to several space-times occupy one space-time and, on the other hand, that relativism, while correctly recognizing the interest-relativity of all conceptual schemes, fails to devise and enforce exclusion principles, welcoming into its embrace fit and unfit, right and wrong versions.

Although no one has ever confused pluralism with monism or skepticism, we have found it useful to distinguish pluralism from both, because in one incarnation or another (psychoanalytic, Bakhtinian, deconstructive, etc.) they are its competitors for attention and adoption. In this section of the essay, the focus is on internal weaknesses, on the inability of the first (monism) to acknowledge and account for the manifest diversity and "rightness" of many of our conceptual schemes and intellectual frameworks and on the incapacity of the other (skepticism) finally to entertain any concepts at all (in taking away or calling into question all justification conditions, it takes away references and concepts as well). As intellectual postures, each is shown to be fatally flawed relative to pluralism, to be either self-refuting or productive in extension of positions whose adoption would require the sacrifice of views we are reluctant to relinquish, views we have found indispensable to the conduct of life.

Because pluralism (as well as many positions within theory, it should be noted) insists on the context-sensitivity and interest-relativity of meaning and reference, it is obliged to acknowledge that many explanations of the "same" thing can be "true" (simply, we can have several "true" explanations or accounts of the *same* text, e.g., true phonological, grammatical, and chemical accounts). Since "truth"—that is, truth relative to a description—cannot provide sufficient justification, however, for choice among accounts, for preferring one account to another, considerable attention is given in the essay to the conditions determining what, *beyond truth*, counts as a good and satisfying, an appropriate or satisfactory explanation. And this concern with the rightness of this rather than that explanation brings us naturally to issues relating to whether and how we can identify *a particular text's interests*, interests that are at once text-specific and constitutive of referential properties and formal features.

Now to address these matters properly we must confront directly the vexed issues of reference and meaning, of stable reference and determinate meaning, the issues, in short, put in deepest question by theory. For example, it is generally assumed, as we have seen, that the notion of stability of reference and meaning is a byproduct of, and possible only to some form of, foundationalism. The prevailing assumption, then, makes an extended discussion of reference and meaning inevitable. Similarly, because various practitioners of theory stress the constitutive power of paradigms, social formations, or interpretive communities, stress, in other words, the determination of facts, things, and values by the conceptual categories of one or another community, "archive," "habitus," or power elite, and hence emphasize the "incommensurability" of schemes, or the impossibility of speaking or understanding outside the historical or categorical framework through which not only "reality" but the speaker him/herself is spoken, *this essay examines at various points and from several angles the possibilities of intersubjectivity across differences in conceptual schemes.* In various ways this essay indicates how facts, references, concepts, and meanings are preserved across various theoretical divides and how we can not only provide *impartial accounts* of the "facts" and "commitments" of rival theories but also *adjudicate* between them, giving the preference to what is demonstrably, according to *shared standards* of judgment, the superior position.

Moreover, to make plausible, against the collective wisdom of theory, the determinate prior interests of the text, this essay is obliged to take up another issue supposedly rendered obsolete by theory, because allegedly it too depends for its meaningfulness upon the suffrage of naive realism or essentialism, the issue of *intentionality* and its role in determining the conditions of interest upon which the textual facts and values depend. At several points in the essay, in connection with different aspects of the problem of "meaning," the indispensability of intentionality to the making and understanding of texts is discussed. This essay returns again and again to intentionality because it is, to deploy a radical expression, a *foundational* concept for this essay.

In the end, then, this essay seeks not to overthrow all theory, to prove that it always undoes itself from within. Rather, it seeks to reclaim senselessly abandoned intellectual territory, by showing that there is nothing in theory's insights into language or culture that has rendered obsolete, meaningless, second-rate, or illusory most of the projects that have excited and continue to excite our interests.

If the modest aims of this essay were allowed to puff themselves with ambition, they would, thus inflated, see themselves as striving to carry us beyond the tedious, repetitive anti- or nonhumanism of New Historicism and deconstruction, among others, to a "new humanism," one fully alert to the taint of the human on all practices and worlds and fully cognizant of our *opportunities* to participate in the making of right and fitting and good texts and worlds and of our *obligations* to contribute to the understanding, the proper, true, and right understanding of all those versions that have designs on us. Restored to modesty, this essay would count itself fortunate if it contributed something to our understanding of the dignity and importance of *practical reasoning* in the creation and interpretation of literary (and, of course, other) works.

In all, this essay is interested not only in elucidating and defending a largely unknown and neglected pluralism, but also in reminding readers of the usefulness of the distinction between theoretical and practical reasoning and of the importance, indeed the indispensability, of practical reasoning to certain kinds of endeavors, especially to the making and understanding of literary texts. Also, and not so incidentally, this essay is interested in making a contribution to that tradition—that largely American tradition—of thought on which it also variously relies and to which it is deeply indebted, that is, pragmatism.

"Pragmatism" is no less vexed and problematic a term than "pluralism," of course, but it is this author's hope that by the end of this work the reader will have no doubts about how a pragmatic pluralist or a pluralistic pragmatist might deal with the most important theoretical issues, or about how he or she might respond to theory and put hard questions to its authority to put into question what it has boldly put into question.

Part One
Problem Setting and Pluralism

Chapter 1
Putting Pluralism on the Map

As a character on the critical scene, pluralism is both an old acquaintance and a stranger, a friend and a derelict, a convivial dinner guest who never heard a story he didn't like and an ancient mariner who, though neither intolerant nor incapable of hearty laughter, prefers to tell and listen to stories that get things right. However much our reputation may suffer by the association, we will treat as a pluralist-worth-knowing only the stranger, the derelict, and the mariner.

Because the pluralist-worth-knowing believes that even in a scene where reason (along with reference, verification, explanation, and so on) has gone "immanent," it is still possible to get many things right and to be right about many things, he is to be sharply distinguished from the "anything goes" *relativist* and the *ingratiating pluralist*—more properly called an *eclectic* or *syncretist*—who finds a little truth in most or many ways of talking. He is also to be differentiated from the *monist* (both the "hard" monist, who, despite what the "immanent reasoners" say, persists in thinking there is one right way of thinking and the "soft" monist, who, while acknowledging the mind-dependent nature of discourse, nevertheless assumes that one kind of talk is to be preferred over other kinds of talk) and, finally, from the *skeptic*, who insists that all ways of talking are at least partially false (the deconstructionist is a special kind of skeptic—an eclectic skeptic perhaps—since for him all languages in place are both true *and* false, possible *and* impossible). Thus, in aligning ourselves with the pluralist-worth-knowing, we at the same time dissociate ourselves from several competitors for our attention.

Unacceptable Versions

Unlike many other "isms," pluralism is not easily pinned to the specimen board with a formulated phrase. Its nature is Protean, altering as it alteration finds in the discourse in which it finds itself. Nevertheless, it assumes, among other things, that "reality" is something we make many versions of and, further, that of the many versions we make some are "true," "good," or "right" versions. Some versions, however, are unacceptable because they are *internally incoherent*, in the sense that they contain elements—propositions, assumptions, or whatever—that violate the standards of acceptability established by the versions themselves (the deconstructionist, of course, assumes that all versions are incoherent in just this way, are fractured within or self-deconstructing), whereas others are unacceptable because they *offend beliefs that we are unwilling to give up*, because they do not make a good fit with other beliefs that, we feel, are just too good to abandon. For example, we can easily imagine a case in which the adoption of one hypothesis (about phlogiston, say) would require the abandonment of another (about oxygen, say) that was just too elegant and attractive and too serviceable to our interests and needs to give up; or, switching areas of concern, we can imagine a case in which the acceptance of one way of reading a textual passage, though entirely plausible and quite compelling, considered locally (that in Shakespeare's *Othello*, for example, at the end of Act IV Desdemona commits the sin of adultery in her heart by considering Lodovico—and men like him, Venetian courtiers—more appealing and more suitable as husbands than Othello), would require the rejection of another way, one equally plausible and compelling but also making a nice fit with all earlier passages and our working understanding of the whole work.[1]

Still others are unacceptable because they are not merely incoherent (internally troubled in one or another respect) but *self-refuting*, creating, for example, a definition of truth or rational acceptability that fails to account for the definition itself. A convenient instance of this sort of self-refutation is provided by the modish cant which affirms that "everything"—all statements, discourses, artifacts, etc.—"is ideological" or by the "positivism" which makes acceptability or meaningfulness contingent upon "testability" by the "scientific method," thereby producing a requirement that is not satisfied by the definition of acceptability itself. The statement that all untestable statements are cognitively empty is itself cognitively empty by the standard of "testability." Of course, all total relativists and methodological solipsists similarly bite the hand that feeds them. Similarly, those critics who insist that *all* our beliefs are determined by a particular, historically determined *archive* ineluctably fall into incoherence or inconsistency when they neglect to apply their wisdom to their own remarks, since, if what they say is true is indeed true, those remarks must themselves be determined by the particular, culturally determined language in place. But if they are determined by the *archive*, then they are not generally true (i.e., cross-archivally), as they are represented to be.

Acceptable Versions

Although the immediate focus here has been on ways in which versions can go wrong, it should be clear that the ways in which they can go wrong is roughly in inverse proportion to the ways in which they can go right. For example, a version can be considered true when, as Nelson Goodman says, "it offends no unyielding beliefs and none of its own precepts."[2] Before proceeding further, we should be careful to note that Goodman is not here defining truth but establishing a basis for accepting a version as a true version. As always, truth is various and interest- or version-relative. There is no one true world against which we can check a version for accuracy, a world prior to perception, description, or interpretation. The only "world" we have is the one which depends upon "right" versions, and all we can "learn about the world is contained in right versions of it."[3] (If there is only one world, it is made up of many different, contrasting versions; if there are many worlds, they together make up the only world we can know.) Needless to say, the pluralist remains a pluralist whether there is one world or many. Needful to say, however, is that from the pluralist perspective versions once accepted can be subsequently rejected or revised, since our beliefs are not invariably unyielding.

Implicated in "unyielding belief" is the view that beliefs do change; "rightness" is a flexible, corrigible notion. The pluralist, then, is always prepared, as Goodman says elsewhere, to amend a rule (a hypothesis, an interpretation) if it yields an inference he is unwilling to accept or reject an inference if it violates a rule he is unwilling to amend.[4] Unpacking everything implicated in "right" versions and "yielding beliefs" will take some time, but something can be done immediately to show that our terms have legs and can walk.

Finding a multiplicity of "right" versions is, of course, a ridiculously easy task, as is showing how any right version could go wrong. In the United States distances are usually measured in terms of miles and speeds in terms of miles per hour, whereas in France, say, distance and speed are measured in kilometers. Both measurements truly measure. Moreover, if it is a matter of convention whether speed is measured in terms of kilometers or miles per hour, it is a matter of *fact* that a given driver is traveling at sixty miles an hour, not fifty miles an hour. If you ask, "But how fast is he *really* traveling?", we cannot answer without a framework, and we certainly cannot say that driving sixty miles an hour in the United States means the same thing as driving sixty kilometers an hour in France.

Meanings, like facts, are scheme-dependent. On the other hand, even without a conversion chart to translate miles into kilometers, we could determine how fast two drivers from the two different countries were traveling if we measured the speed of both cars by a single, *different standard*, if we determined the speed of both cars, for example, relative to a moving airplane. By this new standard, we can say with certainty that two cars with different speedometers are traveling at the same speed, but this standard is simply another version. How fast are they "really" traveling? Well, it all depends. But note that while we can measure speed by many true standards, we can determine "actual" speed in all of them. Choice of standard may be arbitrary (or, more exactly, conventional), but actual speed, within a system of reference, is not. In certain contexts, then, there is such a thing as "getting it right." Clearly, conceptual relativity is not incompatible with the "objective facts of the matter"; within a scheme the *facts* are the facts, and such facts are facts for you and you and you, regardless of whether *you* and the members of your community prefer the "miles per hour" system or not.

That this principle has a bearing on reading literature is obvious. Very few readers would have to be persuaded that *Hamlet*, say, is open to many valid interpretations. The problem, rather, for many readers, is that we have too many interpretations of it. (Others, of course, wish to give up on interpretation altogether.) What is not so obvious perhaps is that a given piece of literature is itself a version and, thus, not any version we would make of it. It is already going a *certain speed*, is already, that is, a system of "meaning" and "reference" as determined by a conceptual system. What obtains in the speed-of-car case obtains just as forcefully in more complicated instances of meaning and reference. It is clear, for example, that if this is the system of rationality we are in, then this rather than that meaning of that word is right and fitting, this rather than that character is the right or appropriate deliverer of the message on this occasion, etc. These are "facts" necessary to satisfy the intentional system of the text; these are, in short, the satisfaction conditions of this instance of intentionality. Although the literary text may accommodate and be accommodated to countless schemes, it is not a site waiting to be relativized to a scheme. Its versional status, however, cannot be discussed in detail until we learn more about right versions and unyielding beliefs.

Mapping Versions and Changing Beliefs

If after the first of the year all maps of the United States were required by statute to be demographic or population maps, the people
in Montana might complain, because, under such a scheme of representation, Big Sky country would be shown to be smaller than
Rhode Island. Civil libertarians all, the Rhode Islanders would insist
that they have been the victims of "area-ism" for too long, that "Little
Rhody" is too demeaning a term for such a large state, made small
only by a prejudicial policy in the Office of Maps favoring *area*. Vic-
timized, but nevertheless fair-minded, the Rhode Islanders call for a
vote, with national mapmaking policy to be decided by a simple majority of votes cast by the citizens of both states. Suspecting something
not quite right in this, the Montanans, in a spirit of compromise, suggest that policy be based neither on *area* nor on *population*, but on
some such "neutral" category as property, cattle perhaps. Property
seems fair to the Rhode Islanders, but they suggest boats. In the
meantime, at the Office of Maps the mapmakers remain indifferent
to the squabble and proceed merrily to design road maps, relief
maps, topographical maps, polar maps, mercator maps, and a hundred other "true" maps. All true maps are true versions, each one
giving a true symbolic account of some interests or features that are
mappable. And to be true, good, or right, a map—at least a certain
kind of map—should fairly and accurately represent the features that
it is mapping; that is, its biases, values, standards, and practices
should be uniformly administered.

From the humble example of maps we can learn much that is ultimately useful to the literary critic, especially the critic who is willing
to look beyond eclecticism, monism, or skepticism for a mooring. As
soon as we think for a moment about the rightness of a particular
map, a road map, for instance, we can then move quickly to an understanding of how it could have gone wrong. Instead of working
fairly and accurately within its scheme of representation, a map
could, for example, supply roads where none were to be found, omit
roads that anybody could find, misemphasize findable roads (endowing a two-lane road, for example, with the sort of thickness reserved
for four-lane, divided highways), reorder or renumber familiar roads
(sending Route 1 east and west rather than north and south or giving
Route 1 the number 95), or otherwise deform the world it is obliged,
by means of an elected scheme, to represent (indicating, for example,
that Boston is one hundred miles rather than fifty miles from Providence).

What an inept mapmaker can do a mischievous reader of maps can also do, with a little help from a "marking" pen or from what the typists call "white-out." And a reader of texts can do much the same sort of mischief by inscribing a "false" scheme of interpretation on a document already inscribed. The question for the critic is not whether he can get along without a scheme, but whether he is going to read a map or make one—more exactly, whether he is going to describe a map already made or one of his own making. Of course, reading a text, especially a "literary" text, is more difficult than reading a map, but by looking at map reading, we can come to an understanding of more general principles and map the way for our more difficult task. At any rate, it is clear that a given kind of map can violate its own precepts in a variety of ways.

A cautionary note: to some it may seem that by suggesting that the accuracy of the lines on a map could be checked against "real" roads we are found by the "correspondence" that sometime we did flee, that there is a real world after all with which to correlate our statements. Radiating from this circle or this "rotary," however, are many routes of escape. When we say that for our present purpose this line will refer to or stand for this road, we are fixing a reference relative to a range of specific interests; we are only doing what we always do when we "fix" a reference, when we ordinarily "refer" or when we refer in the "ordinary," mundane sense. We no more assume that this line *just is* that road or that this road *just is* that line than we assume that water *just is* or *is only* H_2O or that the car *just is* going a certain speed independently of any system of reference. The line has a relation of reference to a road, but this reference relation is clearly scheme-dependent. This is a stipulated reference relation within a scheme of representation; this line stands for this road, but the road has no single "meaning" and no single true representation. This *line* corresponds to that *road* in *this scheme of representation* in much the same way that the word "dog" corresponds to dogs in the "animal" scheme of ordinary reference. Since *words* and *things come into existence together*, it is easy to determine what corresponds to what *in the system*, while still being ignorant of what dogs, say, *really* are. Of course, saying what this line refers to tells us nothing about what the road "really" is or, for that matter, what "lines" really are.

Further, whether a particular road is represented by a dotted, thick, or thin line, or is five or ten inches long, etc. depends upon the scheme of representation—upon the scale and symbol system—adopted by the mapmaker. Nevertheless, the graciousness of the map remains. If you stop by the side of the road and ask it how you can get from where you are to somewhere else, it will tell you with alacrity and without grumbling and, unlike some gas station attendants, tell you the "truth."

To a good map one can put what we might call useful "counterfactuals" or useful "subjunctives," as in the following case: If we are on the road the map says we are on and are at this point on the road, then we should come to the junction of Route 95 in five miles. The delightful thing is that if our "ifs" are "correct," then in five miles we actually will come to that and not some other junction. (Or, to take a quite different kind of example, if Othello really believes that Desdemona has been unfaithful, he will act—or be likely to act—one way rather than another.) Of course, we can misread our map, but, theorists take note, misreading is not inevitable, at least not to the person who knows what *kind* of map he is reading, what system of reference he is in. (Moreover, *Othello*, no less than a road map, is already in a system of meaning and reference when we encounter it; it could not come into existence as a text without meeting the satisfaction conditions of some system of rationality, since it is only relative to such a system that the text has any content(s) at all.) A good map is like a good waiter: both give you what you ask for—provided, of course, you ask the "right" question or make the "right" demand. And what more could you ask for? If you get lost or go hungry, the better part of civility is not always to blame the map or the waiter. As far as "correspondence" is concerned, then, we can say, that our lines (terms, symbols, etc.) do indeed "correspond" to something, but the something they correspond to is something within a system of "immanent meaning." Moreover, the something they correspond to is *roads* (whatever those are *for us*). The point is that lines can and do correspond to many things and that roads exist in many correspondence relations. A line no more uniquely stands for or represents a given road than the word "road" uniquely refers to or corresponds to some underlying, mind-independent *road*. (Of course, "road" and road are coeval.)

But in sending meaning inside once again, we have not at the same time reduced our particular good map to "mere talk." We certainly cannot get along without schemes, but "getting it right" within schemes is not an *inconsequential* matter; "getting it right" has consequences. In the present case, making the right assumptions about the scheme of reference in which you are located makes all the difference between getting where you're going and getting lost. The point within this point (as the subjunctive example was designed to suggest) is that our assumptions within schemes can frequently be confirmed or disconfirmed.[6]

Whether from examination of and reflection on maps we can learn all that we need to know, I cannot say, but by attending to them we can learn at least three more good things. In the first place, they are corrigible, revisable, adaptable to changes in the conditions that under their scheme of representation they are obliged to represent. The 1947 road map, though a true map of its time, is no longer a "true" map for the motorist interested in assessing the driving options in 1992 for a trip from New York to Boston. Just as it is possible to say both that women in the United States are not allowed to vote in national elections and that women over eighteen in the United States can vote in national elections, if the statements apply to different periods of history, so two road maps can both be true versions of the roads at different times (or according to different scales). Which of the two "true" maps I will wish to consult will, of course, depend upon my interests, upon which of the two is, as we say, user-friendly to those interests or has interests of its own which coincide with the kinds of questions I am interested in putting. As a historian of road systems in the period from 1930 to 1950, I am sublimely indifferent to the map of the "Interstate" network that I cherish as a motorist.

As a motorist interested in getting to the beach before the weekend is over, I will certainly find the 1992 road map markedly superior to the 1950 one, and as a scholar interested in a text based on a collation of all editions published in an author's lifetime, I will certainly prefer one based on five rather than, as in the past, on four editions, assuming the fifth has been clearly established as having been published in that lifetime. And if Shakespeare actually wrote a poem entitled "Shall I Die," then an edition that includes it will be more "complete," though not necessarily "truer," than one that does not.

Changing "beliefs" to accommodate changing conditions in what is to be represented (according to a basically unchanging scheme of representation) in order to be, say, "more accurate" is one thing; but changing "beliefs" about the scheme itself (in the process of making the map) or about the scheme you are in (in the process of reading the map) is something else again. Suppose for a moment that in designing a road map for maximum usefulness to motorists who want to get from New York to Boston I employ a scheme in which double yellow lines "stand for" "Interstate" highways, single *black* lines for state roads, and single *red* lines for county roads. Suppose further that it is impossible to get to Boston only by traveling on the "Interstate" roads, that at every point where choice is necessary a red or black route is possible, and that sometimes the red route is "better" (has four lanes, say, rather than two) and sometimes the black route is. (Of course, the "better" road may be the "worse" road when one is interested, for example, in taking the "most scenic," not the "quickest" route.) Guided by utility, lacking any retrograde ambitions (such as a desire to produce distinctly unhelpful maps), and seeing that my scheme yields inferences that I am unwilling to accept (i.e., that the red and the black routes appear to supply equally good alternatives), I wisely and humanely amend my scheme, inserting double black lines where appropriate and double red lines where appropriate (where state and county roads have four lanes).

Suppose now that I am a reader rather than a maker of maps, that I must repeatedly choose between a red route and a black route, that on my map red indicates secondary roads (roads that look fine at the junction but that rapidly deteriorate in a mile or so) and black, primary roads, and, finally, that I cannot tell the difference between the primary and the secondary from the map itself (either because it has no "legend" or because the "legend" has been destroyed). Lacking any clear (to me) guidance from the map, any clear basis for a preferential ordering, but assuming that the color distinctions mark a difference useful to the driver, I "hypothesize" a correlation between vividness or brightness on the map and drivability on the road and, thus, choose a red route, only to discover that dirt and potholes are my fate. At the next junction, I choose a black route and experience those special pleasures that perhaps one has to be a lover of smooth driving to appreciate fully. When choice is again forced upon me, rather than assuming that the one red route I took was the bad apple in the barrel or the runt of an otherwise robust litter, I elect the black route again, thereby amending my hypothesis to accommodate an inference that I am presently unwilling to reject (while preserving, of course, my original assumption that the color distinction indicates a difference in driving conditions).

If I were in an experimental mood, I might make several trials, alternating at successive junctions between red and black routes, but in the end, unless I had complete faith in "accident," I would adopt the "black" hypothesis and stick with it until something unforeseen obliged me to reject it. And since I am not a map "illiterate," since I am map "wise," since, in other words, I assume that distinctions do make a difference and that a conceptual grasp of the cognitive scheme underlying the map is possible (that the map makes a kind of "sense," even though I believe the map would have been more "sensible" if the black lines had been thickened), I will come to a "correct" hypothesis sooner rather than later.[7]

To switch now from map examples to "literary" examples is no easy matter, because we will have to assume the resolution of much that current critical theory puts into question (of course, we make the same assumptions in our talk of maps and mapmakers), but inasmuch as we are now sketching out pluralistic "principles," we can perhaps be forgiven if at this point we do not anticipate and respond to "obvious" objections to our developing case.[8] Holding some of the dogs of resistance at bay temporarily, we can quickly note a couple of "literary" analogues to the tergiversation of the mapmaker and the automobile driver.

Let us suppose for a moment that in its original version Shakespeare's *King Lear* ended with the defeat of the forces of Goneril, Regan, and Edmund, the joyful reunion of Lear and Cordelia, and the impending marriage of Cordelia and Edgar (the King of France, Cordelia's husband, having died gloriously and conveniently in defense of Lear), that this conclusion satisfied a deep though unarticulated desire in the audience for "poetic justice," and that the satisfaction found its emblematic embodiment in a final tableau—Lear embracing Cordelia—of "virtue rewarded." Now suppose further that upon reflection Shakespeare decided that he was not writing a "virtue rewarded" story after all, that his conclusion was "incoherent," that it did not "fit" the version he had been making all along, and that only by revising the conclusion could he end his work in a "fitting" way. Our "possible" Shakespeare does so, and we are the richer for it. Pitching us past the pitch of grief, Shakespeare tosses us into that emotionally rich conceptual space where we can find, if not the "founding gesture," the outstretched expression of such pity and love as beings such as we are capable of and from where, if we can speak at all, we can only "speak what we feel," can only say, with Kent, "The wonder is he hath endured so long," or, with Edgar, "we that are young / Shall never see so much, nor live so long." In the language of our exposition, then, the first version yields an inference that the play cannot accept or, if you prefer, that Shakespeare, working within a version, cannot accept.

From what a "possible" Shakespeare might have done, we can move to what an "actual" Johnson certainly did. In that section of *The Vanity of Human Wishes* in which the young scholar who quits "his ease for fame" is discussed, Johnson invites him, in one version, to "pause awhile from learning, to be wise," and later, in a subsequent version, to "pause awhile from letters, to be wise," changing "learning" to "letters" presumably to avoid a possible ambiguity. A reader or reciter might miss the comma after "learning" and, thus, speak or read "learning to be wise," thereby missing the distinction between being wise and being "lettered" or "learned," a distinction certainly worth preserving. Whether a more subtle explanation of the change might serve better than the "ambiguity" explanation, I cannot say (in part because I cannot think of one offhand), but the "fact" is that "letters" eliminates a possible ambiguity and makes one meaning more probable ("righter") than another. At any rate, an inference that one version may yield is rejected or eliminated by the revision, and, after the change, the reader is in no danger of losing the way, even temporarily.

A convenient example of tergiversation on the reader's part can be found in a possible response to the original version of the Johnson line. Reading past the comma, the reader expects a "to" (or possibly an "and") after "learning to be wise" ("pause awhile from learning to be wise" to do what? "and" then do what?); finding none, a possible reader goes over the line again more slowly and has an "Aha" experience, "correcting" a previous "understanding" by rejecting an inference, correcting a readerly mistake.

To complicate matters slightly, let us now imagine a relatively unsophisticated student who while reading through Akenside's *The Pleasures of Imagination* (admittedly, such readers are not easily found) comes across and is deeply puzzled by the phrase, "God's plastic arm." In an effort to "fix" the reference of "plastic" or to find its "sense," the student imagines nothing more august than a plastic dashboard icon, and finding no "gloss" of the word in the notes, suspects momentarily that what he or she has been treating as a "serious" poem is really a biting, even sacrilegious satire. In trying to reorganize a scheme of interpretation the student finds that satire begins and ends with this phrase, that "ironizing" everything up to the troublesome phrase is no easy matter.

What this student does next will depend largely on his or her individual sensibility, imagination, industry, scholarly proclivities, frustration level, memory, experience, and so on. Let us assume the best. The student does not simply read on, allowing the phrase to float like a cloud in the otherwise unclouded sky of understanding, or simply assume that the author or compositor made a mistake (writing or reading "plastic" for, say, "fantastic," or "gigantic," or, possibly, "pluralistic"). Instead, applying the "principle of charity" to the case at hand, the student gives the writer (or text) the benefit of the doubt and supposes that "plastic" has a "meaning" in this context that has not yet been found. To make this tall story short, let us further assume that, deprived of access to a dictionary (which would solve the puzzle in a hurry), one student thinks of plastic surgery, of what plastic surgeons do, remembers taking a course in what the instructor called a plastic art (pottery, say), and reads what precedes and follows the vexed phrase more attentively, discovering finally that Akenside's God is "creative," is one who forms and shapes and molds a visible universe. And, lo, God's arm loses its risibility and assumes its power, and our student "correctly" reads a "true" version of a story of making that, as a nonbeliever, he or she does not believe to be "true" at all.

Let me conclude this examination of yielding beliefs with another simple case, which while slightly different from those examined above is, like them, chock-full of implications. Briefly, assume a reader who first takes Jonathan Swift's "A Modest Proposal" straight and then, with a little reflection and prodding, "gets it," that is, understands the irony of it all. In this case we have what some Kuhnians might call a "paradigm" shift and some psychologists a "gestalt" switch. The whole work, once read one way, is now read another way, and, as a consequence, outrage yields to pleasure. At the risk of raising hackles, let us say that the reader now sees Swift's version for what it "truly" is, now understands the appropriate context and the system of reference to be dealt with. One belief system yields to another, and the switch is accompanied by a sense of "getting it right." Such conceptual "revolutions" and such satisfactions are common. At this stage, however, we are concerned not with how they come about or how they might be justified, but only with their "occurrence," with the "actuality" of changing beliefs and rejecting inferences.

Standards of Judgment

A long time ago and in a paragraph far away, we mentioned three more good things we could learn from maps, but we have since spent our time on only one. In the interests of economy, we will handle the remaining two with some dispatch. In the second place, then, given the "existence" of many true maps (polar, mercator, demographic, or road), and given that the true maps are true in different ways or different respects, the pluralist assumes that our standards of adequacy vary from map to map. He assumes, in other words, that we cannot judge a road map by standards that apply to a demographic map (or one road map by standards that apply to another road map). More broadly, the operative assumption is that we have different standards for different kinds of discussion. "Literarily" speaking, a novel (however defined) should not be asked to behave as a lyric poem behaves (however lyric is defined, assuming, however, a definition not coterminous with that of a novel), and the *excellence* of "A Modest Proposal" or any other work is neither possible nor recognizable apart from some system of rationality.

The point here is not simply that schemes determine their own standards, that standards are built into schemes (which is "true"), but also that schemes are also *regulated* by the standards they imply. If this were not the case, we would be unable either to detect internal contradiction, incoherence, or inconsistency or to compare the relative merits of any two things that ask to be considered in terms of the same (or a similar) scheme of reference or "meaning," two maps, say, of the same state, both working within the same system of representation. Unless we are willing to give up "truth" (immanent truth, that is), rationality, and explanation altogether, *we are committed to a state of affairs in which our interest-relative remarks must at the very least be relative (i.e., appropriate and accountable) to those interests.* If in the process of making our versions even we cannot tell whether our remarks or symbols are relative to our interests (to our scheme of reference, representation, or interpretation), then it does not matter at all what is tacked onto what, what morphemes or whatever join hands; we make maps with lines, any lines that come our way, and there's an end on't.

Of course, many of our standards, while still context-sensitive and interest-relative, *cut across several schemes*, several projects, and several disciplines, and when they do they are perhaps best understood as "methodological criteria," standards which play a role in both the *emergence* and the *testing* of schemes. For example, earlier we referred to the "fairness" and "accuracy" of maps, thus specifying methodological criteria that individual maps would satisfy in *distinct ways* but that could be used in the *assessment of many maps*. Similarly, certain scientists usefully delimit the range of inquiry by making certain demands of their theories, for instance, that they include no unnecessary entities, that they achieve coherence, that they be simple rather than complex, and so on. Our rational enterprises, in short, have interpretation and value built into them. Nevertheless, no standard or group of standards is "right" or "true" in general or in any absolute sense. Consistency or coherence, for example, is not a master standard ("inconsistency" may be the point of or be right for some versions we make; for the deconstructionist, of course, self-contradiction is always inevitable). Even so, consistency and coherence are often (indeed, usually) deeply satisfying to us, and they often stand front and center in the ranks of criterial equals (as they certainly do in schemes that aspire to rationality). There is no one Archimedean place to stand to make judgments or to move all things, but there are many and various spots of firmness on which at various times we can place our feet.

Although "varying standards" is a full suitcase not quickly unpacked, from it we can take an item or two immediately to shield us from nakedness. We make our standards as we make our versions, but several versions can be answerable to the same standards. The criteria to which we appeal are usually extralocal, extraparadigmatic, are applicable to more than the case at hand. Whether something is right or wrong depends on the *kind* of "language" we are using and the *kind* of context we are in, but we can make our "discourse" answer to itself and can *compare* it with other discourses, so long as at least something remains invariant across the comparison. Comparison presupposes some commensurabilities, some shared reference(s) or concept(s). For example, two road maps of the same state, ordered to different scales and exhibiting striking differences in the number of villages and roads noted, can be compared for "accuracy" in terms of many "common" features. For example, however differently they "mark" their roads, both maps have Allens Avenue running parallel to the Providence River between point A and point B, both situate Pawtucket north of Providence, and so on.

If there is a sartorially splendid outfit in this suitcase, it is this: reason is both *immanent* (located within particular schemes, discourses, or whatever) and *transcendent* (a regulative "ideal" that enables us to compare discourses *inter se*). Those who forget the *immanence* of reason become monists, absolutists, positivists, Hegelian Hegelians, "Marxists," believers, at any rate, in one truth, in one true objectivity, in the "absolute idea," in some final replacement of the "determinate negations" of history by "Absolute Mind," or whatever. Those who forget the *transcendence* of reason become relativists, cultural normists, advocates of "interpretive communities," historicists without an end product, "anthropologists," "arche"-types, "archivists," "anything goists," or whatever, believers, at any rate, in here, there, and everywhere an immanence and only an immanence. Of course, deconstructionists are skeptics/non-skeptics, in a word, "peek-a-booists," to whom the "world" says "now you see me, now you don't."[9]

That immanence and transcendence are not sometime things for reason can be suggested by "literary" cases analogous to the map cases. In the service of expedition, we shall limit discussion to two simple (but nevertheless instructive) cases, one in which a possible text confronts itself and one in which two "hypotheses" are compared. In the first case, the reader is invited to imagine that in the copy of *Measure for Measure* that I own references are fixed and function in a more or less "ordinary" way, that moral terms, descriptive terms, expressive terms and so on are readily intelligible to the general reader (give or take an "oddball" phrase or two and given this reader's easy adaptability to a mixture of verse and prose) without a special translation manual. Now suppose that in one scene in the first act Mistress Overdone, a notorious bawd, tells Lucio that she knows that Claudio has been hauled off to prison and a few lines later tells

Pompey, from whom she has no reason to conceal her knowledge and to whom she has some compelling reasons to tell what she knows, that someone has been hauled away but she knows not who. (Whatever some Shakespeareans may think or whatever may be true in their versions, in *my* version she does and does not know that Claudio is the prisoner.) The text, then, confronts itself and finds itself wanting. The text makes a "mistake," not a devastating mistake (I assume my copy is based on a "bad" quarto or is a stitch and paste job put together from a variety of "foul" papers), but a mistake nevertheless. We have here, then, a completely nonfunctional, entirely evitable, and easily correctable inconsistency in the character of Mistress Overdone. Her two statements make a bad "fit" within the scheme that is this version, and the version itself tells me so.

The second case—barely imaginable but nonetheless instructive—invites us to suppose the classroom presence of a peculiarly truculent and thick-headed student who insists that when Hamlet asks why Horatio is not in Wittenberg, he is referring to a college in Ohio. To make matters worse for the instructor, the fact is that a printed note in the student's text, keyed to the word "Wittenberg" in the play, says—and says "truly"—that "Wittenberg is the name of a university in Ohio." The instructor in turn insists that the term refers to a university in Germany (Horatio's response, "a truant disposition," convinces both of them that the reference is to a "university") and says, additionally, in a tone best described perhaps as convivial sarcasm, that today, as in the past, Englishmen do not refer to Ohio. More seriously, the instructor notes that Ohio did not exist in the early seventeenth century, that a Wittenberg University did exist in Germany at that time, and so on through a long list of "that's" all coming to rest in "thus a college in Germany." Predictably not satisfied, the student, who did not doze through all the sessions of a basic philosophy course, observes that just as water was H_2O before chemistry made it so, so Ohio was surely Ohio before it was officially surveyed, designated, and ratified as such; moreover, Shakespeare is being prophetic here, and he who could "anticipate" so much of what we have come to learn, through Freud, say, about the human mind, could surely "anticipate" something so easy (or not so impossibly difficult) to imagine as a college in Ohio, perhaps one modeled on the university in Germany. Riposte follows riposte, and satisfaction is nowhere to be found. Proving the obvious is often no easy matter.

Our case would have been more significant undoubtedly if our student had a larger "theory" (had argued, say, of another play, that despite the instructor's opinion to the contrary, Iago's hatred of Othello is motivated by a deeply embedded, strongly repressed homoerotic love), but the point remains that without some *context-sensitive, informal criteria of plausibility or rationality* we would never be able to put a limit on the "hypotheses" worth caring about. Whenever we attempt to "justify" our views (or whenever we disagree with someone else), we inevitably appeal to what we can call "nonparadigmatic" or "transparadigmatic" criteria. Less ambitiously than E. D. Hirsch, who has attempted to show that "valid interpretation" is contingent upon the satisfaction of such methodological criteria as *coherence, correspondence, legitimacy,* and *generic appropriateness,* we simply suggest that interpretation and value are intrinsic to rationality and that where there is disagreement (a situation presupposing at least some shared assumptions or beliefs; if two versions are different in all respects, they cannot be brought into disagreement), then resolution is possible only on the ground of shared, however temporarily, "transparadigmatic"—or "transcultural" or "transcommunity"—methodological criteria.[10]

Only the critic who is willing to say "anything goes" can avoid being implicated in a system of rationality or justification not limited to a single version, if only because such practices as accepting, rejecting, criticizing, revising, or inventing versions presuppose "values" or criteria that, while "relevant" to particular versions, are not themselves defined by any single, particular version. How someone could make a denial of the preceding remarks "good" (i.e., convincing) it is not easy to imagine.

Before passing on to one more good lesson (our third and last) to be learned from maps, however, we should remember that our "transparadigmatic" paradigms of rationality are themselves susceptible to change, revision, and supplantation, can themselves undergo "revolution," and that even such durable criteria as "coherence," "consistency," and so on are themselves interest-relative. For example, what counts as coherence in one kind of discussion or version does not necessarily count as such in another kind of discussion or version. The lesson here, of course, is that we have no master paradigm of nonparadigmatic rationality, no supreme measuring stick or ungridlocked grid. Getting on is difficult, but we do get on, improvising as we go in less than haphazard ways.

Diversity and Change

As I have indicated above, we can learn many good things from a consideration of maps, but by the terms of our contract we are restricted to the notation of three good things to be learned from them. Having noted two, we note now that maps do not and cannot change all and everything at once. The corollary is that new maps emerge from old maps, from existing maps, that new maps are intelligible as maps only to the extent that they maintain some contact with some aspects of the possibilities from which they emerge. Presented with a sheet of paper on which there are odd but apparently not random markings, I will get nowhere with it unless and until I assume, for example, that what is before me is a map, and I will get nowhere with my assumption unless what is before me is a map, or is intelligible as a map. Or, in slightly different terms, no place I get with the markings is quite so satisfying as the place I call "map"; getting to "map" is deeply satisfying to me *and* to the markings. Treating the markings as under the command of the cognitive model "map" makes much seem right and fit. And, of course, it will not be intelligible as a map unless it *behaves*, in some respects, the way a map behaves, or unless I can *use* it as a map, unless I can talk to it as a map, get map answers from it, and, finally, get from here to there as a result of this colloquy.

If we ask "how much 'give' maps have," or "how many and what kinds of changes maps will tolerate," we can have no ready answers, inasmuch as there is no and can be no ultimate authority to whom (or to which) we can appeal to decide such questions. That maps have considerable "give," however, is obvious. As far as maps are concerned, we live in an age of their plethorization, an age not of dearth, but of abundance, and we seem incapable of putting limits on what or on how we will map. If *something mentionable* can be situated or distributed, it can apparently be mapped in some form by some means of representation (we can map, for example, people, boats, historic sites, institutions, fast-food restaurants, races, nationalities, creeds, brain waves, "concepts," "ideas," space-time relations, sore spots, pet peeves, schools of thought, or whatever). And if there is a *means of representation*, it can be used in the service of maps (we can so use, for example, lines, dots, stones, triangles, circles, photographs— as in aerial photographs—shoes or anything else that can function "naturally" or stipulatively as a means of reference).

Moreover, our maps are not restricted in terms of mood, tense, class, emotional quality, or . . . (choose any predicate). Our maps can refer to the past, the present, or the future (planning maps or development maps, for example, are future conditional or subjunctive maps). They can be "funny" (i.e., odd, quaint, old-fashioned, adjusted to the prejudices of certain buyers—a map of seats of higher learning in New England, say, with a Harvard writ large and a Yale small), satiric, ironic, comic (e.g., a map of the United States with nothing but wasteland beyond the Hudson River), even "tragic" (e.g., a map of concentration-camp sites, or of sites at which innocent goodness was destroyed by cruelty), hortatory, or almost anything else we want them to be.

Within this diversity there is, of course, still more diversity, two kinds of which are worth noting. For instance, so long as "shape," for example, is the crucial thing, the material embodying it is a matter of indifference. The shape of the United States, for instance, will remain essentially the same, within acceptable tolerances, whether I draw it in pencil on a piece of paper (which itself may be lined, unlined, construction, bond, or onionskin paper), cut it out of a piece of wood (oak, maple, elm, cedar), chisel it in stone (no matter what kind), tattoo it on my arm (his, her, your arm), outline it with my finger in the air, shape it in clay, pie dough, or whatever. Additionally, so long as "shape" is the crucial thing, the size of the "image" is largely a matter of indifference. That is, a large and a small shape will differ in "scale," but not in what for lack of a better term we can call "magnitude" (both will be of a size sufficient to the needs of the representational task, and "magnitude" will enlarge and shrink in relation to what the map is representing and how much and how little of it it chooses to represent—thus, a small, but sharply detailed road map of Rhode Island has less "magnitude" than a large outline map of the United States).

Yet, the internal diversity of maps notwithstanding, maps are maps and are easily distinguishable from fruit stands, boat races, epics, novels, university presidents with truly innovative ideas, graphs, and much else besides. Despite the fact that maps differ in terms of the *objects* (or entities or "things") on which they focus, in terms of the *kinds of materials* they use to focus attention, the *ways* they go about making their information available, and the kinds of *purposes* they serve (descriptive, comic, and so forth); despite the fact that maps do not lend themselves to easy definition (our definitions tend to be either *too narrow*, taking as definitive of the class one or two prominent aspects of many maps—widely shared objects, such as roads—and thus excluding from the class many things that, while lacking roads, are always identified as maps, or *too broad*, making the definitive features so general that it is impossible to exclude from the class things that are never treated as maps—graphs and tables, for example); despite all this and more, we move easily from map to map, adapting our interests to those of the maps we examine, differentiating among kinds of maps, discriminating between "good" and "bad" versions of kinds of maps, deciding that a map once thought "true" is no longer "true," and—so rich is our working understanding of maps—even identifying a new thing as a map, indeed, as a new "kind" of map.

We live then in a map-enriched world, and we move comfortably among the maps of the world or the worlds of maps, switching easily from one system of reference and one scheme of representation to another, as the occasion or the map requires. And although maps can vary along several lines of differentiation, as we have seen, the fact remains that new maps are intelligible because across the systems of variance there is some degree of invariance making translation possible. If it is a map, it is a map of *something* mappable—however ethereal that something may be—something that can be referred to by *some notational device* available to mapmaking in *some systematic, maplike way* for *some reason* or other not incompatible with one or another of the diverse purposes of maps. And by mappable, we mean that every map has reference, refers to something, even though that something is often determined at the moment of reference (and, of course, if it has determinate reference, of necessity it has intentionality). Here, as elsewhere, however, we do not assume or suppose a something that is *real* independently of some interests or a something that has some unique or mandatory description or categories.

Of course, if with all our skill we cannot, after repeated attempts to render the map intelligible, determine either what the map is referring to or how it goes about the task of linking references, then we will have to conclude that the map is inscrutable or that it is not a map. But since maps, as our corollary tells us, come from other maps (where else could they come from?), since we make new maps from old or existing ones, new worlds or versions from the worlds or versions already in place, we will neither make nor encounter maps that are inscrutable. This is so, we think, even if some of the maps we encounter are made by inhabitants of a planet in a galaxy far away. Even they, we assume without a hint of arrogance, map in *maplike ways*. If they don't map in what are for us maplike ways, then their maps just don't map, *for us*. Of course, there is no single attribute or set of attributes that distinguishes maps from all other things, but for all that, "maps is maps"; that is, maps do their duty in systematic ways. If they did not map in any way imaginable to us, then, as noted, we would not be able to understand them, use them, and put answerable questions to them; and, of course, if they were not schemes of reference and representation, we would not be able to make them confront themselves or each other.

Chapter 2
Map States and State Maps

Partially buried within the immediately preceding discussion are two points that deserve a bit more emphasis, because they will be recalled for service later when we apply pluralistic principles directly—rather than indirectly, as here—to "literary" matters. The first point concerns the indifference of shape to material embodiment. In the previous chapter we noted that when the crucial factor is the representation of the "shape" of the United States, the material basis of its realization (in wood, clay, paper, or whatever) is a matter of secondary or incidental importance. A collateral and by no means insignificant point is that what is "crucial" to the representational interest of a map can be represented by something other than a map. For example, the population interest of a demographic map that is indicated state by state with colors coded, say, to millions of people in each state (blue for states with one million or less, red for states with more than one million and less than two million, and so on) can be represented on a graph with bars that extend to different lengths in relation to millions of people within each state, the *lengths* correlating "perfectly" with the *color* designations of the map. By consulting either the graph or the map we can quickly determine the population, albeit in millions, of Connecticut and compare the populations of Montana and Rhode Island. Of course, as with the map of the United States, the graph may have its material basis in wood, plastic, pie dough, or whatever; what counts is a correlation of bar length with population.

The relevance of these examples to the concerns of "criticism" can only be suggested here, but it is worth noting that in both—the realization of shape and bar length with different materials *and* the switch from map to graph—a certain "cognitive sameness," a certain synonymy is preserved across rather remarkable differences in "matter." The matter is certainly *necessary*; it just doesn't matter. To learn what is interesting about these cases we do not simply ask, "What's the matter?" Both cases involve material differences, but in the second case we move, it seems, from one *scheme* to another. In this latter case we have "intertranslatability" from scheme to scheme, or what we might call "interpretive reciprocity."

Cognate with the first example would be, among other things, the following cases:

1. A hand-cranked, cog and wheel computer and an electronic, micro-chip computer running the same "program." In both, the same "information" is produced in the same sequence, and even though the "program" is dependent for its running on the physical properties of a machine, it makes no sense to say that we understand the *program* by understanding the "physics" of the machine, since the program is clearly not reducible to any particular set of physical properties. Moreover, even if the physical properties of the machine impose certain limits on the complexity of the tasks that the machine can perform, those properties cannot themselves create or design a "runnable" program, i.e., a program the machine could run, if it had it.

2. A series of representations—in stone, plaster, and wood, say— depicting the "same" cat. This is too much like the map case to require any comment, but here we do reach "art."

3. Finally and more problematically, different sequences of words expressing the same "sense." This case, at its higher reaches, just might make "genre" talk possible; different works—with, of course, different sequences of words—would belong to the same genre, would have the same principle of form. *Hamlet* and *Othello*, for example, although different in an extraordinary number of material ways, have the "same" form, a distinguishable formal likeness.

At any rate, it is useful to remember that just as the physical properties of machines do not make programs, so pieces of wood or sequences of words do not make cats or sense; sequences of words are what sense is *made of* or *from*—the rules of syntax, for instance, cannot determine their own boundary conditions.

Cognate with the second example (the map-to-graph case) are such common things as the translation of a discursive account of faculty salaries at several colleges into a table, the transmogrification of Rover into a picture of Rover, and, more problematically, the adaptation of a novel to a film. In this latter case we will undoubtedly run bump into some incommensurabilities, some indeterminacy of translation, but even so, some films are better adaptations than others. Furthermore, it is clear that if the "story" is simple enough, a one-sentence story—for example, "The sun rose at six in the morning and set at eight in the evening"—a satisfactory, two-panel, pictorial adaptation of it can be produced by a schoolchild. Interestingly, in this case, we easily adapt to the Ptolemaic scheme upon which both the story and the pictorial account depend—it is, after all, a scheme entirely consonant with the phenomenology of everyday experience—even though as post-Copernicans we have serious reservations about the "validity" of the Ptolemaic scheme. Of course, the truly "sophisticated"—that is, either an astronomer or a pluralist—will resolve the geocentric-heliocentric issue by taking sides with neither of the advocates or with both alternatively, since to him or her what moves around what depends upon one's frame of reference. Still, *understanding* the story and the pictures is not contingent upon *believing* in the world view they represent, as some modern critics seem to think.[1]

Although examples of media switch are easy enough to find, what especially intrigues us in this case is a common but perhaps not so obvious kind of cognitive sameness across material dissimilitude, that is, the persistence of "conceptual" sameness despite differences in "mental content." In the examples noted under the first case (i.e., same program, same cat, same sense), we were concerned with a certain kind of functional isomorphism at the "surface" level or perhaps, more accurately, at the level of direct information, "image," or plain sense, where the same "form" had its constitutive base in physically different materials.[2] At this level, for example, the command, "Go to the store" and the imperative question of an exasperated parent, "Would you please go to the store?!" express the "same" directive, *and* the functional properties of the stone cat and the clay cat cooperate to produce an "image" of the "same" cat. Here, on the other hand, we are interested in a certain functional isomorphism (or isomorphic functionalism) at the level of the concept, where the same form—or concept—can have different "mental" contents or "images."[3]

Before Wittgenstein, it was generally assumed that having a concept was a function of, or equivalent to, having a certain mental "image" or a certain "presentation" in the mind, a certain introspectible content within; in this schema, two people shared a concept when and only when their mental images or presentations were the same. Establishing whether there is a perfect match between "mental contents" is a notoriously tricky, perhaps even an impossible, business; but knowing whether two people share a concept is, if not an untricky, at least a possible enterprise. Basically, we find out by performing or asking others to perform certain operations with the words of which our concepts are made (or with some symbols or some inner "notational devices" with as much potential complexity as language). Simply put, if I say "mow the grass" and you paint the dog, then our failure to communicate is a "conceptual" problem. Having a concept is having a certain ability to put and to answer relevant questions, even if the putting and answering is done "internally," in one's own head. We here give expression to the view, most forcibly expressed perhaps by Quine and Davidson, that "there is no criterion of sameness of meaning except actual interpretive practice"; "the only 'handle' we actually have on the notion of 'same belief' is interpretive practice," because truth, along with meaning and reference, "does not transcend use."[4]

Concepts, of course, are neither words nor abilities, but having the ability to perform certain operations with words (or some other notational system) is a sure (or relatively sure) indication of having or "getting" a concept. Sharing concepts involves sharing an ability to use terms (or whatever) in similar, in mutually satisfying ways. To argue this point would undoubtedly take us well beyond our present concerns; moreover, what we need for our present purposes can be supplied by the exemplary rather than the argumentative mode. For example, in any given use of the phrase "unmarried men," you and I may think of different people (have different images, mental pictures, or perceptual prototypes) and have different "conceptions" of what constitutes the marriage bond. (Your conception, say, is defined by Roman Catholic doctrine, mine by "Well, if it works out, that's wonderful, really wonderful"—in the radical sense of "wonderful." We have, in short, different fundamental *beliefs* about marriage.) Despite these differences in our "mental" contents and in our "conceptions," however, we manage to carry on at some length a gossip-ridden conversation in a state of mutual understanding.

Suppose now you are a "grass" man, someone who knows a great deal about kinds of grass and about plant nutrition, pathology, and other plant-related things, whereas I am a grass illiterate who knows only that grass grows in my front yard, has to be mowed, and is greener in the summer than in the winter. Once again, notwithstanding our different perceptual prototypes and our different conceptions (beliefs), we comfortably exchange grass talk while waiting for our bus. The point here is not that we share no "references" or "concepts." We do share concepts; communication depends upon our having "references" and "concepts" in common, and learning new references and concepts requires a common referential or conceptual starting point. Rather, the point is that our immediate *mental contents* need not be the same for us to share a *concept*. Grass talk would be impossible if, in addition to sharing no prototypes and conceptions, we had available to us no common "lore" about grass.[5]

Simply, regardless of what takes place in your "head" or whether any *image* is called to your mind when the word "grass" is said, and regardless of how much more extensive than mine your knowledge of grass may be, we will get along fine as long as present use requires no more of us than that we know, for example, that grass is a plant, is green (when it is not brown), is flexible rather than rigid (at certain lengths), and so on through a more or less sizable list of conceptual properties. What makes any of this worth our time is that these distinctions bear directly on the issue of whether—and how—we can read and understand the discourse of others (at the level of intended meaning), including and especially literary discourse, as will be shown in a subsequent chapter.

To bring our present business to conclusion, however, it would probably not be out of place to provide a brief "literary" example of conceptual sameness grounded in different mental contents. Among the deeply moving lines in the awful (i.e., awe-full) conclusion to *King Lear* is the following, which Lear utters to an attendant when he knows and desperately struggles not to know that Cordelia is dead: "Pray you, undo this button. Thank you, sir." By itself, the line is not very impressive. Lifted from the play and typed on a blank piece of paper, the line stands ready for service in a wide variety of contexts, including, and perhaps especially, comic contexts, and is ingratiatingly submissive to tonal commands (the line can be said ironically, sarcastically, imperiously, superciliously, etc.). Its comic potential would be realized, for example, if it were said playfully by a college student to a roommate after a long night of "serious" drinking. Indeed, someone might use the line every day for fifty years before hitting upon a place for it in a "tragic" setting.

At the level of what semanticists might call "statement meaning," the line expresses, in the first sentence, a simple request, transparent in its meaning to anyone in a "button" culture (anyone with a working understanding of the "button" concept) and then, in the second sentence, a conventional state of gratitude, the "undo" request presumably having been granted. Of course, at this point, we might talk about possible differences in the perceptual prototypes of and in the fundamental beliefs about buttons underlying Lear's use and the attendant's understanding of the button term (differences that, of course, do not interfere with their sharing of the button concept). What really concerns us here, however, is the "power," the emotional quality, of the line, what the semanticists might call the "utterance meaning" of the line, a meaning which depends upon an imaginative grasp of both the kind of person who expresses it and the kind of situation in which it is said.

The distinction between "statement meaning" and "utterance meaning," without which we could not begin to explain "irony" (among other things), is roughly equivalent to the distinction, once not uncommon in critical discussions, between "lexis" and "praxis," lexis being the kind of meaning that has to do with unbuttoning buttons and praxis the kind that gives this particular button talk its peculiar interest (and emotional force), its interest relativity, the kind of interest to which we would expect an explanation to be relative.[6] (A cautionary note: The reader should recognize that we are not here suggesting that *statement meaning* is some kind of "real," hard fact of the matter *meaning* underlying the sentence. Nor are we suggesting that there is such a thing as an *essential* meaning in the statement. Meanings, like facts, are factitious, including "statement meanings.") We are dealing with a kind of "practical" knowledge, in the case of Lear a kind of conceptual knowledge that is at once moral and practical. We are deeply moved by Lear's remark because we have certain opinions about who he is and what situation he is in, and we have those opinions because we have "sized up" his situation in the way we have.

But what, we may ask in a T. S. Eliot mood, is the "objective correlative" of our emotional response? Well, the answer is the whole text of *Lear*. Not the words of the text, nor the sequence of the words taken together, but the whole text as imaginatively grasped by a sensitivity (ours) alert to the moral dimensions of a person deeply entangled in moral perplexities, the emotional power of which is a reflex of how we have sized them up. We here assume that sizing up depends on "ordinary," "folk" categories, those we ordinarily use in our day to day moral talk. Let us assume that if several people size the play up in similar ways they will have similar responses to the line in question and the play as a whole. Let us assume conservatively only that several people are deeply moved by the play and are moved as they are because their conceptual grasp of the work is roughly the same. If we then ask the witnesses to give an account of their response, we will undoubtedly get as many different accounts as we have witnesses, each drawing inferences from the text not drawn by any of the others, each making slightly different moral assessments, and each calling attention to different aspects of the text or at least referring to the same aspects in different words.

By a somewhat circuitous route, then, we arrive at a somewhat homely truth: radically different critical statements (and essays) can be and often are based on the same conceptual understanding of the text. Moreover, to the extent that our text is already a "true" and "good" version, its properties will be such as to contribute to the functioning of the text as the version it is. And to the extent that our similar responses are based on a conceptual grasp of the functioning of the properties of the version which is the text, our statements will be relative to the conceptual interests of the version, however different they may be in their details or arguments, however different their "contents" may be. At any rate, here as elsewhere we find cognitive or conceptual sameness where mental contents and representations (verbal or otherwise) are strikingly different.

The other point partially buried in the discussion of the map-enriched world in which we find ourselves concerns the sheer diversity of maps as such and what such diversity enables us to do. That is, we can understand, revise, and remake an enormous number of existing maps and create a virtually infinite number of new maps. But before looking at this diversity and its enabling power, we should keep in mind that however extensive our knowledge and skills may be, we still cannot map the unmappable, such as the "real" Rhode Island. (There is after all, no "roaded" Rhode Island apart from some depictions and representations, and there is no single road map which simply is *the* map of Rhode Island *roads*.)[7] A true road map (or several true road maps) may get us easily from Providence to Boston, but no true road map can embody or represent, say, the temporal, auditory, or emotional experience of the trip. Nor can any true road map be used, for example, as a musical score; although it is difficult to put limits on the interests maps may be relative to, some interests remain incompatible and some unmappable.

Also, doomed to failure would be any attempt to make the one true map from all the available true maps by superimposing maps upon maps in a palimpsest or to make all true maps add up to some comprehensive truth about maps by displaying them serially, with each map contributing its sum to the total. Maps are more like roman than arabic numerals. Whereas it is relatively easy to add columns of arabic numerals, it is as difficult to add maps together as it is to add columns of roman numerals; it is perhaps not by accident that the Romans were better orators than mathematicians.

The point here, though obvious to some readers, is still worth emphasizing. For simplicity's sake, let us restrict our attention to all true maps (existing and possible) of one small state, Rhode Island. Our various maps of Rhode Island show not only different but also contrasting conflicting aspects of the state. For example, even the shape changes dramatically as the state is displayed comically, first, from the point of view of the urbanites in Providence and, then, from the point of view of the "sophisticates" in Newport, or as its shoreline reflects the effects of erosion in one or another period, before and after a series of hurricanes, and so on. As the map interests change, so will the state, as it accommodates itself to different entities, emphases, means of denotation, purposes, and so on. And although it is convenient to say that all the maps have at lease one reference in common—Rhode Island—we must not decide too quickly what that Rhode Island really is, inasmuch as the state commonly referred to has no common reference, or has no reference apart from interest; the same state is referred to in many ways, in short, exists in many states of reference. Thus, as the world (version) goes, so goes Rhode Island. We can have many Rhode Islands or one (can have one, however, only so long as we recognize that it is made up of many contrasting, irreconcilable aspects). With these caveats in place, we can return to the main business at hand, diversity and the powers it enables.

The pluralist view of maps is that they have many interests and that they are the way they are because they have the interests they have. Reference is determined by interest, and the significant properties of any given map (both material and conceptual) are functional relative to that interest; indeed, significance, importance, emphasis and so on are interest-relative values. In other words, if an interest is mappable, the map made in that interest will be intelligible and usable (in the *interested* sense) only to the extent that its sensible features make possible a conceptual grasp of the interest. But, significantly (and despite what many theorists claim or seem to believe), a map need not map an interest that I share (or believe in) for it to be intelligible. I can understand a flat-earth map, reflecting *beliefs* that are radically different from my "earth" beliefs and produced in a culture radically different from my own in terms of social and political organization and theological convictions. In short, radical interpretation is possible, despite what some—Gadamerians, for example—might say.

On the other hand, I can make maps with interests that no other map has shown an interest in. For example, I can create two "personal interest" maps, one indicating the streets on which members of my high-school class lived (with "X" marks to signify the approximate locations of their houses on the streets) and another indicating the cities in which they were living ten years after graduation. Stretching even further, I can make a "Twin Earth" map which exhibits how a Twin Earth town would be laid out if it were designed to maximize cooperation among its citizens rather than individuality and entrepreneurship—if it were, that is, informed by political and economic values quite different from those obtaining in its earthly counterpart.

As far as maps are concerned, then, interest-relativity is intelligible across differences in personal belief, culture, and history. To say that the limits of our understanding are coextensive with the beliefs or norms implicated in a particular language, culture, or historical period would be to say what does not seem to be true of our understanding of maps. There are certainly constraints on the making and understanding of maps. Maps are certainly constrained by their interests and by the means available to the realization of those interests. But in saying as much, the pluralist, it is important to remember, is not suggesting or implying that maps, our ideas and beliefs about maps, and our map interests are *not* historically determined in any sense whatsoever; nor is he saying that there is nothing intertextual or "intermapual" about maps or that we cannot discuss or deal with their "intermapuality," nor that maps are always and inevitable without gender bias or an "ideological" component, nor that they cannot be seen as instruments of desire and power, nor . . . much else besides. Further, the pluralist readily admits that the map's interest may often be the least interesting thing to note about the map, may often be, at any rate, what we are at the moment least interested in.[8]

But talk about the interest-relativity of maps, about reference and meaning and the functional properties of maps in relation to or as determined by interest, is misleading to the extent that it suggests that each map has a single interest, a subsumptive, controlling interest, to which everything else is subservient. Maps, of course, may have several interests, though, as we have seen, no single map can map all interests and, unlike many individuals in public life, particular maps are unlikely to be involved in "conflicts of interest."

The road map is a prime example of a multiple-interest map. A given road map may be interested not only in showing what roads go where or how one can get from here to there by this or that particular route, but also in indicating the locations of state parks, historic sites, colleges, beaches, population densities, and so on. From the point of view of the *road* map, however, these are secondary or auxiliary interests, since it has no vested interest in any one of them and remains primarily devoted to roads and locations relative to roads. Nevertheless, any "secondary" interest can become interesting in its own right or can assume coordinate status with the primary interest. For example, a given road map produced by a particular motel chain will naturally give special, detailed prominence to the locations of its motels, thus facilitating the driver's access to them. Thus, it is clearly possible to consider road maps in terms of primary, secondary, and coordinate interests. Analogously, no single work of literature need be restricted to one and only one interest, such as a mimetic or didactic function; but that is another, albeit the same, story: the story within the map story.

To complicate the situation further, just as different maps have different interests and many maps have multiple interests, so *readers* or *users* may bring to them an enormous number of interests, finding maps interesting for a variety of reasons. Of course, some readers or critics of maps may even be interested in revealing interests that maps are interested in concealing or suppressing; maps, they find, inevitably say more and/or less than they "mean" to say. Even to sketch the multiplicity of reader interests would be impossible here, if only because there may be as many interests as readers, but something can be done by way of illustration.

Any differentiable aspect or any secondary interest of a map can be a matter of primary interest to the reader. For example, a reader interested in getting to a state beach can use a map only secondarily interested in beaches to get there. Indeed, even if the map has no interest in beaches as such, an interested reader can use the map to find one by following, say, a shoreline route, just as an interested reader can learn something about the prevalence of certain consonant clusters in a work "uninterested" in such things in any specific way, or can learn about verb tenses, or words beginning with "h," or nature, sickness, and clothing images, or about countless other things. Similarly, the reader may take a particular interest in the kinds of symbols used, in their interrelation, in the kinds of objects denoted or referred to, and so on, and take an interest in any of these only to the extent that it reflects the state of the art at a given time, the policy decisions or cultural prejudices of a certain period, or whatever. The reader who views the particular map as a kind of interpretive discourse caught up in a network of interpretive discourses will be interested in intermapuality, in the map as a mosaic of "quotations" from other maps. Pluralists, of course, give preeminence to no single kind but are concerned with various forms and lines of intermapuality, since they know that maps can be related to other maps in various ways. Maps, indeed, are always already embedded in the map discourse from which they emerge and which makes them possible, but the pluralist recognizes that maps come in various *kinds* and variously bear, openly and covertly, the marks of different kinds and degrees of psychological, social, historical, or class pressure.

To bring this short list of reader responses to maps to an end, we can look for a moment at the reader interested in the politics or in, say, the class, race, or gender prejudices of maps. All maps, of course, have biases, are prejudiced in favor of their interests. A prejudice worn openly by a map is a prejudice worn proudly (or at least unashamedly); but when prejudice is bigotry (or ideology, i.e., the mark of oppression and repression), a map will do the "decent" thing and conceal its nastiness from the general public and often from itself. Some maps are frankly and conspicuously political or racial, for example, maps of missile sites, of nonaligned countries, or of "Democratic" and "Republican" states or, on the racial side, maps of neighborhoods, of states, or countries according to racial predominance or distribution. On the other hand, a general use road map that notes the locations of colleges but that omits the locations, secondarily or auxiliarily, of any women's, black, or Catholic colleges, is either deliberately or inadvertently up to something deserving public exposure. Similarly, a general use road map that locates private golf courses but no public ones, private beaches but no public ones, etc., is undoubtedly interested in serving something other than the public interest.

Moreover, a given culture or society will manufacture, market, and distribute an abundance of maps designed to satisfy the interests it has created in its own interest. And, of course, it is often only by indirection (i.e., by reading through or against the map, by asking the impertinent questions) that we find directions out, the directions that our maps hide from others and often from themselves. If maps make up a kind of knowledge or make possible certain kinds of knowledge, and if knowledge is a kind of power, then it is certainly within the range of ambition to want to define and control the mappable and to determine what does and does not count as a map. Against the success of such retrograde ambition, reading against the grain is our best defense. And impertinence is never more virtuous than when it exposes the "false" and self-serving limits which culture (here map culture) imposes on the imagination. Of course, there is no single rock to which the pluralist Prometheus can be bound by one repressive culture.

Readers are hardly obliged to correlate their interests with those of the maps they study, but to the extent that their speculations or observations depend upon an *understanding* of maps (as do those, for example, of the reader who exposes the racist or political biases of particular maps, the reader who wishes to "deconstruct" maps, or the reader who wishes to "psychoanalyze" maps), map interests cannot be a matter of indifference to them. The preceding, if tautological, is not mere tautology: some inquiries, however far removed from the concerns of particular maps, are impossible in the absence of a prior understanding of map interests. Without the assumption of certain differentiable interests *in* maps, saying something interesting or valuable *about*, for instance, the history of maps, about their part in the definition of the age by which they were also defined, about their participation in the common processes of language or mind, about their inability to avoid deforming the "knowledge" that informs them, and so on, would be impossible.

Nevertheless, the fact remains that not all reader interests are tied to an *understanding* of map interests. We can be interested in a map's *percepts* rather than its *concepts*, that is, in blue lines and red lines, apart from their reference to roads, in the mere appearance of certain elements (town names, say), apart from their map significance, in the kind of ink or paper used, and so on. Similarly, in an examination of "literary" texts, we may be interested in the fact that a clergyman is present in several texts, that the issue of time is raised in several texts, that every sonnet published in 1612 begins with the preposition "of," and so on through a long list of things in which we might take an interest in the process of establishing evidence for a large argument about poetry, history, politics, or whatever.[9]

At perhaps the furthest remove from map interests, we find *user* interests (not reader or ideological interests) that can be satisfied only because an available map has what might be called certain gross physical characteristics; that is, it is flexible, foldable, flammable, and so on. And because maps, like everything else, have meanings relative to interests and can take on any meanings within the functional range of their properties (as determined by or relevant to those interests), they may obsequiously accommodate themselves, within certain limits, to such various and manifold interests as flyswatting, fire starting, fire extinguishing, table leg adjusting, and so on. Asking what a map means, then, is very much like asking how fast the car is going. It all depends. Nevertheless, when we know what it depends upon, we know in no uncertain terms how fast the car is going and what the map means. Moreover, as far as maps are concerned, it is clear that among the interests and meanings they can have are some that are more distinctly map interests and meanings than others. And if we take an interest in such interests and meanings we can get them, as well as all the other interests, *right.*

By directing attention to maps, we have learned that pluralists have many *beliefs* concerning them (and, implicitly, concerning many other kinds of discourse). They have many *beliefs* about truth, reference, meaning, concepts, standards (and even recognize the topic relativity of such general standards as coherence and consistency), about justification, interest, and so on. Yet, amidst this welter of beliefs, they map their way knowing that, while their access to the worlds of maps is through the maps themselves, "true" maps do not make their way inaccessible. They do not ask their beliefs about a particular map, new or old, to square with *all* their map beliefs; rather, they learn what beliefs to have about the map in question in the process of reading the map, assuming all along that it makes some kind of sense in some system of reference not prohibited to maps. But, of course, they bring to the map not uninscribed but richly inscribed minds; and the more various their knowledge and awareness of past inscriptions, the readier they are to narrow the possible range of the inscriptions before them.

Of course, it is important to remember that throughout this discussion of maps I have been chiefly concerned, if somewhat surreptitiously, with some few pluralistic principles and their bearing on discourses of various kinds (creative, theoretical, interpretive). In spite of the ubiquity of maps in the above, I have been more interested in talking *through* than *about* them. By talking through them, I have been able, so I fervently hope, not only to illuminate certain principles but also to highlight what maps have in common with other discourses or symbol systems. Map language, like other kinds of language, uses symbols; has meanings, references, concepts, moods, tenses, and emotional valences; is social, political, historical, and so on. Moreover, a pluralistic perspective on maps reveals much about how pluralists distinguish themselves from others who are likewise situated where meaning has gone immanent and where Truth has been deconstructed.

Without rehearsing or exploring all distinctions here, it is useful to recognize that for the pluralist (but not for many other theorists), *the map is already a version and is the version it is because it has the interests it has.* Just as we can discriminate between the interest-relativity of an essay by Derrida, Foucault, or Richard Rorty and that of an essay by Fish, Booth, or Harold Bloom, so we can similarly discriminate between the interest-relativity of one map and another, and the interest-relativity of *Hamlet* and *Tristram Shandy*. No more than an essay by Geoffrey Hartman or a poem by Yeats is a map loitering about waiting to be versionalized. And if we can differentiate a Copernican from a Ptolemaic explanation of sun, moon, and earth relations, we can similarly differentiate a population map from a road map explanation and a *Four Quartets* from a *Beggar's Opera* explanation. And we can do all this without ever once losing sight of the fact that interests may be multiple or that every version may accommodate itself to a variety of interests.

Additionally, while pluralists countenance countless numbers of versions, they also, unlike many other theorists, refuse to embrace all versions, since among the many versions of the world some are and some are not true, right, or correct. If we make many correct versions, no correct version is made by hammering any old things together in any old way. Of the many right versions we make, some are assimilable or reconcilable to one another and some, of course, are not. There can be several true versions of the same world (e.g., several true road maps of Rhode Island or several true versions of them in paper, wood, pie dough, and so on), versions that differ in real but not crucial ways. For example, two road maps of Rhode Island made to different scales can easily be reconciled to one another, whereas a road map and a population map of the state are not reconcilable, except to the extent that they are both true versions of the "same" state (the state, of course, is not the same in both versions, but for some purposes, we may be willing to accept "state" as a ground of sameness in the two maps).

Similarly, we can join and separate versions in various ways, finding a basis of likeness or difference in any distinguishable feature ("physical" or "mental") shared by two or more maps (or texts). Also, two literary works, for example, may be "materially" different in many ways (use different words, characters, scenes, and so on) but similar in their effects. On the other hand, two works may produce different effects (i.e., depend for their power on radically different kinds of conceptual knowledge) but be similar in many material respects. In short, we can make different versions unite or divide by "enversioning" them in various systems of likeness and difference. (We make genres, for example, by establishing several lines of affiliation or sameness among distinct works, our categories being useful to the extent that they make ruling out as well as ruling in possible and to the extent that the properties identified as similar are actually functional in the works in similar ways, that the similar properties are properties of the functioning of the works as conceptual constructs.) Here, as elsewhere, the pluralist has several choices when confronted with many "true" versions.

On the other hand, when confronted with conflicting versions, the pluralist's choices narrow to three: to reject one as false (the road map, say, that sends an east-west road north-south); to take them both as true but true in different worlds (polar and mercator maps, for example); or to find some way of reconciling them (for example, a 1947 and a 1987 road map of Rhode Island, though conflicting, are both true for different periods). As Nelson Goodman says, "to anyone but an arrant absolutist, alternative ostensibly conflicting versions often present good and equal claims to truth." Nevertheless, he continues, "we can hardly take [geniunely] conflicting statements as true in the same world without admitting all statements whatsoever (since all follow from any contradiction) as true in the same world, and that world itself as impossible."[10]

Finally, then, although pluralists are interested in distinguishing among "true" versions and separating *right* from *wrong* versions, they have no master method by the manipulation of which they can establish or explain some true Objectivity or some one and only true Truth. But though reason, like everything else, has gone immanent, the objectivity of reason (as opposed to the Objectivity of Reason) has not as a consequence also and necessarily been lost. From the pluralist perspective, as Hilary Putnam notes, the "attempt to deny the objectivity of reason leads to self-defeating irrationalisms [such as total relativism, interpretive community-ism, and, indeed, all "isms" that do not allow for the defeasibility of their views], while the attempt to explain the objectivity of reason leads to nonsense, at least if our paradigm of explanation is the familiar reductionist one [the scientific method one or the "historicist" one, for example, which seeks to find and account for true "materiality" and, hence, true Objectivity]"[11]

Having established, or at least announced, in the preceding a significant number of pluralist principles and suggested by exemplification some of their entailments, we are now in a position to consider what makes explanations good and to examine the superiority of pluralist to other explanations.

Part Two
References, Meanings, Worlds

Chapter 3
Eclecticism, or Worlds in Collision

Surprisingly, once the word got out that reason had gone immanent, that truth, reference, justification, standards of judgment, facts, values, and so on were interest-relative and context-sensitive, critics did not rush to pluralism with the same celerity that characterized the hell-bent-for-leather dash of miners to California in 1849 (when, of course, another word got out). If immanent reason was a kind of intellectual gold, pluralism was not, for many critics at least, a kind of California. Claims were—and continue to be—staked in eclecticism, monism, and skepticism, but ever so rarely in pluralism. Why the richest vein should be least mined is a topic deserving attention, but it is not one that can be explored here; our concern is to take a quick, broad look at alternatives to pluralism and to note briefly why these alternatives are unsatisfactory from the pluralistic perspective.

Nevertheless, in deliberately pursuing our course, we shall inevitably, though incidentally, learn something about why the organized confusion of pluralism is deeply offensive to those who hanker for an anchor (one anchor, even though an immanent one) as well as to those who like their confusion unqualified, who like their relativism to be total. Moreover, it should be clear at the outset that in what follows we shall be interested, not in providing a comprehensive survey of contemporary critical views or detailed analyses of particular critical essays or books (though the views of particular advocates will be highlighted occasionally for purposes of illustration), but in outlining broad tendencies and major issues in order better to illuminate not only what the stakes are for which we play but why the pluralist is willing to "call" the highest bidder (and does so with "real" money). This is, after all, a long essay in defense of pluralism as an alternative to prevailing practices and assumptions within a world in which

Truth has been deconstructed and Reality is not simply "out there" independently of our schemes of reference and interpretation.[1]

In the previous two chapters, an attempt was made to present and unpack certain pluralistic principles, but in the process of unpacking we often found what is easier to imagine than to make, namely, another packed suitcase within an unpacked one. And even though I believe that from our map cases we could extrapolate principles and "facts" sufficient to all the problems raised by contemporary literary theory, I also recognize that many of those problems must be confronted directly, problems such as *how* we manage to understand and use versions not of our own making; *where* versions come from ("from other versions" is a right but insufficient answer); *how* we revise and amend old versions and make new ones; *what* counts as a "right" or "good" explanation; *what* constraints on understanding our interpretive practices impose on us; *what* difference *différance* makes to world-making; *how* "meaning" is fixed in a world in which "meaning" derives from schemes of interpretation, in which meaning is interest-conditional; how the pluralist manages to rule versions in and out of court and to avoid being a total "relativist" while persisting in relativizing worlds to various versions, and so on. In this and subsequent chapters the pluralist response to such issues will be given.

Although there are certainly plenty of eclectics on the streets, in the classrooms, at cocktail parties, on bar stools, and in committee meetings, there are no eclectics in the intellectual foxholes. When the shells of critical inquiry start flying, eclecticism is no bunker to hunker down in, because it is, as any building inspector could tell you, a Rube Goldberg, jerry-built sort of contraption. Indeed, it is difficult to find any critic who openly avows eclecticism. For the most part, the eclectics among us prefer to call themselves pluralists, open- and liberal-minded people who believe that there is a little truth in all or most critical positions.

Convinced by something in everything read, or finding a little truth in every critical position or theory, the soft eclectic stitches "truths" together in a crazy-quilt fashion, appealing, in a given discussion, now to Freud and Hans-Georg Gadamer and now to Lacan and Giambattista Vico (or Hartman and Booth or whomever), without suspecting that the authorities or "truths" may conflict with one another, may not be assimilable to or compatible with one another. Attempting to link "truths" in this way is like trying to combine, not an apple and an orange, but an apple and a road (and, as every farm child knows, a roadapple is neither a road nor an apple). For the pluralist, this procedure fails because the separate truths are embedded in different and usually incompatible systems of meaning and reference; they belong, in short, to different versions, which are neither reducible to one another nor reconcilable.

If meaning and reference are relative to scheme of interpretation, then statements deriving from different schemes cannot be adjusted to one another, unless the schemes themselves can be reconciled. Even if two truths refer to the same text, such as *Hamlet*, or to the same scene of the same text, they will not necessarily (or usually) refer to the same "facts" in what, as a matter of convenience, we call the same text or the same scene. The "facts" of the matter will be different "facts," and there are no "facts of the matter" apart from *systems of reference*. The eclectic's procedure here is analogous to that which would superimpose all the maps of Rhode Island upon one another in a palimpsest in the hope of getting a glimpse of the real map of Rhode Island or the map of the state in its full immanence.

The eclectic is being faulted here, not for believing that there are many "truths," but for believing that the many truths are true of the same, the one and only text. The problem for the eclectic is the problem for all of us; none of us can shift to a frame of reference that would allow us to transform a fully committed Marxist reading into a fully committed Freudian reading of Hamlet's character.

In the usual case, however, the eclectic does not make a commitment in one breath to a Freudian reading of character and then in the next to a Marxist reading, overlooking in the process a possible tension in the successive commitments; rather, he or she accepts a "New Critical" reading of the "language" (or some parts of it), a Freudian reading of character, and a Marxist reading of the "actions as a whole." Here is eclecticism in full and unsightly bloom, for to the extent that each of the readings from which such a whole reading is taken is itself part of a whole reading of the text, the eclectic inadvertently produces what is at once a flower, a horse, and a shoe—an amalgamation, not a synthesis of parts. In actual practice, of course, the eclectic is not likely to move systematically or schematically from one derivational base to another, but, rather, to switch from frame to frame somewhat haphazardly as one or another "truth" seems locally appropriate.

The *sceptic* side of the eclectic's faith is that no one method or theory provides a fully adequate account of any particular problem or issue (or text). The *pluralist*, on the other hand, counters such skepticism with the conviction that every true account is adequate to what it is an account of, a conviction not completely vitiated by tautology since it presupposes only what can be readily granted, that is, that a given system of reference cannot account for (or even mention) what lies outside its range of reference and that adequacy is a component of the truth of the account. Upon what remains dark in these remarks a little light can be shed.

The eclectic's refusal to go all the way with any particular theory or interpretation stems from his or her recognition of the sensibleness of very different (often radically different) approaches, from complacence in the face of different versions, and from failure to see that the persistence of similar (or identical) terms in different approaches is no guarantee of shared references or meanings. Two critics, for example, may share a vocabulary (or have many terms in common) without simultaneously sharing meanings, references, or concepts. Even though both "refer" to Hamlet, Gertrude, Claudius, delay of action, or to structure, society, ideology, plot, they will not necessarily be discussing the same play unless their common terms are similarly functional within the same scheme of interpretation. Just as it sometimes happens that *different* terms refer to the "same" thing, are *co-referential*, so it sometimes happens that the *same* terms refer to "different" things. So much depends upon the context or world we are in and the purposes we have in that context or world. If the two approaches are both true accounts of "different" plays, then there is no reason why we cannot go all the way with both accounts of what is commonly called *Hamlet*, why we cannot have two (or countless) plays in one. The "one" in "in one" is, of course, a convenient fiction. There is no "real" play existing somewhere apart from a scheme of reference, just as there is no such thing as *the* meaning of a statement underlying and anteceding some scheme of reference and some system of belief and desire.

To say as much, however, is not to suggest that none of the schemes could be Shakespeare's, that his play is necessarily less accessible than G. Wilson Knight's or Robert Heilman's *Hamlet* (i.e., interpretation of *Hamlet*) or even the hypothetical version that a deconstructionist might make (and then unmake). If such versions can be understood, I see no reason why Shakespeare's cannot also, no reason why the system of reference which is his *Hamlet* should be considered to be inaccessible, when we do not consider the system of reference which is Newton's theory of gravitation or Einstein's general theory of relativity to be similarly inaccessible, as it is not.

Since the critic, like everybody else, cannot talk about or refer to everything at once and is restricted, like everybody else, to discussing only so much of anything as falls within the logical and semantic range of his system of reference, his talk, if true, will be true only within the limits of his selection, his restricted focus of interest.[2] Thus, no critic talks about *Hamlet*, or language, or history as such but only about so much of each of these as can be constituted by and discussed within a delimited range of reference, with the range itself made functional within a particular argumentative system (a system of reasoning or inference) that has as its end in view, either implicitly or explicitly, the resolution of some question or problem.

There is, then, a strict relativity of *statements* to *questions* and of questions to *purposes* and *background knowledge*, that is, the terms, assumptions, distinctions and so on that underlie the asking of certain questions in the first place. Asking this rather than that question implies a certain kind of background knowledge or intellectual framework, and having this rather than that kind of background knowledge implies an interest in certain kinds of questions. Ostensibly conflicting versions (or readings or theories) are troublesome to the pluralist only when they actually collide, for, as we noted earlier, two statements cannot be taken as true of the same world without admitting, as Goodman notes, "all statements whatsoever (since all follow from any contradiction) as true in the same world, and that world itself as impossible."[3]

But *genuinely conflicting true statements* do not collide, because they exist, as it were, in different space-times, are responsible, if you prefer, to different frameworks. They are not actually on a collision course, not in the pluralist's universe at any rate. It is because the different statements (or, more exactly, different kinds of statements) exist in different space-times that they cannot be combined in the way the eclectic wishes to combine them. When they are put together, they do not make a "fit," since they are made up of properties that are *projectible* in different worlds; that is, the statements themselves and the elements of which they are made are implicated in and implications of what some have called different horizons of meaning. Simply put, the *properties* of a Jungian reading of character are not properties from which a Freudian reading can be projected. And it is because this is so that the eclectic's shelter provides no shelter when, as it always does in the meteorological or the trench-warfare world of critical inquiry, the rain it raineth every day or the shells they fly every which way. At bottom, the eclectic is a kind of failed monist—a monist because of a persistent belief that the various references to, say, *Hamlet* refer to the same *Hamlet*, and a failed one because the various "truths" do not add up, do not make the Truth that is sought. Case closed.

Well, almost closed. Before passing on to other concerns, we must say a word or two about those pseudoeclectics (or noneclectic monists) who may be (and are often) confused with "pure" eclectics, that is, those critics who take bits and pieces from many authorities in the process of building their own systems. Such critics—like Bloom,

Shoshana Felman, and many others—take an insight from this one, an aperçu from that one, a little something from Freud, Nietzsche, Lacan, Derrida, Kenneth Burke, and so on and use the various statements and doctrines belonging to and having meaning within radically different systems of entailment as structural components of entirely independent theories.[4] The parts appropriated are no longer parts of their own versions (the versions from which they have been appropriated), but parts of a new version, and the authorities from whom the material is taken are, then, stockjobbers or parts suppliers to a designer with his or her own version to build. The master builder masters the masters and shows that, appearances notwithstanding, they have been working for him or her all along.

Chapter 4
Stable Worlds in Different Space-Times

At this point, it would perhaps be useful to clarify the notion of different space-times and to undermine any suspicion that the *pluralist* simply adds another world to his or her existing worlds whenever coming upon a different version. To some it may seem that if the eclectic foolishly tries to juggle versions from different worlds in one world, the pluralist foolishly makes a new world of any version that is internally coherent or not self-contradictory. At any rate, in making a case against eclecticism, I do not wish to misrepresent the pluralist position.[1]

Two versions occupy different space-times when they cannot be reconciled with one another or when one cannot be reduced to or subsumed by another. Examples of irreconcilable differences come quickly to mind. To begin with large-scale space-time differences, we can consider those old exemplary war-horses, the Ptolemaic and Copernican views of the motions of sun, moon, and planets. This is an especially interesting case because these views, which were once seen to be in conflict, are now rather casually translated into one another, as we adopt now this, now that, and now another planetary frame of reference. At one time more than a little depended on whether one believed the earth went around the sun or the sun, the earth. In a manner of speaking, we can say that the heliocentric and the geocentric views refer to the *same objects* and explain the *same facts*, but we had better not look too closely at precisely what the same "facts" are, since the "same facts" have factual status and meaning in fundamentally different conceptions of motion, in different systems of reference.

Whereas not so very long ago we would have had to say that the heliocentric explanation was false if the geocentric explanation were true, today we can say that, depending on one's perspective, both are true. The explanations are true in different space-times. They are theoretical analogues to the perceptual rabbit-duck, the image that can be seen as either a rabbit or a duck but not as both at the same time; like the competing planetary systems, the rabbit and the duck exist in different space-times. The presence of one in the perceptual field depends upon or is impossible without the cancellation or disappearance of the other in the perceptual field. Thus, only in a manner of speaking can we say that the two explanations or methods give fully adequate answers to the *same* question about the same *facts*. Nevertheless, although we have different theories which differently organize their facts, we are not prevented from comparing them (as we shall see); nor are we prevented by anything in our complex amalgam of present day beliefs from understanding what each theory is trying to explain or how it goes about explaining it. That is, the person in the past who actually believed in the truth of the geocentric view had no trouble understanding what the heliocentric view was all about, and we today have no trouble understanding either the references or explanations of the two theories or how our different views might be relevant to their contestable concepts. Here are "facts" that should not be uninteresting to the literary *theorist*, especially someone whose beliefs are constrained by an interpretive community or archive—a Foucauldian, Gadamerian, or Fishean, perhaps.

The Really Apparent and the Apparently Real

Every writer who has ever proofread his or her own writing knows that one often sees what is not there and fails to see what is there. Many people are also familiar with the common psychological experiment in which the respondent, requested to identify the cards in a deck of playing cards, calls out "five of hearts" when an anomalous *black* five of hearts appears, failing to notice anything "peculiar" about the card. Clearly, we often see what we are prepared to see. What concerns us here is the "thereness" of what is "not there"; if it simply were not there, there would be no "thereness" about it at all. If in most instances we are willing to say that we have made a mistake (slips of the eye probably being even more frequent than slips of the tongue), there are instances in which even when we are told what is "there," we nevertheless continue to see what is "not there." Such instances as these have, I think, interesting theoretical implications, only a few of which can be explored here, as well as relevance to space-time differences.

Under certain conditions, we regularly see motion when it is "only" apparently there.[2] Within certain distances and time intervals (10 to 45 milliseconds), when one spot is flashed and is then followed by a second flash a short distance away, we will normally see, not two flashes, but the continuous movement of the spot from one point to another. Moreover, if the first spot is a circle and the second a square (or any other shape, for that matter), the spot will reshape itself as it moves. If the first spot is followed by several spots differently located around the first, the first spot will divide and move separately and simultaneously to the several locations. More startling still is the case in which one *group* of "images" is flashed before another *group*, for example, a circle-square-circle-square group followed by a square-circle-square-circle group a short distance to the right. Instead of each of the "images" in the first group transforming itself into its counterpart in the sequence of the second group, as we might expect, we find, such is the ingenuity or perversity of our perceptual mechanism, that the last three "images" of the first group (the square-circle-square) move as a block to form the first three images of the second group, while the first circle of the first group becomes the last square of the second group.

In all cases, since we are dealing with successive flashes, the motion seen is "apparent" rather than "real." Since we actually see the spot move, however, it is not clear that we have any warrant for saying that the spot does not "really" move. Indeed, we have only as much warrant for saying so as we have for insisting that we "really" have two spots. At the level of perception the spot *really* moves, whereas at the level of "physical" description we have two flashes. Ruling perceptual talk (or experimental description talk) out of bounds will not change the "facts" of perception (or, on the other hand, the "facts" of the experiment). As Nelson Goodman notes of these experiments in "apparent motion," "The perceptual is no more a rather distorted version of the physical facts than the physical is a highly artificial version of the perceptual facts."[3] The perceptual and physical explanations of the facts occupy different space-times, and they are explanations of the "same facts" only in the sense in which the heliocentric and geocentric versions are explanations of the same facts. They are both adequate explanations of the facts they explain; moreover, they are eminently superior to the explanation that says, for example, that there is *really only one spot* which remains stationary. Relative to this explanation, the other two are correct, right, true.

These experiments, while ingeniously contrived and conducted within severe time and distance constraints, are not so far removed from everyday experience as we might initially think, for we commonly find ourselves confronting analogous perceptual situations in our daily lives. The round dining-room table at which we sit in postprandial satisfaction is regularly perceived from the kitchen (and elsewhere) as oval-shaped. If we ask a child of a certain age to draw the table, he will probably begin by making a circle, drawing what he "knows" to be the case, not what he sees. (And, of course, all adults, compensating perhaps for perceptual "distortion," will, when asked about the *shape* of the table top, say it is *round*, though they almost never *experience*—perceive it—as round.) If the table is rectangular rather than round, the child will begin with a rectangle, not a parallelogram or an even more "correct" image, in which the long sides are represented by lines tending to converge and the short sides by lines of unequal lengths.

Once again, perceived shape is supplanted by "physical" shape, and one kind of knowledge legislates over another. What the child draws is true but somehow "not right" (usually, not even to the child), not because of a failure to see "correctly," but because of a lack of knowledge of the drawing "conventions" (perspective, shading, etc.) that would make possible the overriding of "physical" knowledge and the expression of his "perceptual" knowledge. Of course, perception itself has more than a little of the habitual—cultural, conventional—about it, has value and preference and, thus, "interpretation" built into it. What the child never does, however, is represent the physically "round" and perceptually "oval" table as a square (or rectangle or rhomboid, etc.). Like adults, children know that some versions of the "same facts" are not right.

Of course, the roundness, squareness, hardness, smoothness, and so on of the table are not projectible features of the subatomic physicist's "true" explanation of the table. Such features are not within the explanation space of the physicist's "on-duty" space-time explanation of the table (his or her explanation, that is, as a physicist, not as an ordinary person). The cubist or abstract expressionist painter, on the other hand, despite knowledge of "drawing conventions," may give us a childlike version of the table and the objects on it that suddenly enables us to know what in some sense we may already have known but that *we would never have known we knew without being forced to see it.* The painter enlarges our understanding in the course of giving us access to it; startles us into seeing the world anew or into seeing a new world; redivides, reorders, recombines, reassembles, remakes the worlds we know so that we can inhabit a new space-time that, once we know it, we know as something already latently known or available for knowing by us. (It is this sort of enlargement of our understanding, this sort of *new* and *original* world, that some reader-response, institutional-norms, and intertextual critics seem willing to lose, when they make certain culture-specific categories the inscriptional headmasters of interpretation.)

What else we can learn from these experiments that may be useful to critical theory and to our understanding of knowing and making can only be suggested here. After looking carefully at Paul Kolers's accounts of the high jinks of perceptual behavior, Goodman concludes that the "visual system drives toward uniformity and continuity, constrained by its anatomy and physiology, and influenced by what it has seen and done before, but improvising along the way."[4] At this point, we would note that what is true of perception (itself a kind of interpretation) is true also of interpretive practice generally. Both in making and in reading versions we strive for uniformity and continuity, drawing on what we have seen and done before but improvising as we go, assuming all along, as readers, that what is before us makes some kind of sense in some system of reference, even if it is a sense with which we disagree or in which we cannot believe. We have here not a theory of interpretation, but an observation about interpretive practice. No one theory would be adequate to our practice, of course. Because we cannot know prior to reading what, from out of all that our past seeing and doing has made available to us, will be relevant to the case or text at hand, we cannot create a single theory of interpretation that will adequately accommodate the various ways by which we learn (or guess at) what language is before us and what context we are in.

Looking Backward: Retrospective Construction and Back-Formation

From these experiments I would draw, again following Goodman, one further observation that is suggestively rich in interpretive implications. Since the spot can be seen to move in any direction (to move, even, in several directions at once), it would seem that the movement cannot be determined prior to the occurrence of the second flash (even though the second flash is at the point the spot is seen to move to). If, like others in the critical theory trade today, I were interested in pressing upon this less than obscure point the full weight of obfuscation, I would say that posteriority is the necessary prior condition of the self-actualization of chronicity or periodization, or that the effect is the cause of that by which it is itself effectuated, or, more simply, that the end is the beginning of the end. But not counting myself among those who hope for eminence, as Samuel Johnson says, from the heresies of paradox, I would simply note that the construction of the direction (and the entire course) of apparent motion cannot begin before the second flash, which is presumably *registered* before it is *noticed*. Since it takes up to a third of a second to perceive a stimulus, and since the interval between flashes is less than a tenth of that time, the second flash has clearly appeared before the first flash has been perceived or noticed; the whole event is thus accomplished and, in some sense, "registered" before it is "perceived." To account for the "perceptual experience" of a spot moving steadily from point A to point B (to account, that is, for the moving-dot-of-light experience in a flash-flash environment), Goodman enlists into service a "retrospective construction theory," which simply gives a local habitation and name to what seems to be the case, that is, that the construction of the movement perceived as occurring between the flashes cannot be begun or achieved prior to the second flash.[5]

As applied to apparent motion (and other phenomena), retrospective reconstruction is certainly a useful explanatory principle, but it has our interest because it is a powerful one, applicable to a broad range of interpretive situations and practices, epitomizing, in fact, what is characteristic of interpretive practice generally. Cognate with the situations described by Goodman, for example, are those we confront daily in ordinary reading experience when we attempt to make sense of the stipulated meaning before us, as stipulated.[6]

By way of illustration, we can look quickly at two cases, one a chestnut in the semanticist's bag of examples and the other a nutty product of my own cultivation. Suppose, then, that we have two two-page books with the sentence "The bill is large" on the first page of both but with the sentence "I guess we'll have to pay it, however," on the second page of one and the sentence "It's not as large as the pelican's, however" on the second page of the other. The extraordinary range of possibilities made available by the first sentence (including, in addition to those specified in our books, the bill in a bill of lading, the bill in a tall bill but short Tom situation—lower case "b" here being a "typo," of course—and the bill on a trucker's, farmer's, baseball player's cap) is drastically narrowed by the second sentence, which provides our cue to retrospective construction.[7]

What happens between also happens within sentences, as variations on a periodic sentence will show, this variation, for example: "All the turkeys we saw when we gathered in the hall on that cold November day were well-cooked; were gamboling friskily; were college administrators; were wearing jodphurs," et cetera, ad infinitum. The interest relativity of this sentence is retrospectively determined by the operative predicate. Of course, what the predicate "means" is also a construction (and, thus, possibly a misconstruction), but since life is short, we elect that construction which at least temporarily allows all that precedes the predicate to be retrospectively constructed in a sensibly determinate way, in the way that seems more sensible than some other (barely) possible way.

If the "turkey" narrative were extended beyond, say, "well-cooked" and the next sentence mentioned how delicious the dark meat was and how moist the white, then we would have confirmation of a sort for the adequacy of one rather than another retrospective construction of meaning and reference. If, on the other hand, our sentence concluded with "college administrators" and the next one indicated that, though "well-cooked," the leg meat was "tough," we would have to make a retrospective adjustment in our construction and suppose we were attending a very different kind of thanksgiving feast, one prepared perhaps by a rather macabre satirist (or, perhaps, by an untenured assistant professor). What kinds of and how many adjustments (i.e., retrospective reconstructions) will have to be made in the course of reading an extended account cannot be determined prior to reading; but as we read on, we know with increasing security what sort of context we are in and what sort of language usage we are confronting.

Looking Forward: Recursion and World Reformation

With the last remark, we move beyond retrospective construction to *recursion*, the principle at work when we use our antecedent construction as the ground for subsequent inferences about meaning, as the basis for the subsequent preference ordering of meaning possibilities.[8] At any point the recursive formation (the new operating assumptions about the context we are in) may be inadequate to the incoming information or to the next sentence before us. We run bump into recalcitrance, as Kenneth Burke says, into what cannot be accommodated by our working hypothesis.[9] At such a junction of incommensurabilities, we are obliged to perform a new act of retrospective construction and establish a new basis of recursion.[10]

Generally, however, "recursion switches" occur early rather than late in the reading process because texts, relative as they are to self-interest, tend to stay in context (though where "surprise"—the eruption of the unexpected—rather than "suspense"—the delay of the fatefully rich expected—is the effect devoutly to be wished by a text, the recursion switch, demanded by the text, will usually come late: "Oh, I see, the butler did it," or, "Oh, I see, Wickham is not exactly the swell fella that I, with more than a little help from Austen, imagined him to be"). Also, the switch occurs early or not at all because some readers are simply "determined," incapable of finding and getting on a horse not already bolted to their carousel. If retrospective construction forms the basis of recursion, the looping back on past output for purposes of future projection, then retrospective "reconstruction" is what makes loop-de-looping possible. If we cannot get out of the hermeneutic circle, we can change circles, as we do when texts refuse to submit to the coercive demands of our erroneous recursions or insist on startling us with their own surprises. Recursion, of course, also makes possible our thinking about thinking, our ideas about ideas, our criticism of criticism, and so on. It may even be a concept useful or necessary to our understanding of how we go about using existing worlds to make new ones and to an understanding of how the mind, "reflecting" on its own capacities and skills, builds for each of us a sense of "self."[11]

Prior Restraints on Meaning and Reference

I cannot turn aside from this examination of space-times without indicating, if only briefly and in summary fashion, what Goodman's constructive reflections on Kolers's apparent motion experiments suggest, to me at least, about certain aspects of meaning and reference. Just as the second flash is the logically prior condition of the perceived chronological progression of the spot, so sentence meaning is the antecedent condition of the referential functioning of the words which realize that meaning. In short, words are the cause of our knowing a meaning, but meaning is the cause of the emphasis, value, and referentiality of the words.[12] Reference is inescapably an epistemic and "intentional" (i.e., interest-relative) notion, since words by themselves and sentences in isolation (from context, aim, wish, desire, belief, and so on) are hopelessly, irremediably, and aimlessly polysemous.[13]

What "bill" or "large" or "The bill is large" means, I cannot say in so many words; nor, for that matter, can I say in so many words what someone's swinging his or her arms about energetically means. Is the swinging part of a dance, a warning, part of a warming-up exercise, a segment of a religious ritual, a ceremony of welcoming, a manifestation of a neurological disorder . . . ? Is the impending storm a threat to my well-being or a pleasant relief from the scorching heat? Well, it all depends. What does it mean when at the end of a play the young son puts on the hat of his now dead, long-disliked father? Is this action unspeakably sad, mildly amusing, or uproariously funny? Well, again, it all depends. But knowing what it all depends upon is not to be discovered by giving nights and days to the contemplation of all the meanings the words or isolated sentences might support if their only care were the support of possible meanings. Language-in-use is, of course, always centered, always interest-relative and context-sensitive (as far as I can tell, even "deconstructionists" do not contest this point; they would only insist, with Yeats, that the center will not hold).[14]

We can be said to know what is meant by such and such piece of language when we know the *conditions* in which someone would be *justified* in using such and such language. When we learn a native language, we learn, as Michael Dummett has argued, *practices*, not correspondences. In one of our common practices, for example, the word "chair" corresponds to the bounded entity or the thing "chair"; word and thing emerge together and, hence, correspond to one another, at least in one of our familiar worlds of practice. Here is genuine correspondence and a kind of unmediated vision—the *word* directly denotes the *thing itself* (in this system of denotation, at any rate). If all systems are systems of mediation, the "things" in the various systems are the unmediated things themselves; in our ordinary observation and description system, for example, "chair" refers directly and unmistakably to chairs, whatever they are. (Of course, they are always and only *chairs!*) We learn more "meanings" and "references" as we engage in more *practices* of understanding in increasingly various contexts. Here we simply affirm what Samuel Johnson noted long ago: "as we see more we . . . gain more principles of reasoning [acquire more references and learn more about systems of reference], and found a wider basis of analogy."[15] Relating Johnson's insight directly to the issue at hand, we would say, with Dummett, that knowledge of our native language involves a tacit understanding (an informal, implicit knowledge) of the "conditions under which the sentences of that language are assertible (a sort of recognition ability) . . . ; knowing when a sentence is assertible [is] knowing when it would be justified" to make or utter such a sentence.[16]

Furthermore, what counts as justification is learned in the process of determining what sort of context we are in, what sort of enterprise or situation we are confronting. Thus, a sentence is "true" (i.e., has the meaning that is stipulated or assumed) when the meaning that is stipulated for it is justified by the circumstances in which it is expressed. To say as much is only to say what is commonly recognized (by many Continental philosophers, as well as by linguists), namely, that sentence meaning is prior to word meaning and that context meaning is prior to sentence meaning. More simply still, it is to say what Gadamerians and most "immanent meaning" reasoners have no trouble accepting, namely, that "objects" and "references" are not prior to discourse but, rather, emerge out of discourse, or that "truth" or "meaning" is what reference is relative to.

Where pluralists part company with some other "immanent-meaning reasoners," however, is at the point of locating the contextual determinants of reference in, say, history, politics, gender, ideology, prior texts, or whatever. It is not that pluralists think that none of these contexts or prior conditions determine reference or that they are somehow outside history, apolitical, genderless, or whatever. To them, each and every one of these contexts is from time to time more or less determinate of reference. Nevertheless, to the pluralist, in any given period, each of these contexts or conditions allows for and exhibits a rich diversity of expressions, many of which conflict with or contradict one another. Make the conditions as rigid as you like, and the rules of syntax or meaning generation as precise as you like, and there will still be room within these—and even tighter—constraints for not only diverse but also competing, conflicting, or contradictory meanings, statements, views. Of course, we simply give abstract expression here to what we know from "experience" elsewhere: there are many ways to skin a cat, or every period and every age can say and mean many—indeed, an infinite number of—things, using the "same" lexical stock and the "same" assumptions. Axiomatically, all families (happy and unhappy) are different; or, there are many capitalisms and many versions within each kind. As far as reference is concerned, then, the pluralist is something of a catch-as-catch-can sort of person, one who survives in an extemporaneous, provisional, spontaneous, improvisational sort of way and who is adept at catching the drift of the various languages encountered in a various day, however newfangled or old-fashioned, and at making a drift or two of his or her own, even a new, but understandable and intelligible, drift, as now.

To the issues raised here we shall return shortly, but for now we can note that by the time we are ten or eleven or twelve years old, we are "encoded" and "referenced" up to here. Even at such a tender age, we have accumulated enough contextually determined references to stock several large warehouses, and when we run into new language (or actions, gestures, pictorial symbols, auditory cues, and so on) we have available for constructive use not only sufficient references and contextual resources to dope out the most likely likelihoods of present "meaning" but also a rich working understanding of the various mechanisms by which references can be combined, modified, extended and so on. All this is ours because we have read this, listened to that, been talked to, talked at, been angry, jealous, happy, "in love," watched storms, listened to music, made up games, altered the rules of existing games, laughed at jokes, taken and given directions, and so on, each and every one of these "events" adding something to our interpretive stock and strengthening our interpretive skill. As we see and do more, we gain more principles of reasoning and found a wider basis of analogy, as Johnson wisely observed.

Of course, we live in one, not another, society, one informed by some, not other, political and ideological values that determine in no small way what we will think about and how we will think about it. We have one, not another, gender in historically situated social structures that variously "genderize" not only political, social, and economic opportunity, but also perceptual, imaginative, and intellectual space. We live at one time, in one historical period, not another, a time when some but not other things available for the taking are taken as given; we belong to one class, community, or subculture, not another, with its own network of assumptions and codes. And, to make an end of what could be almost endlessly subdivided, we use a public, widely shared, rule-governed language that imposes its own relatively severe constraints on semantic and syntactic usage. Certainly, no pluralist would deny that wherever there are differentiable social, communal, or individual practices or wherever there are "meanings," there are also codes and conventions or systems of reference at work. Nor would a pluralist deny the importance of some or indeed all of the codes and conventions implicated in the categories above, whether operating individually or in various schemes of coordination, in shaping or influencing behavior, interpretation, and much else. He or she would simply deny absolute or hegemonic authority to any of these codes or conventions *to determine specific meaning and reference.* In every period, we always live in many, in an extraordinarily large number of communities of meaning and reference.

As always, codes and conventions—whether derived from the analysis of language, culture, history, or whatever—supply us with or make available to us a stock of terms or categories capable of entering into a multiplicity of substitutional or combinatorial relations, a stock prodigiously rich in potentiality. But these codes and conventions, however refined and elaborate, cannot determine the boundary conditions of their own operation, of their own "referencing." Obviously, we are here talking about codes and conventions we can talk about; if we are controlled or governed by that which we cannot know to be controlling or governing us—i.e., some ideology—we cannot know enough to talk about it. Our word on this sort of control is, perforce, mum. Just as the system of rules superintending the relations into which chess pieces may enter does not and cannot determine the strategy of any particular game (as Michael Polanyi observes), so the codes and conventions of any language, considered as a relational system of possible combinations and substitutions, cannot determine the nature of any particular essay, theory, sonnet, or other system of reference.[17]

If no game can be played outside the rules, the rules cannot themselves organize a strategy or determine allowable references and reference relations. It is not just that whenever we look here or there, or now and then, we find that as soon as someone has a great notion in some "language" (or domain of concern) someone else has a different, often antithetical notion in the "same" language (or domain of concern), but that, as Hilary Putnam notes, "no matter what operational or theoretical constraints our practice may impose on our use of language, there are always *infinitely many different reference relations* (different 'satisfaction relations,' in the sense of formal semantics, or different *correspondences*) which satisfy all of the constraints," even assuming what we have no right to assume at all, that is, that all such constraints could be known.[18] Because this is so, we are not shocked to learn that even those who share the *same background knowledge* often violently disagree with one another, that complete agreement is difficult to achieve even within narrowly defined interpretive communities, that Marxists argue with many other critics but especially with other Marxists, Freudians with Freudians, and so on.

Thus, even though it would be a mistake to assume that we are not, in a very important sense, played by systems—in that we are all creatures of the terms and references available to us and, as such, limited to working out what falls within the semantic and logical range of our (stipulated and inherited) references—it would be a greater mistake to fail to realize that the systems available to us are many and various and that the boundary conditions for the operation of the relational systems cannot be determined by the systems or the codes and conventions themselves. Hence, it is the very *indeterminacy* or *polysemeity* of language that obliges us, as readers, to decide in a retrospectively constructive way which among the available possibilities makes an appropriate (epistemic or "intentional") fit in the context in which we have some reason to suppose we find ourselves. Of course, we never wait to suppose the sort of situation we are in until we have run through all the situations that the words before us could possibly suggest, just as the scientist does not check out all the strongly falsifiable, possible hypotheses consistent with the "facts" before testing one or some few. In a process analogous to that employed by the reader, the scientist rules out many strongly falsifiable hypotheses at the outset, depending while doing so on some *intuitive* probability estimate or some conception of what Polanyi calls the slope of "deepening meaning," and relying generally on a "default" system, relying, in short, on the usual, typical, or projectible until or unless something changes the conditions of its applicability.

Moreover, it seems to the pluralist that much of what we do when we make or understand references and reference relations depends upon capacities that are ours by evolutionary endowment, that, in not insignificant respects, are transcultural, transhistorical, and transpersonal, and upon language possibilities not restricted to any particular language. For example, there is no reason to assume that if we transported ourselves to different cultures or to different historical eras we would meet a race of people incapable of perceiving apparent motion or of distinguishing a familiar from an unfamiliar face. And there is no reason to assume that the brain has undergone any significant evolutionary changes in at least the last 28,000 years.

Furthermore, moving now to higher reaches of organizational capacity, there is no reason to assume that we have today a severely diminished capacity to size up correctly and respond appropriately to old or brand-new texts. Despite what some critics today affirm about our being spoken by and through a severely restricted range of historically/culturally determined categories, about the categorical controls exerted on our meanings by our culture, archive, or political unconscious, there is no reason to assume that we are prohibited from sizing up correctly and responding appropriately to the pitiful scene in which Oedipus or Lear finds himself or to grasp imaginatively the peculiar nature of the emotional turmoil that afflicts Othello and leads to such disastrous results. At the level of perception and at the level of emotional response (as well as at the level of inference, emotional response itself being a product of inference), there seem to be human saliencies that function in regular ways across differences in culture, ideology, or whatever.

If we size up situations in similar ways, we will respond to them, it seems, in similar ways. Confronted with a scene (sized up as one) of undeserved misfortune, we respond with something not unlike pity; confronted with a scene (sized up as one) of undeserved good fortune, we respond with something not unlike indignation, as I am not the first to notice.[19] To give a point of large currency a small-change exemplification, imagine that on some given day you learn, first, that your brilliant article has been rejected and, second, that your disesteemed colleague's article of nugatory merit has been accepted by a prestigious journal. Here is the stuff of a narrative that would make at least a wife or a husband feel pity and indignation, or at least feign to feel them.

Constrained by our anatomy and physiology and influenced by what we have seen and done before, we make out the context we are in and recognize that the storm in our text is not any storm we would make of it or the storm that necessarily squares with all our beliefs about storms, but *the* storm that threatens to capsize our hero's boat, or *the* storm that ends the drought, or *the* storm that is the outward and physical manifestation of the turmoil within our hero. In short, texts have determinate interests and, hence, meanings, and we can come to know them. The text before us is not a pre-versional site of infinite potentialities, though it is certainly something we can consider in a virtually infinite number of "right" ways, including "right" historical, cultural, or ideological ways.

Language Markers of Change and Stability

About the general constraints that *language* imposes on our theory-building and world-making, little needs to be said here. But, if the syntactic and semantic rules of a given language cannot determine the range of their own operation, they certainly delimit, albeit with somewhat fuzzy lines, the borders beyond which is the "thou shalt not"; they exert some control over the permissible. We cannot (or do not) say, "The man hat on is," or even, "green, big, great tree," as opposed to "great big green tree." We play by the "rules." And across meaning and reference changes, *semantic*, *logical*, or *argumentative* markers do their uniform work to facilitate our understanding of a wide variety of discourses, such markers, for example, as "but," "and," "on the other hand," "if . . . then," "not only . . . but also," "nevertheless," "while," and so on.

Also, across theory differences and, hence, disparities of reference, there are, in addition to some shared methodological criteria of assertibility or justification, shared procedures for linking references, for making *systems* of reference. Such procedures, furthermore, seem not to be characteristic of only a few languages. If one language can embody what cannot be embodied in ours, simultaneity, for example, we find a means sufficient unto our needs to *express* what we cannot embody, translating the efficiently embodied simultaneity (not without some loss perhaps, but without significant loss) into, say, "*While* listening to the music that reminded him of her, he missed the bus that was to take him to her." And if "I think" is not exactly equivalent to "cogito," I think "I think" will serve most of our needs. And if "fleuve" and "rivière" make a difference that is not made by my "river" and "stream," I am not prevented from getting on board an English circumlocomotive that will carry me to the distinction, provided, of course, I can be made to know that one French term signifies a stream-like or river-like body of water that flows toward the ocean and the other a similar body of water that does not so flow. Here, as elsewhere, stating the obvious is a necessary or obligatory act only because the radical claims of many modern theorists have put so much of what is obvious into question.[20]

Space-Times in Review

At bottom, the pluralist recognizes that in the course of any given week he or she participates in, understands, and makes a vast number of systems of reference in the process of going shopping, talking to the hair stylist, arranging to have the car fixed, reading editorial and sports pages, the comics, a novel, a few short stories, letters, and so on; watching movies, visiting an art gallery or museum, listening to music and "talk" shows; and so on through a long list of situations requiring referential leaping and bounding. Nothing the pluralist says, reads, watches, etc. exists (as this something or other) or is intelligible apart from some system of constraint, some constructional system, some organizational system (outside system, there are those objects we stare at when we stare at "nothing," unattached percepts, or perhaps traces of the trace), but the pluralist moves from system to system, from one space-time to another, with comparative ease by guessing the sort of situation he or she is presently in and then retrospectively constructing the "meaning" that would obtain if the words or other symbols were indeed functional in such a situation, not by adjusting all systems to one ready-made, all-purpose system. If, as readers, we guess wrong or, as speakers, we abruptly shift to a new situation of meaningfulness, we will have trouble as we go along making our parts "fit" or cooperate with one another in an intelligible system of reference. When the bill of "the bill is large" must be paid, it becomes a bill that would not be becoming on a duck; it does not "fit" a duck. Of course, we have yet to learn whether the bill not befitting a duck is to be paid to a restaurateur or to a telephone company, but as the plot thickens the range of situational reference and, hence, meaning narrows.

If there is something mysterious in all this system hopping, there is only so much of mystery in it as there is in human creativity, innovation, imaginative capacity itself. In short, there is considerable mystery in it, but, though mysterious, the processes by which we make and understand meanings do indeed function in the making and understanding of meanings or worlds and are indeed intelligible, at least at the higher reaches, in terms of certain suppositions, such suppositions, for example, as retrospective construction and recursion (and others, to be discussed later). At any rate, the mind seems to arrive at meanings in various ways, to work in rather ad hoc ways, selecting out from the many possibilities available for use those that seem most appropriate to a certain kind of (construed) circumstances.

Whatever complications these remarks may contain, the immediate point should be clear: there is no master key to interpretation or creativity, no one place for one Archimedes to stand to become the prime mover of one world (or many worlds). The impossibility here is of a piece with the impossibility of providing a fully satisfactory formal account of inductive logic. It is impossible, at least in practice, to survey and hence to evaluate all the available relevant evidence, and it is always possible to formulate from the available evidence a virtually infinite number of different and contradictory hypotheses consistent with such evidence. Similarly, just as no single theory can account for all the ways the visual mechanism goes about the business of creating various kinds of apparent motion, so no theory is peculiarly suited to account for the various ways we construct and reconstruct "meanings." A meaning is "true," we have argued, if it is justified, if it is assertible in the circumstances, but the circumstances in which it is "true" are themselves constructed, not given, as "present" and determinative of meaning.

We are back, it seems, to the intuitive, the inductive roundhouse, or, perhaps, to the hermeneutic circle, where we cannot know the whole without knowing the parts and cannot know the meaning of the parts without knowing the meaning of the whole, the informing context. As Putnam notes, the "impossibility . . . of formalizing the assertibility conditions for arbitrary sentences [a sentence such as "The bill is large," for example] is just the impossibility of formalizing general intelligence itself,"[21] yet if the sentence before us is to have "meaning," we must be able to know the conditions under which it is assertible. Our first move, then, must be to assume that the sentence before us is not an arbitrary sentence, but an interest-relative sentence, a sentence interested in being adequate to, let us say, some, but not all possible circumstances, frames of reference, or worlds. And our excursus has informed us that in finding the circumstances that make retrospective construction possible, we are guided by our implicit (and explicit) knowledge of syntactic and semantic "rules"; by our anatomy and physiology; by our past successes (what we have seen and done before); by cultural, ideological, and social practices; and undoubtedly by much else of which we are at present ignorant.

Chapter 5
Worlds Unacceptable, Irrelevant, or Incommensurable

The second issue evoked by our discussion of eclecticism concerns population control or, rather, the possibility of an unregulated proliferation of versions in the fecund garden of making watched over by what some would call the tolerant, indeed permissive, eye of pluralism. Put less tropologically, the pluralist, if not the eclecticist he or she is often taken to be, perhaps is that other "ist" with whom he or she is also regularly confused, i.e., the relativist, since, like the relativist, the pluralist seems to be willing to accept within the fold any ambulatory view, any view not crippled by self-refutation. Suspicions notwithstanding, the pluralist finds plenty of room to navigate between the rocks of eclecticism and the whirlpool of relativism.

Basically, the pluralist would insist *that* noncontradiction is a necessary but not a sufficient condition of the acceptability of a theory or version, *that* under some conditions one true version is preferable to another true version, and *that* different versions, existing in different space-times, can be compared and evaluated. Thus, there can be agreement and disagreement across differences in systems of reference. The versions are not, in any radical sense, incommensurable or untranslatable, as some Kuhnians, interpretive community-ists, and historicists are inclined to insist. Versions, then, can be (1) "coherent" but unacceptable; (2) "true" but irrelevant (or otherwise objectionable); and (3) compared though ostensibly incommensurable. And all this can be done without giving up immanent meaning and without rejecting the view that different "true" versions exist in different space-times.

Coherent but Unacceptable Worlds (Versions, Theories)

Our second issue became an issue for us because our critique of eclecticism was based on a conception of different space-times. That is, if the eclectic were guilty of trying to pile a variety of different views on a single bed, of trying to make several versions, each operating within its own discrete boundaries, play within one set of boundaries, the pluralist seemed to solve the problem by simply adding a new bed to an infinitely expandable ward whenever encountering a new, internally coherent version. Recognizing that the projectible properties of, say, a Jungian analysis of character were not properties projectible in a Freudian analysis, the pluralist appeared to make of the difference a difference in world, thereby saving both versions by keeping them discrete and making a world of each.

But, of course, a version does not become acceptable simply because it does not contradict itself or violate any of its own precepts. Even though we have no reason to assume that knowledge from various branches of inquiry is converging toward one point of Truth, we regularly dismiss some coherent versions because they offend (at least at the present historical moment) unyielding beliefs. Some theories that are perfectly compatible with our background knowledge and assumptions we refuse to test or to bother with at all because contingent upon their adoption is the rejection of more than we care to lose. However shaky our grasp of actual worlds may be, we regularly discriminate between actual and "fantastic" possible worlds. Our universe is littered with "false" internally coherent versions, with gods and theories in which we cannot believe, and with views that, though once accepted, are now rejected. Of course, these views are usually not rejected because they have been "proven" to be false, but because they fit less well with what else we believe, because they are less elegant, less beautiful, less economical, or whatever than other views, or because they are less fully consonant than others with our best sense of what a fully exfoliated rationality should be like. If we refuse to ask any particular belief to square with every other particular belief we have, we nevertheless refuse to take on board any belief that can make a case for itself. And when different versions make claims on the same space, space can be allotted to only one version.

Consistent with the general principle of acceptability outlined here is the rejection, of course, of any *monism*, since monism is satisfied with nothing less than claiming all the seats or making all the seats one seat. To the extent that the *eclectic* tries to make many different kinds of explanations explain one thing (one text, say), he or she is a confused monist. To the extent that a critic attempts to give every explanation its own space, he or she is a confused pluralist (i.e., a relativist).

What an acceptable version must accommodate itself to is not "reality" or all other versions, but the space either made available or not occupied by other versions on a bus that continually takes on and lets off passengers. But since neither the eclectic nor the relativist is likely to believe in, say, animism or a flat earth, or, more generally, to give space to versions that no one has granted accreditation status to (despite the fact that neither one seems inherently capable of excluding versions or of supplying grounds of exclusion), we must now consider how we can go about eliminating "true" versions or true explanations from consideration in specific instances.[1]

True but Irrelevant Worlds (Versions, Theories)

For an explanation to be *right* it is not enough that it be *true*, if only because many true explanations are irrelevant to our present interests and, thus, do not explain what we are interested in having explained. Explanation, like reference, is an epistemic notion and, hence, is, like reference, interest-relative and context-sensitive. It follows, then, that what will count as an explanation depends upon interests, frames of reference, the kind of language being used, and the kind of circumstances we are in. Unlike the *monists* and the "always already" *theorists*, for whom the contexts we can be in and, hence, the justification conditions of assertions are already antecedently established, and unlike those *eclectics* and *relativists* who, if not closet monists, have trouble finding grounds for rejecting any versions or explanations, pluralists are regularly obliged to determine which among the available "true" versions are or are not in genuine conflict and which among the available "true" explanations are *appropriate* under the circumstances.

In making decisions, the pluralist obviously cannot allow "truth" to be the sole or primary consideration, inasmuch as he or she must choose among "truths," choose the right, fitting, or appropriate truth under the circumstances. To say, for example, that Hamlet is "upset" is to speak not an "untruth," but a boring, vague, general "truth," that can be interesting only to those for whom it would be a revelation. To say that he is upset because his mother has remarried would be to say a truth that is at once too general and too limited, too limited because, at a minimum, he is upset by his father's death as well, and too general because "upset" is allowed to stand for too many emotional states (to "upset," we would have to add "distraught," "perplexed," "disappointed," etc.). Truth, though necessary to an explanation, is seldom sufficient to our needs, because, as Goodman notes, some "truths are trivial, irrelevant, unintelligible, or redundant [Hamlet is a prince because his father was a king]; too broad, too narrow, too boring, too bizarre, too complicated," and so on.[2]

Of course, deciding when a truth is, for example, too boring or too trivial is not always an easy matter, since what is obvious to one person may not be so to another and what is background knowledge to one person may be an empty room to another. But we edge closer to our most common interpretive dilemmas as readers and hearers when we consider true but inappropriate, wrong, or mistaken explanations, those, for example, pertaining to a version other than the one we are in, "as when a guard" (to take one of Goodman's frequent examples), "ordered to shoot any of his captives who moved, immediately shot them all and explained that they were moving rapidly around the earth's axis and around the sun."[3] If critics could always agree about the version they were in, there would undoubtedly be in our professional journals not only less disagreement but more fruitful controversies. Nevertheless, what is significant about this short story of version-crossed characters is that we can recognize that a "mistake" has been made, that being in the right version sometimes has consequences, that being in the protective custody of an astronomer is, at times, no fun.

Similarly, a parent who assumes that the long-awaited, dreadful day has arrived when a young child asks the trauma-inducing question "where do I come from?" may suddenly discover that in attempting to find a place for a zygote, he or she has not only confused but also misplaced the child. In the midst of the parent's rhapsody about insemination and gestation, the child (as the old joke would have it) says, "No! Joey comes from Cleveland. Where do I come from?" It is impossible to answer the child's question without relying on some ("true") version, some system of reference, and every question allows room for relevant alternatives; but in some contexts, some but not other references and alternatives are just right.

Knowing when to reject a version or an explanation is not something that can be settled by a rule book; it is a skill or ability that is developed in the process of learning what's what, of finding or making a context in which to assert or mean something. To the guard or parent who takes up literary criticism (at least of the interpretive kind), however, we can say, "Don't shoot before determining what system of reference 'move' moves in" and "Don't tell children where they come from before learning where their question is coming from." (In other words, the pluralist critic—unlike many theorists—is reluctant to privilege one kind of talking and unwilling to reduce the multiplicity of possible interests to one interest or one set of interests, the cultural or ideological, for example.)

An Interlude: Rules of Thumb for Rejecting Explanations

Even though publication of the rule book must be delayed until we have a fully adequate understanding of human creativity or complete access to the Truth about making and understanding, we can look to our old friend the thumb for some serviceable rules concerning when to reject explanations. In addition to disregarding those that are too trivial, boring and so on, we can reject those (1) that belong to the wrong version or that simply do not fit the explanation space made available by the version we are in; (2) that "generalize to an uninteresting class of cases"; and (3) that "simply give back what we already know."[4]

First Rule of Thumb: Reject True but Wrong Explanations

Into our first case we would put the guard and the parent and then appeal for additional support to Willie Sutton, who when asked why he robbed banks replied, "That's where the money is." His answer certainly puts something appropriate into the explanatory space opened up by the question, but we should note how different its appropriateness would be if it were said respectively to a priest, a judge, and another robber. Assuming that Willie is not just anybody's fool, we immediately recognize that the reply, as given to a priest, leaps in the direction of sarcasm. As given to a judge, it has about it what the unregenerate might call a certain noble piquancy or a jaunty truculence; and, as given to another robber, it approaches—here humorously and intentionally—the kind of daffy profundity which Yogi Berra and Sam Goldwyn often, quite unintentionally, reached (as in "The game isn't over, 'til it's over," or "An oral contract isn't worth the paper it's written on").

Obviously, there is a strict relativity of "meaning" to version, and much depends upon knowing what version you are in and upon being in the right version. At any rate, it should be clear that an explanation is good or right relative to a version, just as a property (of a text, say) is "essential" relative to a description (for example, going sixty miles an hour is a true and essential property of a certain car in a certain system of description, and Sutton's comment has a certain cognitive or emotional value relative to one but not another description). The underlying point here, as elsewhere, is that Sutton's remark—like a newspaper editorial, a scientific treatise, a critical essay, a novel, and so on—is *already a version* when we meet it, and even though it may be a version in which a given critic, for one reason or another, has little interest, it is a version which only some explanations can account for and which only some explanations will be "right" relative to.

Second Rule of Thumb: Reject Explanations That Lead to Uninteresting Generalizations

To illustrate our second case—that involving the rejection of explanations that generalize to an "uninteresting" class of cases—we can begin by looking at the following example (one cited by Hilary Putnam): a one-inch square peg goes through a one-inch square hole but not through a one-inch round hole. To explain this simple "fact," we can appeal to a variety of "true" explanations. For example, we can find our explanatory base in lower-level, constituent elements or in higher-level, structural features, can find an explanation in microstructure or macrostructure, can appeal, in short, to physics or geometry. An explanation at the molecular, particle, atomic, or subatomic level (achieved by applying the proper covering laws of particle dynamics or quantum electrodynamics to the case) could certainly explain why one "cloud" or "rigid lattice" of atoms (the round peg) cannot pass through a particular hole (another cloud of atoms) in a rigid lattice of atoms (the board), and, of course, a certain kind of positivist might insist that the only *true* explanation is the one which emerges from a consideration of the behavior of "ultimate constituents."

The pluralist, however, would suggest that an explanation at the level of planimetry or geometric structure is equally "valid" and allows us to extrapolate to more "interesting" (because more general) cases. The higher-level, geometric structure explanation is simply that the round hole is smaller than the peg and that the square hole is bigger than the cross-section of the peg; the plain (or plane) geometric fact of the matter is that, no matter what the microstructure of the peg or board is and regardless of whether the peg is made of wood, plastic, or aluminum, the square peg will always pass easily through the square hole in the board and never pass easily through the round hole. Armed with this explanation we can apply it to any situation in which the higher-level geometric "facts" obtain. These structural facts of geometry enable us to explain, for example, why manhole covers are round rather than square or rectangular (the round manhole cover, no matter how you angle it, will not fall through the hole, and this is a piece of news not unwelcome to the construction worker or, as we shall see, to the literary critic). Clearly, both the atomic and the higher-level, geometric structure explanation "truly" explain why one but not another peg will fit through the hole, and both explanations may have our interest if we take an interest in them.

But to see why we might normally or in most cases prefer one to another explanation, we must first look to the class of cases to which we can generalize using one and the other explanation and then look elsewhere. The atomic explanation, though based on what we are fond of calling general physical "laws," will apply only (but always) to those situations which exactly match the atomic structure of our peg-hole-board situation (finding such a match is, of course, virtually impossible), whereas the geometric explanation—the explanation at the level of functional organization—will apply, as our manhole cover case makes clear, to an enormous variety of instances involving an incalculable number of different atomic structures. As interpretive beings, we are more likely to be interested in having available to us an explanation that can be generalized to several cases than in having one that virtually exhausts its utility in its application, especially since, to take an example from our current argument, we are likely to find ourselves in the course of any day in situations in which the geometric explanation, but not the atomic explanation, will come in handy. (Analogous to our geometric case, of course, is one in which we have "cognitive sameness" across differences in "mental content," but we get ahead of ourselves. And analogous to our "atomic" case perhaps are all those critical approaches which start from or give priority to the constituent elements of texts—words, terms, or other "basic" graphemic or lexemic units—as do "new critical," deconstructionist, and many other approaches.)

Nevertheless, it is important to underscore the countervailing point—that on some occasions and for some purposes we may prefer the atomic explanation—and to note, for the sake of some readers, that in disclosing one set of structural relationships, a given explanation hides or, if you prefer, "represses" from knowledge many other sets of relationships; it represses as it reveals relationships. In a manner of speaking congenial to some readers, we can say that it is in the interest of the ideology of geometry to repress awareness of the ideology of molecular structure in pegs and boards, and turnabout is fair/foul play, I'm sure; or, there's no impression without repression. But note that in the systematic repression noted here there is no implicit understanding that one explanation can subsume or be subordinated to the other, that the geometric "facts" are to the atomic as manifest is to latent content, or that geometric structure is to atomic as surface is to deep structure. One explanation is not empowered to explain the other, and one cannot be reduced to the other. Indeed, as we shall see, what is true at the higher level need not even be compatible with what is true at the lower level and may even contradict the lower-level truth.

Perhaps what is at stake in the notion of preferential explanation can be displayed more clearly if we shift our focus from pegs and boards to economics. If economics is a science (call it a social science), it is not a science in the sense or in the way that physics is a science, not a science, at any rate, that looks to elementary *physical* elements for explanations of the motions and events that have its interest. By analogy we can say that it seeks explanations at the geometric rather than the atomic level (or, more exactly, at the conceptual/psychological rather than at the physical/atomic level). Any effort to reduce economic behavior to the activity of elementary particles would be doomed to failure, not because such behavior escapes the physical, but because an indefinite number of physical states are compatible with the behavior and because the behavior, to the extent that it is "rule" governed, depends upon a group of factors that are accidental or incidental from the point of view of physics.

In short, the elementary physical matter of the case doesn't matter. If there are rules and regularities at work in various economic structures ("rules" of supply and demand, for example), they operate across enormous differences in physical conditions and apply to *this country* and *that* and to this group of people and that irrespective of whether the matter of concern is *corn* or *wheat* or *beans* or *oil*, and so on. The boundary conditions in which the economic "rules" work are not coterminous with the boundary conditions in which the physical "laws" work, though it is certainly the case that to be in an economic condition is simultaneously to be in a physical one. Thus, like the higher-level, geometric explanation, the higher-level economic one allows us to generalize to a more "interesting" class of cases, providing us with an instrument by which to understand a diverse number of acts of, say, buying and selling in this and that time and place, since the "rule" applies whenever and wherever the structural relations identified at the higher level obtain.

Moreover—and here we get closer to our main concerns—efforts to explain what has happened or to predict what is likely to happen in economics depend crucially upon sizing up situations in certain ways and upon believing that such and such is the condition we are in. Here, as elsewhere, the boundary conditions for the operation of the "rules" cannot be determined by the "rules" themselves. If the "rules" could determine their own boundary conditions, no one would ever lose money on the stock exchange. What any economic condition "means" depends upon how it is sized up, and knowing when, say, to buy or sell depends upon knowing what kind of situation you are in and upon having certain beliefs, aims, wishes, hopes, fears, and so on relative to such and such situations. If you think the eruption of Mount St. Helens will affect the weather and, hence, the crops in certain ways, if you think the OPEC nations will raise or lower prices on barrels of oil, believe that the rumors about a certain airline's labor difficulties are true, that lower interest rates will induce a buying frenzy, or one of a hundred other things, you will behave this way rather than that; and if you can influence others to believe as you do, you may actually enable mind to control "matter" and determine the boundary conditions for the "rules." At this level, explanations become "interesting" to the extent that they disclose the "interests" that the higher-level structural relations are relative to ("interesting," that is, to those who have an interest in such interest relativity); at this level we are dealing with the epistemic, intentional (in the broad sense of intentional), and, if you will, psychological.

To effect our final turn in this category of explanation preference, we must briefly consider how an explanation at one level may be at odds with an explanation at another level, how, indeed, one structural explanation contradicts or runs counter to another. For a convenient example, we can turn again to our peg and board, which are, so to speak, "clouds" of discontinuous particles or discrete lattice-like arrangements at the atomic level of description and continuous solids at the geometric level.[5] If some might be inclined to say that the peg and board are not, in fact, continuous solids, some others, willing to grant the point for the sake of argument and for the sake of a further point of their own, might say that their lack of solidity is a matter of indifference because *they behave at the level of geometric description the way solids should behave*, and, further, that without the assumption of solidity we would not be able to generalize to the vast array of other cases that are explicable in terms of structural relations at the geometric level, as we clearly can. The point is that *the higher-level explanation, though indispensable, is incompatible or inconsonant with the lower-level explanation*.

Another example (one cited by Putnam) to illustrate the point is taken from aerodynamics. In constructing an aerodynamically efficient vehicle or object (Putnam's example is an airplane wing), the engineer conceives air on the model of a continuous flow, even though "the description of the air flowing around an aeroplane wing as [similar to] a continuous incompressible liquid is *formally incompatible with the actual structure of the air*."[6] The "fact" that the structure of the air is discontinuous at the atomic level is irrelevant to the design of the automobile or the airplane wing, since *the only explanation of air that will account for the efficiency of the design is the higher-level, continual-flow explanation*, and it is because the air behaves as a continuous system would behave that the sleek, new model gets from Providence to Boston on less gas than the boxlike, square-jawed old model.

Thus, it is not just that the higher-level explanation is a good and true one (the atomic one is also good and true), but that it is usually a more interesting one and, in many cases (and especially those that come closest to our minds and bosoms), the superior one. Indeed, it is the one without which most of what we need and wish to have explained (explained at the level of our survivability or our getting-through-the-day interests) would go unexplained, if we were stuck with working out structural permutations at the lower level.

Of course, lower-level worlds are first-class worlds, and for some they are the most interesting of all possible worlds. Clearly, a value like "interesting" is itself interest-relative. Nevertheless, for some interests some explanations simply will not do. And since we spend more of our waking life being practical geometricians, practical economists, and practical readers of many texts than being physicists or connoisseurs of words and their dialectical relations, we tend to have interests that are most fully gratified by higher-level explanations, explanations, that is, that allow us to generalize to a variety of cases and to recognize within some subsequent, locally distinct, materially different event the elaborative power or utility of the textual "generality," to recognize, for example, a Lear-like or Othello-like situation, an unrequited love, an unmerited situation of success or ruin in a new scene, textual or extra-textual. By means of such explanations we gain more principles of reasoning and found a wider basis of analogy, each one adding to the stock of implicit knowledge on which we draw as we try, for example, to determine "meaning" or "reference" or the conditions under which this rather than that kind of assertion would be justified.

Before suggesting why as literary critics we might be forgiven for preferring higher-level structural and psychological explanations to lower-level ones (preferring explanations at the moral action level, at the level of anger or jealousy, for example), we should perhaps consider another case in which a continuous model explanation might be more interesting than a discontinuous one, a case in which what takes place at one level might be irrelevant to what takes place at another level, in much the same way that the "actual" structure of the air is irrelevant to the design of an aerodynamically efficient vehicle. By analogy, then, I would extend the preceding cases, involving the discontinuities of atoms and the continuities of solids and "flowing" air, to the case of brain structure and psychological structure, a case involving discrete, *instantaneous* neuronal states on the one hand and *continuous* "mental" states on the other.

Putnam supplies us with an *opening* move, when he says: "We cannot deduce that a digital model has to be the correct model [of mind or cognition] from the fact that ultimately there are neurons. The brain may work the way it does because it approximates some system whose laws are best conceptualized in terms of continuous mathematics."[7] Although these remarks are embedded in a complex, multibranching argument on the general topic of "our mental life," their relevance to our concerns can be quickly shown. First, Putnam is suggesting that at the level of functional organization (of mental state) the ultimate physics of the brain does not matter. *Form* matters, not *matter*. Just as it does not matter whether a given program is run on a hand-cranked or an electronic computer, as long as the programs are functionally isomorphic (give us the "same" data), so with regard to any particular mental state it does not matter whether its constitutional base is in electrochemistry or, as Putnam says, Swiss cheese, assuming we are interested in mental states rather than ultimate physics.

At this stage (but, of course, not at each and every stage), ultimate physics is irrelevant. Interested in why my grandmother is angry at me, I look for an explanation in my behavior, not in the behavior of her neurons. Moreover, so indifferent are we at times to ultimate constituents that we will call some functions the same regardless of whether they are the "results" of neurons or microchips; so long as functional isomorphism is preserved, neither we nor the I.R.S. agents care whether the figures on our tax form come from a head or a pocket calculator. Or, to revert to geometry, if we have a set of functionally isomorphic pegs—one made of plastic, another of wood, and so forth—we can get them all through the square hole.

But talk of computers and microchips is misleading to the extent that it tends to suggest that, since both neurons and microchips speak a similar yes/no, on/off language, the digital or binary model might be satisfactory after all. Yet to assume a strict correlation between an electrochemical state and a psychological state would seem to be unwarranted for a number of reasons, and thus any attempt to use the computer as a descriptive model of the functioning of understanding would be without justification. But this is to move forward by assertion, not argument.

Second, then, we should note that Putnam is suggesting that a given mental state, such as anger, jealousy, belief, or understanding a concept, subsists within an enormous diversity of electrochemical conditions. Two people can have the "same" emotional response—jealousy, say—and yet be focusing on quite different objects (on Sue and Bob, say), just as two people can share a concept without sharing either the *same mental contents* (the same perceptual prototypes, for example) or the *same conception* of the "matter" in question or under discussion (they have different fundamental beliefs about marriage, for example). At the emotional, psychological, conceptual, cognitive level, a single "state" apparently can be achieved within and across a wide variety of brain states, though, of course, as with our case from economics, we cannot be in a psychological state without simultaneously being in a brain state.[8] And, as with the economics case, the boundary conditions for the operation of psychological states are not coterminous with those for the operation of brain states. At any rate, it is clear that we can give satisfactory and interesting explanations at the higher level and that we can use these explanations to generalize to many other cases, identifying, say, jealousy in this person and that, at work at this time and place and that, in this degree and that, as directed to this situation or object and that, and so on. The structure of jealousy, like the structure of supply and demand, is no partisan of country, clime, age, gender, political institution, or whatever.

If, then, at the higher psychological (emotional, conceptual) level we have *one set* of structural relations, albeit variously individuated by local circumstances, at the neuronal level we have roughly as *many* structural relations or, more exactly, states as we have instances of, say, jealousy. Of course, as we noted, nothing takes place at the psychological level independently of activity at the neuronal level, and nothing in the above is designed to suggest that the higher level cannot be manipulated and to a large extent controlled by chemistry (drugs), electricity, or surgery. What is being suggested is that, though not functional independently of electrochemistry, the psychological level is autonomous, in much the same way that the structural relations of geometry, though always subsisting within some atomic structure, are autonomous, that is, functional across massive differences in atomic structure. And since, as Putnam says, "we are not even at the level of an *idealized* description of the functional organization of the brain," talk of specific correlations between neuronal and functional states is rather more adventurous than wise (even granting that we have made great advances in mapping functions to states).[9]

More important, even if our efforts to establish such correlations were successful beyond our current wildest dreams, *there is no reason to assume that psychological talk would then be any less indispensable to us than geometric (or economic) talk is to us now, despite what we know about the subatomic structure of the many objects participating in geometric relations.*[10] Thus, even if neurons have digital proclivities, a digital (or binary) model would be useless, in practice, for virtually all purposes of explanation, not because it would not explain, but because it would not explain what we are usually interested in and because we could not use its explanation to generalize to other interesting cases, except in the most general and least informative way: this is an on/off state as that is also an on/off state, or this is a neuronal state and that is another one; or perhaps, in theoretical terms, this is a case of aporia and that is another; this term is under erasure and so is that one. Also, we assume that our allegory is transparent throughout this section and, hence, that the discerning reader will understand that geometric or economic talk is to atomic particle talk as plot-character-emotion-psychology talk is to lexeme-word-image-theme talk.

But the model is inadequate for even more compelling reasons than those already indicated, reasons relating (1) to the *simultaneity of multiple states* and (2) to the *continuity of single states. Third,* and finally, then, Putnam is suggesting that even if we were machines a digital "computer" would not serve as an adequate descriptive model of our *psychological* functioning because, for example, a given machine state (brain state) would have to determine not only *that* I feel a pain in my foot, but *that* I am about to step away from the lectern; *that* I'm aware of the pages in front of me, of the student dozing in the back of the room, aware of talking about a poem that says something about hearing a fly buzz when you die; *that* I know my glasses are on and my day far from over; *that* I feel a sneeze coming on and a rumbling in my belly, and so on. It's a busy moment, but, like you, I've been in it.

Moreover, even if there were a machine (brain) state that I could be in only when all this was going on (and another machine state following hard upon the first that would be similarly rich in events), the fact remains that what is *one state* of the machine is *several distinctly different psychological states of knowing, feeling, being aware,* each with an independent interest and each capable of subsumption by one or another class of cases (otherwise, we would not know, feel, or be aware of it as this particular *kind* of something). As Putnam observes, "even if I am a Turing machine [a computer, say], my machine states are *not* the same as my psychological states. My description *qua* Turing machine . . . and my description *qua* human being (*via* a psychological theory) are descriptions at two totally different levels of organization."[11] Furthermore, if machine states are instantaneous, single-state (however complex) states, virtually all of our psychological states are continuous, that is, persistent across what would have to be several machine states, and the complex that makes up the jealousy we feel today (or this morning) will be quite unlike the complex that makes up the "same" jealousy we feel tomorrow (or in the evening of the same day).

The humble point of all this is not simply that the digital machine model cannot do the work we could quite reasonably expect it to do, but that even if its explanatory power were increased exponentially, it would still not explain what we are interested in or render explanations at the psychological level either unnecessary or superfluous. We would still have two necessary, coexistent if not coextensive explanatory worlds, two very different levels of organization, with the higher level remaining at once "autonomous" and, generally, more "interesting." From all this, the pluralist critic can reasonably conclude that explanations of texts at what is for most theorists today the neglected and often forbidden level—i.e., the psychological level, the level of action, character, thought, of persons, jealousies, rivalries, of pain, suffering, hope, etc.—is more often than not talk at the generally interesting level. This is especially so, of course, when the texts in question are organized or "justified" by interests at this level, by psychological and formal interests, are themselves interested in such interests.[12]

To bring all that is contained in this discussion of levels of organization and of the autonomous nature of the psychological level to bear on the issues that most intrigue literary critics, especially those who have not given up on "reading" or "interpretation," would be to anticipate too much of the subsequent argument. Nevertheless, by way of adumbration, we can note here that, whatever else a text may be, it is a symbol system that can be understood at various levels of organization, can be explained by reference to one or another set of structural relations or, alternatively, considered as a hierarchical series of matter-form relationships. Keeping in mind that all levels are "interesting" and that the level we are interested in will be most interesting to us, we would say that with language, as with the other topics we have examined, the general rule is: *the higher the level the more interesting the class to which we can generalize.*

Any text can be described in terms of a large number of structural systems, and the systems themselves can be arranged in a one-way, lower-to-higher order of "dependency." Speaking loosely, and only for purposes of illustration (i.e., not in such a way as to cheer every linguist and critic), we can talk about structural relations at the phonemic (or graphemic) level, the morphemic level, and, moving progressively upward, at the level of syntax, semantics, diction, "style," sentence "meaning," and so on. Speaking even more loosely, we might talk progressively in terms of syllables, words, sentences, paragraphs, whole compositions; still others, of course, might be comfortable talking about the function of a word in a sentence, of a sentence in a speech, of a speech in a scene, a scene in an act, and an act in a whole play, with function being determined by some grasp of the justification conditions that limit "meaning" and "reference" at each level; others still, some other way.

In an effort to make relatively short work of a Herculean project, let us say that the "rules" that apply at one level of organization, though independently interesting and autonomous (in the sense that they can function systematically across material differences) cannot determine their own boundary conditions and that the psychological level determines the boundary conditions for the operation of the lower level "rules," that "reference" and "meaning" are indeterminate below the psychological level, which begins, still speaking roughly and crudely, where syntax and semantics ends. For example, by varying the "letter" preceding the sound system "og" in "dog," I can give my dog something to do in a rhyme scheme that has already found a line-ending place for fog, smog, bog, and log. Actually, my dog belongs in your chorus—the dawg, fawg, smawg, bawg, and lawg chorus—not mine, since my dawg barks out of tune in my fahg, smahg, bahg, and lahg musical system; of course, to me the mutt does not bark at all; he bahks—and quite euphoniously, to my ear.

As a sound system, my dog will frolic with one group of associates, whereas he will frolic with quite another group as a morphemic system (as a word, say). In this system our dog runs not with "bog" and "log," but with pooch, mutt, Rover, spaniel, and so on. These are classes of cases to which I can generalize from "dog" (the word), but not from "dawg" (the sound). And while it is certainly true that there would be no dog (or log, fog, etc.) without a sound system, that system cannot determine either its own boundary conditions (i.e., the ways its elements will link up with one another) or the range of relations in which its morphemically organized components can participate. In other words, if sounds are the *material* basis of the phonemes which *inform* them with determination, the phonemes are the *material* basis of the morphemes which inform them with determination. Thus, what is *material* at one level is *form* at another, and what forms the matter at one level becomes the matter formed at the next level, the whole system being informed by the psychological level which endows the various structures with this rather than that interest-relativity (informed, that is, by aim, purpose, wish, desire, and so on in these rather than those circumstances).

Once we reach what for convenience we will call the level of the "word," we find a dog whose friskiness knows no bounds (dawg's "awg"—i.e., the phonetic string "og"—by contrast, has an extensive but not unlimited range in English). This Rover is a rover, and if grammar, syntax, and semantics put some constraints on his activity, only psychology can keep him first in this yard and then in that one. For the dogcatcher, the problem is that this dog is as many dogs as there are contexts for a dog to be in.

The grammatical dog, for example, takes a plural in "s" and finds its preterite in "-ed" ("My dogs are tired, because me and the sergeant birddogged the guy all night"); but this dog is capable of forming unlimited relationships in countless worlds. We have, for instance, what Kenneth Burke calls the "lexical" dog, the dog defined by the "dictionary" in terms of species and differentia, the dog whose reference is fixed by experts, by, say, biochemists wise to the species-specific ways of genetic material. To this dog, Burke adds the "primal" dog (our first dog, say, or the never-to-be-forgotten dog we first loved, were frightened by, or knew), the "jingle" dog (the previously noted rhyming dog), the "entelechial" dog (the dog of dogs, the "ideal" Platonic dog, perfectly true, good, and beautiful), and the "tautological" dog (the dog implicated by association in such terms as kennel, doghouse, cat, loyalty, and so on).[13]

And, of course, freely consorting with our doggy dogs are all those "so-to-speak" dogs wearing "poetic" licenses. In this pack, we find the dog star; a dog-eat-dog world; firedogs (in the fireplace), which are not to be confused with fire dogs (dalmatians probably, found not in the fireplace, but the firehouse); tired dogs (found at the bottom of the legs of waitresses and infantrymen, especially those who are dog-tired); top dogs; hot dogs (edibles or contemptibles—i.e., showoffs); dog days; the dogs of war; mild oath dogs (the "doggone it" dogs); partial or metonymic dogs (the dogs whose ears give names to the pages of our books or whose legs describe turns in the road); sea dogs (dogfish, seals, or sailors); dogwoods (identified by their bark, not their bite), and, to put an end to a list already too doggone long, a veritable host of lazy, dirty, unconscionable dogs, and so on.

At the level of syntax, we can move, at least in one system of syntactic analysis (i.e., generative grammar) from surface phenomena to deep structural relations and, by so doing, resolve some ambiguities that appear at the surface level. Nevertheless, this grammatical system has no ready means by which to determine whether or not the "dirty dog" at the surface is used ironically or to determine, for that matter, what a particular sentence "means"; it cannot determine, that is, which among the indefinite number of legitimate, alternative possibilities of meaning is locally right, fit, or appropriate. As we noted earlier, in our remarks on Michael Dummett's views, the assertibility conditions for arbitrary sentences cannot be formalized, since every such sentence can adjust to a variety of contexts and be made meaningful relative to a variety of interests (i.e., of psychological imperatives). Moreover, projecting from one sentence to the next (and, of course, from one paragraph to the next) is not a capacity intrinsic to syntactic analysis. Only by supplementing such analysis with assumptions, say, about the kind of context we are in can we project to reasonable possibilities of subsequent "meaning" or understand the sense in which the subsequent sentence is justified. Grammar and syntax make explicit certain "rules" implicit in our verbal practice, grounding what we do in systematic operations, but such rules, however refined, cannot determine the boundary conditions of "meaning" and "reference."

And as it is with syntax, so it is with semantics, at least with the semantic "rules" formalizable from our practice. Undoubtedly, our implicit understanding, for example, of how to order a series of adjectives is rule-governed; and much has been done to bring such rules to the attention of awareness. That, speaking without benefit of counsel, we all tend to say "great big, lazy, brown dog," instead of "brown, big, lazy, great dog" is surely no accident; but no semantic theory, unaccommodated by an independent assessment of the local, operative (psychological) justification conditions, will be able to tell us whether the "great big, lazy, brown dog" has reference to the grotesquely overweight cocker spaniel sprawled on the rug before the fireplace or to that no-account, young, space-filler of a son sprawled on the beach beside his surfboard (or, giving our dog even greater Protean powers, to the Mississippi River on a calm summer day, when the great brown god divests himself of power and becomes the dog that every god by orthographic inversion may become).

So far, we have restricted attention to those systems of structural relation functioning independently and collaboratively within language systems (i.e., texts) that in a broad sense belong to the discipline of linguistics. Furthermore, we have insisted that any attempt to generalize from these systems to principles or conditions of "meaning" and "reference" (to classes of cases determinate of specific "meaning" and "reference") would be, if not fruitless, then, what amounts to the same thing, overfruitful, since only at the psychological level are the innumerable possibilities of "meaning" given their peculiar interest-relativity.

In support of the last point, we would note, for example, that in translating another language or interpreting our own, we cannot achieve an understanding of the interest relativity of "meaning" by relying only on a "translation manual," that is, a knowledge of grammar, vocabulary, syntactical and semantic rules or of the large- and small-scale "beliefs" that are generally accepted in any given culture. To such knowledge we must add assumptions about the aims, desires, wishes, and so on that would justify such and such an assertion in such and such circumstances. We do not ask what do these words or sentences mean but, rather, what is the psychological state or the intentional condition from which the sentence derives its interest-relativity in this context-sensitive situation. The covering assumption is that in expression and interpretation, as in perception and system building, we strive for—without always achieving—uniformity and *continuity*, influenced, as Goodman says, by what we have seen and done before, but improvising along the way.

At any rate, since every differentiable aspect of a text may be the subject of independent inquiry, it is certainly possible as most modern critics have made abundantly clear, to focus attention on lower-level categories and operations. More specifically, it is certainly possible to concentrate on iterative words and phrases or, more exactly, on the possible relations among recurrent terms, "ideas," "themes," and so on, as these are variously determined by the dialectical interests of one or another reader (as "new critics" and some deconstructionists do); on the "meaning" of some particularly characteristic, though often obscured or hidden, tropological or figural maneuvers of a text (as de Man and some other deconstructionists do); or on the diverse and usually conflicting or contradictory "meanings" that the text calls into play by shifting among styles of "discourse" (as many Bakhtinians do). At this level of structural concern (i.e., the level that dominates both critical theory and practice in our period, the level where orders—or disorders—of meaning and significance are derived from an examination of relations among terms, modes of diction, tropes, independent units of meaning, and styles of "discourse"), generalization to certain interesting classes of cases is clearly possible, especially if one is prepared to grant the "truth" of the prior assumptions about "language" or "social reality" upon which discussion at this level is founded and to which each text brings support or confirmation.

If all reading is "hypothetical," in the sense that "meaning" and "reference" are not givens but takens—determined by some construction of interest—reading at this level is peculiarly hypothetical, in that the inherence in the texts of the special features emphasized usually depends upon a habit of reading determined by the hypotheses about language or "reality" one is attempting to establish. The critic finds what he knows is "always already" there, what his dialectic requires. Generalizations at this level are often big-shouldered. They are quite capable of carrying us to the very infrastructure of language or historical becoming, to being and nothingness (or to the traces of nothingness). Criticism or discursive practice here is primarily "dialectical," concerned with binary operations, with division, opposition, or conflict in various pairs of "tropemes" or "ideomemes," and, thus, discussion gives emphasis to tension, irony, paradox, ambiguity, the absence of presence and the presence of absence, alterity or the other, contradictions, cancellations, the dialogic encounter of "ideologemes," the emergence of the "repressed" content from within the expressed content, the insubordination of the element subordinated in traditional orders of value, and so on.

As a matter of necessity, explanation at this level is largely indifferent to all that has prominence at the psychological level, to what we might call the intentional, emotional, affective structure of texts. Hence, in these analyses, the conventional literary categories through which psychological talk (i.e., talk relating to the intentional and affective grounds of "meaning") is filtered, such as plot, act, character, scene, motive, and so on, are disregarded, neglected, or treated, if acknowledged at all, as necessary incidentals, lines on which to hang what has our primary interest. There is, of course, nothing sacrosanct about such categories, and no special privileges attach to psychological talk or to the kinds of generalizations that such talk makes possible. Nevertheless, it is important to remember that in a world of immanent meaning, no special privileges can be granted to the "ideomemic" way of talking, either.

Furthermore, if you believe, as the pragmatic pluralist does, that translation and interpretation, while difficult, are possible, then the sorts of generalizations that psychological talk leads to become especially "interesting" (at least to certain kinds of literary works), since it is to them that we must appeal if we would understand (cognitively and emotionally) what it "means," for example, for such a man as Lear, both king and father, to say in such and such circumstances of abuse that he is "more sinned against than sinning" and if we would understand, retrospectively, why such a "truth," no less true for being more than half made up of pride and self-pity, pales in emotional and moral significance when placed beside his later desire to "expose" himself "to feel what wretches feel" so that he may "shake the superflux to them" and "show the heavens more just." What out of Lear's mouth moves us to pity would out of Goneril's move us to contempt.

And only by some emphathetic grasp of the kind of suffering that is worn and borne by the kind of man Lear is can we understand what it "means" to say what he says and be moved by his saying it. From our encounters with literature, as from our encounters with everyday events, we gain principles of reasoning in proportion to our experience. By virtue of our participation in various social practices and situations, we learn the "truth" conditions that endow sentences and whole works with these rather than those meanings and references, learn to recognize, say, what a "pitiful scene" is and to understand that the "meaning" of a sentence expressed in such a scene is conditioned by psychological state (aim, wish, desire, or feeling).

Explanations at the psychological level, like those at the geometric level, are autonomous, in that they apply across material differences, enabling us to see within new contexts the operations of the "same" "intentions" or truth conditions, of the "Lear-like" in the materially un-Lear-like. The pity that is evoked in one situation of undeserved misfortune will be evoked in another completely different situation of the same kind (in Mary's case as well as in Joe's case).

Ideologemic Explanations: The Example of Bakhtin

The large issues occasioned by the preceding discussion—issues of intention, belief, desire, etc.—will be the concern of subsequent chapters. For now, since our inquiry has been brought to a prospect of possible alternative, higher-level explanations, it might be useful to consider why a psychological explanation might at times be more interesting (or lead to "more interesting generalizations") than an "ideomemic" one. And since we shall later look directly at the explanatory procedures of deconstruction and, more glancingly, "new criticism," our illustrative model here will be Bakhtinian dialogism (or, rather selected aspects of this system). At the outset of this discussion it is important to understand that we are here dealing with different kinds of explanations at the higher level, with different ways of "interpreting" or responding to "whole" works, of informing lower-level structures with determinate emphasis and value. That is, both "ideomemic" and psychological explanations are higher-level organizations of material already participating in several lower-level orders of structure (phonemic, morphemic, syntactic, or whatever).

Nevertheless, it is also important to understand that while each system of explanation may acknowledge the interests of the other system, what has center stage in one system has at best only a walk-on role in the other. For example, if for certain kinds of works, plot and character are central to explanations at the psychological level (because "meaning" and "reference" are relative to the "intentional" states of persons of distinctive character in certain circumstances), they are relatively insignificant to "ideomemic" explanations. On the other hand, if the "ideologeme" (a unit of discourse, embedded in another discourse, that expresses a "particular way of viewing the world, one that strives for a social significance") is to Bakhtin the chief "object of representation" in a novel, it is to the "psychologist," if it is recognized as a discrete unit of "meaning" at all, a material component (in much the way phonemic, morphemic, and syntactic units are material components) whose "meaning" is relativized to the interest in which it is embedded, whose meaning, in other words, is determined by some psychological condition (e.g., anger or jealousy).[14] From the psychological perspective, at any rate, the ideologeme is not an *independent object of representation*, a differentiable unit whose "meaning" is isolable from the circumstantial intentionality in which it is embedded.

For Bakhtinians, a character (as well as the author and the narrator) is interesting to the extent that his discourse is "ideologemic," expressive directly or implicitly of a view with a certain social significance, and the author's primary task is a "stylistic" one (i.e., finding ways to represent artistically "images" of language, ideologemes). In the Bakhtinian scheme, then, "Individual character and individual fates—and the individual discourse that is determined by these and these only—are in themselves of no concern for the novel." What is "distinctive" in such *discourse* "strives" for a "certain social significance," and when such discourse achieves what it strives for, it becomes a "language," an "image of a language," in short, an "ideologeme." Of course, characters act as well as speak, but their action is significant relative to and "always highlighted by ideology," and "is associated with an ideological motif and occupies a definite ideological position." More specifically, "the action and individual act of a character in a novel are essential in order to expose—as well as to test—his ideological position, his discourse."[15] At bottom, the novel is "an artistically organized system for bringing different languages [i.e., ideologies] in contact with one another."[16] As a consequence, "the plot itself is subordinated to the task of coordinating and exposing languages to each other"; hence (and again), the "primary stylistic project of the novel as a genre is to create images of languages" for the sake of highlighting their contradictions and "sharpening our perception of socio-linguistic differentiations."[17]

The kind of unity the novel realizes is, we are assured, an openended one, one in which the "dialogic" contradictions are not resolved but shown for what they are, the work as a whole expressing what ordinary discourse and experience normally conceal, the very conflicts underlying the sociohistorical reality in which the work has its being.[18] If ordinary speech is a heteroglossic mixture of potential ideologemes, novelistic speech is dialogic, still a series of speeches within other speeches, but one in which the ideological potentialities within the mixture are actualized. The unity achieved by the novel is a unity only in the sense that the work is a "concrete" imaging of the dialogic diversity actually constituting a particular stage of "historical becoming."

Ordinary speech and conversation hide what the novelist succeeds in disclosing. We are always involved in speaking somebody else's speech in somebody else's language (more than half of what we say, according to Bakhtin, belongs to others), but the novelist through such devices as parody and hybridization manages to capture the ideologemic in the heteroglossic languages of his narrators and characters and, thus, to get beyond the apparent diversity to the ideological unity of historical diversity. As Bakhtin says:

Novelistic dialogue is pregnant with an endless multitude of dialogic confrontations, which do not and cannot resolve it, and which, as it were, only locally (as one out of many possible dialogues) illustrate this endless, deeplying dialogue of languages; novel dialogue is determined by the very socio-ideological evolution of languages and society. A dialogue of languages is a dialogue of social forces perceived not only in their static co-existence, but also as a dialogue of different times, epochs and days, a dialogue that is forever dying, living, being born: co-existence and becoming are here fused into an indissoluble concrete unity that is contradictory, multi-speeched and heterogeneous; . . . from this dialogue of languages these [ideologemes] take their openendedness, their inability to say anything once and for all or to think anything through to its end, they take from it their lifelike concreteness, their "naturalistic quality" . . .[19]

As documents reflecting states of "historical becoming" (and, implicitly, valuable to the extent that they are explicable in ideological terms), novels are, of necessity, openended.

In this system of analysis, the *author* is crucial to the realization of ideologemic conflicts, which are brought into open conflict only by his conscious and conscientious effort, but he is himself, finally, subordinated to the dialogic contradictions that he exhibits, since his inability to resolve conflicts is directly proportional to his success in exhibiting them. To resolve in any way any of the displayed contradictions he would have to be what he is not, that is, history itself, which tells its complex, multivoiced, and as yet unresolved metastory in its own way. He is subsumed by the forces he inscribes and is himself a mediated mediator. Of course, he could speak with "one" voice—a nondialogic heteroglossia—but not without losing himself as a novelist. He can end his plot (a matter of small moment), but not his dialogue. The plot is not the thing wherein to catch the conscience (or consciousness) of the race; it is the paltry stick on which the golden birds (ideologemes) sing of what is past, passing, and striving to become. Speaking of whole works, with special reference to those by Dostoevsky, Bakhtin says: the novels

in their entirety, taken as utterances of their *author*, are the same never-ending, internally unresolved dialogues among characters (seen as embodied points of view) and between the author himself and his characters; the characters' discourse is never entirely subsumed and remains free and open (as does the discourse of the author himself). In Dostoevsky's novels, the life experience of the characters and their discourse may be resolved as far as plot is concerned, but internally they remain incomplete and unresolved.[20]

To present Bakhtin's views in such a summary fashion is to do not a little violence to the richness, subtlety, and (often) compelling power of his arguments. No one who reads Bakhtin can fail to be impressed by his incisiveness and authority, especially when he works on specific literary texts and identifies the various types of discourse concealed within, say, the author's (or the narrator's or character's) discourse. If, then, we have done less than justice to *his* discourse, we have, nevertheless, fairly exposed what in this mode of analysis is relevant to our discussion, namely, its subordination of the "psychological" to the "ideologemic."

No pluralists would suppose that a "true" world could not be made from the materials found by this approach or assume that for some purposes its explanations would not be preferable to those supplied by an analysis conducted at the psychological level. On the other hand, if such an approach began to claim special privileges, insisting that it was peculiarly suited to the task of explaining, say, novels—because it made available to contemplation or awareness the only world actually constitutive of experience in these times of immanent meaning—then the pluralist would be obliged to ask it to temper its arrogance with a little modesty. Still, after granting the indisputable explanatory power of certain aspects of this way of talking about structural relations within texts, the pluralist (the pluralist-as-psychologist, at any rate) would in an interval of sobriety be bothered by what could be taken to be certain inherent limitations in the approach and have trouble acceding to many of its claims and to several of the assumptions underlying them.

For one thing, the whole approach seems to be focused on too narrow a band of units in the sociohistorical continuum that is the register of historical becoming. More important, the approach seems to be based on a *prior analysis of the conflicted forces*. Indeed, if it were not so based, the "ideologemic" could not be identified as ideologemic; the embedded discourse could not be singled out as a bearer of a peculiar social significance. And if the *reader simply identifies* what the author by conscious effort has made ideologemic in the heteroglossic, then the problem is compounded, for now *both author* and *reader* are implicated in *prior analysis and prior restraint*, since what the author deliberately highlights as significant must be recognized by the reader as having such highlighting and such significance. To be in a position to spot the "ideologemic" in the heteroglossic, one must, in a sense, be *in* socially differentiated time but not *of* it, must, in some sense, already know the contradictions of which one is constituted. It would be reasonable to inquire about the *world view* that makes possible the discrimination of socially significant world views in texts.

But if we put aside this inquiry and assume that it is possible to work, as some are inclined to say, at the margins of discourse, to be where we can *see our seeing* (being), see the eye seeing its seeing, then we are back to the narrowness problem, for we can immediately see that the band of "meaningful units" observed by this approach is too narrow. The band is too narrow precisely because *virtually everything* we say is made up of other people's saying, is compounded of elements already in verbal circulation; it is too narrow *precisely because* the world is so heteroglossic, so multilanguaged, so full of discourses belonging to a rich diversity of "worlds." We make our verbal pots by gluing together the shards of discourse available to us. We inherit a language already "phemed," vocabularized, and syntaxed, and we learn the various uses to which this "rule-laden" (and, of course, "use-laden") language can be put and the various "meanings" it can bear in the process *of using* it to meet our needs in the various circumstances in which we find ourselves and *of striving* to grasp the circumstantial and motivational conditions that would justify the attribution of one rather than another kind of interest relativity to the sentences we encounter in the various enterprises in which we participate from day to day. In using it and understanding its uses, we make and gain access to many worlds.

And, of course, all our worlds are "sociohistoric" in the broad sense (i.e., they emerge and subsist in sociohistoric time).[21] But not all such worlds are specifically "ideological," at least are not singled out as such by Bakhtin, who counts as "interesting" *only* those "world views" (textually embodied as "ideologemes") which have a "social significance," a kind of significance that the world views of, say, genetics, horticulture, sailing, or geometry presumably do not have. (Much in these ways of talking, at any rate, is not determined by or contingent upon some *particular* social formation. At least Bakhtin thinks so, for if he did not so think, everything, every bit of every discourse, would be ideologemic.) To the pluralist, then, Bakhtin gives emphasis to a small group of "emes" embedded in texts.[22]

From the pluralistic perspective, there are within easy reach many worlds available for incorporation into our discursive practices, our sayings and writings. And to the extent that a portion of any of these worlds could be isolated and treated as epitomizing the world view from which it was extracted, that "epitome" so isolated could then be embedded in another discourse and presumably identified by an alert reader as belonging to a distinguishable world of "meaning." In this way, then, we isolate and embed a unit of discourse that strives for something other than social significance, in the Bakhtinian sense; it strives for and presumably exhibits some other kind of significance in some world view other than the narrowly social. If *every* isolable, world-illuminating unit of discourse is understood to strive in one way or another for "social significance," then the force of the ideologemic is lost, and the *social* is trivialized.

And what we can do with one such epitome we can do with many; that is, in one discourse we can embed many discourses, creating in the end a patchwork of worlds that is, in a sense, emblematic of the concrete variety of "experience" itself. But note that in our revised scheme of artistic quilting, there is no reason to assume that the worlds brought together will necessarily be in conflict with one another. Indeed, since they occupy different space-times, they have no reason to contend for territory.

What the preceding amounts to, then, is not a critique of the project as such, but of the thoroughness with which it is carried out. By our lights, the Bakhtinian is simply not thorough enough. At this point, however, the Bakhtinian is only enjoined to add variety to diversity, to cross-fertilize "ideologemes" with other "emes," so that in the end the harvest will be more abundant than it currently is. As of now, the Bakhtinian reaps what the artist sows in but one field of "reality." In short, the pluralist can see no reason why in a world of immanent meaning any special privileges should be granted to "images" of language that betoken "sociolinguistic differentiations," especially when such "images" rather impose limits on than define the range of socially experienced "realities."

But even after granting such privileges to the "ideologemic," the pluralist-psychologist would still be perplexed because, for another thing, the "ideologemic" unit would itself seem to be heteroglossic, compounded, that is, of elements (words) deriving from or capable of entering into a multiplicity of reference relations. Any deconstructionist only half committed to the job could show, for example, how each of the particles making up the ideologeme was itself the bearer of many traces of signification, could show that the stability of the ideologeme was illusory. Since, however, the pluralist is no deconstructionist (though, like one, recognizing that the "reference" of arbitrary words cannot be fixed), he or she would wonder why the *intentional circumstantiality of the context of which the ideologeme is a part would not do unto the ideologeme what the ideologeme does unto the words comprising it, that is, fix the interest relativity.*

Or, more directly, it would seem to the pluralist-psychologist that just as the *words* function in the service of the "ideologeme" (have their reference fixed by the ideologeme), so the *ideologeme* functions in the service of that "intentionality" in which it is embedded. The assertibility conditions of ideologemes, no more than those of arbitrary phonemes, morphemes, words, and sentences, cannot be conveniently delimited, and ideologemes, like these other potentially meaningful units, cannot determine their own boundary conditions. To the pluralist, the ideologemes become in their new (changing and variable) context what the views of other system builders become in the writings of a new system builder, material components of new forms. To treat these ideologemes as though they preserved in their new context the meanings they carried in the context from which they were taken would be to favor them as no other "emes" are favored, as the Freudian "emes" and Emersonian "emes" in Harold Bloom's writings, for example, are not favored. The Freudian "emes" undergo a sea change as they change contexts and are incorporated first into Bloom's and then, say, into Norman Holland's discourse. And clearly these "emes" belong to a world-view as surely as do the ideologemes singled out for notice by Bakhtinians.

Analogously, we could say that treating these ideologemes as irreducible nuggets of meaningful social significance is comparable to treating the "world" from which any given *metaphor* derives its terms or categories of comparison as an independently significant world of meaning. Thus, we could say that when a character is at the zenith of her career, she is astronomically significant, or when a beloved is like a red, red rose, she is horticulturally meaningful, is, in addition to being lovely, fresh, or mortal, inescapably implicated in whatever it is that rose plants do to keep themselves from the doldrums in the world in which they have their significance. Even so, it is perhaps worth noting that if our character were discovered by such a habit of reading to be living now in the heavens—at the zenith—and now in the garden—as a rose—we would not also be obliged to conclude that she lived in conflict or in contradictory worlds.

What an emphasis on what some "old-fashioned" critics would call the *vehicle* (as opposed to the *tenor*) of the metaphor leads to, of course, is "imagery" studies, the identification and analysis of kinds and patterns of imagery, an enterprise that can certainly illuminate hitherto unnoticed aspects of texts and provide the very cautious reader with material on which to base some very tentative generalizations about, say, the character of the author. The critic who adopts this mode of analysis will consider *individual characters* and their *fates* to be of secondary or incidental importance and will not expect the *plot* to "resolve" the images in some synthesizing, grand image. With respect to "psychological" matters, this critic is on a par with (or comparable to) the "ideologemic" critic, for whom plot and character are similarly "uninteresting."

Now, if ideologemes could be identified as readily and as easily as metaphoric vehicles, we would willingly pay unto the studies conducted in their behalf all the respect that we pay unto imagery studies, but, as we have seen, such "emes" have a tendency to lose their specific worldly affiliations in the process of becoming "reworlded," that is, incorporated into new contexts. Moreover, *even* in the "world" in which an ideologeme can have social significance (let us for the sake of convenience say that the "ideologeme" before us belongs squarely in the world of commerce or labor relations or parliamentary proceedings), it is capable of serving as a carrier of various kinds of "social significance," depending on whether, for example, it is the "truth" honored by this faction or the "truth" honored by that faction within the social community from which it is taken. Also, how it is "honored" in its present context may be something quite apart from how it has ever been honored before. The ideologeme is a generalization to a class (commerce, parliamentary proceedings, or whatever), but *it does not apply directly or immediately to any cases in the class*, inasmuch as it only has specific meaning *within a case*. In other words, the ideologemic, wherever found, always has a context-sensitive and interest-relative meaning; it does not belong to any specific world independently of *some* interest relation. Different *ideologues* use the same "ideologemes" in different ways. The ideologeme is not transparently and unmistakably a distinct "world view," but only potentially one.

Thus, we are back to prior analysis and prior restraint, a prior understanding of the peculiar social significance of the ideologemic. Of course, what is said of the ideologeme is largely true of the metaphoric vehicle, except that if we have said enough to carry on with imagery study when by consensus we agree that this or that vehicle is horticultural, we have not said enough to carry on with "ideologemic" study when we agree that this or that ideologeme derives from the world of romance, or satire, or commerce, or parliamentary proceedings, or whatever, since to be truly ideologemic the ideologeme must have a *specific social significance in the world in which it is a world view.* Or, stated more formally, *the ideologeme is always a subset of a set*; it is *not a class of cases but a case within a class.*

But even if we put all this aside and assume that social practice has imposed severe constraints on the "world" meaning that the ideologeme can bear, the pragmatic pluralist-psychologist would still wonder why the critic would be essentially indifferent to the reference relations in which the ideologemic entered as a result of being functional in this or that context of character or plot concern, for example, or of author, narrator, or character concern, especially since the number of reference relations into which it can enter—even assuming its integrity as a meaningful unit—is virtually infinite and since its meaningfulness as a unit is not unaffected by the circumstantial intentionality in which it finds itself. But to wonder why, if the words can be adjusted to the interest of the ideologeme, the ideologeme cannot be adjusted to the interest of that in which it is embedded and which it subserves is to succumb, I suppose, to creeping Henry Higgins-ism, that is, to wonder why the "ideologemist" is not more like a psychologist.

In the end, however, notwithstanding many reservations about ideologemic study, the pluralist-psychologist recognizes that in practice such study, especially when it is undertaken cautiously and with a sensitivity alert to subtle shifts in style (as it usually is by Bakhtin), is often quite compelling. Moreover, no reader would deny that it is peculiarly suited to detecting modes of discourse within discourse or varieties of distinguishable elements of which our language in use is compounded. Such study does indeed bring to awareness (broad) classes of "speech," and by isolating and focusing on these classes we can undoubtedly learn in a general way something not uninteresting about the social (and other) "realities" that underlie our texts. That such study will also lead to a clear understanding of any particular stage of historical becoming seems unlikely, however, in part because the notion of "historical becoming" is itself highly problematic—indeed insupportable—dependent as it is on historicist assumptions about the priority of one world view in a world of immanent meaning, about the preeminence of a possible kind of immanence, and in part because as we extend our survey of cases—texts—we discover in every period not only myriad worlds but also diversity and discord and multiplicity within the very "world views" that we have been willing to treat as constitutive of the stage we supposed we had access to.

On the other hand, it should be clear that nothing in imagery or ideologemic studies precludes discussion at the psychological level and that study at this level allows us to generalize to interesting classes of cases. If imagists and ideologemists (as well as most other modern critics) recognize but neglect, say, character and action for the sake of exploring their interests in relations among images and ideologemes, we are not justified in assuming from such practice that the categories of interest to the psychologist are either unimportant or uninteresting (or, as some theorists seem fond of suggesting, illegitimate or second-rate). In expansive moments, the psychologist would in fact say to all those who would subordinate (at best) his or her interests to theirs: if you are interested in the text as a coordinated system of meaning and reference not of your own devising, you would be well advised to put off your own kind of felicity a while and subordinate your interests to mine.

More soberly, the psychologist would suggest that, since at the psychological level we are concerned with the assertibility conditions endowing the language we use with specific meaning and reference, the explanations available at this level are generally very useful and interesting to those not living in a cave on a remote island. This is so because in general we are more likely to confront situations from day to day in which we are interested in knowing if and why someone is angry or jealous or ironic, whether in the circumstances this or that remark or response is appropriate, what such and such a remark "means" when said by a particular person in a certain frame of mind, and so on, than situations in which it is pressingly important to know something about the kinds of (socially—i.e., ideologically—significant) discourse embedded in the angry speech directed to us or about the derivational base of the imagery in such a speech. Generalizations at the psychological level are like those at the geometric level: they apply to an enormous number of materially different cases, retaining their explanatory power across huge differences in mental contents and "external" circumstances. To size up a situation as one in which jealousy is "warranted" and a remark as one designed to give the jealous speaker a measure of mean gratification is not only to grasp the "truth-conditions" determining the "meaning" of what is said, but also to gain access to a conceptual (psychological) resource not exhausted in its local embodiment but permanently available as a possible conditioner of meaning in a variety of circumstances. It is one of those "principles of reasoning" that Samuel Johnson said we gain from experience.

If all "meanings" in all texts are interest-relative, and if "meanings" not our own can be retrospectively constructed by grasping the assertibility conditions of their expression, then anyone interested in the interest relativity of "meanings" will not be indifferent to explanations at the psychological level, since these explanations are preeminently concerned with *interests*. (We cannot know what Bakhtin's, Bloom's, or anybody's text "means" without knowing its interests.) To be engaged at all by a literary text (at least the kind of text that attracts Bakhtin's attention, in which plot and character figure prominently), we are obliged to figure out, say, what purpose (wish, aim, desire, fear, and so on) would induce a particular person to act or speak as he or she does in a particular situation, or we are obliged to ask what way of sizing up the situation would render intelligible what so-and-so says and does to so-and-so. More specifically, we are invited to inquire what "thin likelihoods of modern seeming" would induce a noble Othello to treat a faultless Desdemona as he does.

As we read a text, we size up the conditions conditioning the way the characters we have sized up in a particular way size up the situations they are in and imagine vividly, and apart from immediate self-interest, the moral and emotional determinants of specific "meaning" in humanly interesting situations. All "phemes," words, sentences, images, or ideologemes, however interesting in themselves as elements in systems of structural relations, are material bases of the interests that they are informed by at the psychological level. Moreover, the situations are humanly interesting *because their intelligibility depends precisely upon the same kind of moral reasoning that we are forced to employ in the world of everyday experience.* There is, then, a powerful, untrivial sense to the notion that literature provides us with "equipment for living." It (or some parts of it) enlarges the stock of concepts and references on which we can draw when the business before us is to make some kind of sense of what we say and do and of what is said and done unto us, when we are impelled to find a fit between what is said or done and what is "meant." Some texts, then, are interesting precisely because they are systems of moral reasoning, systems exhibiting moral reasoning (in characters) and requiring moral reasoning (in the reader), and because in schooling ourselves in their ways of moral reasoning we learn something relevant to the moral reasoning we must employ when we come out of the cave and start running bump into folks who insist on being attended to.

The psychologist's dark suspicion is that the vast majority of literary texts that we find interesting would interest us hardly at all if they were not systems of moral reasoning (and, thus, susceptible to explanations at what we have been persistently calling the psychological level). If such a suspicion were not unfounded, no one, then, would blame the psychologist for preferring on some occasions psychological explanations to a host of other kinds of explanations. If the psychologist insists that we cannot do without psychological talk (intentional, epistemic talk), there is no one who can legitimately gainsay this position without giving up on immanent meaning altogether.

It may be useful at this point to review our route so that we can see where we are and where we are going. In an effort to show that the pluralist can avoid eclecticism without falling into an "anything goes" relativism, I introduced for consideration three kinds of *cases* requiring judgment among different versions or explanations. In brief, I noted that the pluralist was prepared to decide, first, that some versions, though perfectly *coherent*, were nevertheless *unacceptable* (because contingent upon their adoption was the rejection of something not ready to yield its place or because the place they formerly occupied was no longer available; i.e., they were outmoded or superseded); second, that some explanations, though *true*, were *irrelevant*; and third, that some theories, though in some respects *incommensurable*, were nevertheless subject to *comparison* and subsequently to *preference*. At this point, we are near the end of our second case, in which "truth" is tested for relevance by three rules of thumb: explanations are rejected, first, if they do not fit the space opened up by the question (they belong, for example, to a version other than the one we are in); second, if they generalize to an "uninteresting" class of cases (for example, atomic as opposed to geometric explanations); and, third, if they simply tell us what we knew before we asked the question. We will now consult the final rule of thumb and then move on to the third case.

Third Rule of Thumb: Reject Redundant Explanations

This thumbnail sketch of our route reminds us that we cannot get to our third case without conferring again with the thumb. Consulted, the thumb tells the pluralist that no "true" explanation can be called good if it simply rehearses what we already know. Such a garrulous but uninformative explanation is a thrifty banker, one uninterested in interest; we give it an interest-worthy question, expecting a return with interest, but it tells us only that our account keeps pace with our deposits and that we can get back what we are able to put in. Our account "always already" contains what we "always already" knew it

contained. In dealing with this sort of explanation, Putnam frequently has recourse to the example of the professor found "stark
naked" in a dormitory at midnight and to the following indisputable
explanation of his presence at such a place in the vestment of his
nativity: he could neither leave the building nor put on his clothes
precisely at midnight without moving faster than the speed of light.
When the incident and the explanation were reported the next day
in the *Providence Journal*, all the people of Rhode Island were gratified to learn that even uppity physics professors were not above the
law and that once again our system of justice had demonstrated that
"the law's the law" and all are equal before it.[23]

Oddly, some people from Missouri were dissatisfied with the explanation and still wanted to know why the professor had chosen that
time and place to do his imitation of the jaybird. News of a professor's
failure to travel faster than the speed of light was not news to the
people of Missouri, since they were all personally acquainted with at
least one person who had been caught moping along below the speed
limit (just last week so-and-so's uncle had been caught dawdling with
so-and-so's neighbor in the supply room, and so on). In fact, excluding Rhode Islanders, only those who had some doubts about how fast
physics professors actually could move found the story, as reported,
mildly interesting. The rest wanted some other "true" explanation of
his condition, wanted to know something about his motives, aims, desires, purposes, in short, his intentions. (Were they, could they be
honorable, laudable, etc.? Was he attending a conference and using
the dormitory as a residence while the students were on vacation, for
example?)

Putnam's professor brings to mind an anecdote told by Myron Cohen in one of his comic routines, which, under revision, goes like this:
a jealous husband, suspecting his mate of infidelity, comes home
from work early one day and frantically begins to search the house
for an unwelcome (or, only half-welcome) visitor; after anxiously examining this nook and that cranny, the husband finally opens the
door to the wardrobe closet and finds what some in the law enforce-
ment business might call the "alleged perpetrator," to whom this
question is rather urgently put: "What in the hell are you doing
here?" To this query, the "suspect," another physics professor perhaps, replies: "Everybody's gotta be someplace." "Well, now that you
mention it, I guess that's right. Excuse me for asking," the husband
is unlikely to say in return, unless, of course, we are dealing with a
Rhode Islander or someone given to associating with philosophers
and people of that ilk.

In both cases, the explanations clearly do not fill in the space opened up by the questions with anything suitable to our interests. Being unable to travel faster than the speed of light or to occupy some space other than the one currently occupied certainly explains why someone is here rather than someplace else; nevertheless, the explanation resolves nothing that was not already resolved before inquiry began. The information or knowledge given by these answers is part of our *background knowledge*. Moreover, the explanation applies not only to the "closeted culprit" and the naked professor, but also to the spouse, to the witness to the professor's self-display, and, indeed, to all those citizens who found some unproblematic place to be while our protagonists were pledging allegiance to the "laws" of physics in their own turpitudinous way. It is a generous, all-purpose explanation, standing ready to do yeoman's service for all people, in all situations, however incriminating those situations may appear to be. It is the discount-store pantyhose of explanations: one size fits all.

Of course, every area of human inquiry, not simply physics, produces explanations that are designed, like the tarpaulin at Fenway Park, to cover the field, and, Casaubons all, we seem unwilling to settle for anything less than the single key to all mythologies, the one subsumptive term or principle (or the one set of terms or principles) that renders the manifest diversity around us intelligible. At least many of us will be content with nothing less. The speed-of-light explanation is merely a ludicrous example of a way of accounting for things that is, for many, deeply satisfying. Wherever we turn our gaze we see in intellectual life (explanatory life) what Johnson sees in second marriages, the triumph of hope over experience, the compulsion to unite Experiential Diversity and Conceptual Simplicity in bonds that no man dare put asunder. The desire to reduce the many to one, to see this, that, and the other thing as a peculiarly individuated instance of some one very special Thing, is apparently inextinguishable—it is at least in many modern literary critics and theorists, for whom inquiry is largely a matter of tracking down in many particular works the *one* thing that is already known to be there in some form or other.

Any witness to the passing parade that is modern criticism can easily confirm that literature has marched over the years under a variety of banners as now one and now another set of categories has taken charge of paint and brush. Let meaning be ever so immanent, some categories will still insist on being first among equals. The first task, then, is to find some preeminent derivational base of "knowledge," a base complete with "god-terms" and a mechanism for choreographing their movements. Of the many bases available, critics in our period have gone for support most frequently to history, politics, myth,

ritual, anthropology, Freudian psychology, and linguistics, among
others, having recourse, in general, to the social, not the nomothetic,
sciences for their explanatory models. Once selected, the explanatory
model is then sent forward to put questions (for which it already has
answers) to all the sign systems which we have wittingly and unwittingly inscribed or by which we have been inscribed. Not surprisingly,
the method works, for wherever we look, we find the localized manifestation of precisely those features that the model "explains" as it
identifies; inhering in all "texts" (and systems of behavior) are exactly
those traits that the model would require, if it were, as it is assumed
to be, a special conditioner of "meaning." If literary discourse (to
these critics literature is always "discourse") is distinguished by
"irony" or "paradox," then analysis discloses in this and that and the
other work the inherence of irony; if all discourse is characterized by
différance, then . . . , etc.

Moreover, the explanatory power of the model is best seen when
the material to which it is applied seems most resistant to its authority, when what the material *seems* to "mean" directly contradicts what
the model would have the material "mean." In such circumstances the
very "perversity" of the explanation serves as a powerful "proof" of
its "validity"; no one likes to be taken in by appearances, and thus
nothing delights quite so much as the knowledge that things are
other than we had thought them to be (indeed, that they are worse
than we thought them to be or just the reverse of what we had inno-
cently suspected them of being). Satan is Milton's hero and Hamlet,
not Claudius, the play's villain (well, how interesting). There are no
authors, only intertexts (how delightful). There is nothing outside the
text (how wonderful). All texts are—indeed, everything is—ideological (how nice). Long suspected of being the poet of the inner condition, a prince among epistemologists, Wordsworth is *really* the
preeminent *social* critic of the age; and although generally recognized
as one of the chief props or stooges of the Elizabethan status quo,
Shakespeare is, in fact, the primary arsonist or incendiary of the period, at least when he is not functioning as a tool of colonialism (I'll
be a monkey's uncle).

The ultimate authority of the model, however, derives from our
concessions to the "truth" of its claims about the "real" nature of, say,
history, mind, or language. If language or mind, for example, works
this way or that way, then it follows that all "texts" (or "coded" systems of behavior), whether great or small, popular or elite, spontaneous or contrived, whether taking the form of dreams, jokes, epic
poetry, lyric poetry, editorials, or State Department memoranda, are

acting in more or less open complicity with the categorical directives by which the scope of their activity is always already determined.

To prove the bare existence of such modes of reasoning in literary studies would undoubtedly be not unlike giving a speed-of-light explanation to the bare existence of the professor at midnight, in that such a proof is already in the possession of every reader to whom literary studies is not a mere string of vocables. Nevertheless, a quick overview of the mode in two of its more popular incarnations would perhaps not be criminally superfluous.

Knowing Thyself: The Example of New Criticism. The so-called New Critics, for example, begin inquiry, not from some general conception of the nature of language as such (as do many other critics), but from a conception of the nature of literary or "poetic" language, which is sharply differentiated from "scientific," "logical," or "discursive" language. What distinguishes literature from other "ways of knowing" is traceable ultimately to the peculiar characteristics of its medium of expression. Literary (or poetic) language is polysemous, faithful to the rich diversity of experience, and hence especially suited to expressing and exposing by means of paradox, irony, and ambiguity the dynamic tensions or the tensional oppositions that actually underlie our encounters with the world and our attempts to know it. Where irony, paradox, and ambiguity can be found, there too can literature be found; and the critic's task is to show how various texts variously realize their peculiarly "tensed" "meaning" as a result of maintaining some dynamic equilibrium between opposites or countervailing tendencies. The text is a structure of meanings determined by tensions, for example, between denotations and connotations, between the meaning of one term, phrase, idea, or pattern of imagery and that of another. In general, once the basic opposition has been located, the forces it holds in gyroscopic balance can be found at work throughout the text in greater and lesser textual units, in terms, phrases, images, verse paragraphs, scenes, and so on, each unit thus serving as a metonymic epitome of the whole work.

Because the only appropriate vehicle for the expression of the text's "meaning" is the text itself, the linear, propositional reasoning employed in analysis, description, or paraphrase can at best only suggest or approximate what the text embodies. That is, *readings* of texts are no satisfactory substitutes for the internal *meanings* of texts, but they are the only simulacra academics can offer the journals and one another. By means of such "readings," these critics could perhaps suggest, albeit in logocentric, propositional form, the "meanings" that transcended the logocentric or propositional. Like their proper and legitimate heirs, the deconstructionists, they made do with the logocentrism that they canceled or derided. At any rate, in practice this approach, in which the inherence in texts of certain qualities (irony, paradox, etc.) depends upon a habit of reading determined by the very hypothesis about poetic language that is in question, results in thematic readings of texts, in readings that for the most part disclose the dynamic interaction of such general ideas or themes as love and reason, wit and witchcraft, the individual and society, death-in-life and life-in-death, and so on.

And if each text carries a different or unique meaning, all texts go about the business of meaning in the same way, inevitably so, since by prior commitment we know what poetic language is like and consequently what poetic structure must be if poetic language is as we assume it to be. As Johnson once remarked, with reference to a similar mode of reasoning, the whole "system seems to be established on a concession which if it be refused cannot be extorted."[24] Knowing what they are looking for, New Critics quite predictably always find what they earnestly seek (as, of course, you and I and the rest of us always do, though some of us, as we shall see, are occasionally surprised by what we find).

The Abyss in Déja Vu: The Example of Deconstruction. What New Criticism was to one generation of critics, deconstruction aspires to be, it seems, to a more recent generation, that is, the best or most exciting game in town, though it is already prematurely gray and seems to be a prime candidate for early retirement. If the New Critic begins inquiry with a distinction between "scientific" discourse and "poetic" discourse, a distinction based on a conception of the peculiar nature of poetic language, the deconstructionist begins with assumptions about the general nature of language (or sign systems). What applies to poetic language applies as well to "scientific" language and to all other "languages." In brief, language at all levels, from the phoneme or grapheme on up, is a system of differences; no element is positively present because every element carries within it the traces of the system of differences of which it is a part. Presence is always caught up in self-deferral, since "positive" terms can never stand apart from or appear independently of the system that makes them possible; such terms exist *nowhere* apart from a system of differences.

No phone or word or "concept" or whatever can escape the chain of referral or signification, since it is only relative to this chain that its difference is marked; differences are marked in a system of differences. Thus, the "p" of *peak* and the "b" of *beak* are in a sense mutually implicative in that the functioning of the one is impossible without the functioning of the other and both are functional within a class of sound differences. As noted, what is "true" at the level of sound is "true" at the higher levels of "signification," for, as Derrida asserts, "no element can function as a sign without referring to another element which itself is not simply present. This interweaving results in each 'element' . . . being constituted on the basis of the trace within it of the other elements of the chain or system." Thus, "nothing, neither among the elements nor within the system, is anywhere ever simply present or absent. There are only, everywhere, differences and traces of traces."[25]

Deconstructionists are not content to work with sounds (or "graphs") or words in isolation from the larger contexts in which these linguistic elements find themselves, despite the fact that there would seem to be no easy way to maintain contact with the principles upon which the system is based while extending the range of concern to larger units of "meaning," inasmuch as "presence" is never and nowhere to be found. That is, analysis would never get off the ground, if, for example, the "phemes" of the larger units of meaning to be deconstructed were not at least temporarily capable of at least "seeming" to achieve enough presence to subserve the interests (in, for example, words, phrases, themes) that the critic is interested in deconstructing. In short, deconstructionists do not restrict their attention to the irreducible or smallest elements of language, the smallest, differentiable units. They grant to logocentrism the power to impose (apparent) restrictions on the mobility of language *as such*, in the name of one or another power interest. In practice, analysis (or explanation) always begins where traditional criticism leaves off (for "traditional criticism" the reader could without impropriety read "new criticism"), that is, with the theme or with the binary oppositions that give the poetic theme its peculiarly "tensed" equilibrium.

As matters turn out, all writers (and, of course, all others in the sign business) are naked professors, are self-compromised. Just as no naked professor, however determined and willing to do so, can exceed the speed limit set by light, so no writer, no matter how doggedly he or she sets about it, can commit full logocentrism, can really operate outside the limits limiting writing. Less darkly, the writer, regardless how valiantly attempting to come to a point, to express a view, to articulate a philosophy, to defend a position, will inevitably subvert or undermine the positive he or she would establish in the process of establishing it, because the "other" that he would suppress is a necessary condition of the something he aims to express, is part of the system of differences upon which the positive depends. And this we know, because we know that nothing can signify without referring (implicitly but necessarily) to other elements in a system of difference.

But we leapfrog ourselves. We must return for a moment to practice, to themes and binary oppositions. When the New Critic "clocks out," the deconstructionist "clocks in" and begins another shift. Now the deconstructionist, whether relying on the discoveries of the "New Critic" or not, proceeds with the task from some initial conception of the *thematic* aspirations of the text at hand, or of the binary oppositions upon which its "meaning" depends, or of the key concepts, terms, and metaphoric figures that inform it and that serve as the elemental stuff of the text's rhetorical maneuvers. In short, the deconstructionist begins with the supposed (thematic) logocentricity of the text, more narrowly, with its apparent affirmations, and then shows that the meanings it would affirm are undercut by the meanings it would but cannot (fully) repress. Further, he or she shows that the whole system in which the expressed and repressed have functions is itself dependent upon a prior system of differences and, of course, that system upon another system or its trace, and so on, all the way back to the beginning; a beginning or origin, however, cannot be tracked down, because a beginning cannot begin without already having begun, without already having been begotten by a system of differences.

If the text tries to give priority to one of the terms suspended in binary opposition (to reason, not imagination; nature, not nurture; speech, not writing; truth, not fiction; the state, not the individual, and so on), the critic, knowing full well that the "system" is a horizontal rather than a vertical one, can easily turn the tables on the text by claiming, first, that since the primary is positioned as primary by the secondary, the secondary is primary and, then, that mutual dependence makes the notion of primacy or priority a species of arrant nonsense.[26] If, for purposes of deconstructive analysis, some term, concept, or rhetorical figure can be considered as epitomizing the concerns of the text (however marginally important it may have seemed to prior investigators, however subservient to local interests it may have formerly seemed), then unto that figure (and what it "signifies") we can do what we can always do unto any besotted signifier that has delusions of fixing a reference, namely, make it a party to the subversion of what it would affirm. If "parasite" is our metaphor (or trope or figural centerpiece), then by an easy conversion we can make a guest of our host and a host of our guest, revealing thereby the deep-down deferentiality of referentiality to the economics of exchange.

As a practical enterprise, deconstruction, like "new criticism" and Bakhtinian dialogism, is concerned chiefly, not with what determines "meaning" at the psychological level (i.e., aims, wishes, beliefs, fears, hopes, mental "contents," and circumstantial conditions), but with themes, views, key terms, concepts, tropes, images, and so on. Unlike its predecessor or competitor, however, deconstruction is determined to show that the "presences" made so much of in other schemes of analysis are mere shadow presences, illusory phantoms that logocentric prejudice has been willing to call substances because it dare not suppose that the shadows on the wall are always and only shadows on the wall. What the deconstructionist knows before he begins inquiry is that all "texts"—regardless of how determined they are to "mean" this and not that, of how skillfully and diversely they arrange the ruses of figuration to trap this and not that sense, and of how deviously they deploy their rhetorical ploys to catch this rather than that view in its unsupplemented present presence—are, as Derrida says, *textiles*, weavings of weavings, or, more appropriately, unravelers of their own ravelings. No matter how pernicious and retrograde its ambition, no text can successfully revolt against the system of differences or, on the happy side (such is the generosity of the state of language), be found guilty of full logocentricity. Naturally, this can and must be shown by logocentric means; like the New Critics, the deconstructionists are obliged to use the logocentrism they would transcend. Just as we always already know that no professor can travel faster than light, so the deconstructionist always already knows that no text can bypass difference and go directly to presence and always already knows that it disconfirms what it affirms, cancels or erases exactly what it inscribes, turns upside down what it placed "right" side up.

If deconstruction puts all our certainties into question, it does so because it *knows in advance of inquiry* that all sign systems sign themselves with the eraser end of the pencil, inscribe their certainty with uncertainty in the act of inscribing it. At the moment, of course, we are not concerned with the legitimacy, value, or importance of the deconstructive turn from "new criticism," but only with its tendency to find what it is looking for and to ask for what it already knows is there. As an "always already" mode of reasoning, it always gets from explanations exactly what it puts into them, and it shields itself from surprise by digging only where it has already filled the explanatory space with treasure. If the method were a Bible, it would be an infallible and inerrant one.

In making special examples of New Criticism and deconstruction in this way, treating them—and, implicitly, all "always already" modes of reasoning—as particularly hospitable to self-evident explanations, I do not mean to suggest that there is a mode of reasoning that poses *disinterested* questions, that does not in some sense already know what it is looking for in an explanation. Explanation, like reference, is interest-relative. What counts as an explanation or a cause will depend on our interests and our prior knowledge—the assumptions and beliefs that we bring to what presently has our interest. It is only against a background of prior knowledge that our questions can be formulated. There is a strict relativity of questions to operative assumptions, but it is *precisely because those assumptions undergird our questions* that they cannot provide explanations capable of satisfying our interests, our reasons for asking the question. There would be no point in formulating a question if its interests could be satisfied by that which made its formulation possible. A question is interesting, then, only to the extent that its answer is not already contained in the background knowledge.

Chapter 6
Incommensurable Worlds

Incommensurable but Comparable Worlds

The issue we now approach full of fear and trembling—the possibility of comparing and then choosing between ostensibly incommensurate theories—is in a sense the most crucial one we face, since the principles underlying virtually every modern theory of criticism (whether monist, relativist, or pluralist) are, it seems, dead set against the possibility of direct comparison of incommensurables. Deconstructionists, for example, cannot entertain the possibility because, among other things, comparison presupposes centeredness, at least temporary fixity of reference. Furthermore, adjudication presupposes a mechanism for determining that one set of categories can legislate over another set, at least temporarily; it presupposes, in short, what cannot be granted without undermining the whole project to which the deconstructionist is committed.[1]

On the other hand, relativists (or certain kinds of relativists—Gadamerians, New Historicists, or interpretive-community relativists, for example) would lose their name at once if they assumed that different schemes of interpretation or reference could at some points be correlated with one another. Their whole project depends on the assumption that different interpretive communities totally different frameworks make. (Or, what's an interpretive community for?) Across the interpretive divide there is and can be no bridge. A community maintains its identity by adhering to its constitutional imperatives, and it has no choice in the matter, since it is informed by the categories which it informs. We all *see* what we *believe* (our seeing is a function of our beliefs; they are what we see with) and believe what we see; thus to see what somebody else believes is, perforce, *not to believe* what *we see*, which is, of course, beyond belief. And what goes for "we" goes for "thee."[2]

As an aside, it should be clear that the attack "against theory" advanced by Walter Benn Michaels and Steven Knapp culminates in precisely the kind of solipsism outlined here, since if there is no escaping belief, as they maintain, there is no way to stand apart from belief to get a look at different beliefs.[3] To recognize a difference, one must be where recognition is not governed by belief, be, in short, where one cannot be. If "theory" (belief) thus is inevitable, it is also pointless, inasmuch as its meaning is transparent inside and inaccessible outside belief; indeed, from the inside there is no outside, since what is believed to be outside can be believed only from the inside of belief; it is what the outside is to the insider. The true "believer" has no one to argue with, not even himself, for no self-respecting "self" can be divided against itself and be itself; it is beyond "itself" to be beside "its self" with self-doubt.

To be fair to actual practice, we must point out that the relativist will not consent to the reduction of his or her views to solipsism but, notwithstanding the logical implications of these views, will persist in asserting that in a world of immanent meaning there are a multiplicity of mutually exclusive frameworks or systems of meaning and reference. These are exclusive because they do not overlap either in *what* they account for or in *the way* they go about providing accounts. In changing paradigms, one changes not only world views, or organizational structures, but also the particular "objects" of which those worlds are constructed. A change of paradigm always and necessarily involves a change of world, and the "things" of one paradigm are not the "things" of (or things in) the other paradigm. Even though certain descriptive or observational terms remain the "same" across paradigm shifts, the "meanings" of those terms undergo sea-changes in the process of becoming functional within different paradigms. The change is systemic and total, affecting the parts as well as the whole. Although himself undergoing many sea-changes, Stanley Fish in one of his incarnations has held such views, has been a faux-Kuhnian or proto-Feyerabendian. On more than one occasion, he has maintained, for example, that each interpretation is an interpretation of a different text, since the objects or the details of the text are constituted by, are precipitates of, the interpretive strategy in play.[4]

Communication between or among systems is impossible, since the terms of the variant systems, however similar or "identical" those terms may appear to be, have no determinate "meaning" in isolation from the system of meaning that they subserve. In its most radical formulations, then, the relativist position would insist that in moving from, say, a Ptolemaic to a Copernican system, we not only switch to a new world view, but also construe the objects with which we are concerned—sun, moon, planets—differently; the objects themselves are constituted differently as objects in the different perspectives because "reference" follows function and function is determined in systematically different ways in the two cosmological frameworks.[5]

Paradoxes Found: Believing is Seeing

The issue before us is crucial because the notion of comparison or of "objective" knowledge seems to be incompatible with the notion of immanent meaning, which allows a multiplicity of reference relations and precludes appeal to foundational "truth." Indeed, so large and crucial is the issue that we will be obliged to come at it in various ways and in more than one context. In this section, as in later sections, we shall proceed suggestively, not conclusively, taking our cues from actual practice and surmising, on the basis of such practice, how it might be possible to achieve "objectivity" or "justify" decisions without sacrificing our earned sense of the interest-relativity of meaning and reference.

Before proceeding, however, we should perhaps pause for a moment to clarify the general problem. Standing in the way of comparison and decision-making are at least three obstacles, which Israel Scheffler has called paradoxes. There is, first, the *paradox of common observation*, a dilemma occasioned by the "fact" that our *observations* are "theory-laden." If differences are to be resolved, theorists must appeal to common observational "facts," but since the "facts" observed are not theory neutral and are such "things" as the theory determines them to be, any attempt to settle differences by an appeal to the "facts" of the case is doomed to failure.

That such "facts" or "things" are different becomes apparent, of course, when they are described in and incorporated into an articulated theory. Here we encounter the *paradox of common language*, for although different theories may share common sounds (i.e., common words, common observational terms and phrases), they do not share common "meanings." Common words alter their meaning and reference as they find a use in now one and now another theory. As Scheffler observes, the theorist is "effectively isolated within his own system of meanings as well as within his own universe of observed things."[6]

The third and final difficulty is designated the *paradox of categorization*. Simply, what we see or say is not an uncomplicated reflex of merely looking about; rather, our looking about is conditioned by our categories of thought. To look about without categories is to look at what we never see, unformed, undifferentiated, unnoticeable (let us say, for lack of any word whatsoever) "stuff," whereas to look about with categories is to see what can be seen through or with those categories. In either case, our thought cannot be checked or revised or monitored by observation. Of course, to be enthralled by one paradox is to be enthralled by them all, since in practice they work cooperatively and simultaneously. As a matter of analytic convenience, we can discriminate among word, thought, and thing (category) paradoxes, but in practice the subsistence of one is contingent on the "existence" of the others.

Our current dilemma finds its aphoristic formulation in ancient wisdom: believe that you may understand. But, of course, the aphorism is as empty as it is apt, since there is no understanding without belief. When beliefs create worlds and *the* "world" cannot discipline belief, the consequence is that all theorists live within the world of meanings created by their beliefs and are obliged to do their missionary work among the converted, to spread the good news among the faithful; what passes for good words, thoughts, and things in one theorist's world has no currency in another's world of belief, and no set of beliefs can be "justified" to the unbeliever without requiring that it be presupposed. An unbeliever may have a conversion experience or undergo a "gestalt switch" but cannot be persuaded to change beliefs by any appeal to rational norms because the only norms recognized by a belief system are the norms of the system believed.

Such, then, in broad outline are the difficulties confronting the comparativist and arbitrator who would preserve (or even have) a function in a universe in which all worlds are in different space-times. The monist, of course, has trouble with comparison and judgment for reasons quite different from those of the relativist. For the monist the many worlds reduce to one, and if conflict arises in the one world it is the sort of conflict that can be resolved by consulting criteria intrinsic to the operative system of belief. The monist works always at the level of what Kuhn would call "normal science," where the value and efficacy of the "paradigm" are assumed and where all tasks are sanctioned by the "paradigm" because they are made possible by it. To recognize the value of another paradigm requires placing oneself outside the paradigm that determines seeing, and a monist who managed to accomplish this feat of bi-location would be able to maintain preference for the original paradigm only after acknowledging the authority of transparadigmatic criteria to settle competing claims, that is, only after making the decisions of the paradigm subject to review by a superior court of claims. Thus, different as they are, both monism and relativism reduce to solipsism at the theoretical extremes, though, to be sure, relativism continues to insist that every-body is entitled to his or her own monism. Of course, what is *his own* or *her own* or *their own* is always, of categorical necessity, understood from within *my own*. Another's *own* is not understood as the other understands it from within *his or her own view*; what is understood is that view according to *my* view of "it."

In the "real" world, of course, simon-pure monists are as rare as theoretically rigorous, or total relativists. Refusing to claim that a case rests on any genuinely solid foundation (metaphysical or epistemic), the thoroughly modern monist, when pinch becomes crunch, ac-knowledges other possible ways of talking but prefers his or her own way because the others are, well, "uninteresting," "unimportant," or otherwise nugatory in significance. At any rate, the monist has no room for comparison, inasmuch as what is worth accounting for is accounted for by his or her system, and what falls outside its range cannot, by definition, be accommodated within it. Again, our issue is not an issue for the monist (or relativist or deconstructionist or a host of others).

Indeed, once meaning goes immanent, it is difficult to understand how the issue could become an issue for any critic, including the plu-ralist, who, as we have seen, refuses to accept conflicting statements as true in the same world (if they are not true in the same world, they are not in conflict, whereas if they are in conflict or irreconcilable, they cannot both be true in the same world).[7] But notice that even as we restate the pluralist case we introduce the notions of conflict and resolution.[8]

Now, like most modern theorists, pluralists recognize that any at-tempt to compare our discourse (any discourse) with objects as they really are in themselves is futile and that any notion of interpretation that assumes a correlation can be established between what we say and what really is the case (independently of a scheme of interpreta-tion) is fatally flawed. Unlike most theorists, however, pluralists have not given up on the possibility of *comparing* discourses or of *correlating* one discourse with another. Even though reference is relative to scheme of interpretation (as it is), *there is no reason to assume that every change in system of belief effects a change of reference (or function) in every term in that system, or that coreferentiality is impossible, that, in other words, we cannot have many theories about atoms or Hamlet or the French Revolu-tion.* Not quite "no reason," of course, for this is what some Kuhnians and relativists do assume on the basis of what the paradoxes outlined above have insinuated.

Pluralists, however, are emboldened to maintain their view, in part because they *understand* that it conflicts with that of the paradoxicals (i.e., they understand the paradoxicals' view without being *in* it or *of* it). Further, they suppose that it would be impolitic, even perhaps unconscionable, to assume that the *reader* does not *understand* a difference between believing and not believing in the possibility of comparing discourses. That is, pluralists assume that the reader understands a *difference* and what the difference is about without being determined or constituted by a particular belief about the possibility of comparison. In stating the case, pluralists in some (perhaps weak) sense *make* the case. That is, in defining the dilemma, pluralists compare one view with another and assume that all readers, whatever their theoretical commitments, understand that, when conjoined, the views exhibit not only difference but mutual exclusivity. Of course, making this assumption leads to the further assumption that every reader recognizes, at some level of consciousness, that the paradoxical position, a mainstay of theory, is *self-refuting*; otherwise, the reader would not even see the difference between affirming and denying the possibility. But we are here in danger of overextending ourselves by trying to conduct too many campaigns at once.

Trouble in Paradox: The Problem of Self-Refutation

Let us first look at the self-refuting nature of the paradoxical position and then consider how comparison and judgment might be possible where interest-relativity rules the day, might be possible in a world in which conceptual scheme determines reference. If the *theorist* is confined to the world of meanings that his or her system of belief both informs and is informed by, and if those beliefs cannot be "justified" in any world in which they are not already presupposed, then the believer is truly in a fix. This is so because to the extent that this view is true it is false, in that in order to be *convinced* of its truth *I* must become both an apostate and a convert, must violate the belief in the process of acceding to it (give up my prior belief and accept as true what I formerly did not believe), thereby committing sacrilege in the act of rejecting the old and affirming the new faith. Taking the vows is an excommunicable offense, it seems.

By the terms of their beliefs, the paradoxicals can neither persuade those not already persuaded nor even *attempt* to persuade them without violating their own beliefs, if only because recognition of the other, as other, is inconsistent with their beliefs and because appeal to criteria not intrinsic to the belief system itself is not only impossible but also unthinkable. Further, if the position were taken seriously, we would be obliged to reject it on grounds of unintelligibility, since from within our own prisonhouse of language it simply would not make any kind of sense. Finally, *believing* that worlds are determined by systems of belief is not the same thing as (indeed, is inconsistent with) *believing in any particular world determined by belief.* That is, the conviction that all meanings and references are scheme-dependent is not a conviction of the truth of a particular scheme. Belief in belief-determined systems is no part of any system of determined belief, or such a belief is not an implication of any belief system that is a system.

But, of course, the paradoxical position is not unintelligible to us; on the contrary, it is both intelligible and, at first glance, quite compelling. Rather, *it is unacceptable precisely because it is understood.* If it were unintelligible, it would not be understood; but if it is understood, it is, of necessity, unacceptable, because to understand it as a distinct position is to operate outside the borders delimited by the position, is to see the inside from the outside.

The illogical tendency of those inside the position is to say that the entire case against it covertly supports it, since the attack from without is made from within another self-enclosed system of reference. Thus, the prosecutor, they counter, argues for not against the plaintiff. This, at any rate, is how some paradoxicals, including Stanley Fish—at least in one of his critical modes—attempt to take the bait while avoiding the hook.[9] But the mover of this move moves illogically because recognizing and understanding the difference (the argument as an argument within a different system of reference) is recognizing and understanding too much. The paradoxical takes the hook with the bait, as it were, and gasps a rebuttal from within the boat.

Although our present business keeps us from following up on what is implicated in this slide from radical paradoxicalism, it is important to note that as soon as paradoxicals admit that they can recognize different views, they simultaneously acknowledge that comparison and interpretation (or translation) are possible; like others, they can understand and consider several views without being in (or believing in) any one of them. If after surveying the past and present alternatives to his particular view, a paradoxical persists in preferring his approach to others, he must do so on some grounds or other, either rational or irrational. To be rational—or to have the appearance of rationality—the preference would have to appeal to shared or shareable criteria of justification, would have to appeal, in short, to *transparadigmatic criteria.* In this situation, the moment of appeal is the moment of tergiversation; the paradoxical abandons the previous position and becomes, perhaps, a pluralist. If preference, on the other hand, is a matter of arbitrary selection, then the choice is neither justified nor unjustified, and "anything goes."

If the preceding alternative is varied ever so slightly so that arbitrary preference is restricted to those and only those approaches created and thus sanctioned by one's immediate culture or moment in history (as it sometimes is by Fish and Foucault, for example), then we create new problems for ourselves. For instance, how, under this restriction, do *new* approaches emerge? How are they recognized when they do emerge? What mechanism allows understanding to move across different schemes of interpretation *within* a culture, while at the same time prohibiting or preventing such movement across differences no broader in philosophical magnitude *from* culture to culture? Moving across cultures reduces to moving across schemes, and an ability to do one is an ability to do the other. How could it be otherwise? What is a past culture? What was it possible to believe in it, or what is it possible to believe of it? Under this restriction, the beliefs of a prior culture become, in effect, such and such beliefs *according to my present culture's view of them; your* culturally determined beliefs are what according to *my* culture *I* believe them to be.[10] That arbitrary selection, either unrestricted or culturally restricted, is the selection of preference for many theorists today is certainly true, but it is not, as we shall see, certainly right.

What should be stressed at this point is that whether paradoxicals attempt *to justify their preference or not*, they deviate from their position in marking a difference in schemes of interpretation and implicate themselves in comparison in the very process of noting a contrast. Furthermore, it is clear, though less apparent, that that contrast (or mere difference) would not be spotted unless some references and concepts were *interparadigmatic*. Simply put, the difference between one person's saying "tomahto" and your saying "tomayto" would not be registered as a difference in pronunciation if there were no sameness within the difference. Sameness here, of course, is not primarily a matter of being able to point ostensively to the "same" tomato or to share the "same" tomato "concept," but of having a ground of phonological sameness, let us say, against which to paint phonological difference. What applies at this microlevel of "sound," however, applies as well at the macrolevel of "theory," since at all levels "incommensurabilities" are excrescences on the surface of commensurabilities, are the "not-the-same" in the "sameness." If this were not the case, what the deconstructionist said would be mere noise to the reader-response critic and to all others outside the paradigm.[11]

Paradox Lost: Sameness Within Difference

The temptation is strong to cut, rather than untie, the paradoxicals' Gordian knot by saying we know that the view which insists that every theorist is isolated within the world created by a particular paradigm is untrue because we manage every day to translate, understand, or interpret "correctly" a variety of statements and world views with which we disagree. Why should we wonder about whether what we do in practice is possible in principle? But the temptation must be resisted and the wonder indulged because, though what is *practiced* is surely *possible*, though the pie be pie and our bellies be replete with it, the imagination cannot rest satisfied with a pie whose pieness has been called into question. The issue, unlike a common cold, will not go away, and in a world in which meaning has gone immanent, the paradoxical case has been shown to be more than a little plausible by people not easily fooled.[12] One caution, then: because the issue is so prodigious and has excited the attention of so many, the reader should not expect it to be flattened with one cross-body check of an argument, the likes of which no one has ever seen before; nevertheless, we can perhaps impede or thwart the progress of the prevailing view by adding one unprepossessing argument to another until the aggregated pile becomes an obstacle to be reckoned with.

If we are looking for total intersubjectivity from speaker to speaker, reader to reader, or for perfect consonance between text and translation or interpretation, then we are indeed in trouble (in part because we could never be sure we had it even if we happened to find it); in most circumstances, though, we are willing to settle for a good deal less. The less we settle for, however, is usually quite enough, is at once sufficient and negotiable. The striking thing about our symbolic exchanges is not that they often result in misunderstanding but that they so frequently lead to understanding, further exchanges, and agreement or disagreement. Even when the speaker is not, as some used to say, coming from where we are coming from, the "illusion" is strong that we know where the speaker is coming from. We always assume that the speaker is attempting to make some kind of sense (however preposterous that sense may be from the perspective of our kind of sense), and in determining that sense we are obliged to suppose in the reader a rational desire to give intelligible expression to some knowable beliefs; we assume, in short, that there are conditions of belief and desire that underlie, "justify," and determine the "meaning" of what is expressed.

At bottom, the idea of "incommensurable discourse" (i.e., one that we could not understand the "meaning" of, because of our operative categories and our habitual ways of organizing schemes of interpretation) is an unintelligible notion, since as soon as the discourse we couldn't understand is described it loses its incommensurability. If the defender of incommensurability maintains that he or she has found language to describe but a part (and that not the most essential part) of the "other" discourse, then we are obliged to ask what sort of understanding that person has of what is left to understand, or obliged to say that the difference of which we cannot make out the difference is for all practical purposes a matter of indifference. That there is something unknown that would make all the difference if it were known may be possible, but of the difference such a difference would make who can know? Where there are description, comparison, contrast, agreement, or disagreement, there are commensurabilities; these activities—as well as the activities of criticism, judgment, and the invention and defense of new paradigms—presuppose commensurabilities, presuppose some shared references or concepts. Such behavior is impossible where nothing is or can be shared.

In passing, it is perhaps worth reminding ourselves that the issue here has its basis in the paradoxical view that what *is* is constituted as it is by the terms or language of its constitution, and that there is no *is* to it outside that particular terminological or categorical constitution. Some such conception underlies, for example, the "new critical" *heresy of paraphrase* (which asserts that poetry says its say in a way that no other way of talking can say it, even in a paraphrase or in so many other words) and Jonathan Culler's insistence that the French words *fleuve* and *rivière* have no English equivalents because the French words mark a distinction (flowing toward the sea or not) that is not marked in English by, say, *stream* and *river*.[13]

Once meaning goes immanent, once meaning becomes relative to a system of reference or a scheme of interpretation, nothing seems more reasonable than the paradoxical assumption that a change in "theory," in paradigm, changes not just the meaning of a few terms but also the whole system of meaning relations in which the terms participate. It seems reasonable to suppose that in moving from a Ptolemaic to a Copernican view one not only adopts a new understanding of motion but also reconstrues one's notions of sun, moon, and planets; all is changed, changed utterly in a "gestalt" or paradigm switch, and comparison is ruled out because across the gulf separating one view from another there are no bridges of "sameness." From a certain angle this view seems more than plausible; it seems inescapable. Only our *practices* seem to interrupt the pleasures of its authority. But since the interruption is constant and we cannot have both our practices and our paradoxical view, we must consider the possibility that our practices are established because they are "right," not "right" merely because they are established. In other words, having shown the paradoxical view to be *self-refuting*, though plausible, we must now attempt to make a case for the theoretical plausibility of our common practices.

To a large extent, the case for plausibility has been made, at least implicitly, at various points in this essay. For example, we have earlier shown how despite differences in *mental contents* (e.g., differences in conceptions or fundamental beliefs about grass and differences in perceptual prototypes of grass), two speakers can share the same concept (the same grass "concept"). Conversely, we can have the "same" mental contents but different concepts and the same conception of (beliefs about) grass but different concepts. We can easily imagine a case in which the "same" image, the same "mental content" (the image), is shared by two people who nevertheless have different concepts. For example, both are shown the same blade of grass, but one lives in a grass culture (mows the lawn, and so forth) and the other lives now, as always, in a grassless world (a desert, say). We can now suppose that the person who is not a member of grass culture is told everything (more or less) that is currently known about grass; but even so equipped (with more knowledge of grass than the average mower of lawns), he or she would still be unable to share the grass concept with the other, because of the inability to *use* "grass" to *refer* to what he or she has no *experience* of but only *beliefs about*.[14] And cognitive sameness has elsewhere in our analysis been seen to be independent of shared "images" or beliefs; to carry on with a "grass" or "marriage" conversation, it is not necessary that two speakers bring the same *images* to mind or have the same beliefs about the "topic" under discussion; it is necessary only that they have sufficient overlap in the range of their conceptual knowledge to meet the demands of their present purposes. To know whether the speakers are sharing concepts as they speak, we depend on such clues as their ability to sustain the conversation without becoming "lost" or confused, as their continued use of "grass" talk, and so on.

Further, we have seen how two radically different systems—one a hand-cranked cog and wheel computer and the other an electronic computer—can run the same "program," how functional isomorphism is realized across massive differences in material elements, the "sameness" here being comparable to that which occurs when two radically different symbol systems realize the same "meaning" (a map and a graph tell the "same" demographic story). Of course, when we generalize to a "more interesting" class of cases, we acquire the power to discover sameness within an enormous variety of particular instances, to recognize, for example, not only the same geometric saliencies in different materials and situations, but also the same emotional or psychological saliencies in many different human situations. In fact, the indignation evoked by this particular instance of undeserved good fortune serves as an explanatory key to behavior in an altogether "different" instance of such fortune.

More broadly, it is clear that we sharply distinguish between *general* terms or concepts and *particular* applications, *particular* statements or propositions. Moreover, our general terms or concepts exert minimal control over particular use. For example, the directional concepts "up" and "down" can be used to describe an indefinite number of things in a variety of conceptual schemes, and the person who thinks that something is up has no trouble "understanding" the person who thinks it is down. (The former does not believe what is being asserted but has no trouble understanding it; to believe that the sun goes around the earth does not prohibit one from understanding what someone "means" by saying the earth goes around the sun.) An extraordinary number of our general terms and concepts, then, preserve their "meaning" across scheme or theory differences.

Further, it is clear that we distinguish between *language as a body of terms and rules* (as what for convenience we can call a vocabulary and grammar) and *language as a body of assertions*, and that we can make many theories in the same *language* (e.g., English); the same language allows an infinite number of propositions, just as the same chess pieces and the same rules of chess, as Michael Polanyi observes,[15] make possible a great variety of game strategies, all of which are intelligible to those who know the "rules." Indeed, there is no playing outside the rules. Among other things, we here suggest that it is impossible to change everything at once, if only because new meanings and references are not expressible outside a preexisting system of expression; more simply, even the most revolutionary new theory must rely on the stable, transparadigmatic functioning of many linguistic elements, if it hopes to get expressed at all. "Sings" cannot do the work of "dances," for example, and conjunctions (*and, but, for, yet*), prepositions, and argumentative markers ("on the other hand," "nevertheless," "furthermore," "in addition," "not only . . . but also," and so on) must do their *accustomed* work in all systems of reference, as we have noted earlier.

Moreover, in getting from one proposition to another, we are forced to rely on a quite limited number of *systems of inference*; we proceed deductively, inductively, analogically, or by means of some combination of the three modes (except, of course, when we move assertively from fiat to fiat and let the devil of systematic relation take the hindmost), creating in the process the *standards* of sense-making by which our theories are self-judged (not some one particular theory, but our many and various theories).

As it is with our vocabulary, grammar, systems of inference, and so on, so it is with our *categories*. A multiplicity of hypotheses can be based on the same categories; the "world" is not observable apart from categories, but the categories themselves make no truth-claims but are, rather, capable of entering into many widely divergent, even contradictory hypotheses, of being used in the service of many truth-claims, many worlds. Categorization by *state*, for example, imposes no clear limits on the number or kinds of distribution that can be made according to state (we can focus within the scheme of state categorization on beaches, parks, cattle, even-toed ungulates, taverns, and so on), and having categories for beaches, parks, cattle, etc., as well as for states, does not determine how many or what kinds of each we will have from state to state. Just as different states will have different proportions of the several categories (the same categories in different proportions), so *different hypotheses can be built from the same categories*, one subordinating action and character to theme, for example, and another subordinating theme to action and character. For example, we can have many views on or theories about English departments, *Hamlet*, the Glorious Revolution, imagery, or syntax.

Also, if we can have *different hypotheses* and the *same categories*, we can also have the *same hypothesis* and *different categories*, as our demographic map and population chart clearly illustrate. That is, we have the same hypothesis, theory, or proposition about *population* but different *means*—categories—of representation. Sameness is an epistemic, interest-relative thing, but sameness is sameness for all that. We can have different works but the same genre; the same works (as sorted by genre) but different periods of composition; different members but the same English department, and the same members (of the department) but different club affiliations (one member belongs to the National Rifle Association, another to Ducks Unlimited, and still another, an oddball, to the Modern Language Association); the *same words but a different meaning* (Oh, you mean his goose—bird— is really cooked—ready to eat) and the *same meaning but different words* (in some contexts of *use* and *understanding* it doesn't matter whether "his goose is cooked" or "he's had it," and the candidate is out of a job whether the committee *denied him tenure* or he was *denied tenure by* the committee; the passive voice does nothing to change or mitigate his dilemma), and so on and on.

Chapter 7
Paradox Undone: Meaning, Reference, and Cognitive Sameness

Preserving References and Meanings Across Theories

Although throughout this essay we have tended to use "meaning" and "reference" rather casually, treating them at times as synonymous terms, there are very good reasons, as most philosophers know and as most critics should know, for keeping them distinct. Indeed, far too many trees have been sacrificed so the New Critics and many following in their wake could *prove* that different expressions *do not* convey the same "meaning," that paraphrase is "heresy," that every change of words (even, for example, the change from active to passive voice) necessarily involves a change in "meaning," and so on.[1] The sacrifice was unnecessary because the case against sameness of "meaning" could have been granted at the outset of debate, since, as we have seen, the *real* issue concerns not exact or perfect sameness of "meaning," a very scarce commodity, but cognitive "sameness," the sharing of concepts and references. Also, it is absolutely essential to recognize that concepts are not words (though their expression depends upon the use of some symbols, public or private), images, or mental contents (in that *the sharing of concepts does not depend on having some particular words, images, or mental contents in common*). We are concerned with cognitive sameness, not with what, speaking loosely, we might call "material" identity. And, it is important to recognize that where there is difference in "meaning" there can be and often is sameness of "reference," a matter of no small moment to those of us who are interested in comparison and judgment.

Examples of such sameness are easy to find or make, but I will here have recourse to two which use has made conventional. As Bertrand Russell first pointed out, "Sir Walter Scott" and "the author of *Wa-*

verley" differ in "meaning," but not in "reference" or denotation. "Scott" does not "mean" the same thing as "author of *Waverley*," yet what is denoted by one is denoted by the other. Similarly, to take the example first used, I think, by Gottlob Frege (an example in which synonymy plays no part whatsoever), "Evening Star" and "Morning Star" refer to the same "object," but they do not carry the same "meaning." Thus, difference in "meaning" does not necessarily entail difference in "reference," and since this is so, it follows, as night the day or anguish love, that two critics can share references while inscribing (or, as some are fond of saying, being inscribed by) different meanings. The battle waged over the issue of whether *change of words* makes for *change of meaning* can be decided in favor of the "meaning" changers, but when "reference" takes the field the forces of difference are routed and "sameness" wins the war. In my view, however, too much time has been uselessly spent by modern critics on the issue of "meaning," on trying to "prove" that word change necessarily entails meaning change, especially since cognitive sameness is, as I have shown, not dependent on the "meaning" identity of words, phrases, or statements—it is dependent on *use*.

Because in many cases reference is preserved across changes in meaning, we can say with impunity that "theories [or interpretations] do not need to enjoy common 'meanings' to be comparable: it is enough (assuming common referential semantics) that there be sufficiently many terms with the same reference . . . even radically different theories can be compared within the framework of deductive logic and referential semantics."[2] The point here, of course, is not that "reference" points to the "thing itself," whereas "meaning" is hopelessly language-bound, but that some "references," mind-dependent as they are, remain the same across paradigm shifts, while others are singularly bound to a particular scheme of interpretation or expression (are what the scheme stipulates them to be).

We are here dealing with the possibility of sameness within difference and exploring instances in which reference is maintained despite differences in "meaning." The "Evening Star"/"Morning Star" example is particularly interesting because it highlights what Hilary Putnam has referred to as a linguistic division of labor. That is, some of our terms (certainly not all of them, not even the majority of them) have their references fixed (though not permanently) by experts. For example, it is a "discovery" of astronomy, not linguistics, that the "two" stars are one star, and so long as the reference of the terms is fixed by *astronomy*, what can be said of one star can be said of the other star. Cat, dog, cauliflower, and many other terms have their references fixed by experts (fixed, that is, by consensus and relative

to a scheme of interpretation). Having some "things" fixed in reference is, we agree, useful, valuable, or necessary *to us*; we are *interested*
in having such references and are *willing* to treat some people as experts and some categories (for example, chemical or genetic) as au-
thoritative.

The term most frequently used for purposes of exemplification by
Putnam is "gold," which refers to a substance defined chemically (or
atomically) by experts. To use the term "correctly" we are not required, of course, to be able to "define" it expertly (in most instances
of use we are supremely indifferent to the "reference" of gold). What
we "mean" by "gold" is quite different from what "gold" (chemically)
refers to. For example, we may be interested in making a moral
point—"All that glitters is not gold"—and know only that gold is a
precious metal. But, however used, the term is transportable from
situation to situation in large part because its various "meanings" are
supported by a "fixed" reference.

Moreover, and more important, because "gold" is one of the terms
which is understood to admit of fixity of reference, we can say that it
keeps its reference across very large theory or scheme changes. Thus,
although five hundred years ago some objects passed for "pure gold"
which were not by our standards "pure gold" (our tests and standards
for gold are much more sophisticated than those of the fifteenth century), we are justified in claiming that our ancestors were "really" referring to gold. With gold, for example, we refer, then as now, to
whatever gold *turns out to be*; if later tests determine that some of what
I now call gold is not gold, I will still have referred to gold—and not
to something else—when I mistakenly called something else gold.
Gold, and much else, of course, has *durability* but no *essence*.[3] Of
course, all our definitions are made rather than found, are determined by schemes of interpretation, but when we are dealing with
terms that are acknowledged (by us) to admit of definition we can and
do invoke the aid of what is called the principle of charity or the
benefit of the doubt in our interpretive practice to establish referential sameness even while recognizing material or "meaning" differences.

The issue dealt with here is generally more relevant to the interpretation of the terms of "scientific" theories than to the interpretation of the terms of theories of literary criticism or the interpretation
of the terms of literary texts (since, in general, literary critics rather
assume than concern themselves with the references of terms consen-
sually fixed according to a "scientific" scheme of interpretation). At a
time when critics have called everything into question, however, it is
important to recognize that, in spite of their various differences, crit-

ics depend on and regularly assume a considerable amount of referential sameness from theory to theory and text to text and heavily
rely on the principle of charity in their dealings with one another.
That is, they refer *and* understand themselves to be referring to
many of the same "things" and do not confound trees with firecrack-
ers or mistake *Waverley* for *Ivanhoe*, or *Rasselas* for *The Vanity of Human Wishes.*

At this point it is useful to remind ourselves that we are now talking
about a special class of terms, and if they have special privileges, they
have them by our consent, not because they have some special relation to what "is" or to the "real" facts of the matter. As always, objects
and references—or objects of reference—are not independent of or
prior to discourse. They emerge out of discourse, and these are no
less epistemic or "intentional" than other objects of reference by virtue of being derived from a "scientific" scheme of interpretation, of
being fixed in reference by experts. The fact is, however, that we often consent to preserve the references of these terms in a variety of
discourses, thereby simplifying the task of making a host of new reference *relations* in several different theories.[4]

The public use of language for a variety of purposes presupposes
some sharing of references among the users. To understand how in
"ordinary" circumstances sameness of reference can be (indeed, must
be) maintained across wide differences in "meaning," we can consider
an "extreme" case in which *words and references remain the same while
meanings differ.* Suppose one person enjoins another to "hide the
booze" on the following two separate occasions: (1) when the Reverend Billy Bob Shifflet is seen approaching the house; and (2) when
Uncle Billy, the family toper, is seen staggering up the walkway. The
theory—that is, the understanding, the assumptions, background
knowledge, or set of operating concepts—which determines the
meaning of the expression on one occasion is radically different from
the theory determining its meaning on the other occasion, yet across
the divide of theory "booze" preserves its reference.

Suppose now that on either occasion the following exchange takes
place: "Hide the *booze!*" "Where should I conceal the *hootch?*" "I don't
care; just get the *liquor* out of the living room." "O.K. I'll put the *al-
coholic potables* in the linen closet." On this occasion, one might be justified in claiming that the several terms have the same reference and
the same "meaning," especially since a change in the "meaning situation" (a change from a clergyman to an Uncle Billy theory of
meaning determination) would not change the reference or the
synonymy-relations of the terms; that is, the "meaning" of the terms
would be different in the two *situations* (though not the reference),

but the *synonymy relations* among (i.e., the *meaning* of) the terms would be the same in each of the meaning situations. *Within* each of the situations a switch in terms does not require a readjustment of "meanings."

Of course, neither references nor synonymy relations among terms are fixed absolutely for all time or have their "existence" apart from systems of reference or meaning. Nevertheless, *unless some references and meanings were capable of remaining the same (or approximately the same) in different theories, schemes, or discourses, we would never be able to notice discourse differences, create new discourses, or hear anything but noise outside our discourse.* Our task is not to determine which terms can and cannot change reference or which synonymy relations are and are not stable, inasmuch as all terms and all synonymy relations are subject to change from discourse to discourse (there are no permanently privileged references or meanings). Rather, we are bound to employ the principle of charity or the benefit of the doubt whenever possible, guided by the assumption that new meanings and references, like new discourses, emerge from old and that some must remain the same if the new are to emerge. Not all references and synonymy relations can change at once. If they did, no one could understand what was said or written, not even the originator of the statements, for even a totally private language must be intelligible to its maker, which it would not be if there were no means of passing from one language to another or if (assuming there is no other language) there were no "durable" references or meaning relations from one extended statement to the next. As they say at the cryptography school, "We've never met a code *that is a code* that couldn't be broken."

Reference, Meaning, and Synonymy Relations

At this point, having shown that terms can retain their references and meanings across differences in theories or schemes, I should perhaps say something further about meaning and reference, especially since I have rather casually distinguished between the two and, without preparation or explanation, made meaning a function of synonymy relations. Of the two terms, "meaning" is the sloppier, "reference" the more precise, but it is important to remember that in a world in which meaning and reference have gone immanent, both are epistemic and intentional notions, that is, both "mind-dependent."

Briefly, the distinction has our interest largely because it is central to New Criticism (and, not so indirectly or incidentally, to all the postmodern, poststructuralist, linguocentric theory devolving from it), which, reflecting a certain array of philosophical assumptions, insists on separating intension from extension, poetry talk from "science" talk (i.e., positivist talk), meaning from reference, connotation from denotation, and so on. "Science" (positivism), they maintain, is interested in definitions, in fixing references, in testing hypotheses, in "rules" and "laws," in "truth"—it is not interested in metaphysics or "fiction" (poetry), not interested in what is "scientifically" meaningless—whereas "criticism" is interested in "intension," in unique, nonparaphrasable "meanings," in what is connoted, not denoted, in the "tenor," not the "vehicle." The vehicle is a matter of reference; the tenor, of meaning. If "steed" and "horse" can be understood to share a reference, they cannot be understood to share a meaning.

"Meaning" is the thing that counts and that cannot be expressed in "scientific" terms or, for that matter, in any terms other than those used. Different terms make for different meanings. Hence, in this criticism the search for key terms, phrases, images, metaphors, and clusters of the same is a central activity. The critic is on the lookout for clues epitomizing recurrent "meaning," for verbal clues to peculiar "themes," which usually, as we have seen, hold in dynamic tension opposing or countervailing forces or ideas. This "tension" occurs because words, images, and so on are not reducible to their references or denotations but are capable of upholding simultaneously two or more different and usually contradictory "meanings." Despite the emphasis on unique "meanings" and on the nonparaphrasable nature of poetry, this criticism in practice, in its efforts to identify meaning "clusters" and recurrences of meaning in the text, is inevitably led to the notation of synonymy classes and groupings and to the articulation in *discursive language* of special "poetic" meanings, led, that is, to paraphrase, to *explication de texte*, to finding ways of expressing the "same" meaning in different terms. In short, to give readers access to the unique meanings of poetic texts, this criticism is obliged to find ways of explaining and expressing in discursive terms what could only carry meaning in "poetic" terms. Their awareness of this bind, this original sin, is felicitously captured in Cleanth Brooks's fine theological phrase, "the heresy of paraphrase." Paraphrase, the source of pride and shame, is both unacceptable and necessary to this criticism (as is logocentrism to deconstruction). The heretical practices of this criticism are certainly pardonable (they are definitely not hanging offenses); indeed, because they are inevitable, they are excused or pardoned (by us) in their commission.

The reader should note that I am not here justifying either these practices or this form of criticism; rather, I am suggesting that if these critics violate their own principles, they do so because, poor devils, they cannot help themselves, cannot do otherwise. If you ask a student or a critic ("new," "old," or "newfangled") what a literary work—a short poem, say—means, you will not be satisfied with a mere repetition of the words of the work. You will expect—and be satisfied with nothing less than—a response in different words, a response that approximates the "sense" of the work, that in so many different words can explain what the words of the poem refer to and what they connote or suggest.

Synonymy Relations

In general, we have few squabbles about textual references or about, say, the vehicles of the poetic metaphors. The poet whose love is a red, red *rose* refers to—or chooses as his poetic vehicle—what you and I refer to when we talk of *roses*. We argue—or some argue—about "meanings," about "sense" or the connotative or emotional "values" of words, phrases, and so on. And these arguments are inevitably about the synonymy relations of terms and expressions. "Steed" may be just the "right" word (the word that no other single word could legitimately take the place of) for the boy's rocking horse, because, let us say, it suggests, as no other word would, the special "romantic," "heroic" quality of the boy's flights of imagination when he is on it. Let us say it *suggests* all this and more, but of all this and of all the more it may suggest we can have only so much knowledge as can be expressed in so many words (or other symbols), in so many synonymies. Simply, to say what this or that *means*, we cannot merely *repeat* the words or terms; we must supply substitutes, replacements, supplements. Talk about "meaning" is thus talk about synonymy classes and synonymy relations among terms.

Further, all such *synonymies* will be consistent with, tolerated by, available to, or capable of association with *whatever is referred to*, will be, that is, in one or more of these relations to reference under some circumstances, however odd the association, say, may be under "normal" circumstances. (Yes, my love is a red, red rose according to some lines of association that can be established between the flower and a special "she" in some specified or "understood" circumstances.) Moreover, "steed" is just "right" for the speaker or writer because the term is understood as having special synonymy relations with other terms or roundabout expressions or circumlocutions. The word would not be "right" for that particular, speaker/writer unless it conveyed something that was also conveyable in so many other words. The "meaning" is clearly not in (or usually not in) the physical "look"—the physical sound or shape—of the word itself.

Of course, we often choose words not because their "meanings" are just right for the context, but because their "meanings" are more rather than less appropriate, proper, or fitting. We often substitute one word for another not because we find a "better" one or because the first is less and the second more "appropriate," but *because* we used the same word earlier in the sentence or used it one or two sentences earlier (sometimes, of course, when our ready-to-mind "equivalents" are exhausted, we go to the thesaurus, that magazine of synonymy armaments, for an "equally appropriate" word or phrase), or *because* the first word selected makes an unfortunate rhyme with a neighboring word, or because it is too "academic" or "pompous," or for some other reason. Unless such substituted words could in some instances or under some circumstances stand in a synonymy relation to the rejected word, they would be totally inappropriate. A notion of meaning apart from synonymy relations is meaningless. The strange, though not entirely mysterious, fact is that I cannot know whether you have understood my meaning until you somehow say my say in a different saying or respond to my saying so with words (or actions) different from those I used but somehow compatible, in their associations or values, with what I "meant."

Partially buried in the immediately preceding discussion of the dependence of "meaning" on synonymy classes is the further fact that just as reference can remain the same across theory differences, so the same *meaning* can be found in different statements, theories, and, yes, poems. If we can have *different meanings and the same reference* (as in Morning Star and Evening Star), we can also have *the same meaning and different references*. For example, the synonymy relations of "steed" can remain the same even though the reference switches from Tom's rocking horse to Joe's, from Bob's rocking horse to Bill's pony. (And, what is true in these instances is also indubitably true of all indexicals, such as *now, here, I, you,* etc. When I say *I*, I do not refer to the person to whom you refer when you say *I*, as also with *now, here, then,* and so forth.)

Of course, from theory to theory or poem to poem, some synonymy relations can remain the same while others change dramatically (as can some references). Not only can we imagine—indeed, find— two "Petrarchan" love poets who refer to the same sun but to different eyes and different mistresses (when both proclaim, "My mistress's eyes are like the sun"), but we can easily imagine two poets—one "Petrarchan" and the other "anti-Petrarchan"—who refer to the "same" sun and share terms having the same synonymy relations (one "means" by "goddess" and "steed," for example, what the other "means" by them), but who radically alter the synonymy relations of *other* "identical" terms with "identical" *references* (in one poem the eyes are like the sun in their luster, brilliance, and so on, whereas in the other poem they are not like the sun at all because "sun" means sight-destroying intensity of light, scorching heat, and so on). And, of course, in different stages of the relationship the poet's love can be a red, red rose. In an early stage, she is a rose in her "youth," "beauty," "delicacy," "robust good health," ad nauseam, whereas, later on, in a bitter stage, she is a rose in her "thorniness," "prickliness," "short-lived attractiveness," ad infinitum.

As noted above, most of our disputes—critical as well as personal, intellectual as well as ordinary—are about "meanings," not about "references." References not fixed by experts are fixed by community "understanding" or by stipulation (i.e., by local, ad hoc experts; I call my dog "Buster" or "Elliot," and Buster or Elliot is then my dog in one of my systems of reference). What is clear, however, is that our domestic squabbles, like our critical disputes, could not be activated, continued, or resolved, unless across the divide of discourses there were some bridges of sameness in our references and meanings, unless we could come to know what it means to believe something other than what we in our personal and private capacities happen at the moment to believe (or, more radically, come to know that we believe today what we believed yesterday, more or less).

Preserving Meanings and References in Different Solutions

In all seriousness, if we took what the paradoxicals had to say seriously—if, that is, we recognized and understood only those things and meanings (as precisely those things and meanings) that were constituted as such by our interpretive community or our belief network, as Stanley Fish, Hans-Georg Gadamer, and others sometimes insist that we do—we simply would not know how to take it (how to take their saying, that is). There would be nothing in it, *for us* for the taking. If their claims were true, we could not know them to be so, could not even know them to be claims. Oddly, and perhaps even paradoxically, the paradoxicals cause us trouble because we take what they say both seriously and unseriously. Despite their claims, we claim to understand their claims, and we treat their claims seriously by showing how our *practices* take the seriousness out of them, assuming all along, for the sake of argument, that when the claimants yank the hardest they are not really pulling our legs (i.e., we assume *they believe* what they say).

We can perhaps best illustrate how meaning or reference can be preserved across theory changes by consulting the dictionary (any native-language dictionary). The dictionary is a highly useful tool containing a helpfully odd mixture of references and meanings, of

definitions and synonymy classes; it works—often quite successfully—
as both a reference-fixer and a thesaurus. But it would be a useless,
unnecessary, even an impossible book if its meanings and references
could not be *used* in the construction of widely divergent and disparate theories, statements, poems, and so on, if, indeed, its meanings
and references had not been derived from the *use of words* in marvel-
ously different discourses.

When we look up a word that we have encountered in a discourse,
we want perhaps both a reference and synonymies, but we frequently
settle for synonymies (because the reference does not really apply;
our term is used, say, "metaphorically" or "derivatively" in the context we are interested in). The dictionary can be useful as a "meaning-
settler," however, only to the extent that the term in question can
participate in synonymy relations; and those relations are "synonymous" only because it is possible to convey the "same" meaning in
different terms (i.e., *there would be no* "meanings"—no knowable
meanings—*if there were no synonymy classes, and no synonymy classes if*
"meaning" *were entirely a construction of peculiar beliefs or discourses*). This
is not to say, of course, that dictionaries determine the meanings and
references of terms *in use*, of the terms of particular statements and
discourses, but only to remind the radical paradoxicals among us that
dictionaries could neither be made nor used if some references and
meanings were not "capable" of remaining the same across statement
differences, theory differences, poem differences, and so on, and
that discourses (and poems) would not be intelligible constructs (to
others) if some meanings and references did not remain the same (or
approximately the same) from one context to the next.

In appealing to the dictionary to clarify an issue, I may inadvertently have thrown myself into what some might call confusion and
others contradiction. Despite my iterated disavowals, some readers
might think that I am here suggesting what I have elsewhere denied,
namely, that meaning and reference antedate rather than arise out
of discourse, that word or phrase "meaning" is prior to that to which
I have earlier given priority, namely, sentence, utterance, or discourse meaning. Talk of shared references and synonymy classes
seems, at the very least, to imply a reversal of the priorities argued
for earlier: first we have meanings and references and then we make
sentences and discourses out of them, or first we understand meanings and references and then we put together or understand sentences. In my view, however, there is no confusion, contradiction, or
reversal of priorities involved in this switch from "sentence meaning"
to the "meanings" and "references" of *terms* and *phrases*.

As always, specific meanings and references are context-sensitive and interest-relative, are retrospective constructions, are determined as such and such by specific assertibility conditions, that is, certain beliefs and circumstances, as sized up in a certain way, and certain aims, wishes, and so on. To understand a particular statement or discourse, we must have access to something more than a translation manual—a vocabulary and grammar, for example, or a dictionary of "definitions" and "synonymy classes." We must be able to choose from among the *available* possibilities those that would be warranted in a certain "state of mind" operating within a particular construction of a certain set of circumstances. Nevertheless, in the absence of a "translation manual"—what in our native language we might call a vocabulary and grammar (a catalogue of terms and beliefs and the rules of their substitution and combination)—we would be unable to give expression to any particular beliefs whatsoever or to make new "meanings" or "references," which, of course, must come out of old ones or at least out of the mechanisms by which old ones have been made.

Additionally, the burden throughout this section has been to show that the *availability* of "references" and "synonymy classes" is what makes possible the *articulation and understanding* of different, even contradictory theories or sentence meanings. Sentence—or discourse—meaning (particular, contextual meaning) is no more determined by the meanings and references available for use than the strategy of a chess game is determined by the moves available to each of the chess pieces. Such particular meaning is, however, impossible without an available stock of meanings and references (and a system of relational, substitutional, combinatorial moves). If the potential (meaning) is prior to the actual (meaning), the actual has priority of concern when our task is the determination of meaning, current usage. All we are saying here is that if across theory change or change of sentence meaning some *terms* did not remain the same with regard to "meaning" and "reference," we would be unable to understand, for example, the negate of our own assertions,[5] to learn that the John we thought was married is, in fact, still single, that is, *not* married.

Also, if the attribution of terminological sameness of reference or meaning depends chiefly on the principle of charity—as it does—the principle obviously cannot be abandoned without giving up on "sense" altogether. Finally, it should be clear that limitations on the "meanings" and "references" of terms or phrases, be they ever so severe, can impose no discernible limits on the kinds of sentence meanings or theories we may take it into our heads to express.

Sharing "meanings" is more difficult than sharing "references" because "meanings" depend upon synonymies, upon our agreeing to find for present purposes a ground of "approximate sameness" in items manifestly different, whereas reference is fixed by experts, by stipulation (we are the experts of our own stipulations), or by communities; that is, reference is widely, communally understood. Above we noted that many of our common terms, such as "gold" and "water," have their references fixed (i.e., stipulated) by "scientific" experts, but, of course, every field has its experts and consequently its reference fixers. Our fondness for creators, inventors, and innovators is such that we frequently refer to what we owe to them by naming things by their names. For example, in diving, dancing, gymnastics, and figure skating (as well as in medicine, metallurgy, tiremaking, and so on), we know that the "something" before us is nothing other than, say, a Korbut, a Lougainis, or a Crapper. Once "created" and identified, the movement (or instrument, process, or whatever) is fixed in reference, and all those who know what they are talking about will hereafter always know what someone is talking about when that someone "refers to" a korbut or lougainis or whatever. Specifically, this movement and only this movment is a "korbut"; or a "korbut" is this movement and only this movement, and that's that.

Community Reference: The Value of Stereotypes

Before moving to what we might call contextually stipulated reference or locally stipulated reference, I would like to say a word or two about what is perhaps the "messiest" or most complicated kind of reference, namely, what I have identified above as "understood" reference (community shared/generated reference). We have few debates about reference in literary criticism because we generally "understand" what texts are referring to when they refer to "things" (or "actions," "events," "processes," and so on). "Understood" reference, then, is ordinary, everyday, commonplace, transparent, garden-variety reference, the kind of reference we ordinarily and immediately assume, unless we are forced to assume otherwise. It is, thus, what in computer talk we might call "default" reference. "Tree" refers to tree, "cat" to cat, "Denmark" to Denmark, "Polonius" to Polonius, "double play" to double play and so on. When I say, "Before we go to the game, we'll have to drive by my house, so that I can pick up a sweater," the friend to whom I speak is not likely to be baffled or confused by my references, though he might be a little stunned if I subsequently came out of the house not with a knitted garment but with my brother, who, like all my siblings, has a knack for perspiring profusely.

The difference between common, ordinary, "understood" reference and fixed or stipulated reference can be illustrated with the term "water." What we ordinarily call or refer to as "water" may not be "water," as it is defined or fixed in reference by those assigned by common consent to know what "water" is, chemists, say (strictly or referentially speaking, it is not water at all), but it is "water" enough for us if it belongs to the category system "liquid" (category system is sometimes called "semantic marker" by Putnam) and has on this particular occasion of use some properties commonly allied to "water"— it is clear, more or less odorless, drinkable, suitable for swimming in, capable of extinguishing fires, or whatever. This "water," though specific in its reference, does not specifically refer to what is definitively "water."

Common reference is error-prone, though, of course, not always erroneous (sometimes what is commonly referred to as "water" is "water"), whereas stipulated or fixed reference is (of analytic necessity) error-free (from period to period, or until newly defined by subsequent experts). Common reference is a product of the various kinds of community-shared interests a community has taken in the "stuff" attracting its attention, and such references remain stable over long periods of time because, despite massive differences in the "actual stuff" dealt with and called "water" ("actual" as defined by one preferred, community-accepted scheme of reference), the community's referential interests are satisfied if the "stuff" remains, say, drinkable or suitable for swimming in, or whatever. Of course, liquid one can swim in need not be drinkable to be "water"; it is enough that the stuff called "water" have some property or properties that the community has been interested in attaching to it and that that property—or those properties—be "appropriate" or "right" under the present circumstances of interest).

For most purposes, we are not interested in knowing precisely what the "actual stuff" the "water" is that we are swimming in or drinking, but such referential ignorance or indifference rather enhances than impedes our capacity to share "references" with fellow members of our community,[6] to share references even with those in our community who say, it seems to us, the most outrageous, the damnedest, the most paradoxical things. If referring to "things" were contingent upon our knowing the reference (as fixed by experts) of the "things" referred to, we would never be able to say what liquid was in our "water glasses" as we traveled from city to city or country to country, without the help of a municipal or state translation manual. In this municipality there's more of this than that mineral in the water, whereas there's more of that than this mineral in the water of that municipality.

With common or ordinary reference, then, we are dealing with what Putnam has called "stereotypes," and the "stereotype" of any term is simply a composite of the common "knowledge" a community has about the things it denominates. As Steven E. Boër notes, "the community's Stereotype for a term T comprises the community's 'stock answer' to the question [What is (a) T?], the answer that any minimally competent speaker of the language is expected to be able to produce." From the point of view of "actual" (i.e., fixed) reference, stereotypes "may be very superficial and/or inaccurate; for they merely embody what, relative to community-wide interests, is found 'striking' about the (possibly atypical) objects of which the community has had experience. Stereotypes are in no way analytically tied to terms."[7] Hence, whatever "grass" may be (I'm sure, however, that I don't know what it "actually" is, biochemically speaking), "grass" in ordinary reference, in my very broad community, is marked categorically as a plant and understood stereotypically as having such and such features or properties (here the reader should include a long list of familiar features—it grows, can be mowed, is usually green, and so forth).

Thus, by an unfamiliar route we arrive on familiar gound. Once again we find cognitive or conceptual sameness where there may be between two speakers radical differences in fundamental beliefs about and in perceptual prototypes of "grass" (in "mental images" of grass). In ordinary, "understood," community-marked reference, two speakers can share "grass" talk—despite the fact that one speaker knows all about "photosynthesis" and knows what grass "is," whereas the other does not, or the fact that one can distinguish among a hundred varieties of grass, whereas the other cannot—and can "refer" to the same "grass," without sharing the same images (or mental contents) or the same knowledge or beliefs, though they must obviously have some "concepts" in common (such concepts as the referential interests of the community make available). Sharing terms of common reference entails the sharing of certain concepts.

Moreover, it should be clear that differences about "meaning" *depend upon* shared references and concepts, that disagreement presupposes a ground of common understanding about many "things," a ground of common belief about many "things."[8] Indeed, disagreement is impossible in the absence of shared references or concepts. The sea water that is registered as "cold" by the vacationer from South Carolina may be registered as "warm" by the Maine native, but the native, while disagreeing with his guest, has no trouble understanding what his Southern friend "means" when he refers to the "cold" *sea water*.

From such simple cases we learn not only that "translation" (i.e., understanding) across theory change is possible, but also that interpretation requires more than a translation manual—a list of definitions and synonymy classes. It requires also a grasp of what for lack of better terms we can call aims, motives, purposes, or desires, etc., as occasioned by or functional within a certain set of background conditions or circumstances; it requires, in short, sensibility and imagination working in concert with the assumption that the string of words encountered is not an accidental string but one embodying some kind of sense that can be expressed by terms, the actual and potential powers and values of some of which are known to be available to them.

Reference Without Meaning

Before moving to a brief consideration of directly specified, locally stipulated "reference"—what might be called "nonce reference"—we should note that we regularly acquire an understanding of the *references* of terms prior to an understanding of their sense or meaning (their synonymy relations for us in this or that context).[9] For example, the "chair" we first understood to be "chair" was marked for us as such independently of any understanding of an acceptable synonym for "chair" (independently, indeed, of any system of relations, except that of "sound") or any rich conceptual understanding of "chair" or "chairness." Indeed, as Israel Scheffler asserts, if the child were never

to understand any word before grasping some synonymous defining expression, he could never begin to understand any word at all. For each such defining expression would itself require a further synonymous expression in order to be understood, and, barring unilluminating circularity and infinite regress in the chain of synonymies, the initial expression would, in every such chain, remain beyond his reach; the process could, in short, never get started.[10]

If a grasp of the "meaning" of the term involves in this case an infinite regress of synonymy expressions, a grasp of "reference" does not. The chair is immediately "chair" and is "defined" ostensively as such on this first occasion, perhaps by the pointing of a finger; the child acquires a reference in the process of learning a practice.

Stable Meanings, Different References

Let us therefore move from a case involving *reference without meaning* to one involving *the persistence of relatively stable meaning across differences in references*. Suppose a person totally unfamiliar with backed, cushioned, or padded furniture (one acquainted only with backless stools and benches) is asked to help a thoroughly modern friend move into an up-to-date, thoroughly Western apartment. Entering a room in which there is only one object that cannot be conveniently and efficiently moved by one person, he is asked to help move the "davenport" to a location in front of the fireplace. He immediately (or almost immediately) understands the reference and proceeds to lend his assistance. A moment later, the husband enters and says that the "chesterfield" would look better beside the fireplace. Following hard upon one another, the daughter and son enter and say, respectively, "I thought we were going to get rid of that old couch," and "The sofa should be placed against the long wall."

The furniture expert knows that davenport, chesterfield, couch, sofa, and divan (for that matter) refer to five different *kinds* of objects, and, if consulted, he could tell this family that the object in the room is nothing other than a davenport.[11] The quick-witted and helpful friend, however, understands almost immediately that the four terms form a synonymy class in this family and that each member *means* to *refer* to the same thing, even though, as it turns out, only the wife actually refers to the "thing" or refers to the "actual thing" (the *thing* experts refer to) in the living room (front room, parlor). Here, then, is common reference and stable meaning, despite meaning and reference differences. What one means by couch another means by sofa, and all but one refer to the "wrong" thing as they variously express opinions about what to do with the one "thing" that all insist on moving and that the friend is willing to help them do something with. Naturally, without more instruction, this helpful friend would not be much help in the warehouse of the furniture expert; but fortunately, like the rest of us, he is a fast learner. And, of course, the "meanings" and "references" shared by this family can be put to work in the service of a limitless number of contexts and theories.

All references are stipulated—by experts, "communities," individuals—and all stipulations are determined by interests (are interest-relative), are made, not found, and, at the very least, satisfy an interest in calling a spade a "spade." (If we had other interests we simply would not call it a "spade." What would be the point?) At any rate, no references or terms are either required or absolutely right.[12] Once made, they can be *used* in all sorts of ways in all sorts of contexts and subserve a rich variety of special interests while maintaining a shareable, intersubjective interest of their own, as we have seen. As far as *reference* is concerned, we are all experts of our own stipulations, even though our larger or our large-scale interests (our essays and theories, say) depend for their intelligibility on our using many terms and phrases whose references are widely understood. Of course, our local, personal expertise would be socially useless if most of what we said were not already "settled" or ready for one or another known kind of settling or fixing.

Nonce Reference

We can perhaps illuminate our concern here with an example of locally specified "nonce" reference, of extemporaneous spade-calling. Suppose at the outbreak of civil war I decide to call the supporters of the queen the Red Rose Party and the rebels the White Rose Party. Suppose, now, that the designations stick (White Roser refers to a rebel; Red Roser to a loyalist) and that to signify allegiance to one's party each partisan, in a fit of fanatical exuberance, has either a red or a white rose tattooed on his left forearm. In the course of a protracted war, it so happens that, one by one or by twos and threes, those who support and those who rebel against the queen undergo conversion experiences and switch allegiances, so that at the end of fourteen years of struggle all members of the White Rose Party have a red rose on their forearms and all members of the Red Rose Party have a white rose on theirs. If at this point the surest sign of being a traitor to the Red Rose Party is the mark of a red rose on the forearm, what besides confusion is served by referring to those with white rose tattoos as members of the Red Rose Party? Clarity of reference is certainly served, since it is now as it was in the beginning and as it was throughout the long period of transmigratory tergiversation: the Red Rose Party has always supported the queen, and the White Rose Party has always sought her overthrow. Reference is fixed relative to loyalty, not to color of tattoo.

At this late stage in the conflict, the white rose *means* that the bearer of the floral stigmata is a supporter of the queen, even though the queen's party is and always has been, by stipulation, the Red Rose Party. The "meaning"of the tattooed roses has certainly changed, but the Red Rose Party has never changed its allegiance or reference. White-rose tattoo and red-rose tattoo have meant different things at different times (for a time, of course, during the period of shifting loyalties, no one could tell by the tattoo alone what the tattoo "meant"), but by stipulation the parties have retained their distinct reference through all changes in tattoo meaning.

Moreover, those historians who have conflicting or contradictory views of the *meaning* of this *conflict* will have no trouble understanding the party references of one another. If the White Rosers are "freedom fighters" to some historians and "vile usurpers" to others, and if the conflict is characterized as a "struggle for democratic rights" by some and as an "attempt to overthrow legitimate authority" by others, there is no dispute about which party supports and which party does not support the queen. And, of course, because the historians share synonymy classes, as well as "nonce" references, they can agree on the nature of their disagreement about the "meaning" of what they mutually refer to. "Nonce" reference, like all other kinds of reference, can be enlisted to serve a wide variety of meaning interests, of theories. *The uses to which a term is put are not determined in any very restrictive sense by the reference of the term.*

At this point, it is perhaps important to remind the reader that in the immediately preceding discussion of "meaning" and "reference" and of the possibility of preserving both across theory changes, we have not attempted a full-scale analysis of either one or the other (such an analysis would be well beyond the scope and interests of this essay).[13] Rather, we have attempted to distinguish sharply between the two terms and to show that the paradoxical position, notwithstanding its initial plausibility, is difficult to maintain in the face of our interpretive *practices*. Furthermore, it is important to remember that we are still working at the level of *terms* and *phrases*, where we must start if we hope to show that the incommensurability (i.e., the nontranslatability) of different views is an incoherent notion and, further, that it is possible both to compare different views and to choose between them. And if in this discussion we go to great lengths to *prove* the obvious, we do so because the "obvious" is from the paradoxical perspective not so obvious. As we have seen, it is the "obvious" that is regularly called into question by our modern theorists, who continue to assume, for example, that belief in the possibility of recovering determinate, intentional meaning depends upon, is tied to, or is a necessary consequence of belief in a correspondence theory of truth.

Interpretation and the Troublesome Nature of Meaning

Before moving beyond terms and phrases to the possibility of cognitive sameness in different larger structures of meaning and reference (in different statements, views, or theories), however, we should say a word or two about the troublesome nature of "meaning," conceding in the process some gound to the paradoxicals. We have repeatedly acknowledged that in our conversations and in our interpretive disputes, we have more difficulty agreeing about "meaning" than about "reference," about the "tenor" than about the "vehicle" of the metaphor, about "connotation" than about "denotation." We can know what a person is talking *about* without necessarily knowing what he "means." At a slightly higher reach, the difficulty is played out in terms of illocution and locution: statement-meaning is clear enough, but the utterance-meaning is contested. Is "Here come the Red Rosers" a warning or a mere announcement of arrival? There is no question about whether or not the Red Rosers are coming or who the Red Rosers are. The question raised by their arrival on the scene concerns the "meaning" of their coming, and its answer is, at least in part, in the illocutionary force of the remark. Of course, illocutionary force depends not only on the "tone" or emotional quality of the remark, but on much else besides, for example, the context in which it is said, a context informed by a host of assumptions, expectations, or presuppositions about, say, the friend or foe nature of the Red Rosers, the imminence of battle, the prospects of surrender, and so on. Meaning is holistic and a function of use.

We should note that the important point here is that if *these* rather than *those* "justification conditions" prevail, the illocutionary force—the "utterance meaning"—of the remark is *this* rather than *that*. The justification conditions of the remark determine its tone and disambiguate, temporarily, its "meaning" possibilities. *Moreover*, in the case at hand, it should be clear that if the justification conditions remained the same, the speaker would utter the same "warning" (or make the same announcement) whether he said, "The Red Rosers are coming" or "Here come the Red Rosers." Even though abstractly considered the two statements do not "mean" the same thing, they "mean" the same thing *in use*, in practice, in these circumstances. (Of course, "meaning" is never in the words themselves, in their shape or the cut of their jib.) In short, both "meaning" and "reference" are contextually—and conceptually—determined, are determined to be such and such by their *use* in certain conceptually driven contexts. Moreover, if in some cases our *emotion* (attitude, stance, aim, purpose, wish, or whatever) is governed by how we size up a situation, in other cases the way we size up a situation is governed by our emotion (stance, attitude, aim, and so on). Sometimes we choose because we see a value, and sometimes we see a value because we have chosen.

At any rate, translation or interpretation is a global or holistic enterprise, requiring a grasp of the justification conditions underlying and determining the use of statements, rather than a matter of simply understanding the meanings of terms and the kinds of structural relations into which they can enter. More exactly, interpretation depends not only on mastery, say, of semantic rules (mastery of principles of synchrony or principles of substitution) and of syntactic or grammatical operations (of diachronic principles, of structural rules), but also on a knowledge of the conditions, psychological and situational, under which the statements are asserted—in short, on knowledge of the assertibility conditions of the statements.

Without this latter kind of knowledge the statements we encountered would be indeterminate, be rich in possible meaning but poor in specific or utterance meaning, however intelligible or acceptable they might be as locutions. "Close the door," for example, is a perfectly acceptable locution in English, and no native speaker has difficulty with its locutionary force, its terms, or its grammatical appropriateness, but the number of assertibility conditions to which it could accommodate itself is virtually limitless. To know what it means, we would have to know when, by whom, for what purpose, and in what situation it was used. Uttered by someone with a cold, it means one thing, and uttered by a father who has just been told that his prodigal son was approaching the house, it means quite another.[14] There is nothing indeterminate about its meaning in use, however. We here give expression to a commonplace of semantic theory, but its relevance to our *major concerns* (and to the defense of pluralism) should not be missed. As Putnam observes, in translation, as in interpretation, "we construct a global theory which gives reasonable explanations of the speaker's behavior in the light of his beliefs (as determined by the translation manual [an available vocabulary and grammar, say] which is *one* component of the global theory) *and* his desires and intentions (as determined by the psychological theory which is the *other* component.)" In reading, indeterminacy of translation or interpretation "is equivalent to the indeterminacy of the transition from functional organization (in the sense of machine table [e.g., vocabulary and grammar] or whatever) to psychological description."[15]

Our familiarity with many actual worlds and, hence, with the ways in which innumerable available possibilities have become functional in various mind-dependent systems of "meaning" enables us both to *make* and to *participate imaginatively in* (i.e., understand) worlds never previously encountered or imagined. Possibilities available for use derive, of course, from prior use, but subsequent use is, we know, not strictly controlled by such prior use. Otherwise, there would be *no variety* in prior use, no way for what is variously available for revision and extension to become available; variety would never begin. How exactly we go about making and grasping new justification conditions is unknown and is likely to remain obscure at least until such time, if ever, as we have a comprehensive theory of human creativity or a formally complete inductive logic (an unlikely possibility). The hermeneuticist is no more likely to find or devise a surefire key to invention than the nomothetic scientist to find the sort of "prior probability metric" that, according to Rudolf Carnap, would enable us to determine, for example, how "good" theories are formualted (invented) and which falsifiable theories it is reasonable to test and which it is safe to ignore. The trouble is that probability, like consistency or coherence, is context-sensitive and interest-relative; moreover, it is often the case that conflicting or mutually exclusive probabilities are equally consistent with background knowledge.[16]

Comparing and Judging Incommensurable Schemes

Concerning our remarks on intertranslatability and on the stability of some references and meanings across changes in conceptual scheme, some few theorists might insist that we are making too much fuss about too little, about uninteresting and unimportant matters. Some of the theorists might agree that, yes, such things as we affirm are true in the world of everyday, ordinary reference. Some might even say that within schemes words refer to what they refer to (Derrida, for example, would have no trouble with the notion that within a certain logocentric scheme "tree" refers to trees, "yellow-bellied sapsucker" to yellow-bellied sapsuckers, and so on), that meanings are determinate within a given scheme, and that no scheme is privileged over another or has any metaphysical advantage over another. All this can be granted because none of this has much to do with what is for them the only (or the "best") game in town.

What matters for these theorists is not what such and such a statement, thesis, or text ordinarily means, but what it means for anything to have such a meaning; not what the conflicting views are, but what might explain the interest in or the having of this particular conflict in the first place; not what is meant, but what means, that is, what in language, culture, the unconscious, or history does the meaning. Such critics move to the higher ground, transcending the concerns of the groundlings by carrying inquiry to a new level, where they can see how and in what the everyday groundings of the groundlings are grounded. By employing a kind of intellectual bootstrapping, picking themselves up by their own bootstraps (their own categories), or by exercising a kind of highstepping, making their questions the subject of questioning, they take the higher ground (in good Hegelian fashion).

In taking such ground, however, they inadvertently commit a kind of noumenalism (an immanent noumenalism, perhaps, but a noumenalism just the same), since, notwithstanding their opposition to any kind of privileging, they claim to have access to a special (a shifting, historical, but regularly identifiable) realm of justification, of correspondence relations, to have, in short, privileged access to what determines what. Ironically and not uncomically, such critics are to literary and cultural inquiry what the positivists are to scientific inquiry, the High Arbiters of the Meaningful and the Meaningless (or the Interesting and the Uninteresting). What physics is to the positivist, history (or linguistics, psychology, anthropology) is to these theorists. In the New Historicism, for example, there is no historical end product or condition (Absolute Mind, say), as in the older or Hegelian brand, but there is from *epoch* to *epoch* an identifiable *episteme* of the first magnitude, the *chief episteme*, the *archive's archē*, the grand—though local, historical, and, of course, ideological—Conditioner of all systems, whether verbal or pictorial, whether in essay, film, cartoon, State Department bulletin, or whatever. Given this intellectually soft yet aggressively militant *foundationalism* at the *center* of the projects of these theorists, one can only hope that Putnam is correct when he observes that the "incoherence of the attempts to turn the world views of either physics or history [or linguistics or anthropology] into secular theologies have not yet been entirely exposed, but the process is . . . well under way."[17]

The problem of competing interpretations is, of course, a special instance of the more general problem of rival or competing theories. At issue is the putative incommensurability of different theories and, as a consequence, the isolation of each theoretical and interpretive community within a conceptual prisonhouse of its own making. The paradoxical or *theoretical* view is that *since* nothing is discussed or mentioned that is not paradigm-determined and hence paradigm-locked, *since* across the theoretical divide meanings are not shared, and *since* even the theoretical terms that the theories have in common (both use the term "form" or "plot" or "voice," for example) have different references and different meanings, the theories cannot be compared, cannot be discussed or evaluated in any terms not already prejudiced in favor of one or the other of the theories. In literary studies, the view has achieved not a little prominence and authority, especially among various relativists influenced sometimes at first- but often at second-hand by Thomas S. Kuhn's *The Structure of Scientific Revolutions*. And, of course, the view is an article of faith with most reader-response critics and "interpretive community" or "perspectivist" critics, such as Fish (it is indeed the rock upon which the faith is founded).

Because we have already shown how meanings and references can indeed be shared across conceptual schemes (indeed, have shown how, unless we belonged to many and various symbolic communities, *new* and *various* theories, views, and worlds could never emerge, since what is new *cannot even be recognized without appealing to some prior meanings, experiences, and criteria of rationality*), we need not give much space to the issue here. For rival theories to be compared it is sufficient that they have some references in common and concatenate propositions according to some recognizable system of inference and derivation. When these conditions obtain, we can describe what both theories are trying to explain and how they go about the business of explanation, doing so in a language that is *mutually intelligible* and *fair to both theories without being partial to either one*. Our commitment to one or another view or our "impartiality" relative to both does not prevent us from understanding the views of the Copernican and the Ptolemaist, the Marxist and the Lacanian. And in describing their differences, we can easily avoid expressions that presuppose the utility or validity of either, *though not expressions with no presuppositions of their own*, with no presuppositions whatever.[18]

Moreover, if incompatible theories can be compared, they can also be evaluated, with the result that relative *to* a commonly accepted methodological criterion or regulative ideal (comprehensiveness, coherence, appropriateness, or whatever), *to* a set of such ideals, or *to* a commonly recognized purpose or end in view, one is deemed better than or preferable to the other. One can easily imagine a case in which a "chair" or "anger" explanation would be preferable to a "particle" or "wave" explanation, on the one hand, or a "neuron" or "electrochemical" explanation, on the other. Or, one can easily imagine a case in which a "psychoanalytic" explanation would be superior to a "Marxist" explanation of, say, Hamlet's "delay" in executing his charge. In other words for comparison, as well as agreement or disagreement, to take place it is not necessary that the rival theories have all meanings and references in common or employ the same system of inference, as even some pluralists have supposed.[19]

Perhaps our case here can be brought to a close with a couple of brief comments and a couple of "historical" examples. In the first place it is important to remember that when systems differ chiefly in the *organization* or in the *use* and *emphasis* of their elements, they inevitably have much—most references and concepts—in common. Additionally, in literary criticism we are frequently (perhaps usually) dealing in any given period with differences in the *emphasis, organization,* and *use* of a relatively stable critical lexicon of terms and distinctions. Consequently, although many of the specifically "theoretical" terms of the rival theories remain the "same" their uses, emphases, and values are dramatically different.

The criticism of the eighteenth century offers us a convenient example of the reliance of critics on a relatively limited and stable critical vocabulary within and across widely divergent, disparate, incompatible critical systems and approaches. For example, such common terms relating to *critical rules* and *literary types* as "argument," "manners," "fable," "ode," "epic," "pastoral," "thought," "invention," "expression," "arrangement," "sentiments," "middle" and "low" styles *and* such common terms relating to *causes, effects, circumstances, and qualities* as "art," "nature," "the beautiful," "the pathetic," "imitation," "invention," "fancy," "judgment," "imagination," "instruction," "delight," and so on become functional in radically different critical theories; like Englishmen and Americans, the various views are divided by a common language. Further, not only the *terms* but also many of the *doctrines* of this criticism are the "same" from theory to theory. The "sameness" persists, of course, *only so long as the terms and doctrines are isolated from the specific conceptual schemes informing them with particular meaning and emphasis.* Histories of criticism that link critics and theories on the basis of these ostensible similarities, as most literary histories do, inevitably join together what the critics had managed to keep asunder.

The terms and doctrines are, in a sense, the stereotypical "stuff," the relatively tolerant commonplaces of which specific theories are made. Nevertheless, although thoroughly distinct theoretically, the particular theories remain on speaking terms with one another, are, that is, intelligible to one another. We can give perfectly adequate and thoroughly impartial accounts of the radically different theoretical principles underlying and informing Henry Fielding's "Preface" to *Joseph Andrews* and Samuel Johnson's "Preface to Shakespeare," even as we recognize the appearance in each of ostensibly similar doctrines, the emphasis in both, for example, on "species" and not "individuals."

Much the same result is achieved when we turn to a more recent example of theoretical difference and terminological similarity. Both the New Critics and the so-called Chicago critics were identified as "formalists," and both were interested in and used the term "form," yet they developed incompatible theoretical positions. For the New Critics "form" made a pair with and found its antithesis in "content," and this binary unit found a complementary pair or unit in "style and content" or "the poetic and the discursive." On the other hand, for the "Chicago critics" "form" was what gave "matter" its structure and function, and a text was a regulated, hierarchical sequence of form-matter relationships with the "form" of one level becoming the "matter" of the next higher level, all the way up to the synthesizing principle of form for the whole text. As many literary historians have shown, it is possible to describe *how* these critics variously used the "same" terms, *what* they sought to explain, and *how* they went about their explanations without resorting to language partial to either critical position. Indeed, we have just provided such a description, albeit a sketchy one.

Furthermore, in this particular case, we can not only compare the theories but determine the superiority of one view to the other. Assuming a common interest in accounting for the "full formal integrity" of any given literary work and, thus, the appropriateness of "comprehensiveness" as an evaluative standard (everyone familiar with the contests of these "mighty opposites" will acknowledge the legitimacy of our assumptions here), we can say unequivocally, I think, that relative to the Chicago position, the New Critical one is a limited or partial one, is concerned with the justification of fewer kinds of (commonly recognized) particulars and, consequently, that the Chicago position, in accounting for more (commonly recognized) particulars within a discrete structure is superior to that of the New Critics. Generally speaking, the New Critics subsume many works under a single structure, finding the same system of tensions between "logical structure" and "poetic meaning" in all works, whereas the Chicago critics distinguish among many *kinds* of structures and seek, further, to identify the peculiar "principle of form" underlying each particular work of any kind. Of course, this is an "illustration" of how comparison, evaluation, and judgment of rival "theories" could proceed, not a full-scale argument in defense of our "illustrative" conclusion. In other words, the reader need not accede to the conclusion in order to consent to the explanatory power of the "example."

A word or two in passing on the phrase "commonly recognized particulars" is perhaps in order. Although each theory will construe a given particular in the light of or as functional within its conceptual scheme or justification system, each will *recognize* it as a *particular* requiring a justification. For example, the "whale" that makes a fit with camels, baboons, dogs, and the people of Rhode Island according to the imperatives of one theoretical or taxonomic scheme (the "mammal" scheme, let us say) will make a fit with tuna, groupers, clams, oysters, and crabs according to the imperatives of another scheme (the "aquatic" animal scheme, say), but in both schemes the "same," commonly recognized (referred to) whale will be in need of a fitting. Since, as George Lakoff and Mark Johnson have noted, "the truth of a statement [or theory] depends on whether the categories employed in the statement [or theory] fit, the truth of a statement will always be relative to the way the category is understood for our purposes in a given context."[20] Thus, while "piano" will make a fit with flutes and violins and kazoos in the musical instruments system, it will make a fit with refrigerators, interior linemen, hippopotamuses, and armoires in the large-objects-useful-for-blocking-doors system.

As witnesses to this scheme-hopping, we recognize both that the whale and the piano make a fit and that they are too conspicuous to go unnoticed and unaccounted for. A scheme (of the type considered here) without a place for them is not an adequate scheme since they are *recognized*, if recognized at all, as requiring a place, as things that, say, either do or do not belong to or fit the scheme. Even though the piano and the whale may lose their status as bounded entities and become in other versions space-time regions or wave phenomena, our capacity for right categorization and finding a fit remains intact, as well as our ability to work outside our favorite or preferred scheme, the one in which we firmly believe and of which we are inordinately proud. What is commonly recognized is nothing, of course, apart from some system of recognition (nothing recognizable at any rate). There is nothing that the whale "just is" nor any description that captures exactly or corresponds perfectly to the "just is-ness" of the whale. Still, as we move from system to system, we know that where the whale once was there is now a space-time region. We also know, I think, that even though the *whale* and the *region* share no genetic material, they are "deeply related," just as the "chair" as bounded entity is deeply related to the "chair" as wave phenomena.[21] There is nothing "chairy" about *wave phenomena* and nothing "wavy" about the *chair*, but in some contexts (the very one we are in now, for example) and for some purposes (such as ours at the moment), it makes a kind of sense to talk about both as being in some sense the *same* (thing). In doing so, we undoubtedly privilege "thing" talk—and may even betray a deep prejudice for bounded entities—but at the level of present interest and purpose, we are not partial to either description; relative to the matter at hand, we are *disinterested* witnesses. We must be, if we hope to get along in the world (i.e., the worlds we are persistently obliged to understand). And we get along by being unto others what we expect them to be unto us, charitable.

Part Three
Ad Hoc Categories and
Textual Interests

Chapter 8
Interpretation All the Way Down

Just as no single theory seems capable of accounting for the various kinds of apparent motion we perceive, so, in all likelihood, no single theory will adequately explain how we determine the assertibility conditions of the various statements we make or encounter. Nevertheless, in spite of our present (and undoubtedly future) incapacity to develop a single theory to account for our language making and language processing abilities (more generally, our symbol making and symbol processing abilities), there is no question about our capacity either to make "new" sense with language or to make sense of "new" (uses of) language. Nevertheless, if how we do what we do remains shrouded in more than a little mystery, we know increasingly more and more about what it is we do when we do what we do, about the repertoire of skills and abilities (and about the criteria of acceptability) that we bring to bear on our dealings with language (and other symbol systems). Moreover, as interpreters of literary and other texts, we are chiefly concerned with explanations that appeal to this repertoire, and throughout the preceding discussion of meaning and reference and of the locutionary and illocutionary we have been concerned with "continuous" models at the higher levels of explanation (with assertibility conditions as determined by situations and intentions).

Higher-Level Explanations and Justification Conditions

Interestingly, in an essay extending the range of what experimental and clinical studies have shown about the ability of the brain to derive meaning in many different ways, Israel Rosenfield moves suggestively (and analogically) to everyday events at the higher levels of selection and improvisation:

Often in casual conversation we offer explanations with great confidence. Our listener responds with a damaging fact and we quickly drop our explanation, giving in its place a new one with the same confidence with which we proposed our original explanation. Similar processes probably go on unconsciously.[1]

For our purposes, it is of more than passing interest that in the concluding section of what is certainly the most important and comprehensive study of the visual system in print, *Vision*, David Marr speculates on the broader implications of visual selection processes in a way entirely consonant with Israel Rosenfield's suggestions about our conversational maneuvers. Extrapolating from what he has learned about the anatomy, the physiology, and the selectivity mechanisms of the visual system, he turns at the end to an "explanation" of the processes involved in "meaning" selection when we read, the processes involved in grasping the "appropriate" concepts and justification conditions of the sentences we encounter. The importance of the passage obliges us to quote it in full. Presented with the sentences,

"The fly buzzed irritatingly on the windowpane. John picked up the newspaper," [our] immediate inference is that John's intentions toward the fly are fundamentally malicious. If he had picked up the telephone, the inference would be less secure. It is generally agreed that an "insect-damaging" scenario is somehow deployed during the reading of these sentences, being suggested in its coarsest form by the fly buzzing irritatingly. Such a scenario will contain a reference to something that can squash an insect on a brittle surface—a description that a newspaper fits, but not a telephone.

We might therefore conclude that when the newspaper is mentioned (or, in the case of vision, seen) not only is it described internally as a newspaper and some rough [three dimensional] model description of its shape and axes set up, but it is also described [internally] as a light, flexible object with area. Because the second sentence might have continued "and sat down to read," the newspaper must also be described [internally] as reading matter; similarly, it must also be described as a combustible article, as something that rustles, and so forth. *Since we do not usually know in advance what aspect of an object or action is important, it follows that most of the time a given object will give rise to several different coarse internal descriptions.*

Similarly for actions. It may be important to note that the description of fly swatting or reading or fire lighting *does not have to be attached to the newspaper—a description of the newspaper is merely available that will match its role in each scenario.*[2]

As the reader might suspect, I find Marr's "explanation" (his higher-order, psychological-level "explanation") of the processes of "meaning" selection deeply satisfying, in part, I suppose, because it

presents in felicitous epitome so much of what this essay has supported and argued for. Moreover, intuitively, it seems "right," and
one can easily imagine how Marr's procedure could be extended
from "meaning" unit to "meaning" unit in a work of considerable
length (of any length). So extended, the procedure, with its emphasis
on our not knowing in advance what aspect of an object or an action
is important or what emphasis or value the terms employed will carry
(and, as a corollary, its tendency to make and revise justification conditions enroute) would not, it seems, lead inevitably or usually to intertextual, Marxist, deconstructionist, ideologemic (or whatever)
readings or interpretations, would not lead, in other words, to the
kinds of readings generally favored by *theory*.[3]

The reader who has followed the argument this far will immediately see at work in this passage what we have earlier characterized,
following Nelson Goodman, as retrospective construction and recursion. Not much can be made of the "buzzing fly" until we get to "irritatingly," which tells us, perhaps among other things, that this is not
a "fly-perspective" narrative (if the buzzing irritates the fly, then the
fly should stop buzzing). At this point, we conclude only that the
sound irritates some sentient, emotion-prone creature other than
the fly. And not much can be made of John and his newspaper until
a relation—a "fit"—can be supposed to obtain between them and the
irritating buzzing going on at the windowpane. At "newspaper" we
retrospectively construct "meanings" and "references" with our
"insect-damaging" inference (of course, at "buzzed," we tentatively
conclude that "fly" is an insect, not a zipper on the front of a pair of
pants or a fisherman's lure). That is, we supply the justification or
assertibility conditions that at least temporarily render the words
intelligible.

We never ask "what do these words, one by one or collectively,
mean?" We ask instead—ask, that is, *sotto voce*, without formally putting any question to ourselves—what sort of circumstantial and intentional situation would we be justified in supposing to obtain if these
words were to make some kind of sense, given the options made
available by our familiarity with the vocabulary and grammar in use
(and with a variety of human situations).[4] Working from a stock of
available possibilities, we learn our (new) "concepts" along with their
justification conditions. The reader should note that I am not here
suggesting that we process sentences word by word—or even phrase
by phrase, for that matter. What I am suggesting, however, is that
availabilities are not "processed" until retrospective construction occurs—at word, phrase, punctuation mark, or whatever—and that
such construction is a form of justification, is both a constitutive

inference, one determining facts and emphases, and the cognitive basis or ground for the generation of subsequent meaning possibilities (a ground establishing "things" and their projectible properties, setting the conditions of fittingness, of what goes and can go with what). In short, our assumed assertibility conditions function recursively as determinants of our expectations.

Returning to our example, we can note that if after "newspaper" the second sentence went on to say, as Marr suggests, "and sat down to read," we would immediately abandon the construction of meaning under which an insect-damaging scenario was justified and give prominence to another aspect (feature, property) of the "stereotypical," ordinary-reference newspaper, that is, the "reading matter" aspect. Our justification conditions (and, hence, our concepts) turn out to be "wrong," unjustified, in this case. They are *disconfirmed,* even though we were mentally *set* to confirm them. But note that under our new construction of "meaning" (we assume now that John is going to read the newspaper), we are struck with an unexplained and, at least for the moment, inexplicable pest at the windowpane.

Meanings and Intentions

If this were a two-sentence narrative concluding with "and sat down to read," we would be profoundly dissatisfied with it and would feel justified in bringing it before the tribunal responsible for adjudicating cases involving gross violations of the imagination and sensibility on charges of incompleteness or incoherence. If, on the other hand, these two sentences had been written (or had appeared mysteriously) in the sand at the beach, we would, of course, probably not be disturbed by their lack of "fit," their incoherence, though we would be distressed even in this case if we had any reason to suppose that someone had intended these sentences to form a narrative. If they had appeared accidentally, as a consequence, say, of some unusual tidal perturbations, we could make no sense of the sentences at all. For in order to make sense of them, we would first have to assume that they were "intentionally," not accidentally, inscribed on the beach, because assertibility conditions do not and cannot apply to unasserted assertions. Postulation of assertibility or justification conditions assumes intentionality (and intentionality, of course, is a necessary precondition of a statement's "meaning," its being *about something*; and, further, "it is built into the concept of an intentional action that its structure is explicated in terms of a suitable combination of belief and desire");[5] without the assumption of intentionality, the words would be meaningless or, what amounts to the same thing, excessively and limitlessly meaningful. As soon as the reader assumes that the sentences make some kind of sense, he assumes intentionality, and if it turns out that the narrative read as a coherent narrative was accidentally produced, the narrative ceases to be coherent the moment it is discovered to be accidental, since the conditions supposed to justify meaning no longer function as justification conditions, though, of course, the *interpretation*, which is intentional, retains its justification.

Your reading of Shakespeare's Sonnet 55 would be no different from your reading of the "same" sonnet produced by monkeys randomly pecking at typewriters, but only your reading of the Shakespearean sonnet would be (or could be) accepted as a reading of the "sonnet." If you insist that your reading applies to the "monkey sonnet" as well, you simply are willing, for reasons best discovered by introspection, to ascribe intentionality to the arbitrary behavior of monkeys, and from this elevated perspective you should also be able to see hordes of sales representatives for swamp property beating a path to your door. Your reading applies, and can *only* apply to, an *intentional object*; only such an object, grounded in a structure of belief and desire, has a criterion of success built into it.

But wait, some respond while flexing their relativist muscles, we don't deny that the "meaning" is without justification or without intentionality. We only insist that *our* intentionality assigns the justification conditions. There is intentionality here, but it is *our* intentionality. The reading is "true for us," "true" relative to our scheme of interpretation, and this is the only kind of "truth" there can be—mind-dependent, discourse-dependent "truth," as you have repeatedly said. Of course, in making this move, relativists assume that I understand not only their objection *but* the reading that is "true for them," and if after I restate their objection and reading they agree that I have understood them, they then undermine the position they would uphold, for *we* agree that there is a *fact of the matter* about what is "true for them," thereby opening the way for a discussion about what would *count as a justification* of a reading that is "true for them," a discussion that in its unfolding would disclose whether we shared references, concepts, *and* criteria of acceptability, of "fit" or "rightness." Such a discussion, in short, would disclose our agreements and disagreements and would proceed on the assumption that there was a fact of the matter to be settled, a mind-dependent, discourse-dependent fact of the matter to be sure, but one that our mutual understanding had made evident—and potentially resolvable. We would be doing unto the text what we had consented to do unto one another's remarks, that is, treating it as an intentional, meaning-conditional system of sentences, a structure of belief and desire.

Further, assuming that along the way we rejected readings that were possible but unacceptable, we would be not only entertaining possibilities that were, it turned out, not "true for us" but agreeing on *criteria of warranted assertibility*. The happiest, quite possible eventuality would be *agreement* on a reading that was "true for us," on a reading, moreover, that in our personal and private capacities we perhaps both found to be disagreeable or untrue, a reading expressive of a view with which we both disagreed, for example, that the rain in Maine falls mainly on the plain. That is, we agree on what *the text means*, but we reject the "truth" of its meaning—in our view the rain in Maine does *not* fall mainly on what Maine has precious little of. The *reading* that is "true for us" (we read the *same* text and get the same *meaning*) expresses a mind-dependent, context-sensitive *meaning* that is simply not "true" for us (we disagree with the assertion made by the text that we read in the *same* way). Of course, unless we knew what the "text" meant, we would be unable to reject its "meaning." The case made here will be fortified later. For now, we will simply say that "meaning" talk is necessarily "intentional" talk and that "meanings" may be *truly justified* without being "true" for us. Moreover, as far as literature is concerned, we are almost always interested more in what is "fit" and "correct" than in what is "true," and what is "fit" or "correct" or "right" is determined from context to context by some imaginative grasp of the operative justification conditions, the conditions only on the assumption of which the text can be understood to make some kind of sense. To understand better the way constraints are imposed on our assumed justification conditions, we must return to Marr's example.

The True and the Fit

If Marr's two-sentence narrative ended with "He picked up the newspaper," we would have both a kind of coherence and a kind of completeness: the juxtaposed sentences make some kind of sense, and we could assume that the perplexity introduced to our attention was subsequently resolved by the implied but not expressed course of action undertaken by John. Our happiness would be complete or explicitly completed, however, only if our insect-damaging inference were confirmed by an "extermination" sentence, only if what is implied were realized and not left to inference (as it would be with "John stealthily approached and then resolutely swatted the fly, killing it dead"). In this case, we would have all that we could ask for: beginning, middle, and end, the formal resolution of a fully intentional dramatic action.

An inference confirmed is a "right," "correct," or "fitting" inference and, more, a happy exemplification of the coincidence of "fact" and "value" in interpretation. Fact and value are not disjunct but mutually supportive, mutually implicative elements. The reading is "true" because it "fits"; thus, coherence, consistency, appropriateness, plausibility, suitability, and so on are as "objectively" present as "meaning" is. Facts and values are, in fact, codefining or coextensive. To be "justified" as "true" (in context) is to be "fitting" and "right" (in context), and the standard of "truth" is simultaneously the standard of "value." "Value" and "meaning" are both context-sensitive. It may well be true that by some independent standard of euphony "take an ax to the slug's back" is a harsh sequence of vocables. Nevertheless, the cacophonous statement would be perfectly "right" and "fitting" if it were uttered, say, on a certain occasion by a certain character as a further indication of a certain moral quality that was variously exhibited by him, if it were, that is, consistent with our inferences about the "truth-conditions" of his character. Reading is as value-laden as it is theory-laden, and as we read (and write or speak) we are apparently guided (our acceptance of meanings is guided) by such criterial (axiological) imperatives as coherence, consistency, plausibility, and fittingness, so that we treat as "true" (as justified) only what is, under the circumstances, fitting and so forth. Where we lose a "fit," we lose a "meaning." Truth is beauty, beauty, truth (as we long suspected).

Facts, Values, and Meaning Holism

It should be clear that if there are no percepts without concepts, there are neither concepts nor "facts" (neither meanings nor references) without values. If we divide, identify, or categorize in certain ways, we do so because the "products" of such activities (our concepts) have a value for "us" (if the differences we marked—"cat" and "dog," say—made no difference to us, were unimportant or uninteresting to us, we would not mark—or remark—the differences), and if our words and sentences "mean" something to "us," they do so because we have made them fit some justification conditions, have supposed some conditions within which or by virtue of which they make sense, are "necessary," "right," "correct," "plausible," and so forth. To "mean" is to be "justified," and to be justified is to be "right" relative to some conceptual standard. "Meaning" and "justification"—"fact" and "value"—are coeval and mutually implicative. As we have seen, the "meanings" we make do not have to square with what we in our personal and private capacities believe. The "meanings" must be "believable"—that is, justifiable according to some scheme—but it is not necessary that we believe them.

As we read, we move from many possibilities to some probabilities and then to "certainties." In other words, as our justification conditions account for more and more of the text (account for and are accountable to, imply and are implied by more and more of the text), the range of alternatives consistent with those conditions narrows until choice becomes necessity. The "bill" that could have belonged at one time to a duck can no longer function as a duck's bill once the discourse determines that, however large, it must be paid by the diners. And what is true of "poetics" is also true of "hermeneutics." What applies to the *making of a (kind of) text* (or, more exactly, to the *reasoning involved in the making of a kind of text*) applies as well to the *making of a reading*. The reader should note, however, that we are not here principally concerned with determining whether one "justified" reading is better than—more justified than—another "justified" reading, though we are certainly suggesting that if certain conditions can be supposed to prevail, then some readings would be "unjustified" or "unjustifiable" (because ill-fitting under those conditions) and that *interpretation* at the higher, psychological level is certainly possible in a world of immanent meaning. Finally, it should be clear that what Johnson found "true" of experience is similarly "true" of reading: just as we gain more principles of reasoning and establish a wider basis of analogy (become more adept at supplying justification conditions and less prone to superstition) as we experience more, so we gain more principles of certainty (become more confident about the "rightness" of our inferences and justification decisions) as we read more of the text.

Chapter 9
Meaning and Available Scenarios

Justification and Models of Reading

As a first move in the process of elucidating some of the broader implications of the model of reading proposed by David Marr, we can differentiate it, generally, from those models currently in favor with most modern theorists. Throughout the preceding discussion we have given emphasis to the global or holistic character of interpretation or understanding and have insisted that the determination of "meaning" and "reference" depends upon grasping or supposing certain assertibility or justification conditions. Hence, "justified" meaning is specific meaning, and reading "holistically" is reading for specific justification conditions, for those conditions that provide sufficient warrant for the assertion of specific meanings.

Now, it should be clear that, spatially, this model—this pluralist model—is at a considerable remove from the two models favored by the theorists, which are themselves the antipodes of one another. The relativist and the practical deconstructionist[1] have no trouble recognizing the availabilities of ordinary reference, no trouble supposing innumerable possible "meanings" and "references" (the deconstructionist, for example, usually begins with "ordinary," "customary," or "conventional" reference and then exposes the possibilities and contradictions necessarily implicated in the referential system in which the term, say, participates). It is not at availabilities but rather at justification conditions that these critics balk.[2] Their model of reading is long on possibilities but short on assertibility conditions (short at least on a preference among such conditions; there can be no rule of preference when all—or most—available references are equally plausible). Much is available, and nothing is justified, at least in our sense of justified.

On the other hand, the model adopted by the determinists—the ideological, historical, institutional, gender, etc., monists—is short on both availabilities *and* justification conditions. Or, put the other way, nothing not implicated in those justification conditions antecedently determined to be of preeminent importance is referentially available. What counts is known by prior analysis; objects and meanings are subject in a sense to *prior restraint*. Terms, categories, and relations are few and are restricted in movement and association by antecedently determined ideological conditions. Because culture, history, politics, capitalism, or whatever is such and such (discursively considered), meaning and reference are such and such. Meaning and reference are defined by institutional—usually binary—forces that create what they are "embodied" (discursively) by. The worlds we had taken to be many worlds are, at bottom, one world. These critics, unlike their fellow "(post)modernists," do not give up on justification, on "objectivity," or even on immanence; they simply put severe—and, finally, unjustifiable and self-immolating—restrictions on the rich multiplicity of references and meanings available to the pluralist (who, unlike the ideological or institutional monist, has access to many worlds and, unlike the relativist and the decentrist, access to "real"—immanently real—unconflicted worlds).

Locating Meaning in Texts/in Readers

At this point the curious might be prompted to wonder *where* the justified meaning or the effect (the catharsis, say) *is*,[3] to wonder whether the effect is a psychological (or medicinal or physiological) or "poetic" concept. Well, surely, the "effect" or "meaning" is *in* the reader (of course, we use "in" loosely here and mean only that the emotional response is the reader's or that the meaning is the reader's construct), but just as surely the whole drift of our discussion seems to be suggesting that the effect or meaning is somehow *in* the text as well.

We find nothing aberrant in the common notion that a reader has understood the text's—or even Shakespeare's, Fish's, Derrida's—meaning, the meaning that is somehow *in* the text (under one construction or according to one scheme of interpretation). There is, of course, no such thing as *a meaning* independent of some conception, some construal of meaning, for, as Nelson Goodman notes, meanings, like facts, are factitious. In a strict sense, then, meanings are no more *in* the text than *in* the head.[4] On this view, catharsis is a "poetical," not a medicinal, physiological, or "mental" term; catharsis is *in* the ending of the drama every bit as much as—and in exactly the same way that—the pity or fear is *in* the scene or character (or that the "justification conditions" are *in* the construed sentences). What *we experience emotionally* (and experience as satisfaction if the ending is appropriate or fitting) is an *internal achievement of the (construed) drama.* It is a satisfaction condition of the drama, a formal satisfaction, if you will, *within a descriptive framework*, within a *conceptual* system, the system employed by the author. The achievement, though complete in itself under this system of justification, depends for its actualization on our inferences or opinions. Our emotions are products of *inference* in the sense that their specific character is determined by how we size up situations. To respond with pity we must size up the situation *as pitiful*, and we are *angry* because we *understand* or *believe* that the situation is one in which anger is "justified." We can have *reflexes* but not *emotions* without *opinions*—that is, beliefs. Emotional reflex is, strictly speaking, a contradiction in terms, a locution testifying only to the rapidity with which we make certain judgments or construct justifications. The inferences underlying our emotional responses, then, are "justification conditions" by another, more modest name.

Under the ordinance of this view, "meaning" or "effect" is *in* both the text and the reader (in a manner of speaking) but not, even by extension, in the broad social community, which according to some theorists pre-scribes what can count as "meaning." Such an extension would finally be unacceptable because, as we have seen, the community is long on availabilities but short on justifications. The broad social community—like nations, cultures, history, eras, periods—has no intentions (opinions, emotions, or beliefs) and obeys or subserves no justification conditions, no particular, locally functional justification conditions (or, what amounts to the same thing, has too many *possible* intentions).

Perhaps we can take some of the puzzle out of the bi-locality (the bi-lexuality?) of meaning or effect by considering how some ordinary puzzles work. "When is a door not a door?", for example, is a puzzling question, and "When it's ajar" can be accepted as a delightfully felicitous "correct" response by most English speakers.[5] Similarly, most people to whom the question is new will be puzzled by, "How far can a dog run into the woods?" and groaningly pleased by "halfway" (at the halfway point, of course, the dog runs *out of* the woods). Finally, consider this puzzling situation: driving his son to ballet lessons, a man is involved in an automobile accident. The man is killed, and the injured son is rushed to the hospital. At the emergency room the surgeon on duty says, "I can't operate on this boy; he's my son." Up to here with bewilderment, we ask, "How can this be"? A wonderfully "correct" answer to this culture-specific and culture-damning question is that the surgeon is the boy's—well I'll be damned—*mother.*

All such puzzles, it is perhaps worth noting incidentally, depend for their effectiveness on some species of the *unexpected* or *unantici-pated*. What conditions our understanding of the puzzle as a puzzle at the same time blocks our imaginative grasp of an appropriate way out of it, yet the way out must somehow be available to the puzzle and be recognized as a "fitting" way out when it is found. To be puzzled, we must apply (inappropriately, it turns out) the common, usual, famil-iar, or default meaning or emphasis to the object or situation; *dispuz-zlement* comes when we transcend or resist the lure of the "default" invitation and find the neglected but locally "right" meaning or em-phasis hidden within the possibilities available to the object or situa-tion. Interestingly, the puzzle for the paradoxicals—that is, Fisheans, early Kuhnians, and all those who adopt the "paradoxical" position (all those for whom there can be no sharing of meanings or refer-ence, because all things and meanings are scheme-specific, are consti-tuted by and nonexistent apart from a particular conceptual scheme)—begins when the puzzle is *solved*, for the cultural, historically conditioned, institutionally grounded assumptions and categories that are responsible for the *understanding* of the puzzle cannot also find the answer or determine the appropriateness of the answer as an answer. If paradoxicals "get" the answer—or "get" the joke—we are obliged to wonder how they do so, how they recognize a "fit" that only a categorical switch makes fitting. Moreover, cultural relativists who "get" the answer or joke commit themselves, of necessity, to some standard of rational acceptability, some "objective"—though immanent—criterion of coherence, plausibility, or assertibility under the circumstances. The conditions of understanding are such in this case that "getting it" is as a matter of fact "getting it right."

For pluralists the joke or riddle provides a paradigmatic instance of "objective" understanding across theory differences, whereas for paradoxicals the joke or riddle threatens to chew the paradoxical po-sition with its own teeth, namely, *paradox* (the position is consumed by what it feeds on): either its advocates gain a joke at the expense of their principles (i.e., they switch frames and categories midstream, mid-constitution, while constituting objects) or they retain their prin-ciples at the expense of their understanding, preferring, in this latter case, sullen isolation to communal joviality. Correspondingly, relativ-ists find themselves alone by following the crowd, the interpretive community (i.e., they lose by "default," so to speak; they choose a value that the joke transcends or abandons).

Incidental matters aside, we can say about the issue at hand that a puzzled *reader* has found the *question* puzzling. Meaning, inference, effect, puzzlement and so on certainly "belong" (in some sense) to the reader, but the "potentiality to puzzle" belongs to the text (under one construction of text, of course) or, as I would prefer to say, to the textually embodied intentionality of the author, since only persons—not words, sentences, cultures, etc.—can make "meaning." Texts are already—"always already," if you like—intentional worlds or versions of worlds, are at any rate regularly assumed to be such (interpretation, at any rate, is impossible apart from such an assumption—it is that without which interpretation cannot do); otherwise, we would never *argue* about meaning (argument presupposes a rational ground or rational grounds of choice),[6] recognize a "meaning" we disagreed with, or "get" a joke. The reader is actually puzzled and puzzled about a particular matter, about, for example, how far the dog can run into the woods, not just puzzled in a general, ontological sort of way. The *potentiality* to puzzle, however, is an *actuality* of the text or of a "construction" of the text—of a possible, plausible construction of the text.

If a text fell in the woods and no one were around to read it, would that text have, then, a meaning? we might ask in a philosophical mood. Such a text we are obliged to say would *actually* have the *potential* to mean what it *actually means* to the eventual reader for whom it makes some kind of sense to say, for example, that a dog can run only halfway into the woods (the reader, that is, for whom "dog," "woods," and "run" are not inscrutable terms). Here it is perhaps useful to note, following Hilary Putnam, that the "whole justification of an interpretive scheme . . . is that it renders the *behavior of others* minimally intelligible *by our lights*." Or, as Putnam, citing the testimony of Donald Davidson, elsewhere observes, "interpretive practice always requires us to attribute to the speaker [or writer] a substantial number of true beliefs and reasonable desires."[7] What, among countless other things, such a "running-dog" text *does not* have the potential to mean, however, is that the surgeon is the boy's mother. Relative to this meaning (and innumerable other meanings) the text offers only impotentiality, just as the map single-mindedly interested in the roads of Rhode Island is impotent to tell whether there are more people living in Providence than in Newport, no matter how determined the reader is to put population questions to the map.

The actual potentialities and impotentialities of the map (or text or joke), of course, are not *determined by* the actual reading of the map, even though tautology tells us that knowing a map meaning requires reading a map, that apart from reading no meaning is understood. The meaning *understood* by readers is the meaning *they make* (and there is no understanding—no meaning—*for them* apart from this particular making, or for *anyone* apart from some such making), but if they manage to make out the relative population densities of

Providence and Newport from the *map determined to be a road map and nothing but a road map*, they accomplish what those born of woman have seldom been allowed by the fates to accomplish—the miraculous. All this is not to say that readers' interests must or inevitably will coincide with those of the map, text, or joke, but only to suggest that talk of such coincidence is not unwarranted or unjustifiable in an immanent meaning world (despite what some theorists say or imply). Although explanation or interpretation is always relative to some interest, and although the interests we have are certainly always *our interests*, nothing in the "nature" of meaning, reference, or justification prohibits us from taking an interest in or understanding a virtually infinite number of context-sensitive, mind-dependent interests. Only those—not an uncommon few among modern critical theorists—whose retrograde (and self-defeating) ambition is to give up on rationality altogether can aspire to that longed-for felicity of neither understanding others nor being understood by them.

Fortunately, giving up on rationality altogether is impossible, if desirable, and undesirable, if possible. Its abandonment would entail the loss of *our* interests, since, as we have seen, having any concepts or meanings at all depends upon some standard(s) of acceptability, some rationality. Moreover, we certainly could not *agree* or be *convinced* to give up on it, without being supplied with what cannot be given, namely, *good reasons* for doing so. Hence, unless we are ready to give up on rationality and let "mum" be our only word, we are obliged to apply the principle of charity to one another's remarks and texts, including our "literary" texts, and assume that relative to some scheme, some interests, and some "truth" conditions (intelligible to us) the symbol system before us makes some kind of sense, however odd or "novel" that sense might be from the perspective of our own personal and private interests and beliefs.

When Meaning Occurs, Or, Getting the Joke

Before passing on to other matters we should perhaps say a word or two about the metaphorical character of "in" in our remarks about meaning or effect being "in" the text and "in" the reader, about the text's *actual potential* to mean what readers actually take it to mean. If the text is a version of a world, it is a mind-dependent, epistemic, intentional version, as is, of course, the (coincident) version that readers make the version before them out to be. The meaning of neither version is *in* the words or *in* the "things" the version "points to" (rather, the "things"—and their "mental equivalents"—are *in* the version), though, certainly, there are no versions without "symbols," or internal, "mental" symbol-analogues. Briefly, then, both versions (the author's and the reader's) are intentional "objects."

Nevertheless, it would be unwise to assume that there was *some (mental) thing* in the minds of the author and reader that both shared and that, when shared, constituted the "real meaning" of the two versions, that *some mental entity* was, make no mistake about it, *the* "meaning," because the sharing of concepts neither presupposes nor depends upon any identity of mental contents. To make a "meaning," writers have to have some justification conditions in place or in mind (*otherwise, the text would be without concepts or references*). Similarly, if readers are to "get" the joke (the "meaning"), they must grasp or supply the (justification) conditions that give meaning or reference to the words of which the joke is made. But there are no peculiar mental contents underlying the text (and, thus, "in" it, so to speak) or in the (mind of a) reader that are *the* meaning of the text (no contents, at any rate, that are recognizable or that could be identified as just the right contents if they were accidentally found). Something must be "in mind" when the "meaning" of the text is first created and then subsequently understood (meaning is not "contentless"),[8] but what is *in mind* can vary greatly without affecting the "intended" meaning (the system of justification). For example, not only do we regularly make many versions of the same interpretation—for example, tell different students (in different classes) our "reading" of the "same" text in different terms, or write the "same" piece differently, now as a talk and now as an article—but we also have the "same" meaning in many different moods, many states of mind. Also, we have earlier seen how speakers working with different perceptual prototypes of grass and different conceptions or beliefs about grass can converse at great length about a common "grass" in a state of mutual understanding.

But, we may now properly ask, if there are no meanings without some mental contents and if mental contents do not have to be the same for meaning to be the "same," where, then, or in what exactly is the meaning to be found? According to our present account, it seems to be neither in the text nor in the reader. Speaking somewhat cryptically, we can say that the "meaning" is "in" whatever conceptual container is considered to be sufficient to contain it. Less cryptically, we can say that whenever we have an instance of cognitive sameness we have the ability to move back and forth between discursive, representational, or symbolic systems, so that it is a matter of indifference, as far as "meaning" is concerned, which system we use. For example, we can move quickly, efficiently, and without loss of "meaning" between a chart, a map, and a graph to learn the "same" something about the population of Providence. Put bluntly, we *agree* that saying such and such is (roughly or essentially) equivalent to saying so and so. Ultimately, then, we are more concerned with "when" than with "where" meaning is. Location of meaning is subordinated to the *ability to use signs in such a way as to participate in conceptual exchange*. Paraphrase is, hence, no exegetical heresy but a fundamental condition of understanding and, as investigation and reflection will show, of expression.

In our ordinary dealings, we can quite comfortably continue to say, without fear of rebuke, that "meaning" is "in" both the text (in the capacity of the text—as construed—to bring certain *kinds* of concepts to mind) and the reader (the reader's grasp of justification conditions), as long as we recognize that *meaning, while impossible in the absence of some specific mental contents and some specific signs (or some inner notational system) is independent of any particular contents or signs* (i.e., there are no contents or signs that *just are* the meaning). What counts as cognitive sameness depends upon *an agreement* that, across differences in mental contents and often differences in symbolic representations, there is a sharing of concepts and references.

Instead of asking what and where a concept—or meaning—is (in particular mental contents or particular words or in readers, authors, signs, texts), then, we can more profitably ask whether the concepts are alike or different, whether the inquiry or dialogue can be sustained employing these assumptions. What determines whether or not the conceptual assumptions are "correct" is the kind of fit they make with the other concepts at work in the unfolding discourse, for it is clear that "correctness," plausibility, coherence, and so on are "holistic" judgments requiring that the concepts in use imply or entail one another, the whole discourse making up a *system* of entailment, a reticulated fabric of implication and "confirmation" or verification. In slightly different terms, *there is no understanding without* "translation" ("interpretation" is the term for, say, English-to-English translation), and although translation is inconceivable apart from some specific signs and some specific mental contents, cognitive or conceptual sameness is not a matter of identity relations among *words, internal images*, or *mental contents*, but a matter of *agreements* on likeness/ difference relations, agreements underwritten by the principle of charity and ratified by whatever context-sensitive, shifting methodological criteria (e.g., coherence, plausibility, and so on) we agree to apply to the (construed) circumstances at hand.

Thinking in terms of "when," as opposed to "what" or "where," meaning is (and thinking of meaning as "holistic," as a system of entailments and a set of agreements about those entailments), we confidently and quite tautologically say that meaning occurs whenever someone "gets it" (i.e., for a meaning to exist a meaning must be gotten). "Getting a joke" is a form of getting a meaning, and in everyday conversation we know we "get" the concepts and meanings "intended" by speakers when we display an ability to participate in the conversation, to talk about whatever is being talked about. We need to know what *kind* of talk is in use; we need to share a certain kind of background knowledge if there is to be intersubjective understanding.[9]

What Begets the Joke, What the Joke Begets (Or, Conversions, Re-versions, and Sub-versions)

Although "getting" what is "gettable" is certainly possible (as this essay has endeavored to show; if the "gettable" can't be gotten, then I don't know what can), there's a good deal more to be gotten from a joke, say, than the joke, and sometimes getting the joke is just not good enough. Sometimes we are more interested in either *what begets the joke* or *what the joke begets* than in getting the joke (of course, far too many critics tend to confuse what begets or what is begotten by the joke with the joke's joke). For example, suppose a joke gotten is not taken to be funny, but taken, rather, to be offensive, an instance of bad taste, of sexist bias, of an unconscious wish to dominate or intimidate the listener, of suppressed hostility toward the listener, of power and authority relations in a certain economic system, or of whatever.

Now, it should be clear that whenever we talk about (1) the conditions (in language, mind, society, gender, ideology, etc.) making possible the constitution of the joke; (2) the "real" (i.e., the deep, latent, buried, suppressed, repressed, psychoanalytical, cultural, ideological) *meaning* of the joke, whatever the source of its constitution; or (3) the broad social, cultural, or philosophical *implications* of the joke, we subordinate one set of epistemic interests to another, one kind of intentionality to another. In such circumstances, it is perhaps not unfair to say that a new or different version is being made of a "gotten" version, that the version *made* of the version *gotten* is parasitic (to use a highly esteemed critical term) on the gotten version, that many versions can be made of the version gotten, and that no "sub-version" or "re-version" of the gotten version is possible without the aid of some preferred "con-version" scheme. First we translate or interpret, and then we produce our "re-version" or "sub-version," our subsidiary or auxiliary version. We can make nothing of the joke not gotten (it should—but unfortunately today does not—go without saying); and until the interests of a particular map, say, are made out, nothing can be made of its peculiar cultural biases (its references, for instance, to many men's but to no women's colleges in New England). In any case, it is easy to see that intersubjective understanding of the joke or map forms the necessary "background-knowledge" condition of an understanding of the cultural, ideological, or whatever meaning. That is, for me to understand what the "converter" makes of the joke (or map), there must be between the "converter" and me, at a minimum, an intersubjective understanding of the joke's joke, which is the shared "background knowledge" to which the converter's explanation must accommodate itself if it is ever to be seen (by me) as "justified" for that person (or even for me).

"Re-version" or "sub-version" is, then, translation at one remove (is the translation of a translation), that is, translation from one system of equivalences (the joke's "meaning" is one equivalence system, since different words, "images," and mental contents can carry the same meaning) into another system (the cultural, social, psychoanalytic, ideologemic, or whatever system). The distinction between version and "reversion" (text and palimpsest, or text and over- or under-text) is similar to that which E. D. Hirsch has made between "meaning" and "significance," with "re-version," like "significance," being a relation of the construed version (or meaning) to something else. Construed "meaning" is given a peculiar *significance* by virtue of its being taken to convey something or other about the nature of, say, mind, language, history, politics, ideology, or whatever. Before "reversion" or "subversion" can take place, however, a version must first be gotten. Usually, or often, the version gotten is understood to be to the construct created by the preferred "conversion" chart as the *manifest* is to the *latent* content, the overt to the covert, the surface to the deep, the superficial to the "real" meaning; and the aim of exegesis is to show that this meaning on the surface really means this on the social, cultural, psychoanalytic, ideological level, with a two-fold system of interpretation being substituted for the fourfold system of medieval scholarship.[10]

Nothing in the foregoing account is designed to suggest that such "conversions" are necessarily illegitimate. Such "converted" knowledge is better than legitimate—it is necessary and irrepressible. Trouble arises when the advocates of a preferred conversion table claim that its categories and operations give special access to the real meaning or the only really important meaning of the version. At this britches-bursting point we encounter a species of indecency which for convenience we can call the "noumenal fallacy" or, when the enthusiasm fails to reach beyond what is graspable in an immanent meaning world, the "quasi-noumenal fallacy," which is nothing more than the conviction that the preferred categories enable us to penetrate to the substance beneath the appearance or, alternatively, to the ultimate though still immanent ground of all symbolic activities, all surface operations (at bottom, we are assured, there is cultural, historical, ideological, or linguistic bedrock). Of course, in the pluralist's world of immanent meaning there is no bedrock on which an Archimedes can stand to get an unencumbered view of what's what before undertaking the great task of world moving and shaking. Since each of the claims for the preeminence of certain categories (and hence meanings) *presupposes*—rather than establishes—the rationality it would impose on debate and can recognize no independent or transparadigmatic standards of argumentation, there can be no impartial court of appeals to which the several claims for superiority can be brought for adjudication. What counts as a reason in one scheme does not count as one in another; and since everybody shows up on a different field, everyone wins by default, if anything can be won when nothing is contested.

But we stray once again from the business at hand, which is not the legitimacy or illegitimacy of particular conversion schemes, but the distinction we quite easily and readily make between getting the joke or understanding the map's interests and getting at what the understood joke or map is "really" or "ultimately" up to or, even, getting at how the joke, say, cancels or inverts the "sense" it seems to affirm (creating, thus, an "in-version"), inadvertently but ineluctably honoring, for example, the very ethnic, racial, or cultural group it aspired and seemed to denigrate. As we have elsewhere seen, even the practical deconstructionist honors the distinction by starting analysis from some community sanctioned, logocentric meaning, some "traditional," "conventional," or widely accepted "reading," or some culturally inscribed trope, figural device, or set of oppositions (e.g., nature/nurture, speech/writing). At this point, we would insist only that the joke or map is a version of the (or a) world and that its mind-dependent interests are (approximately) knowable (knowable with as much "certainty" as we can know anything else) and distinguishable from other interests, including those we are personally interested in believing.

Of course, even in insisting on only so much we are obliged to assume, without sufficient warrant, that what is before us makes some kind of sense. We assume that the conceptual scheme before us is indeed a conceptual scheme and that it works pretty much the way our own would work, if it, rather than our own, were our own. For instance, what is said or written would not be "justified" unless so-and-so "believed" what I personally do not happen to believe (e.g., that the earth sits on the point of a pyramid or the back of a whale);

only on such and such an assumption would this or that be plausible, intelligible, or coherent. We adjust our standards of, while preserving our confidence in, plausibility, coherence, and so on; and thus as Putnam says, seconding a point made by Davidson, "an interpreted conceptual scheme will necessarily turn out to be for the most part like our own, however violently it may contradict our own in its higher reaches."[11]

Putting aside matters of "significance" for the moment and returning to the temporality of the text (to *when* it is a text), we can quite confidently affirm, in puzzle language, that a text *is not* a (literary or artistic) text (a system of conceptual entailments) *when* it is, say, a *doorstop* or what an interior designer might call a piece of *decor*. For instance, a "coffee-table" book has properties that contribute to the functioning of the room, not the text, as a symbol. Only when such a book is "read" does it have conceptual properties that contribute to the functioning of the text as a symbol or version. Moreover, a text *is not* a text (in our sense) *when* it is exhibited merely as an example of something produced in a certain historical period; or by a particular author; or in a specific kind of typeface (Baskerville, say); or by a particular typesetter; or in the service of certain production or marketing interests, and so on. Nor, to move to another level of concern, is a text a text *when* its conceptual and referential properties are considered in isolation from their contribution to the functioning of the (whole) work as a symbol or version, when they are considered, for example, with regard to the prevalence of "nature" or "power" images in eighteenth-century poetry; the persistence of "love and honor" themes in late seventeenth-century literature; or certain political, cultural, architectural, or whatever other interests. In these cases the text is a *resource* of materials that can be used in the justification of one or another thesis. The text is poured through a special interest sieve so that conceptual properties useful to the functioning of the thesis can be trapped and inutile properties filtered out. Of course, even here, the properties deemed useful to the thesis must be justified as those properties by some prior construction, though clearly justification here is *not* a *global* or *holistic* business; it is enough that the properties be locally warranted and serviceable to the thesis, that they have, say, common reference or referentiality.

In Sum

From all these "negative" moments we are led to conclude that a text *is* a text (in our sense) *when* it is *used* in a certain way and *is not* a text *when* it is *used* in other ways. We conclude that it is a text *when* and *only when* its conceptual properties (be they ever so complicated and rich or ever so political, cultural, psychoanalytic or whatever) *contribute to the functioning of the work as a version*, as a system of entailments answerable to some context-sensitive justification conditions.[12] A jar is never a door, except when, as ajar, it is an answer to a specific puzzle; and a red line on a piece of paper is never a road marker except when it is used (by mapmaker and mapreader) as an indicator of a route from Providence to Boston. Only when "ajar" and "red line" are *used* in certain ways (or are construed by the reader as *used* in certain ways) do they function as properties, respectively, of puzzle and road worlds. Of course, the principles at work in interpreting puzzles and road maps are also at work in our more complex, "literary" interpretations; and this is simply another way of saying that as our entailments become more entangled and our justification conditions accountable to more properties, our disagreements about "meaning" increase (or at any rate, are likely to increase), without becoming incapable of resolution, however, as long as there is some agreement about what will count as methodological criteria in the case at hand, which agreement, in turn, depends upon the sharing of some concepts and references.

Chapter 10
From Readers to Writers, Interpretation to Making

If the *text* is thoroughly conditioned (if, that is, its various elements are justified by a particular conceptual scheme or "make sense" relative to this rather than that principle of entailment or "meaning," to a flyswatting rather than a firestarting scenario, say), *readers*, on the other hand, are ready customers for the text's hard sell. They are ready because they are accustomed to learning and adapting to new conceptual schemes. In the process of negotiating their way through each and every day, they are obliged to understand and adapt to a rich assortment of conceptual schemes (employing many different kinds of references and concepts) and a wide variety of systems of organization (using the "same" references and concepts in different ways). Moreover, at the moment of contact with the text they are usually not committed to one and only one way of projecting "meanings." In this encounter, the strength of commitment of the parties is unevenly distributed: the text is determined, whereas the reader is complaisant and open, as always, to suggestion.

The position outlined here is, in my view, entirely compatible with that expressed by Kenneth Burke many years ago in "Lexicon Rhetoricae" under the concept of "margin of persuasion." In subsequent works Burke talks about what is to me a companionable, indeed a cognate, concept, the author's "rottenness for perfection," that is, the tendency to carry to term or "perfection" whatever possibilities the author's conceptual scheme opens up (even if such a "pathological" determination to be "fully justified" means that the hero must die or that the worlds predicted to collide by the theory will collide), but here he speaks, as I do, not of the rottenness, but of the "thoroughness" of the author and, on the other side, the malleability of the reader. The "margin of persuasion" is available because

First, there is the authority of the expert. The artist possessed by a certain pattern of experience is an "expert" in this pattern. He should thus be equipped to make it convincing, for the duration of the fiction at least. By thoroughness he should be able to overwhelm his reader and thus compel the reader to accept his interpretations. For a pattern of experience is an interpretation of life. Life being open to many interpretations, the reader is open to many interpretations. Only the madman or the genius or the temporarily exalted (as the lover, the terrified, or the sick) will have a pattern of experience so pronounced as to close him to the authority of other patterns of experience. The thoroughness of the artist's attack can "wear down" the reader until he accepts the artist's interpretation, the pattern of experience underlying the Symbol [i.e., the work]. . . . This "margin of persuasion" is further made possible by the fact that our modes of experience are ambiguous or fluctuant. That is, the normal person has a variety of feelings attached to the same object. A thunder-shower can cause terror if one is caught far from shore in a rowboat, or relief if it tempers the heat.[1]

Here, I submit, is wisdom incapable of being rendered chill and lifeless by the cold currents of our present problematizing climate. Despite structuralist (and other) claims to the contrary, the author turns out to be a perdurable and necessary "fiction" in many kinds of talk we cannot seem to do without.

Ad Hoc Categories and Fitness

What David Marr's model of reading looks like from the writer's side can perhaps be happily illustrated by drawing briefly upon some recent studies in cognitive psychology. In *Women, Fire, and Dangerous Things: What Categories Reveal About the Mind*, George Lakoff discusses, among many other things, categories based on "holistically structured activities," especially those investigated by Lawrence Barsalou. Of particular concern to us are what Barsalou calls "ad hoc categories," which depend upon some grasp of a large, complex, but nevertheless well-structured intentional situation. Barsalou has considered such categories, for example, as *things to take on a camping trip, foods not to eat on a diet, clothes to wear in the snow,* and *what to do for entertainment on the weekend.* How many such categories there are even a supercomputer with workaholic proclivities, after a lifetime at the job, would be hard-pressed to say. Indeed, anyone who still has a couple of neurons firing will immediately be able to come up with ten or twelve such categories in any ten second segment of time, perhaps these, for example: *statements likely to outrage an academic Marxist, items in the house that might be used as a doorstop* or *that might qualify as blunt instruments in an emergency* (a shoe repair emergency, say), *kinds of feathers you will undoubtedly never wear in your cap, kinds of discount stores the sultan of Brunei is unlikely to patronize, things that get your goat,* and so on. Left alone for a few minutes we could generate hundreds of these ad hoc, made-up-on-the-spot categories (and continue to do so every few minutes for the rest of our lives). Moreover, it is worth noting that:

1. Every area of human concern—fishing, cooking, vegetables, sub-atomic particles, and so on—offers limitless opportunities for the creation of new, never-before-thought-of categories.

2. Almost everyone I am familiar with or could conceivably have a conversation with would understand (immediately in most cases) these categories, understand each sufficiently well to be able to determine whether any proposed item belonged in or to it (whether it "fit" the category or not).

3. Such categories are not restricted by mood, mode, emotional quality, and so on (there can be comic, tragic, neo-platonic, hypothetical, and you-name-it categories).

4. To bring this series to a stop, if not an end, the category of kinds of categories that can be registered under the rubric of "ad hoc categories" is so capacious that it can include a category comprising elements that I cannot imagine the existence of, that I am in fact categorically prohibited from forming any image of whatsoever (e.g., "alien life forms that I cannot imagine"; this is a rich and densely populated category, but no alien life form my imagination enables me to have an image of will belong to the category).[2]

Now, to suppose that all or most of these emergent, respectable, bizarre, drunken, stolid, friendly, bitter, or phantasmagorical categories are determined in their specific nature (except perhaps in some extremely large and uninformative sense) by some specific Culture, History, Discourse, Profession or whatever is to use the capacity to suppose very parsimoniously or unimaginatively and, among other things, *to entertain a supposition that is itself not warranted or determined by history, culture,* or whatever. Thus, if the supposition (all our thoughts, speeches, acts, concepts, references are determined by our culture, epoch, episteme, or whatever) is true, then it is false, since the supposition itself is not culture-specific, culture-determined, or culture-limited. Although this is an easy objection, it is also, I think—despite the efforts of some to evade it or laugh it out of court—a *deep* one.[3] Our business now is to look into some striking and as yet undisclosed features of such categories; but in passing I would quickly note that there is no History, Culture, or whatever that is knowable or capable of being understood, apart from some scheme. There is no special relation that is the correspondence relation between our words (signs) or thoughts (mental representations or whatever) and what unmistakably *just is* History or Culture and so forth. To *know* what History or Culture *warrants* or *authorizes* (in any specific case of determination or justification) is to have access to what would be—if Reality were our concern—the *noumenal*, to have access to what *just is*. As always History or Culture warrants, authorizes, or legitimizes too much, and much of that authorized much contradicts or is incompatible with much of what else is authorized. There is now—as there was in the beginning and as, alas, there ever will be—only practices or inscriptions (or makings) and re-scriptions (remakings) that are more or less true, right, or fit.[4]

Most of our concepts, of course, involve categories rather than particulars or individuals (dogs and trees and horses rather than Buster, the oak outside my window, and Citation); and our most common, workaday, "normal-science" understanding of a category goes perhaps something like this: there are certain particular *entities* (or things) that have certain *properties* in certain *relations* with one another; those things with similar properties in similar relations belong to the same category. Whether a thing belongs in the category or not is a matter of making likeness/difference decisions according to some relatively stable, conventionally fixed notion of appropriate properties and relations.

Putting aside the value or validity of such an understanding of categories, we can say that our ad hoc categories are not at all like our "normal" categories. However dependent such categories may be upon "preexistent," conventional elements, they are themselves neither fixed nor conventional, since they are created on the spot to serve some local, emergent exigency or purpose. Moreover, the items making up or belonging to an ad hoc category are extraordinarily heterogeneous, sharing virtually no common properties in necessary and predictable relations. For example, the *things* in the category "things to take on a camping trip"—sleeping bags, tent poles, matches, bug spray, marshmallows, etc.—have, as objects, virtually nothing in common, though they all certainly belong to the camping trip category every bit as securely as Buster belongs to the dog category. And as the interests and conditions of the camping trip change, so too do the appropriate or right things. Since Bill and Betty are not taking a camping trip for the reasons that Frank and Shirley are taking theirs, one trip but not the other will have room for walking shoes, 35mm cameras, the children, Biff and Beth, and so on. To understand what does or does not belong we must know, in this case, which couple is going on what kind of camping trip for what reason.[5]

What the items in the ad hoc category have in common, then, is not some common property (or set of properties) or some internal structural relation but an interest relativity, an intelligible connection to some subsumptive purpose or some controlling context of delimited concern. Of such categories, Lakoff notes that they

> must be constructed on the basis of one's cognitive models of the subject matter under consideration. . . . such categories have prototype structure—structure that does not exist in advance, since the category does not exist in advance. Barsalou argues that in such cases, the nature of the category is principally determined by goals and that such goal structure is a function of one's cognitive models [conceptual schemes, schemes of interpretation].[6]

Interestingly, the description that applies here to ad hoc categories has a fitting analogue in that applied to meaning in frame semantics, as discussed by Charles Fillmore. Reporting on recent work, Lakoff notes that Fillmore has demonstrated that the "meanings of lexical items—words and morphemes—are characterized in terms of cognitive models." In short, "the meaning of each lexical item is represented as an element in an ICM [an Idealized Cognitive Model]"; this model "as a whole is taken as the background against which the word is defined."[7] And, of course, all this is perfectly compatible with our previous discussion of assertibility conditions and of the determination of references and concepts, objects and meanings, by interests, background assumptions, and purposes, which together provide, from discourse to discourse, the standard or test of rational acceptability (i.e., references and meanings are admissible or not relative to these).

Ad Hoc Categories and Motivation

That voices from various intellectual and research communities are coming together to make up something like a choir is not a matter of distress to the friends of euphony (and pluralism). Nevertheless, we should perhaps absent ourselves from any open displays of our felicity awhile and consider briefly one or two more tonal qualities in the register of ad hoc categories. For one thing, it is important to recognize that in general these categories are based, as Lakoff says, on "holistically structured activities," such as shopping, camping, removing articles from a burning building, writing a lyric poem, etc., and undertaken in certain circumstances for certain reasons or purposes. As we have noted above, these circumstances and purposes establish conditions of inclusion or exclusion for items. Moreover, and this is worth underscoring, although we can almost always determine immediately whether an item belongs in or fits the category, we can *never predict all*—and rarely predict many—*of the items that will be included in any given locally emergent category* (of the holistically structured kind). Unlike the items in what for convenience we have called "normal science," workaday categories, those included in these categories are neither *arbitrary* nor *predictable*. Rather, the items included are, as Lakoff says, *motivated*.[8]

Now what logical positivists, certain "scientists," all monists, "epistemists," "arche-writists," and most historicists want are not "motivated" but arbitrary or predictable ("always already") items in categories that function in predictable ways in preestablished systems of entailment with (usually) clearly spelled out computational rules. For some "just-is-ists," for example, what particular things will go into the "dog" category has been determined for ever and ever, apart from any or all particular circumstances and purposes, by specifying just what common properties in what relations just are essential to "dog." We know, of course, what "dog" or "History" or the "episteme" or the culture is prior to our examination of cases. More broadly, what *makes true* any statement or assertion is something known about the nature of, say, history or culture beforehand, or, to put the case more damningly, what *makes true* (or *interesting*) any statements about, say, this or that literary text are "facts" (about economics or colonialism, say) known independently of and apart from the specific scheme of representation in hand, a specific, interest-relative text, say. Meanings and references are subject to prior constraint, prior justification, so that, oddly, conditions anteceding the assertibility or justification conditions that determine specific meaning and reference are taken to determine locally specific meaning and reference. Statements within one conceptual scheme are *made true* by the "facts" of another scheme, a primary or subsumptive scheme—economics, psychoanalysis, or colonialism, for example.

Of course, nothing in these remarks is designed to suggest that our ad hoc categories and other holistic structures *are not* situated in history or culture or whatever—a camping or shopping trip is one thing at this time and in this culture and quite another thing in that time and that culture. What these remarks do affirm, however, is that *within every culture, however restricted its range of terms and rules of inference and reference, there is always room for an indefinite, a virtually infinite number of different and even contradictory statements and views.* Discussing a related issue, Lakoff notes that "It is often assumed that conceptual systems are monolithic, that they provide a single, consistent world view . . . but [the fact is] that people can have many ways *within a single conceptual system and a single language* of conceptualizing a domain." "It is simply a fact that it is possible for an individual to understand the same domain of experience in different and inconsistent ways."[9] Of course, Hilary Putnam makes a similar point, as we have seen, when he says that "no matter what operational and theoretical constraints our practice may impose on our use of language, there are always infinitely many different reference relations . . . which satisfy all the constraints."[10]

To say that an item in a category is "motivated" (and implicitly, therefore, that it is neither arbitrary nor predictable) is simply to say that it fits the conditions that it is authorized by, that it can serve as an appropriate answer to a question legitimately implicated in its intentional situation. For example, "can of pork and beans" is one of the many appropriate answers built into the questions implicit in the "things to take on a camping trip" category. More directly, we can say that the item "satisfies" a condition made possible by the intentional situation. Moreover, its "appropriateness" or "fit" is what makes it "true."

Intentional States and Satisfactions

To clarify what is embedded in the notion of "satisfaction" as it is used in the context of holistically structured activities, we will have to review quickly some of the fundamental features of intentionality, at least those relevant to this discussion.[11] In the first place, the purpose of our having mental states is to represent the world (or, more properly, to make representations of worlds) to ourselves, so that we can have something (some things) to be concerned about or interested in. Being *about something* is what makes a mental state *intentional* (intending, of course, is but one of the psychological types of intentionality and has no preeminence among the other types, such as, hoping, fearing, believing, desiring, being thirsty or hungry and so forth).

Now since we can have various kinds of "attitudes" toward the same "world" and the same "attitude" toward different "worlds," it is helpful to differentiate between the "content" and "psychological type" of any intentional state, with "content" being the "world" the state is about and "type" being a modal relation to that "world." For example, with regard to the *drink* in front of me, I can "believe" *it* is coffee, "wish" *it* to be hot, "fear" *it* to be cold, and so on. In short, about the same drink I can have many attitudes (just as I can have the same attitude toward many things: I can "wish" the Red Sox would win a world series, "wish" it would rain, and so on). Moreover, because intentional states take a stance or have an "attitude" toward a "world," they will be *fulfilled* or *satisfied* or *true* in that world depending upon how well they work or function *in that world*. Less cryptically, the large consequence of our having intentions in a world is that

> our beliefs will be true if they match the way the world is, false if they don't; our desires will be fulfilled or frustrated, our intentions carried out or not carried out. In general, then, intentional states have "conditions of satisfaction." *Each state itself determines under what conditions it is true* (if, say, it is a belief) or *under what conditions it is fulfilled* (if, say, it is a desire) and *under what conditions it is carried out* (if it is an intention). In each case the mental state represents its own conditions of satisfaction.[12]

Finally (at least for our purposes), and perhaps most important, it is often the case that the "intention" occasions or realizes the state of affairs it "intends." In such cases, thinking so is what makes so (causes to make so). For example, my *wish* to have a complementary balance weight on this side of the canvas to the mass and color on that side of the canvas will *cause* or bring about the very state of affairs represented in the mental state or intention. Or, to take a homelier case, my desire to raise my hand causes my hand to shoot up. Thus, the state of affairs represented as desirable in my mental state causes the state of affairs that is the satisfaction of that representation. In few, it frequently happens that the state of affairs in the representation is brought about by the representation, and when this happens (when, as John Searle says, "the mind brings about the very state of affairs it has been thinking about"),[13] the "mind" creates its own conditions of satisfaction.

For our purposes, such internally occasioned conditions of satisfaction, such examples of what Searle calls "intentional causation," are relevant to the making and understanding of coherence in holistic structures, such as ad hoc categories, essays, epics, critical theories, etc. To avoid or forestall the charge that I have inadvertently slipped back into the world of foundationalism, or naive realism, by differentiating between type and content and talking about the way *the world is*, I perhaps should point out that the distinction is an analytic convenience, that, of course, in any state of intentionality there is never a content apart from a type—or a type without a content—and that the view of intentionality outlined here privileges no particular world or version. More important, at least for the moment, although not privileging any world, the view does assert that where there is a world there is an intentionality and that where there is intentionality there are conditions of satisfaction, and where there are conditions of satisfaction there is rationality. And, certainly, it is never the case

that "anything goes" where there are conditions of rational acceptability. Where "fit," "cohere," "appropriate" are, "getting it right"—in
this world—is *in* and "anything goes" is *out*.

Texts and Theories as Ad Hoc Categories

Returning now to holistic structures, I would suggest that the dynamics at work in such smaller structures as ad hoc categories are the
same as those operating in such larger structures as essays, poems, or
novels. The "intentional causation" and "motivation" characterizing
small-scale, ad hoc, intentional structures characterize large-scale
ones as well. Indeed, extrapolation and analogy invite us to observe
that the various texts, oral and written, with which we all deal from
day to day—including our letters, editorials, epics, novels, theories,
harangues, sermons, directives, and so on—are, speaking pejora-
tively, overreaching and self-inflated ad hoc categories or, speaking
melioratively, the selfsame categories informed by noble ambition. In
a manner of speaking, then, ad hoc categories, the products of holistically structured activities, are minimalist versions of our maximal
forms, including our theories and literary works. Our literary works
and our critical theories are the artifactual consequences of *extended*
holistically structured activities.

In the larger models, as in the smaller, we find "intentional causation" and "motivated" items. Of course, since the larger structures
often or usually involve argument or narrative progression and development, not only are their constituent elements *motivated* but so
are the order, sequence, arrangement, and emphasis of those elements. As any given text unfolds it brings about, it works out and
toward, in good "intentional causation" fashion, its own conditions of
satisfaction. To the extent that the text is to its own self true, it regularly deploys its elements (terms, figures, images, characters, actions,
propositions, or whatever) in ways that are neither arbitrary nor predictable, but motivated—by the scheme, system, the overall intention.
Otherwise, nothing would come of nothing; nothing would be expressed because there would be nothing to say and no reason (or justification) for saying it. As readers of such justified large-scale
structures, we have the satisfaction of knowing that the satisfaction
conditions of the text are knowable.

Moreover, supported by the foregoing understanding of what is
involved in understanding a version that would not—and could not—
be a version unless it were justified by some intentionality/rationality,
we can say, anticipating ourselves slightly, that what takes the abysmal
out of the abyss, the unending chase of the trace out of the reading

of the text, the endless "textile" out of the weave of signification, is "fit," "rightness," "appropriateness," etc. The journey through the labyrinth of deferred signification is interrupted by finding a fit (a fit that really fits the scheme). Virtually every constituent element of the text could "be" something other than what it "is" under this particular description (this scheme, this system of intentionality) or could function in some way other than how it does under this description, but if this is *this* rather than *that* kind of holistic structure, then the "bill" is the duck's, not the customer's and not just maybe or possibly the duck's, but the duck's absolutely, within this constitutive, intentional scheme. The "fact" is that "duck," but not "customer," is an *essential* property of a certain intentionally organized or structured description. "Duck," but not "customer," makes a *necessary* contribution to the functioning of the work (the intentional construct) as a whole, necessary in the sense that "duck" is a "state of affairs" that *necessitates and is necessitated by one but not another overall intentionality.*

Essentialism in Immanent Worlds

Here, then, are "essentialism" and "objectivity," but essentialism and objectivity without "foundationalism," that is, without a ready-made world of things to which we are obliged to accommodate our thoughts and language if we want to speak meaningfully and not just metaphorically or "poetically." We are talking about knowable, internally necessary, highly motivated particulars within an internally coherent (more or less), thoroughly justified (more or less) intentional system, about the cooperative functioning of interest-determined elements within the system of their interest (their meaning and reference).

Because the text before us, as the product of a complex series of holistically structured activities, is interest-determined all the way down, not just any conceptual scheme that happens to interest us will suit the interests of the text. If *our interpretive scheme* is a system of rationality (a system which makes references and meanings as it makes assertibility conditions—as it inevitably is), whereas *the text* just intransigently happens to be conditioned or determined by another, entirely different system, then it is extremely unlikely that, even with very strenuous pushing and shoving, our "alien" system will be able to make the whole (self-satisfied and self-interested) text fit within the contours of our scheme's desires and interests. The situation here is analogous to one described by Putnam, in which the task is to translate from one language to another. As Putnam notes, "if what we are doing is forcing our pattern of thought on a linguistic scheme which doesn't have structural similarities to ours, one which doesn't 'map' onto ours under any mapping that is 'natural' (to us), we would expect to pay a price later on, when we try to extend our first translations of isolated utterances to a scheme for interpreting the whole language."[14] What applies to translation applies as well to interpretation: we would expect to run into trouble later in the reading process if what we were doing initially was forcing a pattern of thought with its own justification conditions on a system of language governed by quite a different pattern of thought with its quite different justification conditions. The text before us would become "strange," *even to us*, if we persisted in our deluded ways and tried, say, to burden our "duck" with a bill that must be paid to the cashier (or our cashier with the "bill" of a duck).

Running Into and Getting Beyond the Hermeneutic Wall

From the time we were pups we have heard about how we more than half create what we see, about the activity of the reader and the passivity of the text. From way back when we have heard about the willingness of the text to adjust to the categorical demands of our always already formed schemes, about the pliability and ductility of the text, about, to put a fine point on't, the hermeneutic circle (i.e., the tendency to see subsequent events or meanings in the light of our antecedent determinations, to see or find what we are categorically prepared to see or find, to self-fulfill our prophecies in predictable ways). Now my ambition here is not so retrograde as to wish to teach old dogs brand-new, never-heard-of-before tricks or to suggest that there is nothing but legerdemain and illusion in the old hermeneutic-circle tricks. More modestly, I seek only to submit a brief on behalf of the unrepresented (or underrepresented) plaintiff, insisting therein, among other things, that though the reader is certainly busy, the text is just as certainly not passive, that the singlemindedness of the reader is not always—or even usually—sufficient to overwhelm the bullheadedness of the text, and that against the rush of the categorical imperative on the track of the hermeneutic circle there is frequently raised by the text the obstacle of the "hermeneutic wall."

If, on the reader's side, the "hermeneutic circle" is an irresistible force, then, on the author-text's side, the "hermeneutic wall" is an immovable object. Sometimes object yields to force (some trains simply will not become untracked and some minds will not be persuaded or admit defeat), and sometimes force, to object. When force yields to object (when, that is, the reader revises a working hypothesis or governing conception of the holistic structure to accommodate material that recalcitrantly refuses to adapt to what now seems to be a "misconception"), the "wall" ceases to be an obstacle, a wall, and becomes a transfer depot, a changeover stop that at once prevents the hermeneutic traveler from going further astray and sets him or her off in the "right" (or "fitting") direction. Until the wall becomes a depot, however, it is a wall, an obstacle. What it erects in the path of the reader's locomotive (or "logo-motion") is a barrier that the reader, in order to have his or her way, must either deny (burst through) or explain away (get around), and the recalcitrant material—phrase, statement, action or whatever—is experienced as recalcitrant because it will not yield and cannot be ignored. It cannot be seen—even by a determined or resolute reader—as *arbitrary* or *accidental*. It is not *predictable* from within the reader's governing scheme of interpretation, and it is not—or cannot be seen to be—motivated by the preferred scheme. The material has a place (a justification), it seems, but the reader cannot find it, cannot find a place for the material within his or her system.

Curiously, but quite appropriately, then, the more successful readers have been in negotiating their way from text to text, situation to situation, and motivation to motivation, in developing and assimilating linguistic practices, in exercising their empathy and their imaginative capacities generally, the more susceptible they become to the wily insinuations and seductive blandishments of each new text. As they extend their knowledge and refine their skills, learning more and more as they go about the devilishly devious devices of duplicitous dealing in various worlds of denotation, depiction, and description, they become progressively better and better victims of each new trick practiced upon them.

Simply, readers (1) know that there are no constraints built into a Language or Culture that prevent it from expressing many quite different and often quite contradictory things; (2) have read with understanding many different texts written in many historical eras from many different, often conflicting, points of view; (3) know that their survival—or, more modestly, their getting on from day to day—depends on accommodating themselves to a variety of holistic structures (people say things to them, and they usually act in response in ways that do not seem to be displeasing or incomprehensible to them); (4) are often satisfied from day to day (they say things to others, and the others act in ways not disappointing to their expectations). Because all these factors (and more) obtain, readers are prepared to understand and accommodate themselves to any number of new and, in some respects, unique holistic structures with their own peculiar assertibility conditions. Readers are not, however, absolutely and unalterably disposed to read every new text one way rather than another, to approach every new text or situation as though it were always already interpreted and as though they always already understood it (or "they" and "it" were both already spoken for by some socially/historically/politically/culturally coded system of terms and transformation or substitution/combination rules).

Our readers are predisposed to make some kind of sense of what is before them, to find some principle(s) of reasonableness at work in the text, to suppose that others go about the business of making their kind of sense in pretty much the same ways our readers go about making their kind of sense (such a predisposition, they find, is a paying policy, and the coin it pays off in is satisfaction, mutual satisfaction; thus they are satisfied to learn the satisfaction conditions of the text). But these readers are not programmed to produce or generate, according to some algorithm, these and only these specific interpretations.

Writing as a Holistic and Practical Activity

What should be apparent is that writing and interpreting are differently located and sponsored instances of similar processes. If interpretation is, as we have earlier shown, a *global enterprise*, writing is a *holistic activity*. That is, in neither case can we get very far by concentrating on words, objects, references, statements, or any parts or group of parts considered independently of that rationality which endows such parts with their specific meaning and significance and the objects with their aspectual functionality.

Moreover, from our consideration of large and small scale ad hoc categories, it should also be apparent that writing (speaking/making) and reading (interpretation of all kinds) are *practical* not theoretical endeavors and that the kind of reasoning necessary to both is *practical* not theoretical reasoning. Now practical reasoning is always a kind of cognitive or mental barnstorming, a flying by the seat of one's pants, an activity requiring, at any rate, imagination and sensibility, a gift for trial and error, for visions and revisions, for choosing among alternatives, for making quick adjustments in mid stride, and so on. Such reasoning is, of course, goal-oriented, demanding of its practitioners an ability to imagine, revise, and judge options, to formulate and evaluate choices in the light of need, wish, expectation, or desire. In our mind's eye, we can catch practical reasoning in characteristic power and act by watching it run creatively and with moderate speed across a shallow stream: it avoids a fall into the drink by quickly imagining and assessing the available options and then choosing to step on those rocks that best seem, under the circumstances, to facilitate progress and thereby best satisfy the desire to get to the other side. Now if we imagine such reasoning crossing several streams, each with its own unpredictable configuration of partially exposed stones, climbing several hills, negotiating for food with several farmers, finding shelter in a variety of inhospitable terrains, devising means to span several chasms, and so on, we will quickly understand, I think, why there can be no foolproof, fail-safe model, machine, or (structuralist) mechanism for generating either ad hoc categories ("meaningful" categories, that is) or interpretations of them.

It is certainly possible, of course, for a certain properly "programmed" machine or a certain particularly constituted culture to produce the familiar sentence "I didn't say he stole it," but it is not so easy for the machine or Culture to mean anything in particular by it. The sentence is but the verbal part, the verbally expressed (or exposed) part, of the total (global) context determining local, specific meaning. As parts of the inexplicit or indirectly and inaudibly expressed meaning of the sentence—more properly, the *meaning conditions* of the sentence—we would include kind of background knowledge understood, kind of situation assumed, purpose or intentionality presupposed. In a fundamental sense, the *verbal* part is the least important part of the "meaning," since it determines virtually nothing in itself and is determined in its specific nature, value, and emphases by all that is *unexpressed* or *uninscribed*. This, of course, is not to say that these particular words are unnecessary or unimportant; words of some kind are absolutely necessary to the meaning, and these particular words are not unimportant, only less important than some other things.[15] And sometimes, of course, these very words are necessary, are just right, in the sense that on this occasion or under these circumstances no other words we can think of would work or fit quite so well.

There is all the difference in the world (at times at least) between saying "The remorseful prince carried the dead statesman from the queen's closet" and saying "The mad, ignoble prince lugged the guts of the dead old fool from the shameless queen's dishonored bedchamber," but the difference is not a function of the words, but of the context and conditions establishing the appropriateness and choice of the words. In both instances the referential situation could be the "same" (Hamlet, for example, removes Polonius from Gertrude's room), but the "meaning" of the situation is different in the two cases. What interests us here is not "reference" (though it is important that the two situations share references), but "meaning," and the "meaning" is determined by the *whole situation*, by whatever *complex* it is that makes "lugs" appropriate to one and "carries" appropriate to the other description. And even if we factored into our machine or Culture a sort of "ordinary reference" or "stereotype" semantics (i.e., a list of standard beliefs about various things) and a deductive reasoning capacity and declared inadmissible all "funny" possibilities (i.e., all metaphoric, poetic, ironic, or other possibilities), we would still have these possibilities, among innumerable others, for our "I didn't say he stole it" sentence, possibilities emerging simply from giving successive emphasis to each of the six words in the sentence: *I* . . . (it wasn't I; somebody else said so); *didn't* . . . (my opinion has been misstated, misquoted); *say* . . . (I may have suggested it, but I didn't say it); *he* . . . (I said someone else stole it); *stole* . . . (but he does have it in his possession, doesn't he?); and . . . *it* (I said he stole something else).[16]

Given that there is apparently no limit to the number of conceptual systems or systems of "meaning" we can devise and understand; that there is no way of deriving all these systems from or reducing all of them to some particular basal mechanism (some one structural model with its stable sets and rules of transformation), whether neuronal, sexual, social, political, economic, or other; and that there is no immediate (or even long-range) likelihood that we will come up with a Grand Unified Theory (a GUT or a super-GUT) of creativity (or of epistemology, explanation, coherence, imagination and so on), it is not surprising that we frequently misunderstand one another (that coming from where we are coming from, we fail to see where someone else is coming from). On the other and truly startling side, however, it is wonderful, awesome, and amazing that we understand so much, indeed, most of what we see, hear, and read, despite the fact that we disagree with (or reject as "not true for us") so much of the much we understand. Against our theoretical shortcomings, then, we can place our practical successes in making and understanding conceptual systems. If we have inadequate or insufficient *theories*, we have remarkably successful *practices*. And if we are unlikely ever to develop a single, coherent theory to explain fully how we do what we do, we can nevertheless provide a fairly satisfying account of what it is we seem to do when we make or understand.

Chapter 11
Human "Nature" and Language "Universals"

For the processes of making and understanding to work so well, there must be some durabilities or stabilities underlying our "symbolic" activities. Talking and writing to others and understanding others depend upon having some references, concepts, and conceptions of rationality in common. We could neither make nor understand sense unless we had some notion of what it was like to make sense, some working notion(s) of what intelligibility requires.

Body Language and Conceptual Schemes

Recent work in cognitive psychology—especially that on category formation and classification systems—has done much to illuminate the "material" bases of our conceptual schemes, showing, for example, that our *forms of reason* have their bases in our bodily experiences. Moreover, it seems that whatever imagination is (like creativity, it is undoubtedly many things), it is indispensable to the shaping of our basic categories and perceptual gestalts into forms of reason. This, at any rate, is the view of George Lakoff (among others), who observes that "imagination, especially metaphor and metonymy, . . . transforms the general schemas defined by our animal experience into forms of reason." Summing up much of his research on what categories reveal about the mind, Lakoff identifies the kinds of schemas or concepts that underlie conceptual systems, thereby disclosing the kinds of human saliencies we can reasonably expect to persist across vast differences in actual conceptual schemes:

What kinds of concepts is one most likely to find as one surveys conceptual systems? First, kinesthetic-image schemas: concepts like UP-DOWN, IN-OUT, PART-WHOLE [top-bottom, center-periphery, here-gone . . .], etc. Second, basic-level concepts for things, states, activities in one's immediate experience: body parts, plants and animals, basic-level artifacts, basic colors, basic emotions, etc. [N.B. We are not talking about any irreducible, primitive, underived "out there," but about "concept" or "category" persistences deriving from our physical nature and our forms of social organization, our ways of valuing and being interested in "things."] Third, metaphorical concepts based on universal experiences: thus it would not be surprising to find MORE being UP, or ANGER being understood in terms of HEAT or PRESSURE. There are a fair number of such things that one would not expect to vary much. All of these are tied very closely to well-structured experience. I would not expect radical variation in these three areas. I *would* expect a fair amount of variation in organization and use.[1]

Whatever "stuff" we are ultimately made of or however variously we may discuss our selves and our relations to others (in terms, for example, of atoms, molecules, neurons, electrochemical states, commodities, balances of power, and so on), it seems to be the case that there are a good many relatively stable kinds of *phenomenal* experiences underlying and supporting our various conceptual schemes, such as our wave, particle, and other abstract schemes of one kind and another, which remain attached to phenomenal categories and metaphors in their expression or articulation (in descriptions and explanations). Although intersubjectivity among speakers increases proportionately to the number of background assumptions they share, we all know first hand of our inexhaustible capacity to learn new conceptual schemes, to move with ease from one scheme to another. This capacity—this conceptualizing ability—eludes formalization, but it is clearly the energetic issue of the union of bodily (phenomenal) experience and imagination.[2] Our forms of reason and representation (even our abstract forms) are, then, very much *our* forms, systems rooted in our carbon-based, nutrient-rich clay.

The Body and Systems of Reasoning

In full foliation, of course, our systems are strikingly different from one another in their "entities," emphases, ordering principles, in their structural configurations, and in their aims, but before we consider what Lakoff stresses at the end of the passage quoted above, that is, variations in *use* and *organization*, we should look briefly at other durabilities or persistences in our systems, along with their possible connection to somatic or phenomenal experience. To what has been noted above, we would want to add, for example, the relatively stable procedures we follow in building or establishing arguments, the stabilities in our systems of inference or reference. Simply put, we tend to work inductively, deductively, or analogically; these are our principal *modes* of reasoning, and if we are not using one, we are using another mode or some combination of them. To understand a conceptual system (one expressed in words) we need to know not only *what* is talked about but *how* the subject matter under discussion is talked about (what kind of account is given of what is talked about). In short, we need to know not only what the speaker/writer talks *about*, but what he or she talks *with*—the system of reasoning.[3]

If these are the three (or are among the) basic modes of reasoning (of concatenating propositions or connecting inferences), then a little reflection will speedily disclose, I think, their affiliation with the common soil. At any rate, it requires no very turbulent imagination to suppose that the inductive and deductive modes are but metaphorically refined and extended versions of what Lakoff has called kinesthetic-image schemas (down-up, up-down; lower-higher, higher-lower; less to more-more to less; . . .), whereas the analogical is easily conceived as a metaphorically refined version of "basic-level" category formation, where likeness and difference are measured against a best exemplar, say, or where two perceptually discrete things are linked together by virtue of some perceived ground of similarity.[4]

The Body and Systems of Depiction, Expression, and Representation

And what goes for our forms of reasoning or argumentation goes also for our various forms of description and depiction, of representation and narration. Even such a simple narrative as "John ate the apple" is a rich presuppositional complex based on an assortment of "phenomenal" interests and values, interests for example, in gestalts, bounded entities in space (Johns and apples), in before/after, here/gone states, in priority, sequence, etc. Our basic descriptive patterns—top to bottom, bottom to top, center to periphery, least to most important, chronological, and so on—wear their origins as openly as the son wears his mother's prominent nose (or, say, eye color) on his face.

Also, most of the forms and devices of disclosure and representation found, say, in novels and dramas—consecutive, consequential action (this happens which leads to this which leads to this), flashbacks, flashforwards, parallel lines of action or subplots, and so on—can easily be seen as complex variations on or imaginatively developed versions of the structural patterns exhibited in various "image schemas," for example, those concerned with the perception of simple causation and near-far, before-after states. In these and other patterns, whether verbal, pictorial, or otherwise, we find highly elaborated versions of "kinesthetic-image schemas." Thus, not only the forms of reason but the various forms of depiction, description, and representation (in literature, painting, music, etc.) undoubtedly have a grounding in the features of phenomenal, bodily experience. (Of course, it should go without saying that such experience is interested and value-laden; it shows us what sorts of "bounded entities," basic concepts, and relational possibilities we are interested in and supplies us with the sorts of materials we will need in forming our various representations of various worlds or versions.)

The Durability of Markers and Stereotypes

Concerning various kinds of stabilities on which we can depend in the creation and understanding of new conceptual systems, we have already said much, especially in the earlier discussion of the preservation of some meanings and references across theory changes. Nevertheless, it is perhaps worth recalling that there would be no such thing as linguistic competence among the users of a given language if a certain indefinitely large number of *syntactic, semantic*, and *logical* markers did not retain their functions within radically different schemes of description or representation. Every competent speaker of a given language knows, for example, how indexical words like *me, I, here*, or *there*, can maintain identity of reference while changing meaning: when *you* and *I* are alone together talking about *you* and *me*, we both know that "I" mean by *I* what "you" mean by *you* when the person of reference is *me*.

Of course, the terms and phrases of any given language most immediately connected to the concepts of our "kinesthetic-image schemas"—that is, those relating for instance to time (now, later, earlier, in a minute, when, while, and so on), space (before, after, beneath, beside, on top of, and so on), and "quantity" (more, less, greater than, in addition, moreover, furthermore, and so on)—are generally quite indifferent, functionally speaking, to the specific interests of the scheme in which they find themselves (they are mercenaries rather than patriots), as are as well all such "logical" markers or "argument" movers as "if . . . then," "not only . . . but also," "first," "on the other hand," etc.

Also, we have previously discussed how some of our references, some of the extensions of our terms, are fixed by experts, by those whose determinations we have consented to trust (we have privileged for purposes of reference some descriptions—the chemical ones—of gold and water, for example), and we are all the experts of our own nominations (I call my dog Buster and my car Bob, and in all contexts they remain and are referred to as Buster and Bob). Moreover, we have noted that what enables people with different *perceptual prototypes* and different *conceptions* of the subjects under discussion to carry on successful conversations are "stereotypes," arrays of widespread, general notions about the subjects (water is wet, a liquid when not a solid, suitable for swimming, etc.), availabilities and aspects that make sustained discussion possible. Without "stereotypes" there is no conversation, no sharing of concepts; individuals are *joined* by "stereotypes" and separated—often at least—by perceptual prototypes, mental contents, and conceptions.

Immanent Domains and Domain Competence

Now from linguistic competence and "stereotypes" in general, we can move easily and naturally, by way of analogy, to a consideration of our "stereotypical proficiency" in a vast, indeed incalculable, number of domains of experience. This proficiency in various domains we might appropriately call our "experience competence" or, perhaps even more aptly, our "domain competence." As we acquire more experience, we gain more principles of reasoning and establish a wider basis of analogy. We gain, in short, more competence in more domains. Wherever our understanding has traveled it has brought back from each excursion materials of competence, which remain available for subsequent use or pleasure. To be familiar with a domain is to have learned the conditions determining meaning and reference in that domain, is to have acquired a practice and a body of "knowledge." The more we experience and read the more extensive our competence becomes. So extensive and diverse is our working knowledge that no satisfactory summary account can be given of it. Nevertheless, something of its nature can be suggested by considering in a very sketchy fashion what we might all dependably know about the weather or transportation, say, and its various modes. Special kinds and degrees of weather smartness aside, large numbers of us know that generally speaking it's warmer in the summer than in the winter, that London gets more rain each year than Phoenix, Arizona, that snowblowers are not a necessary expense in Cuba, that ground fog decreases driving visibility, and on and on. Concerning transportation and its modes, we know about all kinds of vehicles (cars, trucks, boats, planes, trains, chariots, coaches, horses). Additionally, we know much about when various forms of the various kinds were in use (in what century or among what ancient people, say), about their speeds, sources of energy, susceptibility to breakdown or exhaustion, and so on and on. And as it is with these domains, so it is also with commerce, forms of government, sailing, shopping, baseball, scientific theories, religions, ad virtually infinitum.

Further, and perhaps more important, because the various domains are capable of subdivision (cooking, say, has various branches and hence various elements and protocols within each of its branches), our competence is similarly divisible. And because the actual number of domains under the command of any individual is never fully specifiable (if only because we may continue to think of additional, new domains within our competence—each "ad hoc category" is, in a sense, a specialized domain of competence with its proper entities, relations, and inclusion and exclusion conditions), we are always more competent than we know. Moreover, as we narrow the domain (by focusing, for example, on one of its subdivisions), we restrict the number and kind of stereotypes that can appropriately obtain: the "swim-in-ableness" of water does not obtain when the domain of concern is fire extinguishing. Even at its tightest and most restrictive, however, when ready intersubjective understanding depends on the sharing of very specific background assumptions, the particular domain does not become permanently inaccessible to the layman, become so paradigm locked as to preclude translation, if only because, tight as it is, it cannot escape involvement in the general durabilities noted above (and cannot elude the grasp of the imagination, which extends its reach by stretching exercises).

At this point, where moving from one specific domain to the next determines or affects the applicability of the "stereotype" knowledge, we begin to confront the dynamics of specific making and understanding. Here, a change of domain brings with it a change of meaning and reference, a change in justification conditions or conditions of reasonableness. In the domain of fishing, the "fly" is quite a different thing from the "fly" in the domain of an entomology lab or of a zipper factory. Although clearly there are circumstances in which all three (domain) "flies" could be in a single scenario (an insectual fly could buzz about a fly fisherman's unzipped fly), our weakness for efficiency, our desire to shorten the mental work week inclines us to find in the "usual" situation the "usual" fly. Unless something emerges to suggest that the "customary" does not obtain, that the prevailing winds are not blowing, we tend to assume, as "computer talk" would have it, that the "default" function is on, the "default" value in effect; in other words, the most common meaning or reference applies.

Of course, we immediately know when the "default" value is not in effect, because the assumed meaning does not "work" or "fit." In more than nine out of ten cases, the fly we swat will not be in a fisherman's gear box or have interlocking teeth and be on the front of a pair of trousers. Because the "default" values of the terms found in any given domain usually obtain, we initially choose them. But because those values do not always obtain, we are occasionally surprised by incongruity, by ill-fittingness, at which point we scramble about in an effort to make the fit we do not immediately find.

Textual Domains and Literary Competence

Concerning domains of competence, it is important to recognize that while a vast number, perhaps even a majority, of them emerge from our persistent and mostly successful negotiations with the events of quotidian existence (we have competence, of course, in visual, aural, olfactory, tactile, and gustatory domains, as well as in "language" domains), virtually all that we *know* about much of what we know comes from "texts" of one kind or another (verbal texts as well as, say, movies, soundtapes, videotapes, museum exhibits, maps, or graphs). In these "textual" domains, as in others, our "default" knowledge grows in proportion to our competence (or our competence grows in proportion to our default knowledge). Historians of science, say, become adept at reading about and understanding a good many "ancient," "outdated" theoretical constructs with which in their personal and private capacity they may disagree, and even though they personally would no longer use such *terms* (phlogiston, say) in such *ways* to describe such *things*, they have no trouble understanding what any given theory is trying to give an account of and how it goes about accounting for it, or even how it differs from a variety of similar accounts vying for supremacy at the time. Moreover, they can indicate how the default values of certain terms have changed over the years.

To a general "literary competence," which, of course, exists in various degrees of range and refinement, we can add such specialized competencies as an Austen competence, a Shakespeare competence, and a sonnet sequence competence, each of which enables its bearer to spot almost immediately the typical or characteristic quality or to determine with ease whether, say, a given unattributed or contested passage belongs in the Austen "canon" or even whether a given passage could have been extracted from a particular text, such as *Emma*. Even if the passage in question was not in fact taken from a Shakespearean or Austenian text, we would expect the reader with Shakespeare or Austen competence to be able to give a reasonable, well-justified answer to the question of whether the passage had—or could be read as having—a place in *Othello* or an appropriateness coming from the mouth of Elizabeth Bennet. Our specialized competent reader knows much about default values and about what is fitting. *Othello* cannot accommodate some things and meanings and be *Othello* still, and Elizabeth, given the fact that she has this and not that character, cannot say some things and still be Elizabeth.

Similarly, the reader who has a competence based on reading a lot of texts, both literary and otherwise, produced in *a given historical period*, will quickly find a default value where the undercompetent finds only confusion or ambiguity. For example, if this is the middle of the eighteenth century, then the "plastic" modifying "arm" in this poem will carry the "shaping," "forming" value, not the oil byproduct value. If, on the other hand, this is the *early* eighteenth century, then "fabric" most likely refers to the product of the architect-builder's efforts rather than to that of the weaver-textile manufacturer's efforts.

The "default" value has a value, of course, because it rather than some other value makes sense in a particular system of rationality or scheme of description or representation. It works here more or less as it worked there. Having the abilities that competence presupposes means that one is skilled at knowing what sorts of questions are worth asking in a given domain and what sorts of answers can be deemed acceptable, are justified. What we are more than suggesting here, then, is that we can have real, objective knowledge within systems. If this is the system we are in, make no mistake about it, this rather than that is "true," "right," "fit," or "appropriate," true for me and true for you.

Ordering Principles and Boundary Conditions

As far as broad "headings" are concerned, we would note that the versions or conceptual systems that we make or interpret differ primarily in terms of, first, the number and kind of *entities* or *objects* brought into play; second, the kinds and degrees of *emphasis* given to the objects (we can have, for example, different emphases but the same entities, similar emphases but different entities, and differences in entities and emphases); and, third, the kinds of *ordering principles* governing the objects and their emphases. Relative to "fruit" as ordering principle, apples and watermelons make a more felicitous match than apples and baseballs, whereas relative to "roundish objects suitable for hurling considerable distances with relative ease" apples and baseballs consort together more respectably than apples and watermelons or baseballs and medicine balls.

Of course, underlying and determining the specific nature of these grounds of difference in any particular conceptual system is some purpose, aim, intention, or end in view; it is owing to this that there are such particular objects arranged in such a fashion with such an emphasis. It is this overall end in view that makes and "makes true" the objects and meanings of the conceptual system, the interpretive scheme, or representational symbol (i.e., the work as a whole); for it is relative to this that everything is justified. In this complex of mutual implication, the particular parts—in their nature, emphasis, and structure—imply and are implied by some comprehensive intentionality, and the intentionality (or principle of rationality) implies and is implied by the parts. Thus, we arrive at this seeming paradox: there would be no purposes, aims, intentions, or ends, unless there were worlds for them to be in and about, but there are no objects and worlds apart from our aims, purposes, or ends, since the objects and worlds of our conceptual systems are not "made true" by their consonance with mind-independent states of affairs, but by their satisfying conditions internal to the systems themselves.

But, of course, we have not come this far only to discover that we are paradoxicals after all, victims of the roundhouse we would escape, for, as we have repeatedly seen, our various worlds are arranged in a series of matter-form levels, with the higher providing the boundary conditions for the operation of the materials of the lower level. We move progressively to increasingly complex principles of order, since each stage must order whatever precedes it. Crudely put, we move, for instance, from phone to phoneme to morpheme to sentence to paragraph to section to whole composition. It is because of this lower-higher arrangement—the dependence of the higher on the materials of the lower and the top-down determination of the "meaning" of the lower by the interests of the higher—that we are usually able to compare, say, two different, conflicting views or theories, since however uniquely or peculiarly they may use *some* of the "same" terms—and even though those terms have different meanings and references in the two systems—both have many references and meanings in common and both depend on many of the "same" material conditions for the making of their separate boundaries.

The materials of one level cannot determine their own boundary conditions, cannot by means of any internal principle determine the form they should or must take on any specific occasion (of occasions the materials know nothing at all). The material bases of any given sentence (the lexical stock, the words) cannot determine their own interests, values, emphases, arrangements. As at least some critics, as distinct from *theorists*, have recognized, words are the cause of our knowing a meaning, but meaning is the cause of the words in their selection, emphasis, value, and arrangement.[5] Similarly, without clay, there is no pipe, but without now "pipe," now "cat," now "pot," etc. as boundary conditions, as ends in view, there is ever and always only "clay." It is because a principle must be a principle of something other than itself that the words cannot be a principle of their own arrangement (or their specific meaning on a particular occasion).

This stratification of "boundary" conditions also explains why we cannot *understand* the theories we use from *within* the theories themselves (to talk *of* our theories is to talk about them from *above* or from the *outside*; such talk is always "metatalk," as the theoretical hipster might say). From within the theory everything is justified ("internally" justified as fitting, proper, right, or whatever, if it is justified at all, if the theory is not self-refuting), but the theory itself cannot be justified by appealing to its reasonableness, since it presupposes reason rather than explains it.[6] Of course, most (all) of our talk is conducted from within some theory. For example, our day-to-day survival talk (i.e., the talk we use to get through each and every day), is conducted for the most part within a practical, rough and ready, "correspondence-theory" worldview, one in which our observational terms, for instance, take for granted a rather uncomplicated view of how words and thoughts correspond to things. The word "chair" simply stands in for the chair out there. Hence, the issue of the justification or the reasonableness of our survival talk does not come up. (It just makes sense to call grass "grass," spades "spades," chairs "chairs," anger "anger," and so on. What else would it make sense to call them, for heaven's sake?) But as soon as we start to *argue* about our schemes, about what rationality is or about what reasonableness entails, or about whether this *scheme* is justified or is more justified than that (or to suggest that this way of talking is to be preferred to that way of talking), we implicitly acknowledge our reliance or dependence on transcultural, nonparadigmatic criteria, on notions of justification broader in application than those relevant to any particular scheme, notions which can enable us to decide (at least for the time being) contested territory.

An Interlude on Reading and Interpretation

It is perhaps worth noting that, for the most part, critics are not interested in interpretation, in the text as a rational system of interests, beliefs, and desires. Rather, they are interested in such other things as history, class, language, discourse, culture, gender, mind, signs, and signifiers, and in texts as more or less peculiar or individuated exemplars of general facts or tendencies in mind, language, or history.

Explanations, as we have seen, are interest-relative, and there is absolutely no reason why the critic's interests need to run parallel to those of the author-text. And, of course, when the "same" text is seen as supplying satisfactory and satisfying answers to different questions arising from different conceptual frameworks, it is doing so in response to different systems of rationality, which, though perhaps equally acceptable or intelligible as systems, cannot equally account for the *functioning within the symbol*—the work—of the meanings and references that are shared across conceptual frameworks. In short, not all acceptable conceptual frameworks will serve equally well to justify parts—categories, references, and meanings—that are recognizable across theoretical differences.

Thus, though we can look at texts in various ways and bring various interests to them, *most of those interests do not and cannot satisfy the interests of interpretation, since they cannot within their system of rationality account for many details that even their system of rationality recognizes as requiring an account*. That is, these interests, while capable of recognizing that so-and-so in the text is a priest and that he brings bad news at such and such a time, cannot account within their system (of interest) either for his *being a priest* or his bringing such news *when* and *as* he does. Such "facts" (the priest, his news), though recognizable by every reader—when shown—as functional to the working of the text as a symbol are not functional within the critics' various conceptual systems—their systems do not crucially depend on the news coming when it does or by means of a priestly agent. What counts in the alternative schemes is, for example, that the news *is about* political conditions, *reflects* power relations, *betrays* a certain kind of "primary-process thinking," *stands in for* the news that cannot be expressed, the news that must be repressed or suppressed, and so on through a vast array of ways of accommodating "shared facts" to special interests. In a text *relativized to the interests of language or culture or history*, such and such a particular detail is not required in its particularity where it is found, whereas in this text *relativized to the functioning of the work as a symbol*, to this internal system of rationality, such and such a detail is understood to have a necessary function as and where it is.

One of the reasons there seems to be so much conflict or disagreement in criticism is that the "same" categories or the "same" references and concepts are serving a variety of assumptions, schemes, interests, or systems of organization. That is, because a good many terms preserve their meaning, reference, or categorical value *across theory or system change*, there is a tendency to assume that between the views using the "same" terms there must be conflict or, at a minimum, clear disagreement, when most often there is only difference between them. The views are concerned with different questions, make different assumptions, and organize the "same" material according to different conceptual directives. Thus, we have the same or similar terms, references, or meanings but different conceptual *systems*. We have different *organizations* or *uses* of similar (or identical) *materials*. Although the critics share many references and concepts, they are involved in different holistic structures with different justification conditions.

In fact, despite assertions to the contrary, very few critics are immediately and persistently interested in *interpretation*, as opposed to being interested in *reading* loosely interpreted texts in the light of their preferred interests, if by *interpretation* we mean the satisfaction of this ideal: only if this (hypothetical) system of justification were in effect would the text be as it is in all its particularity. In other words— and this is worth stressing—whereas *interpretation* can be "right," *readings* can hardly ever go wrong, at least so long as the critic is faithful to *his* interests. For all the squabbling and ostensible conflict, there are fewer disagreements among critics—as opposed to differences among organizational schemes or conceptual systems—than there generally appear to be.

Chapter 12
Intentions, Interests, Preferences, Choices

Best Choices, Or, Satisfying Interests

Having such and such a goal, aim, end, plan, or project in view in some world means that some possibilities are conducive to its realization and a whole lot of others quite certainly are not. The intentionality opens and narrows, indeed, narrows as it opens the range of possibilities. Simply, if, while talking to the ex-husband of a colleague in the corner of a crowded room which is directly opposite to the room in which the bar is set up, I discover I am in the intentional state of thirst (a state which is satisfied with nothing less than its own extinction, nothing less than quenching), I can do this, that, or some other thing to quench it, but not a countless number of things else. I can zig past this person, make a quick cut and then zag past that one. I can zip through that opening, hang a left past the kitchen, and make my attack from the rear. Or, I can take the relatively straight-line route, moving convulsively forward with one hand on my stomach, the other over my mouth, all the while suggesting that I can no longer contain what until now I have had the decency to keep to myself and trusting that where a moment before a passage could not be forced it would now as if by miracle instantly appear.

Moreover, since nothing pleases thirst quite so much as self-immolation (and the quicker the demise the better), the best of the many available options or appropriate, right, fitting choices will be that which brings me *soonest* from the aridity of the far corner to the liquidity of the collegial oasis. As it turns out on this particular ad hoc occasion of practical reasoning, the best, and I mean absolutely the best choice (*and this is an objective fact, a matter of fact within the operative system of reference and the intentional condition of thirst*) is the one involving the *longest* route, the through-the-kitchen, rear-guard route, since it provides the *quickest* way to the desired end. The zig-and-zag route entails an "Excuse me" here and a "Pardon me" there, as well as the risk of being buttonholed by someone who wants my opinion on such and such a matter here and now, whereas the route opened up by the simulation of digestive tract distress includes a side-trip to the small room with porcelain appointments, a trip necessitated by the emergent need to "legitimate" or "make good" the deception.

Now, clearly, getting to a makeshift bar in a colleague's dining room is not quite the same thing as putting together, say, *Paradise Lost*, but the two have much in common, in principle and in practice, in that both are practical, problem-solving, justified activities reflecting the procedures necessarily involved in all our efforts to *make* and *understand* some kind of sense. Inextricably entangled in all our acts of doing, speaking, and writing something are several elements:

1. a kind of "inductive logic" (a plan, project, or intentionality whose attainment is either highly probable or surely possible in some world; as a *probability*, it is currently the best or most favored, and as a *possibility*, it is consistent with what one knows about this world and what one has done in it before);

2. a kind of "deductive logic" (a range of "relevant" options or choices made possible by the plan or intentionality and a tentative preference ranking of them according to some implicit standard of value); and, underlying the ranking and guiding behavior throughout,

3. a general "rule of action," which, stated baldly, is "to maximize essential utility" under the prevailing circumstances of referentiality and intentionality.[1]

Although for convenience we can divide the activity (or activities) into components, it should be clear by now that we are talking about a complex of mutually supporting, mutually reinforcing, mutually defining elements. For utility to be maximized there must be a world with options. *World, options,* and *effective utility* come into the world together, or together constitute a world, so that *fact, value,* and *logic* (system of reasoning) are equally meaningless apart from this or that constitution or conceptual system. And, of course, without *beliefs, intentions,* and some *rule of action* we would never make or understand any world or version whatsoever.

Reasonableness and Transparadigmatic Rationality, Or, Getting What You Want in the World You Want It In

Taken together, what these views contribute to, finally, is an *image or conception of reasonableness* that "transcends" particular versions, transcends in the sense of informing not one version but all (or a great many) "reasonable" versions. The principle of reasonableness, acting in cooperation with the principle of charity, affirms that just as in making *our* versions we never try to shoot ourselves in the foot, to thwart, impede, or otherwise make difficult or impossible the satisfaction of the conditions upon which satisfaction in the version depends, so in the making of *their* versions—the versions we interpret rather than make—others take aim at their targets, not their feet. In short, if what is in front of us makes some kind of sense, it will be a reasonable composite of belief, desire, and "right" action (or so we assume).[2] Imagine cultures as bizarre as you like and you still will not hit upon one in which there are, say, recognizable artifacts or intelligible speeches apart from beliefs, desires, interests, and rational preference rules for action. If it's footwear you're about, for example, with all that such an aboutness suggests about beliefs in body parts, movement, causality, and so forth, then you had better not attach what I would call the "heel" to what I would call the "tongue," not, at any rate, if you would make what I would call a shoe.

In the plainest of plainspeak, what we are saying comes down to something as homely as this: We act or speak as we do because we believe we can get what we want (in the world we want it in) by doing so. And the world we at the moment want something in is a world we *believe* in, whether it be the world of quantum mechanics, field theory, sense data, loving relationships with parents, fair play and honesty in our dealings with others, horticulture, drag racing, or whatever. Our belief in it is indispensable to our getting or doing what we want, and, generally, we want the *best* in the immediate, local world of interest that we want something in and want it as soon as possible. And if it turns out that we get what we want in the world we want it in, then there is good enough reason to believe (success is reason enough) that what we believe *about* and *in* that world is *true*.[3] Moreover, by accumulating true beliefs in this way we build a foundation for making and finding more true beliefs. If there is no one, ultimate, total World of Truth that is the guarantor or certifier of all really true truths, with which all truths must be squared to qualify as truth, there are *many true worlds* in which we can have true beliefs. Many of our beliefs, then, are true, in that without them we would not get what we want, in that they are indispensable to our getting what we want or where we're going.

Messages from the (Real World) Beyond

All this makes up what we can call a "rational preference theory" of making, doing, understanding. To talk about what *the* world contains, what objects, properties, and relations exist in the world, or about what is true and believable in that world independently of some choice of a conceptual scheme is to talk nonsensically, is to talk without terms, references, or concepts. Wherever there is a world (for us) there is a human interest, and in every world or domain that continues to be interesting to us we have true beliefs, even though these beliefs (and worlds) are always subject to revision, alteration, reformation, deformation, addition, subtraction, cancellation, or always susceptible to takeover bids by or merger deals with other worlds.

What saves all this from linguistic idealism[4] or soft, anything goes relativism is one or another kind of *recalcitrance* or *resistance*. On the positive side, we have the test by correctness—or fit, appropriateness. For example, if *this* is the language or conceptual system we are in, then we are going fifty, not sixty miles an hour; if *this* one, then, make no mistake about it, she is definitely *angry* with me. (What matters is that she is angry with me, not that x, y, and z neurons are firing in region "O" of her brain, even though it happens that such neurons are indeed firing in such region.) Moreover, if we have the *wrong* belief about the world we are in, we will not—I repeat *not*—get what we want. That is, the *external*, the *outside* world does make a real contribution in our pluralism. Our pluralism allows room for mistakes, real, make no mistake about it, mistakes. If you believe you can get to Boston from Providence in about an hour by taking I-95 south, then your belief is in for a bruising. Or, if you believe that a casual, throwaway, parting remark is a real invitation to "do lunch" sometime, as they say, you will undoubtedly be stunned by the repeated rejections your subsequent offers encounter.

Of course, that *external, outside* world is no world that we can know or talk about at all without some concepts or apart from some conceptual system. Still, unlike what obtains presumably in the linguistic idealist's world(s), in our world(s) it hurts when we hit our thumbs with a hammer or, to switch to a moral world, when the "friend" we had counted on fails to come through in our time of need, or, to switch to a "literary" world, when the text before us fails to satisfy appropriately and in specific ways the interests it had specifically activated or excited. The pluralist worth knowing lives in real worlds, in which there are *real facts* and *facts of the matter* and in which doing one thing or another has real (sometimes even fatal) consequences.

Thus, we have many true beliefs about many things in many worlds, true beliefs, for example, about how to start a car engine, what photosynthesis is, how to score a baseball game, how to send a package to a sister in California, where a never-to-be-forgotten and ever-to-be-loved grandmother ranks in our hearts, how many martinis are too many at one sitting, which team won the World Series in 1986, and so on, as well as many beliefs about many things that will turn out to be mistaken or false, of course.[5] These views about true beliefs are entirely compatible, I think, with those advanced by Hilary Putnam and Donald Davidson. Indeed, addressing similar issues, Putnam observes that

. . . the attempt to deny the objectivity of reason leads to self-defeating irrationalisms [to "anything goes" relativism or the hypermonadism of interpretive community-ism, for example], while the attempt to explain the objectivity of reason leads to nonsense, at least if our paradigm of explanation is the familiar reductionist one [the reductionist one offered in the name, for example, of psychoanalysis, physics, Marxism, anthropology, linguistics]. Of course, there is a good deal of philosophical work that philosophers who do not seek any sort of reductionist theory of rationality have been doing and will continue to do. We have many beliefs about truth, about explanation, about counterfactuals, about coherence and simplicity, about belief and desire, and philosophers are engaged in discussing and describing these beliefs and their function in our life. Some of the beliefs we have about *truth*, for example the belief that *speakers' beliefs about certain kinds of topics tend to be true*, and that *speakers are more likely to attain their goals when they act on true beliefs*, play an important role in interpretation [and in action and making], as Donald Davidson has taught us. The beliefs that we have about belief and desire and their connection with action (in an idealized way, these are described in rational preference theory) also play an important role in interpretation [and in doing and making]. All these beliefs together: our general beliefs about truth, our beliefs about belief, our beliefs about desire, form a kind of informal system, an overarching mentalistic theory, which gives material content to such notions as truth, reference, belief, and desire, as a number of philosophers have argued.[6]

Standards and Practices Acts

We are now in a position to bring to conclusion the discussion that began a decade or so ago with David Marr's newspaper and buzzing fly. And we can do so with a reflection or two on the thirsty colleague case. In the particular situation we outlined, belief, desire, interest, and action were interlocked in the circumstantial setting in such a way that the rear-guard, through-the-kitchen route was the quickest

and thus the best, absolutely the best route to thirst-quenching satisfaction, even though it was also the longest route, in distance (in our
case, the shortest was the slowest and the longest the fastest route).
Had the people in the rooms achieved a slightly different configuration, the shortest route could well have been what it usually is, the
quickest and hence the best route.

What has our interest here is the security and certainty of our *value
judgment*, and this in turn has our interest because of what it seems to
suggest about the "objectivity," as distinct from the "subjectivity," of
some values and value judgments. Many values, it seems, are *properties
of the system* or of the *things* in the system, not merely subjective attitudes or feelings of spectators/readers. They are values for everyone
working within the conceptual system. Every system has what the
movie and television industry has, namely, its own "standards and
practices commission." In other words, our *standards* of value and our
practices (our worlds) arise together. Our standards are every bit as
much our own making as are our practices, our conceptual systems.
Our standards are as ad hoc as our categories, our holistically structured activities. In a way, of course, we have known this all along or
for a good while now, since "just," "fit," "right," and "appropriate" are
all *value* terms. As we have seen, whatever is "just," "fit," etc. is "justified" within and by the system—if it is *justified* and hence *right* or *fit* at
all—and, consequently, whatever is justified contributes to the functioning of the system as a system or as a symbol.

The wrinkle within this wrinkle of our argument is that the operative standard—while appropriate, emergent, and context- and
interest-specific in its authority—is not just a standard for any single
action, text, or context alone. Rather, it remains available for service
in other contexts and systems. It is another item in the stockpile of
our availabilities, one item in the heap of *available standards*, taking a
place among such others as plausibility, coherence, expedition, ex-
pedience, simplicity, and so on. The standards arise with discourse,
but despite having so arisen, they are not restricted in their functioning to that discourse. In brief, they are both immanent and transcendent. In the case at hand, the *best* route is the *longest* but *quickest* route.
Now, the "quick" standard arises in and emerges from the whole situation; that is, "quick" has value and makes sense as a standard relative to this specific situation. But without working up a sweat the
imagination can easily see that this standard is at once *ad hoc* or *immanent*, in that it has immediate and peculiar relevance to the case at
hand, and *extraterritorial* or *transcendent*, in that it could serve just as
well in a variety of nonthirst situations, albeit with a peculiar twist of
emphasis or "meaning" in each. That is, what is "quick" in this con-

text is not "quick" in that one, just as what "coherence" means in this context is not what "coherence" means in that one, though we are dealing with "quickness" or "coherence" in each and we know what we mean in each, be the differences in operative force ever so many or ever so subtle.

Clearly, two critics who disagree about the meaning of a given sentence, for example, can share the same standard of judgment, can agree that of two or more possible meanings the most plausible (under the agreed-upon circumstances) is the best one. Further, they can agree that if the situation the sentence is relative to is such and such, then this rather than that meaning would make a better fit and thus be more plausible, whereas if the situation is some other such and such then some other reading would be more plausible. The specific nature of, say, plausibility, coherence, and simplicity may shift, but the criteria, along with some references and concepts, remain the same (or sort of the same) across the differences in meaning (or theory). Thus, even though a given criterion arises with (and within) the discourse and has its being so to speak within a specific context, *plausibility* and *coherence* and *simplicity* remain distinctly different criteria to which appeal can commonly be made by those with different views and by reference to which disputed claims can be adjudicated. Indeed, to *argue* with someone about whether *this* is better, more rational, more plausible, more likely, or more efficient than *that* is to presuppose at least some methodological ground of arbitration (*without which there could be no disagreement at all and no hope of a settlement*). We can easily imagine, then, how the "same" standard could apply to different *situations*.

Conversely, we can easily imagine how the *same* intentional situation or circumstance could evoke different satisfaction standards. For example, on the "immanent" side, in which we have the simultaneous emergence of practices and standards, it is clear, for example, that even though thirst is an intentional state with a strong death wish, with, indeed, suicidal tendencies (it seeks its own undoing), some conditions of thirst are not best satisfied by a "quickest route" line of action. That is, if the default *value* of "thirst" or "thirst scenarios" is "the quickest (and shortest) route to satisfaction," every reader can easily imagine dramas or narratives in which the interests would be lined up by the *author* in such a way that the *reader* (and *text*) would be best satisfied by the extended and repeated deferral of the hero's satisfaction of his thirst. In one of many possible hypothetical cases, satisfaction is withheld until the time is ripe, until there can be some significant equivalence established between the hero's suffering and reward. The reader, knowing all along that the ethically worthy character will not die of thirst (and suspecting or hoping that the reward will be perfectly commensurate with such great and manifest goodness), thus reads on to discover not *whether* but *when* the thirst will be quenched. Hopes are repeatedly raised and dashed until, when we least expect it, satisfaction comes from a most unpromising quarter in the best of all possible forms (a favorite drink) by means of the best possible emissary (the hero's best friend, for whose sake he has sacrificed his own interest and endured his present suffering), that is, until the drink can be the drink that most refreshes the deserving hero, the empathetic reader, and the intentionally interested text. Even in our cocktail party example, the default value of thirst was significantly altered to fit the peculiarities of the specific occasion. Since the shortest was not also the quickest route, the best choice simply had more quickness than shortness about it, simply gave up on shortness and deferred to the interests of quickness.

Worldly Satisfactions

Perhaps we can conveniently illustrate how standards and practices arise together by considering a couple of neglected aspects of the ad hoc activity of getting to a makeshift bar at a crowded cocktail party under the generative and constitutive impulse of thirst. In the world of practical reasoning we have presented, "thirst" means what we ordinarily mean by the term, "kitchen" refers to kitchen (to the room we generally designate to be the kitchen when we refer to that room), "bar" to bar, "ex-husband of a colleague" to her ex-husband, and so on. These terms are "primitives" in this world, and there will be satisfaction in *this* world of reference or no satisfaction at all. While we are in this world, that is, while this world has our interest, whatever is possible or done is possible or done in this world; all options are options in this world, and only those descriptions and explanations will count as descriptions and explanations that are relevant to the interests of this world.

Thus, although innumerable descriptions or explanations of my thirst-driven behavior (my getting to the bar by way of the kitchen) would be true, truly true, only one *kind* of account would be relevant to the world I was in. For instance, we would surely rule out as irrelevant any of the following "true" responses to the query "What is he doing?"

1. he's causing air and dust particles to move violently about;
2. he's executing a military marching maneuver;
3. he's heading first in the direction of Paducah, Kentucky, and then in the direction of Raleigh, North Carolina;

4. he's creating a bustle in the motor centers of his brain;
5. he's fulfilling his plan to abuse his liver;
6. he's playing his part in one of the commonest scenes in the farce of late capitalism;
7. he's deviating from the instructions of the Reverend Billy Bob;
8. he's enacting a repetition compulsion;
9. he's expressing solidarity with his colleague (by abandoning her ex-husband in the corner of the room);
10. he's participating in the great cosmic dance;
11. he's rolling round in earth's diurnal course with rocks, and stones, and trees;

and on and on through explanations taken from each and every domain of interest known to featherless bipeds.[7]

If the version we are in rules out of bounds countless true descriptions or explanations of our behavior, it also places rather severe limits on the behavioral choices available to us, even as it opens up to us an indefinite number of appropriate, fit, right choices. In other words, if many explanations are *irrelevant*, many actions (choices of action) are *inappropriate* (or otherwise unacceptable, on grounds, for example, of goofiness, inutility, counterproductivity, etc.). Sticking to possible actions within "ordinary," day-to-day, garden-variety experience, we would not be ashamed to stigmatize with some such unhandsome epithet as inappropriate or goofy any of the following actions, elected in preference to walking to the bar by the quickest route:

1. twirling aimlessly about;
2. pacing back and forth;
3. jumping up and down;
4. rubbing the top of my colleague's ex-husband's pate energetically with the knuckles of my best fist;
5. doing Julia Child impressions;
6. whistling "Dixie";
7. saluting anything that moved;
8. yelling the names of left-handed relief pitchers;

and so on and so on to the edge of doom. And, of course, the social background knowledge that we bring with us to the party, the "amenities" knowledge that even the basic course in civil interchange equips us with, tells us that many actions, though efficacious, are socially unacceptable, yelling "fire" or shoving out of our way those who are in it, for example. In short, because our focus is always selective, because we are and can be concerned at any given time with those things and only those things within the logical, semantic, and axiological range of our terms and interests, in other words, because no view or aim or theory can account for what it has no terms for and thus no awareness or conception of, we are obliged to work with ad hoc standards in ad hoc worlds, making do with what we have and scuttling worlds and standards when and as we see fit (or fail any longer to see a fitness).

Textual Interests and Prior Restraint

In our view, then, every text is an ad hoc system of terms, interests, intentions, a conceptual system which makes some kind of sense. The differentiable parts of the system are justified, and the text as a whole is self-satisfied. It is not some wimpy collection of graphemes, lexemes, morphemes, or whatever waiting docilely for some cultural or historical martinet to come along to whip it into shape, to teach it some close-order drill. This is not to deny, of course, that every reader has an inalienable, constitutionally protected right to read any text he pleases in the light of any interests or categories or imperatives that please him or that he happens at the moment to be interested in or to deny that any text can usefully be examined and discussed in the light of an indefinite number of categories. We assume the text has interests that it has attempted to satisfy in the best way imaginable at the time. To assume otherwise, we find, would be to offend too many of our unyielding beliefs and to insult too many of our practices. The perhaps surprising and odd but nonetheless deep and persistent fact—which pluralists but so few other theorists can explain—is that in the course of any given day we switch from one to another conceptual system with ease, even to systems prepared long ago and far away, systems, moreover, which you and I and Hume and so-and-so agree to read in pretty much the "same" way, in terms of the "same" justification conditions. Together, extending a little charity here and granting a little benefit of doubt there, we pretty much agree on what Derrida, Fish, Foucault, Horace, Dryden, Sir Joshua Reynolds, et al. are saying and on how they go about saying their various says in their various ways.

To this belief in our capacity to understand new and old systems, we add another of our favorite unyielding beliefs for which the pluralist but so few others can make accommodations, namely, the belief that no matter how rigorously and narrowly, say, the "archive" or the "episteme" is defined, no matter how severely the operational rules for derivation and declension, for substitution and combination are formulated, no matter how precisely the language and its rules are expressed, it is always possible to imagine or express an indefinite number of conflicting or incompatible statements or hypotheses that are completely consistent with the constraints specified.

There is nothing in the preceding, of course, that obliges us to deny that interests have their seasons or epochs or that one kind of knowledge or knowing has a tendency to suppress awareness of another kind of knowledge or knowing, or even that, for instance, thinking of literature in terms of historical periods has some large and important effects on the structure of the curriculum and the composition of the teaching staff. People tend to think about what those around them are thinking about, and they continue to do so until they decide to think about something else with some others who are interested in thinking in some other conceptual terms about something else. Sometimes many of us want to know how the manifest physical and moral evil in the world can be squared with the notion of an Omnipotent and Benevolent Father. Sometimes it is phlogiston that excites the collective attention of some of us; sometimes it is "taste," or "intuition," or the "trace" or "intertextuality," or this or that. Of course, nothing is so necessary to heterodoxy as orthodoxy, and nothing evokes multiplicity, diversity, contrariety, complication, contradiction of views so readily as the articulation of a view—*by someone else*.

And, as we have repeatedly seen, there is nothing in the "topic" (whatever the topic) or in the "rules" (logical, syntactic, semantic rules, say) by which the topic must be discussed that precludes or can preclude infinitely many different, even conflicting accounts of it. If our *rottenness for perfection* prods us to raise the ante again and again, to track down the full implications of our ways of talking,[8] our *saintliness for disorder or chaos* or perhaps our simple low-flying *hunger for novelty* urges us to undermine or explode any standing intellectual fortress, to reject the established solely because it is established, or, more modestly, to take a new perspective on things, to take, as Kenneth Burke says, a "perspective by incongruity."

Certainly there are blowing at various times prevailing winds of one sort or another in one area of interest or another, but few winds prevail for long, and no winds prevail everywhere at once without opposition or without themselves provoking independent gusts and whirlwinds. Oddly, certain winds that *do* prevail, those that we breathe in every day and that, thus, inspire our everyday accounts of things—our ready and working notions of things physical, social, ethical, political, and so on—are generally disesteemed by many of our *theorists*. Generally, these are treated by our *theorists* as second-rate, even though, for most of the tasks that concern us most and most often, such winds are, well, indispensable, as well as refreshing and burden-easing, and even though we have not yet found and have no present prospects of ever finding a "first-rate" vantage point from which to rate our various accounts of things.[9]

Objective Value

Since the pluralists we are concerned with assume that speaking and listening, writing and reading are practical, participant activities requiring imagination, ingenuity, and agility at each and every step (i.e., the ability to execute ad hoc corrective maneuvers as the situation from moment to moment seems to require), they are easily distinguished from those among their colleagues who assume a perspective at some remove from the text—a perspective, for example, from above, from the outside, from the margins of the dominant discourse, despite the conviction of many of them that there is no outside, that they never *speak* but are *always already spoken for* by the episteme or whatever that is functioning as the power broker, as the thing- and self-maker in any given historical era. The perspective of the pluralist, then, is that taken traditionally by the pragmatist, namely, the *agent* as opposed to the *patient* or *spectator* perspective. As both writer/speaker and reader/hearer (interpreter), the pluralist is engaged persistently in the practical, problem-solving business of trying to make or find a fit under these or those (supposed) conditions of assertibility or justification. Thus, as we have seen, reading is always a *global enterprise*, an attempt to determine, for example, what beliefs and desires it would be necessary to suppose in order to render such and such behavior reasonable, and writing always a *holistic activity*, an option-riddled exercise in getting where you want to go by what are under the circumstances the best means possible.

We are now in a position to bring this ad hoc discussion to a conclusion with a few more words on the thirst-motivated behavior at the cocktail party. That everything we say and do in the course of any intentional, ad hoc activity is a consequence of practical reasoning or is an achievement of problem solving is frequently obscured, because the choices we make (the words and phrases we choose, for example) often, perhaps usually, seem so automatic, so easy, so "natural," so, well, right and fitting, once we get what we "want to say" under way, and because sometimes the best choice is the only choice, under these particular conditions of intentionality (if this is a "fly-swatting scenario," the newspaper functions absolutely and certainly as a weapon, not as reading matter). Yet, clearly, since everything is necessitated or justified by some particular system of intentionality or some conceptual system, everything included in the activity, and especially what is "easy," "natural," or "inevitable," is chosen by and for the intentional system, apart from which nothing is anything in and of itself and nothing is easy, true, or natural.

If this or that is natural or easy or fit or true, it is made so, not found so. Such and such a choice is right or fit or appropriate only on the supposition of such and such a system of belief and desire. Or, under such and such circumstances of belief and desire, this rather than that choice is more or most reasonable. At any rate, it is clear that what is fitting, right, or appropriate is a matter of choice under local intentional conditions, not a consequence of some general features of language, mind, culture, history, or whatever. And, of course—and here is what has our immediate interest—the issue of choice is inseparable from the issue of value, since selection is meaningful only where there exists a range of better and worse possibilities and where the choice makes a (qualitative) difference.

Moreover, it is important to recognize that in allowing for degrees of fit or rightness and of better and worse "fits," we are not at the same time acknowledging the subjectivity of our value judgments. The judgments are "objective," in that they have reference to *properties or features of the activities* to which they are applied and not to our subjective feelings. *A property or feature has value* (is *good* or *bad* in greater or lesser degree) *to the extent that it contributes to the satisfaction of the intentionality* (or, in another case, *to the functioning of the work as a symbol*, as Nelson Goodman says).[10] In our cocktail party example, an important point made but not stressed was that the best route was just that, the objectively best route. Among the many available better and worse possibilities the absolutely best route was taken under the circumstances of congestion and the condition of thirst. Had the configuration of the rooms or the guests been altered ever so slightly, the conditions of satisfaction might have changed dramatically. Under a different alignment, the best route might have involved going out the back door, around the building, and then in the front door, just beyond which and to the left stood the bar.

Making Do and Making Out

The inherence of the values *in the properties of the situation*, not in the feelings of the participant or interpreter, can be conveniently illustrated in the example of the local movie theater. Relative to the quality of audio and visual reception, the best seats are those smack dab in the middle of the auditorium, whereas relative to what was called "making out" in my (relatively) innocent high school days of yore, the best seats are those located in the far corner of the last row, where,

seeing but unseen, two could do much to compensate for the defi-
ciencies of a bad movie and avoid, if not suspicion, at least detection.
And, of course, the objective nature of value has not been lost on the
stage and concert theater managers downtown, who turn the values
inhering in the architect's design into cash distinctions at the box office. It costs a whole lot more to see and hear, to see and be seen from
these seats than to do the very same things from those seats. Relative
to the ad hoc standards created by this intentional situation or this ad
hoc activity (the audio/visual standards, let us say), these seats are a
whole lot better than those, which are themselves a whole lot better
than those in the fourteenth balcony situated just below the ineffec-
tual but not unnoisy fan, whereas relative to these quite different, ad
hoc standards created by the intentional ad hoc activity of *Othello*, this
remark dropped casually by Iago is best suited to activate the doubt
that will prove most destructive to the noble Moor's peace of mind.

Whether you like going to the theater or not is perhaps a subjective
matter (though even here preference is undoubtedly grounded in
some reason or justification; indeed, liking to go is sufficient reason
to go), but there is nothing "subjective" (in the pejorative, idiosyn-
cratic, quixotic sense of "subjective") about whether, having gone to
the theatre with smiling or frowning countenance, you can see and
hear well from your expensive seat in the first balcony or about
whether what you hear Iago say is just the right sort of thing to say
to the green-eyed monster dozing within Othello. It is simply a matter of "objective truth" (i.e., it is objectively true "within the system")
that relative to the quality of audio/visual reception the seat is a pip
and that relative to the aim of inciting an overwhelming jealousy in
Othello the ostensibly casual remark is a humdinger, is remarkably,
perfectly apt, right, fit. The structure of goodness is coextensive and
coincident with the structure of intentionality. If what is is justified,
then what is justified is good (as justified).

Of course, both theater and text can be asked to participate in
many orders of goodness (or evil)—civic, social, historical, cultural,
and so on (the text, for example, may be said to promote or perpet-
uate sexual stereotypes, may be seen to reflect patriarchic patterns of
dominance and control, to exhibit power relations in early capitalism,
or, in the case of Desdemona's handkerchief, to display the deleteri-
ous consequences of the commodification of the emotions, and so
on). *But* as intentional, conceptual systems, text and theater are already systems of justification and value (or so we assume). And if the
level of justification is also the level of interest (the interest-relative
level), as we further assume, then, from the perspective of interpretation, this is a level of interesting questions and explanations, a level

at any rate where interesting and valuable questions can be formulated and answered (here we simply wish to make space for what most kinds of modern criticism have in their insufferable and unjustified arrogance proscribed).

The Problematic Method of Interrogation

From the standpoint of reading or interpretation, we have in place of a theory or a set of rules a flexible set of practical procedures of what I call the "positive" and "conditional" kind. What we are talking about, finally, I suppose, is a certain habit of reading (a habit that, because it can be taught, has important pedagogic—i.e., classroom—implications), a certain method of, as the popular phrase goes, "interrogating texts," the *problematic method*. In short, we get in the habit of asking of any differentiable element of the text *either* what it is doing where and as it is *or* what difference it would make if something else obtained where it obtains. We are interested in determining what it would be necessary to suppose to give the element a function or justification, in determining what description or conception it would be an essential or useful property of, in determining how it, in this or that particular form and location, contributes to the functioning of the work as a symbol or as a system of intentionality.[11]

When and how we hit upon a working understanding of the conceptual imperatives of the system we are in it is impossible to say since each text offers new challenges to our problem-solving skills and since each individual can—and probably does—use a different textual launching pad for a working hypothesis. However hit upon, though, this understanding remains in effect only so long as it continues both to imply and be implied by the details with which we question its subsumptive power. For example, in reading James Joyce's "Araby," in *Dubliners*, we quickly assume that we are dealing with the everyday world of ordinary reference and with a complex of experiences for the description or elucidation of which ordinary ethical, moral, social, religious (Catholic, in this case) terms will serve (i.e., "neighborhood" refers to the young boy's Dublin neighborhood, "Mangan's sister" to his friend's sister, "aunt" to his aunt, and so on; and his condition of "confused adoration" is one which beings such as we can "experience" and discuss in ordinary emotional terms, as opposed to chemical or clinical terms, for example.

Assuming intentionality at the level of ordinary reference and experience, then (without forgetting, of course, that the scene is set in a particular time and place and thus that the ordinary is rehearsed before specific background conditions), we ask, for example, *positively*, why the former tenant of the boy's house was a priest or, *conditionally*, what would have been the case or the difference if the former tenant had been a butcher or turf accountant; *positively*, why the boy is the only passenger on the train to the bazaar, why the accents he hears at "Araby" are English ones, why he lives at the blind end of the street, why there are so many religious and "romantic" terms in the story, or, *conditionally*, how would the story have been altered or affected by having someone other than the boy as an adult narrate it, by raising the lust quotient of the boy slightly, by representing Mangan's sister not as a brown-clad, rather plain schoolgirl but as a ravishing beauty fond of garish clothes and scarlet accessories and actively engaged in attracting the attention of the young boy, and so on.

We ask, *positively*, why the information we get is presented at this time, by this means, from this point of view, by this character, why this term, image, phrase is used here and then used again in a slightly varied form later and still later, why this character is a priest or doctor, why he is introduced at this time, why the events are ordered as they are, and so on. And we ask, *conditionally*, what the consequences would have been if this rather than that had happened, if this rather than that character had given us this rather than that information at this rather than that time, ask how different, to take another case, our response to Lear would be if he were indeed more sinning than sinned against, and so on. We ask such questions, we interrogate our texts in such ways not only to discover the justification conditions that the various parts are satisfying, but to test, revise, enlarge, and refine our understanding of the system as a system of self-satisfaction. And we do all this because such *understanding* is, well, pleasurable, is satisfying. It gives to the conceptual muscles what tone presumably gives to the muscle muscles. Making and finding conceptual systems are distinctly human pleasures, it seems fair to say. Whenever we find a fit, the pleasure is genuine and immediate.

Making Use of Interest

The manner of interrogating texts advocated here, the problematic approach to texts (the "why this, why that" or the "what if this, then what" approach) can easily be taught to and learned by others. Indeed, some form of the approach is necessary to understanding of any kind, though it tends to carry on its operations sub rosa or sotto voce. Once taught, it becomes a permanent possession of the student, which can be used at will with utmost abandon independently of the instructor's assistance. And if used, it brings what every user immediately recognizes as real benefits, since few things elate quite so much as finding a fit and knowing with unshakable confidence that the fit found (made) is truly fitting and thus is a true find. And surely most of what we read, certainly most of the "literature" we read, we read not for its "truth" value, its propositional content, not for what we can learn about the truth of epistemology, ontology, society, economics, or whatever (the pluralist, of course, would be suspicious of any system of statements claiming access to *the* truth about this or that, though he would certainly be interested in knowing what various self-proclaimed soothsayers were saying), but for its *conceptual interest*, for what it allows us to *contemplate* and *imagine*.

Now, whether in our personal and private capacities we believe in the Christian dispensation, the great chain of being, or the epistemological notions advanced by Wordsworth, for example, we continue to read with pleasure and instruction *The Divine Comedy*, *The Essay on Man*, and the "Immortality Ode." We continue to read these with pleasure, *because*, among other things, understanding conceptual systems, versions, worlds is inherently satisfying to beings such as we; *because* such reading enlarges the stock of our resources, of the materials we need to make and understand *new* and *subsequent* versions (here's what because of my prior reading I can call a particular circle of hell situation, here's a ruling-passion case if I ever saw one, here's a circumstance in which it might be useful to think of the child as the father to the man, or here's a Cordelia-like or Lear-like emotional condition); and *because* it is pleasurable, interesting, and potentially useful to consider what it would be like to think within the terms and bounds of this or that controlling conception of this or that, to contemplate what life would be like if such and such obtained, to imagine vividly the ethical and emotional perplexities and possibilities that would follow from such and such assumptions, hopes, fears, etc.

Ultimately, of course, we are all interested in knowing *what to believe* and in learning *how to live*, but the makeshift complex that serves as the variable, flexible ideal model of our knowing and living is accountable to many worlds and versions. At any rate, for our purposes here, at the end of our long discussion, it is perhaps enough to recognize, with Goodman, that

Discovery often amounts, as when I place a piece in a jigsaw puzzle, not to arrival at a proposition for declaration or defense, but to finding a fit. Much of knowing aims at something other than true, or any, belief. An increase in acuity of insight or in range of comprehension, rather than a change of belief, occurs when we find in a pictured forest a face we already knew was there, or learn to distinguish stylistic differences among works already classified by artist or composer or writer, or study a picture or a concerto or a treatise until we see or hear or grasp features and structures we could not discern before. Such growth in knowledge is not by formation or fixation of belief but by the advancement of understanding.[12]

Textual Durability

Despite striking changes in many beliefs about this and that from one period to the next, the text that the younger or succeeding generation wakes up to is pretty much the text that the older or preceding generation went to bed with, at least so far as the text is considered at the level of its interest and justification. If we can understand what Newton or Copernicus or Harvey or Boyle or Priestley was referring to and trying to explain and how he went about explaining it, despite the fact that we no longer refer to such things exactly or actually believe in such things (at least not in the same way), we are certainly not prohibited from understanding "literary" works written in earlier periods (or written yesterday, for that matter), especially since—but not only because—such works assume and depend for their articulation upon what we can call ordinary reference and meaning. The worlds referred to are the familiar, durable, everyday, folk worlds of ordinary objects, properties, and relations (rocks, stones, trees, houses, curates, mothers-in-law, priests, shoes, hats, below, above, on top of, instead of, because of, against), and the concerns activated and the explanations required are those expressible in the familiar, everyday terms of folk psychology (anger, love, hate, hope, ambition, envy, greed, jealousy, fear), in the terms, in other words, that have remained remarkably stable over the long years (thanks in large part to the principle of charity—what we call a hat is not remarkably similar to what so and so calls a hat in such and such a work, but we "know" or "allow" that what so and so puts on his head is a "hat").

Additionally, we assume that the *rule of action* that we recognize as guiding our behavior in our ad hoc activities guided the behavior of our predecessors as well, and that what counts as motivation for us is not unlike, in some respect or another, what counts as motivation for our predecessors. And even when the text is concerned chiefly, not with ordinary references and relations in ordinary contexts of social, moral, and psychological perplexity, but with special systems of belief or peculiar ways of knowing (science-fiction ways, for example), it is no more inaccessible than any other strikingly different conceptual system is, than Copernicus's or Harvey's or Boyle's system is. Furthermore, as we have elsewhere seen, most of the conditions of understanding that apply to literary texts apply to these texts: across the differences in our "frameworks" many references, meanings, and

functions remain the same, and every system depends for its motivation and hence its self-satisfaction on some form of intentionality not
alien or unfamiliar to us (we, at any rate, cannot know anything about
such a completely alien system; such a system is not a conceptual system *for us*).

Seeing More and Seeing Deeper

While not restricting his focus to the text's internal conditions of self-
satisfaction, Goodman reminds those of us who "read" the same texts,
paintings, or musical scores again and again that there is nothing de-
grading or demeaning in coming to a progressively deeper and richer
understanding of how *King Lear* or *Paradise Lost* works, of how the
various parts of Pope's *Essay on Man* function as elements of a complex system of analogical relations, of how *Don Giovanni* achieves its
effects. It has been reserved for recent critics to discover that, since
what counts is what in language, culture, or history speaks texts or
authorizes speech, any text is really as good as any other text for purposes of analysis or discussion, and that authors (when or if allowed
to participate at all) and readers are mighty opposites struggling unto
death for conceptual supremacy, or that the only interests texts are
relative to are those determined by various communities of interpretation.

At the hundredth reading the pluralist critic and teacher sees what
at the ninety-ninth reading he missed, for example, that the terms on
which France takes Cordelia in the first act are precisely the terms on
which we shall soon have Lear and on which he shall deserve to be
taken by us, as he is so taken by Kent, the Fool, and Cordelia. He is
later, as she is now, "most choice forsaken, and most loved despised,"
and as Burgundy's neglect leads to France's respect for the "unprized
precious" Cordelia, so soon the "cold'st neglect" of Goneril and Regan will kindle our love for Lear to "inflamed respect." The earlier
scene does not so much prepare the way for or bring about the later
scenes as exemplify the "generic" conditions of moral discrimination
necessary to full empathetic understanding of the play's ethical and
emotional interests. And what is finally seen is satisfying, not because
it leads (in this case) to a new understanding of the work (though,
certainly, coming to a new and presumably "better" understanding of
the text's assertibility conditions is no doleful thing), but because it
enriches and enlarges the understanding we had been working with
all along, the understanding we had at the ninety-ninth reading.

The pleasures accompanying deeper and deeper participation in
the system's system of entailment and justification are certainly not

the only pleasures the pluralist as reader of texts looks for or could be satisfied with, but such pleasures are real pleasures (as those who know them know). Moreover, since such pleasures cannot be driven away by philosophic argument (certainly not by the arguments of the skeptics, relativists, and closet monists—the linguists, anthropologists, historicists, and psychoanalysts—among us), they should not be scared away by the menaces of intellectual ruffians who persist in saying "boo" to *authors* and *books* and *intentions* in their public and official capacities while getting on quite familiarly with them in their personal and private capacities, when they are, as it were, off-duty.

The Suppression of Interests and the Dangerous Prevalence of Language

Finally, in taking an interest in texts at the level of their interest and justification, at the level where explanations show the reasonableness of choices and the interrelatedness of properties in the functioning of the whole symbol, we manage to avoid the sorts of reductive explanations (so characteristic of modern criticism) that seek to make one world of many, especially perhaps those that find the key to all systems in some particular "facts" of language. In one form or another, the "linguistic" explanation has proved to be the most popular and durable of our modern explanations, finding practitioners in, among many others, New Criticism, stylistic criticism, and deconstruction. For all their up-to-datism, however, the purveyors of such explanations seem closest in intellectual style and method to the materialists or physicalists, to the naive realists and foundationalists that they most persistently denounce.

They seem closest, in short, to those nomothetic scientists who assume that if we and everything else are ultimately matter, if even our minds are reducible to material, electrochemical operations, then the best explanations—the only respectable or true explanations—of things will be physical explanations, explanations in materiophysical terms. To these reasoners, all other explanations are pseudo-explanations. Similarly, our language/discourse theorists reason that if literature (and, recently, philosophy, history, and everything else in which signs or symbols have a part—i.e., everything) is language, words, signs, then the only useful explanation of things must be "linguistic" (or semiotic), must deal with tropes, ironies, paradoxes, traces, themes, or whatever else is true of or implicated in language as a system of signs or as a rule-governed set of operations. All other explanations are considered to be false, jejune, hopelessly naive, or worse.

At the inspissated darkness of mind exhibited in such uninformed arrogance, we would weep if we were angels and perhaps smile indulgently if we were mere mortals. What such a preoccupation precludes, of course, is an interest in a host of interesting explanations—those, for example, at what we have elsewhere characterized as the higher, psychological levels, those focusing on, say, emotion, thought, action, character, intention, and so on. It shelters itself from—indeed, it excoriates, gives the Bronx cheer to—a rich assortment of explanations that, despite our intellectual snobbism, we continue to find not only *interesting* but *indispensable* to the living of our lives and *necessary* to the needs and pleasures of our imaginations. Furthermore, under certain conditions of interest, these just happen to be the best explanations possible, the most philosophically respectable and relevant explanations we could possibly find. After all, what sort of explanation could be more relevant or philosophically respectable than an indispensable one?

There is, of course, nothing wrong, illegitimate, or moronic about neuronic, electrochemical explanations or about tropological, linguicentric explanations. It is just that sometimes they are simply uninteresting or irrelevant, since what we want to know is not what neurons are firing but why so-and-so is angry at us or why Othello is ripe for jealousy. Moreover, only by employing some form of the practical, problematic approach outlined here, with its emphasis on finding the reasonableness underlying and informing ad hoc activities and its concern with conceptual systems at the level of their interest and justification, can we come to know a text from inside its making, so to speak, since it alone obliges us to participate at every step in the *rationale of construction*. Only this approach allows us to generate the text, albeit after the fact, because only it culminates in an hypothesis (about justification conditions) which both implies and is implied by all the details of the text, an hypothesis only upon the assumption of which would the text be as it is in all its particularity. If the *trope* or *paradox* or *terminological conflict* identified as central cannot explain, for example, why this speaker is a spinster and that one a rake, or why so-and-so's argument takes this particular form and is introduced at this particular point, then it obviously cannot elucidate the principles of the text's making. All this the problematic approach can do, and while a whole lot of other things remain to be done and are eminently worth doing, coming to know the monuments of intellect from within their reasonableness is no mean achievement; it is enough to make students young and old clap their hands and enough to make a golden bird on a golden bough sing.

Part Four
Worlds Well Founded
and Worlds Well Lost

Chapter 13
Making Mistakes, Making Amends, Making Do

In our efforts to rehabilitate such currently discredited notions as coherence, intention, translation, interpretation, and objectivity and to show that understanding texts at the level of their interest and justification is both possible and desirable, we may at times have given the impression that all texts are always and necessarily fully and most felicitously justified, are always thoroughly saturated with rightness or fitness, with what is perfectly appropriate to their relatively single-minded intentionality. Of course, however, we clearly recognize that writers do not always choose best or even appropriately. Subsequent choices are not always consistent or even compatible with earlier choices, and often one system of justification is abandoned midstream for another system. Some texts break apart, fail to adhere consistently to their own ad hoc imperatives; some centers do not hold. Some works split, some fracture, and some may even cancel at one point what they affirm at another, erase here and now what they had inscribed there and earlier. And if Homer can sometimes nod, lesser makers can sometimes doze. Where virtually every step requires a choice, it is not surprising that attention sometimes wanders or diligence sometimes relaxes and that as a consequence we sometimes choose incorrectly, inappropriately, or ill-fitting; nor is it surprising that we sometimes forsake one path to pursue what an emergent sidepath seems to promise. And so on.

What is surprising, given what we have been told and what from our own experience we know about the Procrustean proclivities of our hypotheses (given the dependence of our "facts" and "worlds" upon our constitutive assumptions, our readiness to apprehend those features and only those features that are implicated in or consistent with our cognitive models or conceptual schemes), what is surprising, given all this, is that we can recognize the breakdowns as breakdowns or the mistakes as mistakes at all. Nevertheless, as surely as we know that in a rightly ordered universe the Mets would not have won the 1986 World Series, we also know not only that some things break down or go wrong, but also where and how (and sometimes even why) they do so.

In the midst of understanding a text one way, we run into what cannot be adjusted to or accommodated by our governing conception of justification conditions. What we run into simply does not fit the complex intentionality that until now all the details had, it seemed, been satisfying. Such a nodule of recalcitrance we are inclined to call a mistake, if it persists in refusing all invitations to subserve some sense-making system of entanglement, some system of satisfaction, however odd or morally reprehensible such a system might seem to be to us in our personal and private capacities. As an aside, we should perhaps note that there are those who insist that this never happens, who say that we can always make a fit, always adjust the docile and submissive text to our hypothesis or scheme, since, it is affirmed, we never meet a fact or detail that is not of our own—or of our scheme's own—making. We can even make nonsense strings of words—or, say, a disjunct list of proper names—make sense.[1] That we can impose a sense where there is none, or where there is another minimal one, is neither surprising nor particularly noteworthy; for, as the barstool philosopher says, it's a free country, and you have an inalienable, constitutionally protected right to invest morphemes with whatever sense you please. But securing the agreement of others is more difficult than imposing on oneself. Self abuse is always a ready consolation, but making a community-pleasing sense where there is no antecedent system of justification in place is, generally, much more difficult than some theorists take it to be. Moreover, even when we succeed in pleasing ourselves, we can never quite shake the knowledge of our imposition, the knowledge of our own ingenuity in performing a tour de force. And, of course, successfully imposing an "alien" sense on a string of words already fully justified in "meaning" is also possible, but not within the domain of *interpretation*.

What causes our dismay at the point of recalcitrance is not something in the nature of language or history or culture or whatever, but a "glitch" in the local, ad hoc system of intentionality. The "glitch," however, is not an inevitability (a result, for example, of the fact that *exotopy* is inescapable in language, that the *other* or *opposite* always unreads or unravels what its doppelgänger reads or ravels), but a species of accident or carelessness or dumbness to which our frail nature is susceptible, if not natively inclined. We and our systems are rotten for perfection, though seldom perfect. Usually our systems are thoroughly without perhaps ever being completely saturated with fittingness or rightness. Even so, if we do not *always* choose best, we *usually* choose appropriately, usually choose what is fitting, since it is by so choosing that we get what we want or where we're going.

And against our susceptibility to dumbness and accident the forces of what we can call *symbolic inertia* are working. Our terms and systems are narcissists, preoccupied with taking care of number one; that is, the thirst that sends us to the makeshift bar tends to keep our interests and actions usefully focused, and the interests our works succeed in exciting are the interests they remain determined to satisfy. If we have given emphasis to the possibilities of satisfaction, of coherence, of internal plausibility, and so on, we have done so to redress the balance, which has been weighted by so much in modernist and postmodernist thought on the side of breakdown, contradiction, self-cancelation, self-immolation, and so on.

What we have come to recognize is that if there is no Foundation, there are innumerable *foundations, worlds and versions in which words and thoughts or concepts correspond to things within systems of justification.* Truth is rational acceptability within a system of belief and desire or intention. Outside such a system of rational acceptability there is nothing; there are no concepts whatsoever, not even the trace of one. Nothing clears the head quite so completely (nothing leaves us quite so emptyheaded and emptyminded) as the elimination of all conceptual schemes and all standards of rational acceptability.

Although sometimes the text cracks, the bough breaks (and the baby falls) and sometimes the center will not hold even when the best are rich in conviction or passionate intentionality, there are in our practices happinesses as well as cares. More often than not the architect's blueprints happily meet the conditions of their own satisfaction (the sign system of which they are made does not crack, split, or otherwise undo or unread itself), and when they do so satisfy themselves, more often than not they facilitate the construction of a bridge that satisfies the contractor's best hopes and, finally, the driver's immediate driving interests. The bridge has within its sign system of steel girders, suspension lines, and other elements no internal principle of self-destruction or self-contradiction, no principle for the car driver to be alarmed about, at any rate. Even if oxidation is burning up steel, there is time enough to get across the bridge and time enough to put out the rust. As it is with the bridge in blueprint and steel, so it very, very often is with many other plans and projects of mice and men.

The ankle bone connects to the leg bone, the leg bone to the thigh bone, and so on, until the plan of the man is the man of the plan.

From Hume, Quine, Derrida, and many others we can learn that our efforts to establish firm (non-epistemological) foundations (or a firm Foundation) for our various epistemological claims are useless expenditures of energy, and from many thinkers we can learn that of the many possible last norms and values available to us there is no "maker good and true" of one or of one set of them. From all this, however, we are not obliged to learn either that "anything goes" or that "nothing holds." From a particular vantage point (a Humean one, say), it is certainly the case that there are no durable objects interacting causally with one another in the world, and from another (a Derridean vantage point, say), it is the case that there is no signified underlying and making good our designations (no signified, at any rate, that is untainted by the conceptual, the intentional, the mental, no signified that does not, as Gerald Manley Hopkins says, wear man's smudge and share man's smell).[2] But none but the truculent skeptic has been content to know no more.

With Hume, and to the Derrideans (if not to Derrida himself), we can say that the beliefs that philosophy undermines are indispensable to the conduct of life. And, more important, if they are indispensable to life, then we can perhaps go Hume one better and say that they are indispensable to philosophy as well. Certainly, what is indispensable cannot be second-rate; and certainly nothing in contemporary critical theory has emerged that can serve as a rating scale of critical activities, that can rule out, on grounds of legitimacy, say, such activities as interpretation or practical criticism, despite the often bullying assertions of some purveyors of theoretical opinions.

Inadvertence

To bring our reflections on these matters to a close, we can note that for the most part it is only by considering works at the level of their interest and justification, at the level of interpretation and practical reasoning that we can show how works may at various points and with more or less significant consequences deviate from their own interests. Clearly, some mistakes are more important to the overall intentionality, to the ad hoc activity as a whole than others; clearly, if we persist in admiring a work that is more or less severely flawed (internally flawed, flawed with respect to its own conditions of satisfaction, that is), we do so not because of its peccadilloes, but in spite of them.

No work is deemed great because of its flaws, but because, flawed as it is, it still enlarges our conceptual stock or deals with human issues at what we take to be a significant and important intellectual, conceptual, or emotional level, because it deals with what are to us important matters or vividly presents moral dilemmas and perplexities that are for us persistently engaging and interesting, without compromising what we take to be their power, subtlety, or complexity. It may well be, for example, that *Measure for Measure* cracks in two, exciting and satisfying one set of interests up to the Duke's interview with Isabella in Act 3 and quite a different set of interests after the interview. But, granting for the nonce the validity of the case against the integrity of the play, we continue to value the work above, let us say, "lesser" but more clearly unified works because, among other things, it presents not only the rival claims of justice and mercy in their argumentative power but also the human circumstances calling for adjudication in all their richness and complexity, in the circumstances, that is, that put our views on the "proper" relations between justice and mercy to their severest tests.

Since perfection is seldom the consort of human beings, most of our schemes and works are corrigible, perfectible in one way or another at one point or another. And although some mistakes are faux pas of heroic proportions (as the *Measure for Measure* mistake would be, if it were one), most are merely matters of casual inadvertence, details that cannot be assimilated to the current or to a new working hypothesis, but that are easily neglected or quickly forgotten. For example, at one point in the description of the convocation in the woods, the narrator of Nathaniel Hawthorne's "Young Goodman Brown" asserts that "some affirm that the lady of the governor was there," thereby inadvertently introducing the possibility of extranarrative, multiple witnesses to—and thus the possibility of testimonial confirmation of—events the functional effectiveness of which depends upon their uncertain status. As soon as we are introduced to "some" from whom, *hypothetically*, we could take depositions relating to the events in the woods, we close down the illusory aspects of the events, upon which our subsequent judgment of Goodman Brown's character is suspended. After wrestling with this line for a few moments, we recognize that the better part of interpretive wisdom counsels neglect; we stop seeking a justification within the textual scheme for what we are now inclined to see as a slip of inadvertence.

Similarly, when, in the middle of "A Modest Proposal," Jonathan Swift's social scientist observes that the landlords would be interested in eating the young infants, since they "have already devoured most of the parents," he speaks feelingly and bitingly but uncharacteristically and thus wrongly. As a friend and coreligionist of the landlords, whose interests he elsewhere rather openly supports, he cannot say what he now says and mean it (either literally or figuratively), without ceasing to be who he is, without violating many of the conditions upon which his character and his (and Swift's) case depend. Swift has clearly made a mistake here, but if the comment dents the artistic integrity of the essay, it does so with our forgiveness, since the artistic inadvertence betrays the author's outrage and enhances his dignity as a moral being. At any rate, we learn from these and countless other mistakes that our conceptual systems are at once knowable, various, corrigible, and perfectible, And we learn that *knowing what does and does not fit is contingent on our imaginative participation in the reasoning upon which the works as systems of justification depend.*

Poetic Practices and Internal Goods

We know we are participating in the text at the level of its interest relativity, understanding its particular features within the system of their justification when our interpretive practice is successful, successful not only in finding fitting accommodations for the various details as they emerge, but also in withstanding the scrutiny of independent investigators and the test of competing conceptual systems, in being more satisfying than any alternative possible system similarly concerned with *internal satisfaction conditions*. Participation in such rationality is deeply satisfying, of course, even when, as often happens, the understanding we achieve is of something that in our personal and private capacities we cannot accept or agree with.

Because we cannot be certain beforehand what conceptual system is responsible for bringing what is before us before us (unless we are very determined readers, mindlessly obedient to a very rigid program), we are obliged to learn our texts—our paintings, poems, versions—pretty much the way we learn a language or the meaning of the various new sentences that we encounter every day. We learn these by acquiring a practice, by relying on what we have learned and used before while improvising along the way, by guessing at justification conditions until we find the fittingness that seems to work best, acquiring thereby our concepts and references and meanings simultaneously with our justification conditions. We call our guess, our justification hypothesis good when it both implies and is implied by everything we encounter. Moreover, everything we encounter is itself a *good* (a good internal to the system) to the extent that it supports, serves, or otherwise contributes to the functioning of the system as a system of self-satisfaction.

It is perhaps worth remarking here that what Kenneth Burke says about poetic practices and what Alasdair MacIntyre says about the "internal goods" of such "practices" as portrait painting and chess can be seen to have a bearing on our discussion. If not exactly apposite to, their views are compatible with those developed here and elsewhere in this essay. In "Poetics in Particular, Language in General," speaking of "poetics" and using the word "principles" where we might use "justification conditions," Burke observes: ". . . the poet makes a poem; and his ways of making the poem are *practices* which implicitly involve principles, or precepts. The critic, in matching the poetry with a poetics, seeks to make these implicit principles explicit." He seeks to "bring out the modes of judgment implicit in the decisions which the poet's work exemplifies. . . ."[3] By a "practice" MacIntyre means a "coherent and complex form of . . . activity through which goods internal to that form of activity are realized in the course of trying to achieve those standards of excellence which are appropriate to, and partially definitive of, that form of activity. . . ." Such goods are to be distinguished from "external goods," from wealth, fame, or power, for example, which pursuit of the activity might bring. External goods can be achieved by many means; "their achievement is never to be had *only* by engaging in some particular kind of practice." Internal goods, on the other hand, cannot be achieved except by engaging in the activity, by playing chess or painting a portrait, for example. The goods are internal in that they can only be specified in terms of the activity (the goods are virtues of the activity, are powers and values within the possibilities of the system) and in that "they can only be identified and recognized by the experience of participating in the practice in question."[4]

Adjusting the focus slightly for purposes of illustration, we would note that if to consider a text as a doorstop or as a financial investment (or perhaps as a reflection of power relations, of social/ideological "realities") is to consider it *externally*, then to consider it as a system of rationality, as a novel, say, with its own imperatives and conditions of satisfaction, is to consider it *internally*. Certainly, many things other than the text could function as doorstops (including many other texts) or as investments (including many other art works), but no other "thing" could be quite so right, quite so peculiarly appropriate in all its particulars under the operative conditions of satisfaction as this work, or this work fully justified in its interests. Unfortunately, few critics today have much belief or interest in the *principles of practice* or in the *practices of virtue*.

Interpretation and Reading

We have seen above how it is quite possible for a work to fail to be unto its own self true, how writers can slip Lethe-wards and forget their and the text's own best interests. Usually such slips are not fatal, and we continue to admire and to be moved, delighted, and enriched by the work in spite of our finding here and there a peccadillo or two. And surely it requires no flapper from Swift's Flying Island to remind us of occasional lapses in ourselves, when in the midst of our projections (as readers) we discover that we have been working from an incorrect conceptual hypothesis, a misconception of the system of rationality in place. We are going along smoothly when something we encounter forces us to recognize that our bill cannot belong to a duck, or to realize that "God's plastic arm" is a term of praise, not of abuse or satire. Cases such as these are not particularly problematic, since we either discern how the *text* (and author) went "wrong" or correct *our* misunderstanding; and the net result in each case is a handsome dividend for the understanding.

What causes trouble are those special cases in which two or more readings seem equally compelling and fully "justified." To many, perhaps most, critics today such cases are not special but paradigmatic. For these critics, literature is by nature or by virtue of its dependence on language open to many, indeed an indeterminate number of interpretations. A given text is a site of interpretive activity, a site on which much can be erected because there is no stable edifice in place (in some versions, of course, it is a site always already occupied by the Powers That Be).

At this stage, it is unnecessary, I hope, to rehearse again the arguments in favor of treating the text as a rationally structured consequence of practical reasoning, which with the aid of our natural, human, genetically based conceptualizing abilities and our acquired skills at learning new practices we can (ideally or in principle) come to understand in all its rationality. It may be worth remarking, however, that most of what is called interpretation is not interpretation at all, if we take interpretation to be restricted to the very rigorous enterprise of providing a full or reasonably full account of all particulars (or an account from which any particulars not discussed could be derived in a fuller treatment) and of their relations of value and emphasis in terms of justification conditions or of providing a reasonably full account of the internal goods of a particular system of rationality.

As used in this essay, interpretation is a very distinct kind of effort, one sharply distinguished from "reading," the practice commonly confused with interpretation. For our purposes "reading" is not "interpretation," because it presupposes interpretation, presupposes *an* interpretation. Most critics today are well "beyond interpretation" at the outset, since texts, to the extent that they are discussed at all, are subordinated to interests in "power" or "culture," for example ("Culture Studies," as anyone who is with it knows, is where it's at today). But even those who do "readings" of texts are also beyond interpretation in that what has their concern depends upon some prior conceptual understanding of the text. For example, many psychoanalytic readings (at least those of the sort practiced by, for example, Norman Holland) and many "deconstructionist" readings (at least those prepared by, for example, G. Douglas Atkins and virtually every other "practical" deconstructionist) presuppose and depend upon what are essentially "new critical" "interpretations" for their "surface" or "manifest" details or for their initial terms, categories, or tensions.[5] They begin with a presumption of the interpretive importance of such terms or categories as "authority," "legitimation," or "supplement" or such binary opposites as speech/writing, nature/nurture, individual/society, reason/passion, and so on.

Justification and Textual Ambiguity

Nevertheless, once the above allowances have been made and interpretation has been distinguished from reading, the fact remains that for some texts (far fewer than we are accustomed to think; such texts are quite rare despite the many assertions to the contrary) two or more interpretations seem to be "fully justified." In relatively recent critical discussion the chestnut cases of textual tolerance in the face of conflicting or incompatible interpretive designs are Wordsworth's "A Slumber Did My Spirit Seal" and James's "The Turn of the Screw."[6] Since what has our interest here is not the specific nature of interpretive controversy but the fact of controversy itself, the fact that more than one system of rationality seems to be fully justified, we can neglect the subtleties and nuances of critical debate and simply outline in general terms the incompatible schemes to which the texts have been variously adjusted before commenting on the relevance and importance of such special cases to our ongoing argument.

Briefly, then, with Wordsworth's poem (which is short enough to be quoted in full),

> A slumber did my spirit seal;
>   I had no human fears;
> She seemed a thing that could not feel
>   The touch of earthly years.

No motion has she now, no force;
  She neither hears nor sees;
Rolled round in earth's diurnal course,
  With rocks, and stones, and trees.

one controlling conception assumes that the poem expresses and gives painful immediacy to the speaker's realization of irreparable loss, to the speaker's unavoidable wakefulness to the permanent un- wakefulness of a loved one, whereas the other controlling conception finds in the poem, especially in the last line with its culminating stress on the organic vitality of "trees," a comfort as well as a care, a large consolation for the speaker's loss in the pantheistic affirmation of the ending, finds indeed a macrocosmic compensation for his microcos- mic loss. On the other hand, with James's story, under one synthesiz- ing conception the work is a ghost story involving young children in supernatural or unnatural doings, told by a reliable, sober, imper- sonal narrator who is also the governess of the children, whereas un- der the competing conception the work is a psychological horror story, a study, as Edmund Wilson has asserted, in "the hallucinatory effects of repressed sexuality," presented through the voice of the sexual neurotic herself, who subjects her young charges, Flora and Miles, to "all the vagaries of her progressively more and more de- ranged mind" until they are brought to destruction. Wilson makes the case a hard one by asserting that "almost everything from begin- ning to end can be read equally in either of two senses."[7]

About these cases, assuming for the moment that in each instance the alternative interpretations are justified and incompatible, the fol- lowing points relevant to our developing argument should be made. First, if writers can sometimes offend or violate the conditions upon which their text's satisfactions depend, as we have seen in the Swift and Hawthorne examples above, they can also fail to realize them fully, inadvertently leaving their text open to legitimate—that is, al- lowable—but unfortunate and unwanted construals, as when the text—the "I didn't say he stole it" text, for example—neglects to in- dicate the word on which the emphasis should fall. Taken by itself, ambiguity of this sort (accidental, unintended ambiguity, as distinct from determinate, intended ambiguity, which is not at all ambiguous about what it is ambiguous about) cannot be made to pledge alle- giance to one system of rationality, though it is easy to imagine how a certain contextualization or a certain change in background condi- tions could make a patriot of the quisling.

It is easy to imagine, for instance, how the goofball possibilities in the sentence "The stolen painting was found by the tree" could be eliminated in a jiffy by an inquisitive associate: *"Where* was the stolen painting found? By the house? By the river?" "No! The stolen painting was found by the tree." Or consider how one interpretation of "A Slumber" would be affected by changes in background knowledge, the discovery, for example, *of* five more poems mourning the same death, *of* an authentic letter testifying unequivocally to the poet's unmitigatable grief at the time of composing the poem, or *of* an essay expressing the poet's lifelong, unwavering antagonism to pantheistic views. Changes in background conditions do nothing, of course, to change the susceptibility of the poem to divergent interpretations, but they alter utterly the plausibility conditions of the rational acceptability of the interpretations.

Second, if writers sometimes fail to mark the emphases crucial to their versions, to evoke those and only those aspects of stereotypical knowledge essential to their meanings, or to signalize the categories of understanding necessary to their conceptual schemes, thereby creating the conditions for diversity of interpretation, readers for their part sometimes fail on the side of premature articulation or of partiality, making large pronouncements on the basis of their early and small findings and then adjusting all that comes within view to the exigencies of their preferred adolescent hypotheses, with the result that two or more interpretations seem to be "fully justified." If in the first instance the text is insufficient to its "intentionality" (is not fully "satisfied," is ambiguous), in the second instance readers are sufficient to the wrong intentionality (are sufficient only to their own). Altering the ground rules slightly, we here assume not a radical ambiguity in the text but an insufficiency in readers to come to a satisfactory understanding of the full rationality of the text. In general, the insufficiencies of the competing conceptual hypotheses do not become glaringly apparent as insufficiencies until a superior hypothesis appears and is adopted or until one of the competitors strengthens itself from within, adding new to previously established justifications, or receives unexpected support from without, becoming the sole beneficiary of the will of newly discovered "facts."

Third, it is important to recognize that nothing in our position suggests that the justification conditions determining the references, concepts, emphases, and meanings of existent texts will be quickly, easily, or *inerrantly* gotten by readers, will come to readers as easily as leaves come to the tree, disappointment to the lover, or anguish to the Red Sox fan, or that all readers will agree that the gettable has been gotten, even when it has been gotten. On the other hand, what is more than suggested, what is affirmed, is that if the text is a text, then it is a system of rationality, one that can be understood as that system, even though it may be for us an unacceptable, unwholesome, or otherwise disagreeable system.

And perhaps here it is once again necessary to observe that nothing in our position suggests that we are not bound more or less tightly in various ways by historical, cultural, class, or gender categories that affect more or less immediately what we make and what we make of what we meet, but our successes in participating in diverse and disparate, early and late, foreign and domestic schemes convinces us not only of the indefinite flexibility of our conceptualizing abilities but of the over- and underdeterminateness of all the postulated constraints (the gender, class, cultural, historical constraints) on those abilities. Such constraints, we find, determine both too much (i.e., allow for or make possible a wide range of different and conflicting systems) and too little (i.e., are incapable of explaining the appropriateness or necessity of a considerable number of particular details in any given system). Where they have precision, they lack scope (they can account for this or that aspect of the text but not these or those aspects or the text as a whole construct; that is, the whole text cannot be projected from the interests of the locally appropriate explanations). And where they have scope, they lack precision (they can account, say, for all the various productions of a given epoch—be they ever so various, be they car designs, filmscripts, cartoons, the length of Santa Claus's beard, and whatever—but they cannot account for very much of anything in particular).

Fourth, although by the terms of the present discussion allowance is made for the possibility of rival and conflicting *interpretations* of the "same" text, the self-interestedness of texts is such that irreconcilable conflict, when not occasioned by radical, linguistic ambiguity, usually betokens the insufficiency of both conceptual schemes (or of at least one of them). Where there is local ambiguity in a given text—where, that is, an expression or passage refuses to give up its willingness to serve more than one master, despite the not inconsiderable blandishments of the prevailing and very satisfying interpretive hypothesis— we apply to the troublemaker ad hoc, makeshift tests, giving up the "full coherence test," say, for the "preponderance of the evidence" or the "all-things-considered" test, making do improvisationally as we make out and make up the sense as we go along. All things considered, despite the intractablility of the ambiguity, this rather than that justification system seems to provide the best or fullest explanatory model of the text as a whole. What our working understanding allows for, then, is a "tolerable incongruity," a wrinkle in the otherwise smooth cloth, a pea under the still-comfortable mattress.

In passing I would note that insufficiency of conceptual grasp

seems to apply to both of our illustrative cases. The pantheistic interpretation of "A Slumber" is finally less able to withstand scrutiny than
the "grief" interpretation, though even it is insufficiently refined.
Nevertheless, the brevity of the poem and the richness of its "stereotypes" (rocks, stones, trees, slumber, thing, fears) make radical ambiguity seem almost inescapable (its symbols are very *dense*, i.e., capable
of serving many systems of meaning). The poem almost approximates the condition of an arbitrary sentence, the assertibility conditions of which cannot be surveyed, as we have seen.

On the other hand, "The Turn of the Screw" resists enlistment under one or the other (or any single) interpretive hypothesis, because
it is, in my view, a radically flawed text, one that remains interesting
to us not in spite of its flaws (as, say, *Measure for Measure* would remain even if it broke apart in the middle as some critics suggest), but
because of them. It is neither a duck nor a rabbit; nor, on the other
hand, is it quite a rabbit-duck. Wilson is quite right when he says that
"*almost everything* from beginning to end can be read equally in either
of two senses" (my emphasis). The "almost" in "almost everything" is
both right and, I think, devastating. No matter how singlemindedly
one reads, alien possibilities bleed into one's conceptual fabric,
possibilities that cannot be bleached out with ad hoc, "all-things-
considered" explanatory expedients.

Although perhaps possible, it is very difficult to make a highly detailed rabbit that is also a highly detailed duck, and the constructional
problems are compounded when, as in verbal as distinct from pictorial representations, the duck must walk and talk like a duck and the
rabbit hop and carry on like a rabbit, as well as interact with one another in one plot scheme or another. What we had taken to be a duck
is forced to act in unducklike but very rabbitlike ways. However tolerant we may be, this, we must confess, is too odd a duck even for us.

Fifth, and finally, it is worth remarking, I think, that no matter how
disparate the rival interpretations are, no matter how deeply committed they are to no matter how radically different or antithetical assumptions, we have virtually no trouble understanding what they are
trying to explain and how they go about the job of explanation. Incompatible interpretations are readily understood, and the nature
and bases of the incompatibility are easily discerned. We switch with
ease from a ghost-story interpretive paradigm to a psychological
horror-story paradigm, and if the "rocks," "stones," "trees," "fears,"
"thing," and "slumber" function now in the service of cosmic affirmation and now in that of unappeasable grief we have no trouble
preserving references and concepts as we alter emphases and uses,

preserving "entities" and (some) relations as we change "meanings" and reorganize values.

In Sum

The large or deep consequences of these humble, peasant-faced "facts" have not gone without their (perhaps mind-numbing) iteration in this essay, but since, as Johnson observes, we need more often to be reminded than informed, the generous will perhaps forgive us the following summation, mercifully presented in the pithy mode. In ascertaining the distinct interests of the different interpretations and recognizing across their radical conceptual differences the persistence of (many of) the "same" references and concepts, we affirm the following at least implicitly (among other things):

1. the determinateness and stability of "meaning" within a particular conceptual scheme (endorsing, hence, a kind of *internal foundationalism*, in which within the scheme we know in no uncertain terms what refers to what and what relates to what in what emphatic and normative ways);

2. the impossibility of references and concepts apart from a system of rationality;

3. the dependence of our understanding of differences on the principle of charity (we share concepts and references across schemes; our schemes are not monolithic, not self-enclosed monads, emitting no light without and admitting no light within themselves);

4. the inevitability of authors, intentionalities, texts, justification and assertibility conditions, truth (within the scheme), justice (within the scheme), and goodness (and hence beauty, within the scheme);

and much more.

Chapter 14
Conclusion: Worlds Without End

In a very important sense this essay has been one long reclamation project, an attempt to recover for use much that has been discarded as worthless by recent critical theory, discarded primarily because it was assumed to be attached—either ignorantly or sentimentally—to an outmoded, thoroughly discredited metaphysics and epistemology, the metaphysics of naive realism and the epistemology of direct knowledge, of unmediated vision. What we are left with in the end, I hope, is a more spacious field in which to conduct a vast array of activities requiring a multiplicity of critical tools, a field, moreover, full of folk with diverse and sundry interests, who are now able to undertake an unlimited number of projects, without fear of being driven from the scene of their useful industry by the self-appointed thought police of theory, who, despite their awareness of and insistence on the immanent nature of meaning, still seem to know what language or history *just is*—to know, in short, what's what. Something has been done in this essay, I hope, to rehabilitate or reinvest with dignity many critical enterprises and practices that have undergone the lash of excoriation and suffered the shame of excommunication in recent years, largely because they were *supposed* to advance, promote, or be supported by heretical, officially condemned ontotheological, phallologocentric (or ontotheophalloethnologocentric) principles and assumptions, because they were informed and driven by the antichrist's antichrist, the creating word, the principle of Logos in the religion variously denominated Foundationalism, Essentialism, Correspondence, Naive Realism, Objectivism, or Humanism.

Finding Centers, Or, Turning from the Linguistic Turn

For many long years many a hipster of theory has assumed that once meaning goes immanent (once things and thoughts and all the rest go inside conceptual schemes, inside the language by which they are constituted what they are), then objectivity, determinate meaning, truth, justification, and so on disappear from the scene, along with authors, stable texts, and standards of value (since these are all nothing but precipitates of always already in place categories and systems of meaning). And the theorist has further assumed that the only way out of the prisonhouse(s) of language is by a leap or fall into the abyss.

Concomitantly and coordinately with these assumptions there has emerged the virtual supplantation of the poet by the critic as a locus of interest, and not just any critic, but the critic elevated or exalted to theoretician or poet-theoretician. To trace the lineage of the prevailing views back to this and that Romantic poet or philosopher, to this and that Roman rhetorician, or to this and that pre-Socratic thinker shall be for us a pleasure deferred. For our present needs, we shall only glance immediately behind us and note that the linguistic turn in critical thinking has not been an unmixed blessing. For better and worse ours is (among many other things, of course) a discourse-crazed, a sign-soaked, sign-entranced age.

Taking the exemplary rather than the survey or overview road, we can observe that what logical positivism was—and in some quarters may still be—to the nomothetic or "hard" sciences, structuralism was (and in some quarters may still be) to the human, social, or "soft" sciences, namely, an attempt to get beyond the distracting and finally inconsequential babble of authors and speakers, of individuals, to the principles and conditions of meaning in "language" or other sign systems, the diachronic, synchronic, substitutional, combinatorial rules and operations through which all that is spoken or meant, including authors, is spoken or meant. In our pursuit of signs, we have managed to transcend those stultifying, maudlin attachments to *self, person, individual* (and all their noisome progeny and relatives, will, choice, deliberate action, intentionality, determinate meaning, and so on), managed to move beyond humanism to the worlds of systems, of terms, doctrines, and ideas in various relations. There is now no fleeing what sometime we did seek, however, for we are absorbed by the object of our inquiry and shaken out, if we are needed at all, as tokens and counters of the structures or code systems that we had believed to be our creatures—and thus under our protective care—in the prelapsarian days of delusional grandeur, when all the animals and plants, the great and the small, proudly and contentedly wore the names we gave them and either gladdened under our ministrations or responded with alacrity to our instructions.

And once everything went textual (once what *is* became only *semes*), it was easy to drive a *post* in before structuralism and to show that no center or mooring would hold. In short, once the sign of the thing became the "thing," it was not far to learn that everything is really intertextual, since there is no *here* but for *there*, no *this* but for *that*. Nor was it far to learn that the prevalence of any this or that at this or that time was not founded on Truth or Right, but was—and could be nothing other than—a consequence of the power of (some logocentrically deluded) authorities, oppressors, imposing their wills, that is, categories, on (some logocentrically deludable) others, the oppressed, and doing so in such a way that the dominated could be entrusted with the keys to their own cells. In all historical practices and all the practices of history (i.e., all practices), all the parties acted "naturally" and in the best interests of the best good. Power was exercised and endured according to the nature of things, and the plantation was a happy plantation, until a new notion of the natural put "nature" into question. When the dust occasioned by the inevitable conflict of power claims finally settled, all were pleased to learn that the spoils had gone to the party with "nature" on its side. Obviously, language in our time is a highly ramified tree, and we have here barely sketched but one line of ramification on but one of its brachiations.

Despite the obvious limitations of this way of talking "at large" about complex issues, it does have the virtue of highlighting prominent features in the theoretical topography. For example, from this perspective it is possible within the bounds of fairness to say that if the "hard" science view of "things" as matter or material has led ineluctably to the privileging of physical, preferably electrochemical or subatomic, explanations (with all other explanations or ways of talking being consigned to magic or myth), the human or social "science" view of "things" as language (or semic) has led persistently, if eluctably, to the privileging of linguistic (or semiological) explanations. If there is nothing apart from "writing" and no writing apart from the linguistic units of which writing is made up, then explanations in terms of such units—their nature, possibility, rules of association, and their "meanings" when associated—are inescapably necessary. All other explanations—including and especially, of course, those of the "hard" scientists and the secular humanists—are consigned to magic or myth, or are the oppressive products of western, white, male hegemony.

If all literature is discourse and all discourse linguistic (or semiotic), then the injunction of inquiry is clear: follow the language. Following the language in one direction has led to the abyss ("all roads lead to the abyss" is the abysmal view of some, of course), whereas following it in other directions has led to preoccupations with various terms, tropes, figural maneuvers, rhetorical operations, and, always and ever, theses, themes, claims, propositional assertions, doctrinal bulls and bullies. Beginning with assumptions about the distinctiveness of "poetic discourse" from scientific, logical, nonpoetic discourse and, hence, about the importance of such figures or tropes as irony, paradox, or ambiguity, the New Critics locate the dynamic tensions, the special ideational oppositions (e.g., rich/poor, wit/witchcraft, burial inside/burial outside the church, etc.) that epitomize and crystallize the peculiar nature of the work. And of course, many psychoanalytic critics, most notably, Norman Holland, begin their discussions of transformation and displacement by taking the New Critical, "thematic" reading as the manifest form of a latent, suppressed fantasy. In this scheme, the "central meaning" has its analogical counterpart in a "central fantasy." Moreover, as we have seen, the traditional or conventional reading from which the deconstructionist, in his practical mode, works to effect his reversals of emphasis and his erasures is almost always the New Critical one—one, at any rate, featuring antithetical elements or some *one* element which invariably discloses the *other* it would hide, suppress, or repress. Logocentricity is ever and always "propositional," "discursive," or "figural" in some way or other.

Indeed, wherever we turn our view—for example, to Marxist, historicist, Bakhtinian, or other categories and "readings"—we are greeted by opposed pairs or by bearers of antithetic propositional content. Any aspect of the text worth discussing is an implicit or explicit messenger or representative, as many have grown fond of saying today, of *ideology*. Everything, we are told, is ideological—from the perspective of what ideology this ideological statement, or its negate, is made no one, of course, can say. Anyone who has raised his head for only one sand-clearing moment and looked about the contemporary critical scene quickly and dartingly knows that no *relation of terms* (and ideas) has proved more durable or been employed more often than the "antithetic" one; and no set of operations more durable than the binary one. Of course, our preferred mode of reasoning is the dialectical mode. We are always dealing with *the* (antithetic) other, and then with the other's *other*, or always buffeted about within a tensed system of dynamic oppositions, for example, master/slave, nature/culture, city/country, male/female, individual/state, wit/witchcraft, yin/yang, love/reason, fancy/understanding, and on and on, ad infinitum. Either the antithesis (or the alterity) is a surface phenomenon, proclaiming itself openly in the text as, say, a love/honor conflict, or it is a beast of two essences, one announced and one suppressed. In this latter case, the critic usually fastens onto some abstraction mentioned in the text either prominently and repeatedly (or even incidentally)—for example, authority, repetition, supplementation, legitimacy, and so on—then talks about it generally and as it appears in a number of works (some by the author initially under scrutiny), and finally shows how in various ways its power or value is regularly undermined by the "other," antithetical abstraction it would silence ("authority" is always subtly deauthorizing itself, losing its certainty in tentativeness and doubt, for example). Abstract terms are related to abstract terms, and we are the beneficiaries of some new insight into language, mind, society, history, politics, class, gender, ideology, or whatever.

Critics are empowered to say what the words, terms, phrases, and doctrines "mean" in this or that or any context (in any given era) because they know what language, history, class, or ideology is, know at least what units of meaning and value go with what other units of meaning and value and what can be combined with or substituted for what to effect what "meanings" or possibilities of meaning. At any rate, it should require no strong-arm rhetorical measures to convince the reader of what he already knows from his own experience and probably from his own practice, namely, that "thematizing" is today the most common (indeed, the most "natural") critical activity. Self-effacing shyness itself can without trepidation boldly say that many readers—the vast majority—do not think they are doing criticism at all unless they are thematizing; and for them "interpretation" (if it is indulged in at all) is a matter of locating the thematic navel or the thematic principle of the work, or of finding an abstraction to ring the changes on. Of other critical activities they either know nothing or know little more than that they have allegedly been caught *in flagrante delicto*, discovered in criminal association with disreputable and thoroughly discredited views (caught in compromising positions on the Foundation's grounds, one might say).

What we have been arguing, of course, is not that all linguistic-discursive-thematic approaches are wrong, wrongly directed, or wrongheaded, though certainly all those with global or totalitarian ambitions are wrong, misguided, or just altogether too big for their britches. The view, for example, that everything is ideological and thus requires an ideological explanation is no more interesting or compelling than the view that everything is geometrical and requires a geometric explanation; for even if in some vague, general, and trivial sense everything could be said to be ideological, every ideology permits—because it cannot exclude or preclude—many diverse, even conflicting formulations, expressions, and practices. And, even if the ideology were as stern a conceptual taskmaster as one could imagine, there would still be room for an indefinite number of conflicts of interest within the regime or archive—and family disputes (disputes within conceptual systems) are real disputes, which as quickly and as often as others turn from smoke to fire, from anger to violence. More important, however, is the fact that we are interested in many things that cannot be reduced to ideological talk and that call for many kinds of explanations that are not ideological in any sense, unless "ideology" is thoroughly eviscerated of meaningful content and becomes an empty category. We have not argued that they are always and necessarily wrong; rather, we have shown that they are just too narrow in their interests, just too circumscribed in their prospects and projects. Additionally, we have argued that most modern critics have practiced, at best, a form of premature articulation in proclaiming many practices ill-suited for placement on the site of criticism (and theory) and that, the thunderousness of their assertiveness notwithstanding, they have no *foundation* for doing so, no grounds for doing so.

In making room for all "right" thematic versions, we have also made room for many kinds of "rightful" activities. And we have done so by defusing the foundationalist charge with which the condemned views and activities were to be exploded. With our fellow (post)modernists we have insisted that there is no Archimedean place to stand, no place outside all conceptual systems from which to move or get a fix on things, and no conceptual system specially endowed with the right or capacity to pass judgment on other systems. Indeed, it is because there is no conceptually uncontaminated place to stand and no contaminated place of special privilege that *we* have been unable to rule out of court most of the "old-fashioned," humanistic practices summarily dismissed by our linguo-semio-thematic justices.

While recognizing the importance and the necessity of focusing (sometimes) on terms, figures, abstract categories, rhetorical values, themes and so on, we have regularly emphasized the importance and value of other interests, especially the higher-level interests of various versions of various worlds. Consequently, we have frequently been interested less in terms and their permutational and relational possibilities within a conception of language or a conception of the categories of power in a historical era or political unit than in principles of organization and use, in motivations, in purposes, in ICMs (idealized cognitive models), in conceptual systems, in the conditions of satisfaction internal to intentional states, in rightnesses within ad hoc categories, in justification and assertibility conditions. In short, we have been interested in the *invisibilities* (the mental and conceptual "foundations") that underlie and give visibility and power to the visibilities—the "things," emphases, and values—in our various ways of talking and making.

Essential Foundations of Relativism

Although, like our thoroughly modern (or postmodern or meta-postmodern and poststructuralist) colleagues, we have given up on the transcendental signified, we have not, like them, given up on "objectivity" and "rightness" and much else prematurely, unjustly, and unwarrantedly ostracized from the commonwealth of acceptability. Thus, we have not been obliged to take refuge in eclecticism (the Rube Goldberg contraption of criticism, in which every part works against the interest of some other part), skepticism (the Word [dis]incarnate, the principle of unrule working to bring about its own immolation in its successive failures to find any standards of rationality acceptable), or relativism (the sort of relativism, at any rate, that never met an intellectual sailor—never met an idea, system, version, or world—that it didn't like or that it could find any reason to take the least exception to). In place of a Foundation, we have discovered many foundations, and found them to be "real" foundations, capable of supporting structures in which beings such as we can actually live and laugh and do much else.

Dropping essentialism, we have nevertheless found much that is essential, many things, categories, references, concepts, and so on that are essential to a version, much that is essential relative to a system. And turning from correspondence—the grand Correspondence—in which words or thoughts had themselves validated and confirmed by the world of preexistent things, we ran bump into a rambunctious crowd of "correspondences," of "real" correspondences between words or thoughts and things within systems. In each of these systems words and things necessarily corresponded because they came into existence together—words and stuff were coeval with world and hence coterminous and mutually dependent. Moreover, these "real" correspondences are functional, we found, in worlds of "real" consequence, worlds, that is, in which being "right" or "wrong," having "true" or "false" beliefs, had real—sometimes fatal—consequences and made a heap of difference to one's well-being or satisfaction, for one was not likely to get what one wanted or where one wanted to go without having the right belief in the right world.

And we found that one was not likely to *make* a good and right version (text, interpretation, bridge, shoe, or whatever) unless one kept within the categories of understanding of one's version and its interests and made sure that one's categories continued not only to belong but to fit together, and *fit in such a way as to enhance the work-ingness of the whole intended,* so that in the end the desires one formed within the operative system of beliefs would be blessed with a most satisfying satisfaction. In such happy circumstances we have true rightness, hence "truth." What is "right" is "true"; what is "true" is "justified," and what is "justified" is "good," good for you and good for me and, thus, good for us, for, that is, folks like us—at least under these emergent circumstances and for these contingent purposes.

"Good for us" is crucial because we have been concerned through-out with *our* interests and what are good explanations *for us* under these and those circumstances and given this or that purpose. We have been concerned with "human" explanations at the level of our present interest. Sometimes a chemical or neuronic or political or ideological explanation—as good and as humanly interesting as it is under some circumstances of interest—simply is not as good as an anger or jealousy explanation, just is not what we had in mind, just is not what we had a mind to mind.

And if we have let go of realism in its naive or physicalist version, we have managed to hang on to a kind of realism, the kind which Putnam has called "internal realism." This is a "realism" of "real" things in real versions, entailing right and wrong decisions and real consequences. Although versional, the real we encounter here is re-ally real, and if you don't want to bark your shins (or worse) and you do want to get what you want, then you had better take now this and now that real world seriously for what it is.

In all, then, we have abandoned foundationalism, essentialism, cor-respondence, naive realism, and objectivism, without slipping into eclecticism, into undiscriminating or total relativism (the open-admission-ism, the "ism" without admission standards), into skepti-cism (the no-admission-ism) or into monism (the admit-one-ism). And we have given all this up without losing facts, things, standards, justification conditions, right and wrong, without losing *foundations* (on which structures good and true can be built), *essential features* (es-sential to the description, theory, version, system), *correspondences* (of words or thoughts and things in versions), *realities* (internal real reali-ties), and, of course, *objectivity* (shifting and various objective stan-dards and methodological criteria). From this cost-benefit analysis we learn in the end that our account is deeply in the black—in that we have gained much at little cost. What we are left with is a huge stock-pile of opportunities and availabilities for the making and under-standing of no one knows how much. What we are left with is a *relativism with foundations and standards,* a relativism whose productiv-ity of systems of delight and instruction is rather advanced than impeded by employment regulations and standards and practices acts. We are left, in short, with pluralism.

Of course, what all this means at the level of critical practice is that we are free to undertake with a clear and untroubled conscience not only many of the kinds of projects most recently favored by the "professionals" and the "political terrorists" among us but also most of the projects that had formerly, in the prepoststructuralist days, excited our interests, activated our energies, filled our minds, and satisfied our hearts. On the other side, we are perhaps no longer obliged, in an effort to attract a publisher or win an audience, to suit up the "traditional" project that we are really interested in and have in fact produced in some garish terminology or some chic categorical apparel currently in vogue, or no longer obliged to paint our seascape on the velvet terminological background supplied by some popular logodaedalist.

Interpretation and the Deepdown Fittingness of Things

In this essay we have regularly stressed first the *possibility* and then the *importance* of *interpretation*, of understanding texts within the system of their interest and rationality, in large part because "interpretation," "determinate meaning," "intentionality" and related concepts have been repeatedly "put into question," "problematized," or simply dismissed out of hand in recent discussions. Although some today suppose we are so far "beyond interpretation" that there is no going back, we have argued that interpretation is much like the wag's democracy, that is, often discussed but seldom practiced, at any rate seldom practiced in any rigorous and thorough way. What passes for interpretation is more often than not a form of special pleading on behalf of one's preferred categories or favorite antithesis (and, often, its self-erasure) or an exercise in adjusting discernible features of texts to the exigencies of one's hypothesis or tracking down the relations in which specially selected terms and concepts can stand to other terms and concepts, the whole entrepreneurial effort aspiring not to "rightness" or "accuracy" but to a kind of "Look, Ma, no hands" ingenuity and cleverness.

As presented here, interpretation involves coming to an understanding of the text's categories of understanding in their functional relations within a system of rationality. And we have persistently, if quietly and obliquely, insisted that the richness of the literature that we have come most to value is such that our understanding is enlarged with each renewed contact and perhaps never enlarged to fullness or completeness. In reading *Othello* for the fortieth time, we are struck by a new rightness or appropriateness that we had not noticed before. And, of course, our pleasure is not diminished upon rereading even when we make no new discoveries of appropriateness, because, whatever our retentive powers, we cannot keep the whole text in mind and because we cannot, further, even assuming the whole text in mind, have our successive pleasures in their proper order except by reexperiencing the text sequentially, temporally. Coming to such an understanding or enlarging our understanding within an existent understanding, we have argued, is a good (for us), a good in the sense that finding (and making) a satisfaction is always good, that is, satisfying. And it is always pleasurable in proportion to the satisfaction. And being justifiably pleased is always deemed good (by us). The skill part of such an understanding can be developed and refined and, to a large extent and in its main features, taught. Moreover, those to whom it is taught can develop and refine it on their own, largely because in all the cases of its application it admits of right *and* wrong, because the hypothesis from which we project meanings and possibilities is right and adequate to the (always already) justified structure, *or it is not*; our projections can be *disconfirmed* as well as confirmed, and we can be regularly surprised by sin and especially *virtue*, that is, the text's own goods.

And surely those of us who give days and nights to the study of, say, literature can be forgiven for focusing at least some of our attention *on* what we ought not to be embarrassed to call "artistic" or "aesthetic" values, *on* the rather uncommon, wonderful, and remarkable fittingness and workingness of things in certain texts, once they are considered under this or that conception of justification. Perhaps we can even be forgiven for allowing ourselves *to value more highly* than other works those which not only manage to fit much in but to make so much of what fits in *contribute significantly* to the working of the whole work. Surely, we can be forgiven for continuing to admire and honor *Paradise Lost*, the *Essay on Man*, *The Prelude*, and *King Lear* as monuments of unageing intellect, as "masterpieces" even, *even though* as bodies of ideas or systems of thought they are if not philosophically bankrupt, at least intellectually poor, and *even though* most of what is politically, ideologically, historically, etc. interesting in them can be found in many other earlier, contemporaneous, and later works (both serious and comic, both popular and elite, as well as in other cultural artifacts, like trade routes or jokes or whatever) and found perhaps in purer, starker, bolder form in them.

In addition to admiring these works for the largeness of their conception, the extent of their understanding, the importance of the matters they raise and deal with (notwithstanding the attachment of some of them to what are for us outmoded, discredited, disvalued, or bizarre notions), we recognize as we applaud in each of them a superior kind of formal or artistic achievement; we discern in each rightnesses and appropriatenesses that are widely distributed and deeply embedded, that make the whole work, finally, a rare and, hence, especially valuable achievement.

Further, it is worth stressing again that in such works of uncommon achievement it is not simply that the parts are appropriate and, thus, fit in or belong to the scheme, but that they *enhance the workingness of the whole*, that they actively contribute to the special integrity of the whole. Everyone who has read Shakespeare's Sonnet 73 ("That time of year thou mayest in me behold") knows that while each of the three quatrains plays a variation on the "same" idea, says essentially the same thing (i.e., "I am on the verge of death"), the order of the quatrains cannot be altered without subtracting from the achievement. It is not simply that we move metaphorically from a time of year (late autumn) to a time of day (late dusk) to a moment late in the evening, thus contracting the time as we proceed, but that all the categories of exemplification in the poem—primarily space, color, and heat—are making similarly appropriate contributions to our sense of the imminence of death.

What we witness here in the short poem is found as well in works of great extent, such as Pope's *Essay on Man*, in which we find not only a complex and fitting "logic" in the order of the four epistles, as well as within the argumentative structure of each of them, but a peculiarly happy echoing of universal order in the images and analogies by which the argument is sustained in each of the sections, so that in the end we have within the rich integrity of the poem a model—and, thus, a kind of poetic proof—of the order that is the poem's subject. Or, to take an example from drama, the kind of artistic integrity found in Sonnet 73 is also found in *Othello*, in which every scene, virtually every word, not only contributes to the forwarding of the action and to our understanding of the bases of behavior, but also enhances and enriches our sense of the internal goodness and virtue, of the architectonic or symphonic cohesiveness of the work as a whole. One after another every scene, image, or phrase finds itself involved with predecessors or successors in a complexly appropriate system of interimplication. Encountering these words, we are transported to a new order of accomplishment. If the making of such richly self-satisfied, abundantly coherent works is a huge accomplishment (as it is when measured against the standards established over the years by the accomplishments of other toilers in the same fields), then the participation, by means of understanding, in such achievements at the level of their interests and justifications is a huge pleasure, which many today do not experience but which, fortunately (in an odd sense of fortunately, the sense in which ignorance is bliss), their theoretical principles keep them from knowing they are not experiencing.

To talk of these pleasures and these accomplishments to the cognoscenti is undoubtedly to talk unnecessarily; that is, it is to talk to the sailor of the sea, to talk to those who already know what one is talking about and who do not need to be convinced of the pleasure of pleasure. But something is surely awry when one is repeatedly invited to deny the pleasure, or to confess that it is second-rate, insignificant, illusory or impossible, because language is such and such or because what really counts or what everything boils down to is ideology, undoing, colonialism, or whatever. Or if the pleasure is allowed, it is allowed only as a guilty pleasure, one inseparable from one's toleration of or complicity with oppression, racism, or whatever. It has been our goal, in part, to reclaim the pleasure and take the guilt out of it by showing that the text is already an uncommonly rich or dense system of justification and that the system it is is knowable as that system (though coming to know it is no easy or automatic task). It is a system made and recovered by the more or less strenuous exercise of practical reasoning upon materials within grasp or available to reach.

Ethics: Living and Learning

Of course, we are interested in texts for other than artistic or aesthetic reasons, and even our artistic, internal, formal, structural interests are necessarily entangled with the "things," interests, ideas, and values that are the "contents" or the material bases of the successful and satisfying functioning of the work in part and in whole. Indeed, any differentiable part, any isolable element of the work can become the focus of independent interest and inquiry, and anything so isolated for attention can be examined and discussed in connection with any number of things linguistic, social, political, philological, semantic, ideological, anthropological, patriotic, mechanical, biographical, or psychological.

High among our interests in those works not motivated primarily by a system of *ideas* or *themes* but focusing on morally differentiated individuals in humanly interesting situations is an interest in what speaking broadly we can call "ethical quality." Most of our novels, dramas, narrative poems, as well as the majority of our lyric poems, for example, invite us to witness clearly and then to consider carefully and disinterestedly what it would be like to think and feel in such and such frame of mind and live in such and such circumstances, allow us to see vividly and to participate imaginatively in moral perplexities, in situations of moral choice and moral action, to confront those perplexities, not as as a system of ideas or as a corpus of theses or moral propositions, but as a complex of social, personal, emotional circumstances impinging on or otherwise affecting and affected by particular character. What we witness and are moved by are ethical possibilities of living, and we are interested in what it would be like to live in them and live them out (i.e., to know the consequences of their adoption and use).

Upon the moral harmonium more tunes than we can imagine are possible, are consistent with what is implicated in our experience and prior reading. For all the accounts of moral engagement hidden in our availabilities, we are ready and waiting. And for many simple reasons within easy reach, all of which are connected in some way or another with our insatiable interest in ourselves, we are tirelessly interested in "new" exhibitions of moral perplexity and possibility. Such exhibitions enable us to add to the stock of our conceptual storehouse, to enlarge our understanding, and to fit ourselves for further and future understanding.[1]

Life is short, and, like Bottom, we cannot be in all roles or know much about the roles available or possible. These works provide us with "ethical samples" of ethical possibilities, and they are, in a very large and untrivial sense, the schools of our moral sensibilities, teaching us surreptitiously much about the nature and bases of right behavior. As we read these works the line of our sustained interest is the line of moral entanglement, complication, and usually, resolution. In other words, the line of our interest and satisfaction follows the line of the text's moral concerns, and these concerns supply the categories of rightness and the conditions of justification that make up the text's interest and make for artistic fulfillment. But as we move beyond the texts we carry from them conceptual resources serviceable in the making and understanding of many new worlds, and in the making of the good life. Reading literature at the level of its ethical concern (which is, for many works, the level of its justification), with empathetic understanding, will not necessarily make us better people, of course, but it will *exercise our capacity for and improve our skill at moral discrimination*, provide us with concepts useful to the formation of a *regulative image* of the good life, and, thus, make us better equipped for *right action*.

This is certainly not the place to launch a discussion of the ethical dimensions or implications of literature (and other arts), but the argument advanced in this essay clearly indicates the importance of inquiries into the ethical aspects of literature, even as it clears space for them on the site of criticism and theory by showing that there is nothing in an immanent meaning world that precludes such inquiries. Those who reject such inquiries have no *foundation* for such rejection, as we have seen, and once we have refused (on good and sufficient grounds) their charge of foundationalism, there is nothing left in the *theoretical* bag of tricks to pester or trouble our renewed interest in a host of proscribed projects except the bluster of paper slogans (proclaiming, among other things, the death or destruction of authors, of interpretation, of books, of this and that and of all the dreckish liberal stuff that goes into the making of that bloated dragon of error, Secular Humanism).

From this long essay it would not be unreasonable to draw, among others, this inference: inasmuch as literature is made by, for, and of human beings, there are unlikely to be many inquiries into it from which it, offended, will turn away or which will not enlarge our understanding of it or enhance our ability to make and understand new instances of it. Critical ingenuity has been sufficiently prolific not to require specific suggestions for topics from me; but it might be useful to remind ourselves of some broad possibilities, especially of those that have been rather brutally set upon recently by some toughs of theory.

Poetics: Kin, Kind, and Kinkind

From examining works in terms of their internal systems of justification, at the level of their motivation, functioning, and effect (i.e., from meeting the responsibilities of interpretation in some rigorous fashion), we can move quite naturally and easily, for example, to *poetics*, to a consideration of formal lines of affiliation among works as *kinds*, in terms of similarities and differences in their principles of reasoning and conditions of justification. Once we have understood the principles of workingness in first this and then that and then again that work, we can begin to establish categories of likeness/difference discrimination, aligning works, for example, which use similar *means* in similar *ways* to bring about comparable *effects* in similar *conditions of distress or perplexity*. Since we can make relevant statements about similarities in the essential features of several texts (we are not confined to "particulars"), and since works use their linguistic medium in distinguishable ways to express, represent, or disclose what they are interested in expressing, representing, or disclosing, we can begin to outline the *poetics* of distinct forms or kinds of literature.

And if we can do *poetics* (and I see no reason why we cannot), then we can perhaps undertake a history of forms, tracing changes and variations over time in the constructional conditions of forms and noting instances of refinement and innovation in the use of one or another kind of essential feature, as generations of writers respond to the achievements of their predecessors and the possibilities implicit in the formal features themselves.

At this point, discussion can move *from* a concern with the internal, constructional causes within schemes and kinds of schemes and with the changes brought about by refining and "perfecting" the possibilities inherent in the discernible and defining features of the various forms *to* a concern with any number of "preconstructional," extra-literary causes of literary change in social, political, historical, philosophic, gender, musical, or whatever conditions. Here we are especially interested, for example, in the various ways social formations of one kind or another impinge on textual interests, structures, emphases, values, purposes, on kinds of topics discussed, kinds of characters presented, kinds of situations represented, kinds of dilemmas confronted, kinds of diction employed, and so on. We would be interested here in, among other things, how Hobbes or Locke or landscape gardening or the Glorious Revolution or early capitalism or shifts in the nature of audiences or in means of production or distribution impacted, as we say, on this or that literary feature or this or that piece of literature or kind of literature, or created the conditions for the emergence of this or that piece or kind of literature, as well as doing much else besides outside the range of our current "literary" interests. The reader should note well that we are not here specifying how "social formations" or "historical material" or "epistemes" or whatever are to be used or discussed; we are simply talking about a certain kind of talking or writing—a kind not much cultivated today but still estimable.

Criticism: The Wilderness and Beyond

These concerns take us to the border of *poetics* (internally and externally considered), beyond which lies the vast territory, mostly wilderness, of *criticism*, where texts can be seen in their larger artistic, social, political, ideological relations, or as subsumed by one or another domain of interest or value (the psychological, psychoanalytic, linguistic, anthropological, chemical, rhetorical, philological, semantic, or whatever domain). Here ingenuity roams at large and can make literature relate to whatever it wants and can make of literature (or anything else) whatever it wants, as long as in the making it does not shoot itself in the foot (or hoist itself on its own petard, i.e., refute itself) or create that which we cannot have without giving up something that we simply will not and cannot give up. In the Big Sky Country of criticism there is room for—you name it: for source and influence studies (of the traditional and anxious kind), for biography (of various kinds), for reading (of various kinds), for new or old historicist studies (though these are very difficult things to manage, and its practitioners are always on the ledge, always in danger of falling into reification or hypostatization or of expending their energies in the pursuit of the self-generated categories of their own dialectic), for figural, image, and diction studies (at the ordinary, run of the mill, garden variety level and at the meta-, mega-, supra-, infra-level), for all this and, of course, more.

Further, in identifying likenesses and differences among works, creating with each line of association a classification, we are not restricted, *in criticism*, to the deep or full classification required by *poetics*, which has genre identification and definition as its object. Any distinguishable feature, any projectible property or feature can serve as the ground or condition of filiation. As Catherine Z. Elgin observes: "We [can] classify [works] by *subject*, as crucifixion pictures or medical bulletins [or domestic tragedies]; by *style* as impressionist paintings or symbolist poems; [by, we might add, *manner of representation or disclosure*, as first-person or omniscient author narration]. And we classify them by *medium*, as watercolors or news reports; by *author*, as Monets or Flauberts; by *historical or culture milieu*, as Renaissance or Victorian works."[2]

There are undoubtedly many other classifications that ingenuity can contrive in its efforts to contextualize features, and there is undoubtedly no way of classifying works that cannot, at least hypothetically, contribute to our understanding of the work under present scrutiny and, of course, the works we encounter subsequently, since these classifications add to the stock of "availabilities" on which we can draw when we are once again called on to understand or discuss (or make) a new work.[3] In the outback of criticism, then, there is space for an indefinite number of projects to situate themselves, including the following three, with which we will conclude our speculations.

First, we can do something to refine our understanding of the peculiar features of *thought, emotion*, and *expression* that characterize the productions of a given artist or writer. Something there is in various artistic works that enable us to recognize with remarkable sureness, for example, the characteristic Johnson or Donne or Wordsworth quality or to determine whether a particular unidentified piece can be attributed to a particular author. Concerning such attributions, disputes rage and passions are inflamed, but there is scarcely any reader who has read much by one writer who does not feel qualified to judge the authenticity or spuriousness of a document of uncertain provenance but attributed to the writer of his concern. What is even more surprising is that there is considerable agreement among "specialists" about the legitimacy or illegitimacy of any given attribution. And for the most part, this agreement, while often supported by, is not usually grounded in numerical, statistical, or other computer-generated evidence, but in what for lack of a better term we can call the critic's sensibility. It is, I think, reasonable to hope that the bases of this tacit understanding can be made more explicit than they currently are by applying both computer and sensibility to the differentiable qualities of thought, emotion, and expression in the works of various writers. And they can be made more explicit by reasoning back, in good Longinian fashion, from the achieved effects or from the motivations or justification conditions of many works by a single author to the habits of mind, feeling, and expression upon which they necessarily depend, reasoning back, in short, to the material grounds of distinguishable, differentiable achievement. (In the language of understatement, such studies have tended rather to languish than to prosper in this our "post-authorial," "intertextual," and "code-relational" age.)

Second, what can be done for the writer can also be done for the productions of his or any other "age" (with "age" discriminated in the way all our categories are discriminated, i.e., by habit, practice, and agreement, by our seeing a value in such discriminations for certain purposes). With remarkable sureness we are able to distinguish a given work as a production of a given era or period, undoubtedly by bringing our sensibility (our accumulated knowledge and skill) to bear once again on peculiarities of *thought, emotion,* and *expression* that we have come to recognize as characteristic of the era. It is important to understand that we are not here sneaking in the back door the zeitgeist or the historicism we kicked out the front door earlier, not welcoming now with open arms what we gave the bum's rush to earlier. While avoiding the narrowness of vision, the paucity of constitutive categories, and the incoherent determinism of historicism, we here acknowledge that from time to time across wide variations in a rich multiplicity of conceptual systems there are certain persistencies in questions entertained and in idioms and terms employed. For all the manifold diversity of theoretical production in the eighteenth century, for example, there is within this mass of variety and conflict a persistent interest in a certain range of topics and a persistent reliance on a rather stable critical vocabulary (as we have earlier noted). Similarly, however various and different the literary productions of, say, the first thirty years of the nineteenth century are (in style, genre, topic, diction, ambition, range of concern, etc.) they (or many of them) are sufficiently distinct as a group not to be confused with the productions of an earlier or later period. Although intertextualists have not been reluctant to drive their Land Rovers across this terrain, much remains to be done, employing categories of discrimination more capacious and habits of inquiry more responsive to subtle nuances than those currently in use, to illuminate the grounds of our intuitive determinations, our tacit judgments.

Finally (for our purposes of illustration), where wilderness yields to jungle, there is room in criticism for commentary—largely suggestive and speculative but anchored as firmly as possible in the categories of understanding actually informing particular works—on the social, political, ethical, ideological, religious, or cultural values implicit in literary and other artistic works. The concern here is with what the works may have to contribute to our understanding of, say, ways of knowing or ways of living, of ethics, polity, epistemology, and so on. Intellectual roving in this territory is always difficult and always full of danger, because we are always working from restricted evidence to large conclusions and because we are trying to give clarity and precision to the conceptions of the good, the true, and the beautiful that are implicit in works primarily interested in more local and mundane matters. Underlying our artistic versions (as all our other versions) are visions (or conceptions) of what we can know or do or what would be good for beings such as we to know or do. If such things are difficult to discover, their value to and interest for us is proportionate to the difficulty of their attainment, for when it's right down to it that we get, what we most want to know something about is what's to know and how to live.

The World Well Lost

That these and many other projects are possible and worth undertaking it should not be our daily or weekly business to prove. Nor should those worthily engaged in such worthy undertakings be obliged to demonstrate again and again that such projects do not draw their life-substance from a world, alas, gone bust, namely, the foundationalist, essentialist, objectivist world. Rather, it seems that those projects and views sponsored or underwritten by one or another form of eclecticism, skepticism, relativism, or monism (as most of our most common projects today are) should be on the defensive, considering that they have situated themselves on theoretical sites that are minefields, ready to self-explode. Moreover, it should not be the job of every generation (those who come of critical age every ten years or so) to point out once again the fatal weaknesses of historicism, the incoherence and bone-deep irrationality of it.

The jobs available for the doing are, as we have seen, many and sufficient to the abilities of the most energetic and intellectually acute genius, and it has been the aim of this essay on pluralism to promote the getting on with these enterprises. What pluralism—the pluralism-worth-knowing, at any rate—underwrites is a relativism with muscle, with standards of rightness. It is an "ism" that acknowledges the mind-dependent nature of all the versions we make and all the worlds we inhabit, even as it recognizes that some versions cannot be lived in, because they are about to implode, and that others, while possible, are either not worthy of habitation or not capable of being occupied as long as we prefer some other address. Pluralism of the pragmatic, constructional, internally realistic sort that we have described and defended in this essay is the only ism in which the loss of the transcendent signified does not entail as a necessary consequence the sacrifice of interpretation, determinate meaning, "true" and "right" versions and worlds, justification, standards of value, methodological criteria, regulative ideals, and all the facts and things on which we depend to get through each and every day. In the end, then, pluralism is the only Cleopatra for which the World is well lost.

Notes

Introduction

1. I long debated whether to retain the designation "pluralism" or to come up with some other term, one not already deeply injured by custom and abuse, by misunderstanding and misrepresentation, but in the end I chose rehabilitation and recuperation over surgery and prosthesis, in part because it is as pluralism that I first met "internal realism" (Hilary Putnam's term) and "constructionalism" (Nelson Goodman's term), and in part because I wished to preserve its association with the broad categories from which it is traditionally—and in this essay—distinguished, namely, monism, eclecticism, (total) relativism, and skepticism.

2. J. Hillis Miller, "Presidential Address," *PMLA* 102 (1987): 283, 291. My emphasis on "always already." It is perhaps not unfair to say that the quoted material is not uncharacteristic of the cogency and lucidity of expression in *theory*.

3. Robert Scholes, *Textual Power: Literary Theory and the Teaching of English* (New Haven, Conn.: Yale University Press, 1985), 4.

4. Especially the most economically and professionally vulnerable of them—students and untenured faculty.

5. Miller, "Address," 285. Emphasis added.

6. Culler, *The Pursuit of Signs: Semiotics, Literature, Deconstruction* (Ithaca, N.Y.: Cornell University Press, 1981), 33.

7. Jacques Derrida, *Of Grammatology*, trans. Gayatri Chakravorty Spivak (Baltimore: Johns Hopkins University Press, 1976), 159.

8. Stanley Fish, *Is There a Text in This Class? The Authority of Interpretive Communities* (Cambridge, Mass.: Harvard University Press, 1980), 284.

9. Fish, *Is There a Text*, 14.

10. I here borrow from Samuel Johnson's *The Vanity of Human Wishes*, lines 307–10. All these are dismissed or neglected because of their alleged attachment to the old foundationalist drama. Fredric Jameson, for example, finds in Wayne Booth's discussion of the point of view of the "implied author" a yearning for certainties and a nostalgia for middle-class stability. For Jameson's discussion of Booth's views, see *Marxism and Form: Twentieth-Century Dialectical Theories of Literature* (Princeton, N.J.: Princeton University Press, 1971), 355–59.

11. Virtually all the contributors to a special issue of *Critical Inquiry* "Pluralism and Its Discontents," rely on a popular, relatively unsophisticated

notion of pluralism, mistaking it persistently for eclecticism or melting-pot "liberalism." See *Critical Inquiry* 12 (1986).

Chapter 1

1. In general we are interested in what is possible in actual worlds (or in actual possible worlds), not in what is merely imaginable. The science-fiction writer invites us to participate in "unbelievable" possibilities, but he does so for the sake of illuminating actual worlds of human interest. For a philosophical, rather than a science-fiction account of possible worlds, see David Lewis, *On the Plurality of Worlds* (Oxford: Blackwell, 1986).

2. Nelson Goodman, *Ways of Worldmaking* (Indianapolis, Ind.: Hackett, 1978), 17. Throughout this section I am indebted to Goodman (indeed, "version" talk is Goodman talk) and, in varying degrees, to Hilary Putnam.

3. Goodman, *Worldmaking*, 4.

4. Nelson Goodman, *Fact, Fiction, and Forecast* (Cambridge, Mass.: Harvard University Press, 1979), 67.

5. For some maps, as we shall see, "fairness" and "accuracy" are not crucial matters; there are no universal or absolute standards. Fairness and accuracy are not useful standards for comic maps, for example.

6. What we say can often be tested by and against our say-so; our scheme may get things wrong and fail to satisfy our interests.

7. For those interested in theory and in literary interpretation, it is perhaps worth noting that even though my *beliefs* about representation or reference—about what kinds of lines should refer to what, for example—do not coincide with the mapmaker's, his are perfectly intelligible to me.

8. It is important to keep in mind that we are not peddling some naive, metaphysical realism and that the pluralist does have something to say to those who believe that institutional norms or languages already in place create texts; who believe that maps and literary works are texts and, as such, are made up of and made possible by other texts (are intertextual); that "authors" are themselves inscriptions, etc.

9. For much of the material in this paragraph (indeed, in this section), I am indebted to Hilary Putnam, *Realism and Reason* (Cambridge: Cambridge University Press, 1983); see especially 234–37.

10. For Hirsch's criteria, see *Validity in Interpretation* (New Haven, Conn.: Yale University Press, 1967), especially 236ff.

Chapter 2

1. See Steven Knapp and Walter Benn Michaels, "Against Theory," *Critical Inquiry* 8 (1982): 723–42.

2. For a related discussion of functional isomorphism, see Hilary Putnam, *Mind, Language, and Reality* (Cambridge: Cambridge University Press, 1975), especially the "Introduction," vii-xvii, and chapter 1, "Language and Philosophy," 1–32.

3. If at times the two kinds of cases sometimes merge or suggest a distinction without much of a difference, then so be it. No real harm is done so long as the concept of functional isomorphism is preserved. What counts is the preservation of "form" across "material" differences.

4. For a recent debunking of the "pictures in the mind" view, see Nelson Goodman and Catherine Z. Elgin, *Reconceptions in Philosophy and Other Arts and Sciences* (Indianapolis, Ind.: Hackett, 1988), 84. The quoted material in this parenthetical aside is taken from Hilary Putnam, *Representation and Reality* (Cambridge, Mass.: MIT Press, 1988), xiii, 104, 115.

5. For an interesting discussion of related issues, see John Searle, *Minds, Brains, and Science* (Cambridge, Mass.: Harvard University Press, 1984), especially 31–38 (on translating Chinese), and Hilary Putnam, *Reason, Truth and History* (Cambridge: Cambridge University Press, 1981), especially chapter 1, "Brains in a Vat," 1–21.

6. As used here, "lexis" and "praxis" have been appropriated from Elder Olson, "An Outline of Poetic Theory," *Critics and Criticism: Ancient and Modern*, ed. R. S. Crane (Chicago: University of Chicago Press, 1952), 546–66.

7. Moreover, we cannot superimpose all "true" maps on one another to produce the *one* true map of the state. And a " 'road' is a road," after all, if and only if a 'road' is a road.

8. What the pluralist is not, however, is a *monist*, and what the pluralist cannot imagine is how an "always already," however construed (e.g., in terms of language, discourse, culture, or history), could put severe limits on reference and meaning, could make disagreement within the "always already" impossible (it is always possible to see, as Iago does, from the "seamy side out," or simply to say the inverse of or something other than what one has said before). Further, the pluralist cannot imagine how "always already" categories could control the boundary conditions for the operation of their component parts.

9. Those who insist that maps have no interests apart from those with which readers invest them will have our attention later.

Chapter 3

1. As all diluvians know, the critical landscape is currently flooded with such surveys and overviews, including, among many others, the following: William E. Cain, *The Crisis in Criticism: Theory, Literature, and Reform in English Studies* (Baltimore: Johns Hopkins University Press, 1984); Frank Lentricchia, *After the New Criticism* (Chicago: University of Chicago Press, 1980); Terry Eagleton, *Literary Theory: An Introduction* (Minneapolis: University of Minnesota Press, 1983); William Ray, *Literary Meaning: From Phenomenology to Deconstruction* (Oxford: Blackwell, 1984); Vincent B. Leitch, *Deconstructive Criticism: An Advanced Introduction* (New York: Columbia University Press, 1983); Christopher Norris, *Deconstruction: Theory and Practice* (London: Methuen, 1982); Jonathan Culler, *On Deconstruction: Theory and Criticism after Structuralism* (Ithaca, N.Y.: Cornell University Press, 1982); Raman Selden, *A Reader's Guide to Contemporary Literary Theory* (Brighton: Harvester, 1985); Peter J. McCormick, *Fictions, Philosophies, and the Problems of Poetics* (Ithaca, N.Y.: Cornell University Press, 1988); Christopher Norris, *Contest of Faculties: Philosophy and Theory after Deconstruction* (London: Methuen, 1985), and Adolf Grunbaum and Wesley C. Salmon, eds., *The Limitations of Deconstruction* (Berkeley: University of California Press, 1988). Of course, in the past ten years we have been overwhelmed with journal essays (far too many to notice

here, even selectively) devoted to summarizing, attacking, or defending particular movements, views, "isms," or theorists.

2. With Hilary Putnam, I assume that there are "only the various points of view of actual persons reflecting various interests and purposes that their descriptions and theories subserve," and, further, that "no theory or picture is complete for *all* purposes." See *Reason, Truth and History* (Cambridge: Cambridge University Press, 1981), 50, 147.

3. Nelson Goodman, *Ways of Worldmaking* (Indianapolis, Ind.: Hackett, 1978), 110.

4. For clear examples of this kind of independent system-building, see, among many others, Harold Bloom, *A Map of Misreading* (New York: Oxford University Press, 1975) and Shoshana Felman, "Turning the Screw of Interpretation," *Literature and Psychoanalysis: The Question of Reading: Otherwise*, ed. Shoshana Felman (Baltimore: Johns Hopkins University Press, 1982), 94–207.

Chapter 4

1. Also, the preceding discussion of eclecticism supplies a convenient opportunity to review and revise two principles traditionally propounded by some pluralists, namely, (1) that more than one approach can deal adequately with the same question about the same material; and (2) that there can be real disagreement or agreement only within the same system of reference. In subsequent pages we shall challenge the first and qualify the second principle.

2. For Paul A. Kolers's detailed analyses of several "freaks" of perception, see his *Aspects of Motion Perception* (Oxford: Pergamon, 1972). I am also indebted in this section to Nelson Goodman's discussion of Kolers's experiments in *Ways of Worldmaking* (Indianapolis, Ind.: Hackett, 1978), especially chapter 5, "A Puzzle About Perception."

3. Goodman, *Worldmaking*, 92–93.

4. Goodman, *Worldmaking*, 79.

5. Goodman finds an analogous situation in the dream in which the dreamer constructs a scenario within his dream that leads to an actual knocking on the door, which interrupts the dream. That is, the dreamer incorporates into his dream the knocking that wakes him from his dream. See *Worldmaking*, 81.

6. The reader should understand that I assume that all meaning is, in some sense, stipulated meaning; that no given sentence has meaning apart from some stipulation (assumption, belief); that the list of meaning possibilities for any arbitrary sentence is indefinitely long; and that whether the reader makes or recovers a meaning he does so by stipulation in a retrospectively constructive way.

7. One illuminating use of the chestnut, "The bill is large," can be found in F. R. Palmer, *Semantics* (Cambridge: Cambridge University Press, 1976); see especially chapters 3, "Context and Reference," and 7, "Utterance Meaning." Of course, I am entirely responsible for the uses to which the chestnut is put in this chapter.

8. "Recursion" talk is familiar to computer specialists, of course. The pro-

cess we are concerned with is analogous to that by which a computer program might use the result of one computation or operation as the input for the next one.

9. For an example of Burke's use of the phrase in connection with hypothesis revision, see "Poetics in Particular, Language in General," *Language as Symbolic Action* (Berkeley: University of California Press, 1966), 25–43.

10. It is perhaps worth noting that much of what we assume here runs counter to much of what is said or suggested in contemporary theory. We assume, for example, that the interest-relativity of most texts is knowable, that we can be *surprised* by what texts disclose, that meanings are usually not historically or culturally determined in any very specific sense, and that the meaning of a text is not antecedently determined by some arche-system, some ideology.

11. A discussion of recursion in relation to the construction of a self can be found in Philip N. Johnson-Laird, *Mental Models: Toward a Cognitive Science of Language, Inference, and Consciousness* (Cambridge, Mass.: Harvard University Press, 1983). Also, for much in this section on recursion, I am indebted to "Under Construction," Jerome Bruner and Carol Fleisher Feldman's review of *Of Mind and Other Matters* by Nelson Goodman, *New York Review of Books*, 27 March 1986, 46–49. See also Jerome Bruner, *Actual Minds, Possible Worlds* (Cambridge, Mass.: Harvard University Press, 1986), 93–105.

12. I here slightly alter Elder Olson's view of the relationship between words and meaning. This view is presented in several essays; for one clear expression of it, see his "William Empson, Contemporary Criticism, and Poetic Diction," in *Critics and Criticism: Ancient and Modern*, ed. R. S. Crane (Chicago: University of Chicago Press, 1952), 45–82.

13. As an aside, I would suggest that polysemeity has come to function as the Covering Cherub of much twentieth-century criticism. Where there are words and sentences, there polysemeity has raised its banner. At any rate, the preoccupation with "language" and "discourse" in our period has led to an almost pathological preoccupation with irony, ambiquity, paradox, and so on, producing "language" criticism, multiple "readings," much semiotic criticism, an obsession with thematizing (of a social, political, cultural, psychoanalytic kind), and even the "deconstructive" attacks against what is rather sweepingly called "logocentrism."

14. Derrida, for example, would certainly acknowledge that there is a "present" meaning within a particular (logocentric) system of meaning. Going beyond such acknowledgment, however, he "brackets" or "suspends" that acknowledged meaning or presence to consider the illusoriness of presence itself, to consider the systems of "deferentiality" in which signs inevitably participate, to consider, in short, the (logocentrically) meaningful signs as players in the differ-/defer-entiality of all sign systems.

15. Samuel Johnson, *A Journey to the Western Islands of Scotland*, ed. Mary Lascelles, vol. 9 of *The Yale Edition of the Works of Samuel Johnson* (New Haven, Conn.: Yale University Press, 1971), 40.

16. I here quote Dummett's position as it is summarized by Hilary Putnam in *Realism and Reason* (Cambridge: Cambridge University Press, 1983), xvi. Those interested in a fuller account of Dummett's "anti-realist" views on assertibility conditions should consult the "Preface" to his *Truth and Other Enigmas* (Cambridge, Mass.: Harvard University Press, 1978), ix–lviii.

17. Polanyi uses the example of chess strategies in several works. For one such use, see *The Tacit Dimension* (Garden City, N.Y.: Doubleday, 1967), 29–30.

18. Putnam, *Realism and Reason*, ix. Of course, Putnam is here referring to formal systems or set-theoretic models, but his point applies equally strongly to our case.

19. For similar, and slightly earlier, remarks on *pity* and *indignation*, the reader, of course, could consult Aristotle's *Poetics* and *Nicomachean Ethics*.

20. The *fleuve-rivière* distinction is taken from Jonathan Culler, *Ferdinand de Saussure* (Harmondsworth: Penguin, 1976), 15–16.

21. Putnam, *Realism and Reason*, ix.

Chapter 5

1. It is perhaps worth noting that with regard to the Jungian, Freudian, and Marxist explanations referred to earlier, the pluralist would be likely to reject each of them, if in any particular case acceptance were contingent upon acceding implicitly to its broader, "monistic" claims about what *mind, nature,* or *social structure* "really" is or upon acknowledging its "scientific" status.

2. Nelson Goodman, *Ways of Worldmaking* (Indianapolis, Ind.: Hackett, 1978), 120–21.

3. Goodman, *Worldmaking*, 121.

4. Hilary Putnam, *Meaning and the Moral Sciences* (London: Routledge and Kegan Paul, 1978), 47.

5. Here, as elsewhere, I use the term "atomic" loosely.

6. Hilary Putnam, *Mind, Language, and Reality* (Cambridge: Cambridge University Press, 1975), 302. Throughout this section, I have borrowed both examples and arguments from chapter 14 of this book, "Philosophy and Our Mental Life." I have everywhere tried to make Putnam's examples serve my interests and purposes. Thus, although I am deeply indebted to his essay, he is in no way responsible for the uses to which I have put it.

7. Putnam, *Mind, Language*, 302.

8. In a discussion of the mind-body problem, John Searle provides a stronger version of the point made here when he observes that in "the case of liquidity [of water], solidity [of a table], and transparency [of glass], we have no difficulty at all in supposing that the surface features are *caused by* the behaviour of elements at the micro-level, and at the same time we accept that the surface phenomena *just are* features of the very systems in question." By way of clarification, he goes on to note that with regard to these phenomena and mental states "the surface feature is both *caused by* the behaviour of micro-elements, and at the same time is *realized in* the system that is made up of micro-elements." See *Mind, Brains, and Science* (Cambridge, Mass.: Harvard University Press, 1984), 21. The case we make stops just short of Searle's *just are* equation.

9. Putnam, *Mind, Language*, 303.

10. Would such knowledge take the romance out of romance? Perhaps, but only if we could all quickly learn to assess our state and take quick corrective action, with a pill or an electric jolt, for example. But to what system

of values would we appeal to determine that corrective action was necessary, and what is the brain state in which such values subsist, and who will be assigned to place a value on those values or, rather, those brain states, and who will determine which brain states are valuable?

11. Putnam, *Mind, Language,* 298–99.

12. With John Searle, it would be important to note, among other things, that the "computer" or the "computer program" is strong on syntax but weak to the point of emaciation on semantics. For Searle's remarks on the "semantic" weakness of computer programs, see *Minds, Brains, and Science,* 28–41.

13. For Burke's discussion of linguistic "dogginess," see "Mind, Body, and the Unconscious," *Language as Symbolic Action* (Berkeley: University of California Press, 1966), 73–74.

14. M. M. Bakhtin, *The Dialogic Imagination: Four Essays,* trans. Caryl Emerson and Michael Holquist, ed. Michael Holquist (Austin: University of Texas Press, 1981), 333.

15. Bakhtin, *Dialogic,* 333–34. The quoted material is taken from these pages, with emphasis added on "discourse" here and elsewhere. It is important to note that in Bakhtinian—as in new critical, deconstructive, and many other kinds of—analysis, literature is treated "rhetorically"—treated, that is, as a kind of "discourse." As discourse, it is concerned inevitably and chiefly with *meanings* or themes, theses, ideas.

16. Bakhtin, *Dialogic,* 361.

17. Bakhtin, *Dialogic,* 366.

18. The not very astute reader recognizes here, albeit outfitted in different terminological dress, the logical distinctions and argumentative maneuvers that characterize New Criticism. The method of reasoning is the "abstract" or "dialectical" method; it deals, as Hume would say, in "matters of relation" (in the logical and dialectical relations of terms).

19. Bakhtin, *Dialogic,* 365.

20. Bakhtin, *Dialogic,* 349.

21. Though certainly the assumptions about *time* and *history* underlying most sociohistoric talk are not everybody's cup of tea; these assumptions are not acceptable, for example, to every physicist and holy man (who have their own views of time and history). In short, such talk presupposes *a view* of history and presupposes its *truth.*

22. Although our focus here is on texts and verbal meaning, we should not forget that we make worlds out of more than words. We depict as well as describe worlds, for example, and sometimes we prefer pictorial or imagistic "explanations" to verbal ones, as when, for example, we dope out our pool-table situation at a glance and try out "imagistically" several options before taking our next shot, imagining our future as it would be determined by playing the cue ball off this or that cushion.

23. In Rhode Island justice is swift, especially in matters having to do with violations of public trust, as everybody knows who is even casually familiar with the celerity with which the state pounces on any offender, however high-placed or influential and however minor the peccadillo.

24. Samuel Johnson, "Review of a Free Inquiry into the Nature and Origin of Evil," in *Johnson: Prose and Poetry,* ed. Mona Wilson (Cambridge, Mass.: Harvard University Press, 1967), 355.

25. Jacques Derrida, *Positions* (Chicago: University of Chicago Press, 1981), 26.

26. Of course, I here use "text" and "its *efforts* to fix emphases" as convenient *fictions*. Nothing would get done if, as *strict deconstructionists*, we put everything *sous rature*.

Chapter 6

1. Actually, of course, at the higher levels of "meaning," two or more works can be compared in terms of their common engagement with a particular set of *antitheses*; in the end, however, because of the nature of language *as such*, all such works will be seen to dissolve what they aspired to resolve and to reverse and then erase the order of command they hoped to institute.

2. Such egalitarians are indistinguishable from what philosophers call "methodological solipsists"; they differ from "real" solipsists only in their affirmation of reciprocal insularity, in their recognition of being alone in the same boat with everybody else. Simply put, just as I cannot know you or anything else except by means of my way of knowing, so you too are similarly restricted. Methodological solipsists give *you* the same privileges they take; they acknowledge that *you* are as scheme- and category-bound as they are. With the relativist—either the old-fashioned kind or the new "cultural norm," "interpretive community" relativist—we have roughly the same options and the same results that we have with the solipsists. To both we can say, with a good deal more wisdom than flippancy, what the philosopher Alan Garfinkel is reported to have said to his students in California: "I know where you're coming from, but, you know, Relativism [Solipsism] isn't *true-for-me*." (The deep sense of this snappy rejoinder is not soon exhausted.) Garfinkel's remark is reported by Hilary Putnam in *Realism and Reason* (Cambridge: Cambridge University Press, 1983), 288.

3. For the full argument, see Steven Knapp and Walter Benn Michaels, "Against Theory," *Critical Inquiry* 8 (1982): 723–42.

4. For one such expression, see Stanley Fish, "Normal Circumstances, Literal Language, Direct Speech Acts, the Ordinary, the Everyday, the Obvious, What Goes without Saying, and Other Special Cases," *Critical Inquiry* 4 (1978): 625–44.

5. For the most part, I have tried here, as elsewhere, to focus on general principles rather than on the views of particular theorists or critics, in the belief that the reader could easily find particular feet to fit the shoes to which I refer (or, sometimes, allude). Still, a hint or two might not be inappropriate. At the moment, for example, readers would not be forced to stretch the leather too much if they found in their shop, in addition to Stanley Fish, Paul Feyerabend, the early Thomas Kuhn, and some reader-response critics (among others). See, for example, Paul Feyerabend, "Consolations for the Specialist," *Criticism and the Growth of Knowledge*, ed. Imre Lakatos and Alan Musgrove (Cambridge: Cambridge University Press, 1970), 197–230, and Thomas S. Kuhn, *The Structure of Scientific Revolutions*, 2d ed. enlarged (Chicago: University of Chicago Press, 1970); for some relevant reader-response views, see *Reader-Response Criticism: From Formalism to Post-Structuralism*, ed. Jane P. Tompkins (Baltimore: Johns Hopkins University Press, 1980).

6. Israel Scheffler, *Science and Subjectivity* (Indianapolis, Ind.: Hackett,

1982), 17. Scheffler outlines and discusses these paradoxes in the first chapter, "Objectivity Under Attack." Throughout this section, I am indebted to Scheffler's rich, subtle, tightly argued book.

7. The principle articulated here is taken, as I have indicated earlier, from Nelson Goodman, *Ways of Worldmaking* (Indianapolis, Ind.: Hackett, 1978), 110.

8. At this point, it is important to remember that this discussion began a good while ago in a determination to distinguish the pluralism-worth-knowing from both eclecticism and the "anything goes" sort of relativism so popular with theorists and to show that for the pluralist not every difference made a *world* of difference.

9. A convenient example of such table turning can be found in Stanley Fish, "Anti-Professionalism," *New Literary History* 17 (1985): 89–108.

10. What we witness here, then, is a form of *cultural solipsism*, the lack of parity being not among persons, but among cultures. The *you* (your culture) that *I* recognize is always the *you* possible to *my* culturally determined scheme of observation or interpretation.

11. What the interpretive-community relativist can say to all this will have to be deferred until later.

12. Here, of course, we have in mind not only the views of those critics who, like Fish and Kuhn, assert that references and concepts, facts and the interrelations of facts are constituted by our interpretive strategies and that our various strategies are "incommensurable" discourses, but also the views of those critics who insist on the indeterminacy of translation or interpretation. For a useful and pertinent discussion of the whole issue of "incommensurability," see Annette Barnes, *On Interpretation* (Oxford: Blackwell, 1988), especially 78–82.

13. See Cleanth Brooks, "The Heresy of Paraphrase," *The Well Wrought Urn: Studies in the Structure of Poetry* (New York: Harcourt Brace, 1947), 192–214. For Culler's discussion of this distinction, see *Ferdinand de Saussure* (Harmondsworth: Penguin, 1976), 15–22, and for a collateral discussion, see his *Structuralist Poetics: Structuralism, Linguistics, and the Study of Literature* (Ithaca, N.Y.: Cornell University Press, 1976), especially chapter 1, "The Linguistic Foundation," 3–31. To some it may seem that our objections to the views of the paradoxicals (which have various particular embodiments or exemplifications in modern theory, in, for example, new criticism, deconstruction, interpretive communityism, certain Gadamerian and Foucauldian principles, etc.) are at once *obvious* and *easy* and, thus, not very telling or noteworthy. Our point—quietly and persistently made here and throughout—is that the objections, if *easy*, are also *deep*. They go, we think, to the marrow; and no one has thus far shown in print that the objections are *invalid*.

14. For related discussions, see John Searle, "Can Computers Think?" *Minds, Brains, and Science* (Cambridge, Mass.: Harvard University Press, 1984), 28–41; and Hilary Putnam, "Brains in a Vat," *Reason, Truth and History* (Cambridge: Cambridge University Press, 1981), 1–21.

15. *The Tacit Dimension* (Garden City, N.Y.: Doubleday, 1967), 34.

Chapter 7

1. Such views are staples of modern theory; for convenient illustrations of most of them, see Stanley Fish, *Is There a Text in This Class? The Authority of*

Interpretive Communities (Cambridge: Harvard University Press, 1980), especially chapter 1, "Literature in the Reader: Affective Stylistics," 21–67.

2. Hilary Putnam, *Mind, Language, and Reality* (Cambridge: Cambridge University Press, 1975), 281.

3. For a related discussion of "continuity through change" as it applies to "meaning," as well as to "reference," see Hilary Putnam, *Representation and Reality* (Cambridge, Mass.: MIT Press, 1988), 11–18.

4. We do so, as we have indicated, because we have agreed that, say, gold will be whatever our experts, using "scientific" criteria, determine it to be. This is a *social* agreement, one that the ancient Greek accepted and that the modern European still accepts. If it turns out that some of the stuff that the ancient Greek called gold doesn't satisfy our present test for gold—as our gold may fail to satisfy future tests—the Greek and I nevertheless both *refer* to gold when we speak of gold, since we agree that it is whatever our experts—and their tests—determine it to be.

5. We would be unable to understand, for example, *both* "the store is open" and "the store is *not* open."

6. "Community" here is not to be confused with "interpretive community"; different "interpretive communities," in the literary criticism sense of the term, can belong—do belong, for the most part—to the same "common reference" community.

7. Both quotations are taken from Steven E. Boër, "Substance and Kind: Reflections on the New Theory of Reference," *Inaugural Lectures: 1984–85* (Columbus: Ohio State University, College of Humanities, 1985), 61. For Putnam's discussion of "stereotypes," see "The Meaning of 'Meaning,' " *Language, Mind, and Knowledge,* ed. K. Gunderson (Minneapolis: University of Minnesota Press, 1975). Throughout this section I am indebted to both Boër and Putnam.

8. As well as, in most cases, a common conceptual grasp of what is being referred to.

9. The importance of this point should not be missed, if only because it has some bearing on one of the central premises of the deconstructionists, complicating, if not overwhelming, the notion of *différance*. (Of course, nothing can overwhelm or nullify *différance*, since "presence," we have been informed, cannot be marked as "present" without carrying a "trace" of the presently unmarked "other"; if there is a "chair," there must be, at the very least, that which is "non-chair," and, of course, "chair" is *always already* a function of a system of "sounds.")

10. Israel Scheffler, *Science and Subjectivity* (Indianapolis, Ind.: Hackett, 1982), 57.

11. I, of course, make all of this out of whole cloth. At any rate, I certainly do not know whether these terms *refer* to different *kinds* of objects, and I could no more distinguish a davenport from a couch than I could tell whether it is samba or rhumba (or one of a hundred other varieties of dance) music that I hear in the background.

12. I here play a variation, I think, on a view expressed by Nelson Goodman in "Notes on a Well-Made World": "No organization into units is unique or mandatory, nor is there any featureless raw material underlying different organizations. Any raw stuff is as much the creature of a version as is what is made out of that stuff." See *Partisan Review* 51 (1984): 279.

13. For example, we have been talking throughout about reference as gen-

erally used in our quotidian dealings with words. We have not been dealing with reference formally or technically.

14. For this "close the door" example I am indebted to my friend Ralph Rader, who has used it on many occasions to make companionable points. He, of course, is in no way responsible for the sense I have made or the uses to which I have put his irrefragable views. For one such use, see Ralph Rader, "Fact, Theory, and Literary Explanation," *Critical Inquiry* 1 (1974): 245–72.

15. *Meaning and the Moral Sciences* (London: Routledge and Kegan Paul, 1978), 41, 49.

16. This is why, in part, we regularly have trouble *predicting* what will happen next, predicting, for example, what our friends will do, determining what we ought to do, what is the "right" thing to do, etc., even though we are sure that what we or they do will not be completely arbitrary. What is done is unpredictable but also "reasonable" and "motivated."

17. Putnam, *Realism and Reason*, 303.

18. Perhaps the most persistent, intransigent, and common mistake committed by theorists is the assumption that any attempt to discuss conflicting views impartially necessarily presupposes belief in some form of essentialism or foundationalism; the pluralist, contradistinctly, supposes that the language used to describe rival claims can be *at once* fair to both claims without being partial to either *and* partial to some interests without being unfair to the rival interests—and, thus, the descriptive language is fair *and* impartial, without being uninterested. It is just that its interests are not relevant to the conflict, to the matter under dispute.

19. Both R. S. Crane and Elder Olson, for example, have argued that there can only be agreement and disagreement when critics are working within the same system of reference and inference. For expressions of these views, see Crane, "The Multiplicity of Critical Languages," in *The Languages of Criticism and the Structure of Poetry* (Toronto: University of Toronto Press, 1953), 3–38; and Olson, "An Outline of Poetic Theory," *Critiques and Essays in Criticism, 1920–1948*, ed. Robert Wooster Stallman (New York: Ronald, 1949), 264–88.

20. George Lakoff and Mark Johnson, *Metaphors We Live By* (Chicago: University of Chicago Press, 1980), 164.

21. The phrase "deeply related" is taken from Putnam, *The Many Faces of Realism* (La Salle, Ill.: Open Court, 1987), 20.

Chapter 8

1. Israel Rosenfield, *New York Review of Books*, 11 October 1984, 55.

2. Emphasis added. David Marr, *Vision* (San Francisco: W. H. Freeman, 1982), 358.

3. The reader should note that in saying so I am not also suggesting that such readings—and countless other readings—are unwarranted or illegitimate by virtue of our constitution or the nature of language as such or our settled ways with "meaning" and "reference." Indeed, such readings are especially interesting when the focus of attention is on the critic's sensibility and the ingenuity with which he manipulates the terms of his dialectic. I am simply stating that the way of *reading* outlined in Marr's passage is defensible in

a world of immanent meaning and is not predisposed to lend unequivocal support to any particular "always already" mode of interpretation.

4. For a similar and related formulation of the question we internally ask, see Ralph Rader, "Fact, Theory, and Literary Explanation," *Critical Inquiry* 1 (1974): 245–72, especially 250–51; and Rader, "The Concept of Genre and Eighteenth-Century Studies," *New Approaches to Eighteenth-Century Literature*, ed. Phillip Harth (New York: Columbia University Press, 1974), 79–115, especially 89.

5. The material quoted is taken from Bijoy H. Boruah, *Fiction and Emotion: A Study in Aesthetics and the Philosophy of Mind* (Oxford: Clarendon Press, 1988), 34. Moreover, it is worth noting that as a system of rationality *intentionality* has an internal criterion of success. As Ronald de Sousa reminds us, "Any concept of rationality must be founded on a criterion of success. Success in this sense is defined as the attainment of the formal object of the state in question; for example, truth is the success of belief, good of want." For this remark, see *The Rationality of Emotion* (Cambridge, Mass.: MIT Press, 1987), 142.

Chapter 9

1. As well as the Empsonian (and some New Critics). It is not surprising that William Empson—especially the Empson of *Seven Types of Ambiguity*—is much admired by many deconstructionists.

2. They have trouble in ruling readings *out*, not in ruling them *in*. Deprived of *grounds*, they can find no grounds of defeasibility.

3. Since, as we have seen, the meaning is *not* in the *words* or, for that matter, in the *head* (in the sense of being in some particular *mental contents* that *just are* for *you* and *me today, tomorrow,* and the *next day* perfectly equivalent to *the meaning*).

4. See Goodman, *Ways of Worldmaking* (Indianapolis, Ind.: Hackett, 1978), 92–93.

5. Of course, "when it's a jamb"—a jam—simply will not do, because a door is never a jamb.

6. Argument presupposes, for example, that one reading is more *appropriate*, more *adequate*, etc., than another, though *adequacy* could in a given instance be seen as relative to any number of "internal" or "external" standards (coherence or patriotism, for instance).

7. Emphasis added in the first quotation. See Putnam, *Realism and Reason* (Cambridge: Cambridge University Press, 1983), 196, and "The Craving for Objectivity," *New Literary History* 15 (1984): 233. See also Donald Davidson, *Inquiries into Truth and Interpretation* (Oxford: Clarendon Press, 1984), especially the chapters in the sections on "Truth and Meaning" and "Radical Interpretation," 1–76, 123–180; and Davidson, *Essays on Actions and Events* (Oxford: Clarendon Press, 1980), especially section 1, "Intention and Action." For some part of this discussion of *actuality* and *potentiality* I am indebted to Elder Olson, "On Value Judgments in the Arts," *Critical Inquiry* 1 (1974): 71–90. The reader interested in the larger implications of this distinction should consult this important essay.

8. The *epistemic* or the *intentional* is certainly not contentless. The *intentional*, after all, concerns content, directs us to the "external," is about something. For a useful overview of and introduction to intentionality, see John Searle, *Intentionality: An Essay in the Philosophy of Mind* (Cambridge: Cambridge University Press, 1983), especially chapter 1, "The Nature of Intentional States"; Daniel C. Dennett, *The Intentional Stance* (Cambridge, Mass.: MIT Press, 1987), especially the first four chapters; and *Intention and Intentionality: Essays in Honour of G. E. M. Anscombe*, ed. Cora Diamond and Jenny Teichman (Brighton: Harvester, 1979).

9. In this discussion of the "when" of meaning, I borrow from (or, more properly, allude to) Nelson Goodman's "When is Art?"; see *Ways of Worldmaking* (Indianapolis, Ind.: Hackett, 1978), 57–70.

10. For one of Hirsch's discussions of the distinction between "meaning" and "significance," see *Validity in Interpretation* (New Haven, Conn.: Yale University Press, 1967), especially 61–67. Hirsch's views on these terms have changed over the years; for his most recent reevaluation, see "Meaning and Significance Reinterpreted," *Critical Inquiry* 11 (1984): 202–25. And for a review and analysis of this new position, see James L. Battersby and James Phelan, "Meaning as Concept and Extension: Some Problems," *Critical Inquiry* 12 (1986): 605–15.

11. Putnam, "The Craving for Objectivity," *New Literary History* 15 (1984): 233. Here Putnam is reviewing and summarizing Davidson's views on interpretation, for which, see Davidson, *Inquiries into Truth and Interpretation* (Oxford: Clarendon Press, 1984), especially 1–76.

12. For a discussion of related matters, see Goodman, *Worldmaking*, 57–70.

Chapter 10

1. The quoted passage is taken from Kenneth Burke, "Lexicon Rhetoricae," in *Counter-Statement* (Chicago: University of Chicago Press, 1957), 176–77.

2. And, of course, this category itself can be seen to be an item in the ad hoc category, which includes such other categories as "the number of kind acts I will never have the opportunity to perform," "the shortstops who have driven on the Newport Bridge," etc. For George Lakoff's discussion, see *Women, Fire, and Dangerous Things: What Categories Reveal About the Mind* (Chicago: University of Chicago Press, 1987), 12–57.

3. For one such attempt to deal with this deep (and, I think, devastating) objection, see Barbara Herrnstein Smith, *Contingencies of Value: Alternative Perspectives for Critical Theory* (Cambridge, Mass.: Harvard University Press, 1988), especially chapter 7, "Matters of Consequence."

4. History, culture, epoch, episteme, genre (as construed) can be consulted to determine whether such and such work or practice (as construed) fits or belongs to the epoch or genre. That is, *we determine* what likenesses and differences count (as well as what counts as a likeness or difference) in our categories or subsumptive headings. But, no history, culture, episteme, genre, or whatever can determine a *specific practice*, can supply the justification

conditions of any specific work (or, put the other way, every episteme, genre, etc. can supply justification conditions for too many works or determine—in the loose sense of "allow"—too many conflicting or incompatible practices).

5. That the making, as well as the understanding, of such categories is a holistic enterprise can be clearly seen, I think, if we consider the kinds of things that, say, "baseball" can appropriately modify. We must know something about the activity as a whole to know that glove, field, shoe, manager, bag, score, diamond, and bat are right and fitting baseball things but that type-writer, elevator, car, corn, etc., are not. It makes good sense to put "baseball" before these but not before those things.

6. Lakoff, *Women, Fire*, 45–46.

7. Lakoff, *Women, Fire*, 289. The essays and studies by Fillmore relevant to our concerns are "An Alternative to Checklist Theories of Meaning," *Proceedings of the First Annual Meeting of the Berkeley Linguistics Society* (Berkeley: Berkeley Linguistics Society, 1975), 123–31; "Topics in Lexical Semantics," *Current Issues in Linguistic Theory* (Bloomington: Indiana University Press, 1976), 76–138; "The Organization of Semantic Information in the Lexicon," *Papers from the Parasession on the Lexicon* (Chicago: Chicago Linguistics Society, 1978), 1–11; "Towards a Description Framework for Spatial Deixis," in *Speech, Place, and Action*, ed. R. J. Jarvella and W. Klein (London: John Wiley, 1982), 31–59; "Frame Semantics," *Linguistics in the Morning Calm*, Linguistic Society of Korea (Seoul: Hanshin, 1982), 111–38; and "Frames and the Semantics of Understanding," *Quaderni di Semantica* 6 (1985): 222–53.

8. Lakoff, *Women, Fire*, 106–9.

9. The quoted material is taken from Lakoff, *Women, Fire*, 317, 345.

10. Putnam, *Realism and Reason* (Cambridge: Cambridge University Press, 1983), ix. Putnam is here referring specifically to *formal languages*, to set-theoretic models; but the point admits of general application and is relevant certainly to the "cultural," "historical," "structural" case. Any system of rules (or meanings) capable of covering or applying to more than one case (one system of justification) is vulnerable to polysemeity.

11. Here I borrow generously from John R. Searle, *Intentionality: An Essay in the Philosophy of Mind* (Cambridge: Cambridge University Press, 1983), especially chapter 1, "The Nature of Intentional States," 1–36; and his *Minds, Brains, and Science* (Cambridge, Mass.: Harvard University Press, 1984), especially 60–67.

12. Searle, *Minds*, 60; emphasis added.

13. Searle, *Minds*, 61.

14. *Meaning and the Moral Sciences* (London: Routledge and Kegan Paul, 1978), 55.

15. For similar views, see Elder Olson, "William Empson, Contemporary Criticism, and Poetic Diction," *Modern Philology* 47 (1950): 222–52; and James L. Battersby, "The Inevitability of Professing Literature," in *Criticism, History, and Intertextuality*, ed. Richard Fleming and Michael Payne, *Bucknell Review* (Lewisburg, Pa.: Bucknell University Press, 1988), 61–76.

16. The "I didn't say he stole it" example I received from a former student, Wayne De Young, who in turn received it in some promotional material from a publishing company, which shall remain nameless, because forgotten.

Chapter 11

1. George Lakoff, *Women, Fire, and Dangerous Things: What Categories Reveal About the Mind* (Chicago, University of Chicago Press, 1987), 368, 336.

2. I here play a slight variation on Lakoff's "conceptualizing capacity." For a more detailed discussion of this "capacity," see *Women, Fire,* 309–12.

3. This distinction between "about" and "with" is appropriated from R. S. Crane. For his discussion of this distinction and related matters, see "The Multiplicity of Critical Languages," *The Languages of Criticism and the Structure of Poetry* (Toronto: University of Toronto Press, 1953), 3–38. For a related discussion, see Elder Olson, "The Dialectical Foundations of Critical Pluralism," *Texas Quarterly* 9 (1966): 202–30.

4. For further discussion of both "basic-level categories" and "kinesthetic image-schemas," see Lakoff, *Women, Fire,* 267–75.

5. I have particularly in mind here critics such as R. S. Crane, Elder Olson, and Kenneth Burke; in this sentence I paraphrase remarks in Olson, " 'Sailing to Byzantium': Prolegomena to a Poetics of the Lyric," *University Review* 8 (1942): 209–19. Kenneth Burke articulates a similar view in his discussion of chronological and logical priority. For Burke, the words have chronological priority (for the reader-interpreter), in that they are the first things encountered, but the meaning has logical priority, in that it is the antecedent condition of the sequence and, hence, of the references and emphases. For one discussion of this distinction, see Burke, "Poetics in Particular, Language in General," *Language as Symbolic Action: Essays on Life, Literature, and Method* (Berkeley: University of California Press, 1966), 34–41.

6. For much in this section I am indebted to Olson, " 'Sailing to Byzantium': Prolegomena to a Poetics of the Lyric," and "William Empson, Contemporary Criticism, and Poetic Diction," *Modern Philology* 47 (1950): 222–52, as well as (especially at this point in my argument) to Hilary Putnam, *Meaning and the Moral Sciences* (London: Routledge and Kegan Paul, 1978), 135–38.

Chapter 12

1. I am here adapting to my own purposes and argument views frequently expressed by Hilary Putnam (and others). To see how Putnam uses the phrases and terms within quotation marks, see *Meaning and the Moral Sciences* (London: Routledge and Kegan Paul, 1978), 66–80.

2. Of course, we are not here dealing with the deep irrationality of those who insist that authors do not write texts but, instead, are written by them, that texts are written not by authors but by other texts. Of such irrationalists, we can say that if they really believed that what they said was true, then what they said would be false, since they could not believe it *from within their belief.* If what they said were true *were true for them,* they would not be able to say it was true for them. For a full elucidation of the self-refutation inherent in such irrational views, see Putnam, "Brains in a Vat," in *Reason, Truth and History* (Cambridge: Cambridge University Press, 1981), 1–21. In this chapter, Putnam explains how it is the case that if we *were all just brains in a vat,* we would not be able to say we were brains in a vat. In my view, the argument

about brains in a vat admits of wide extension and applies quite forcefully to the views of those many theorists who deny agency and will to "authors" and insist that instead of speaking we are spoken. For a related and equally devastating argument (this one directed at the sort of "criterial rationality" favored by Richard Rorty and, in some at least of his shapes, Stanley Fish), see Putnam, "Why Reason Can't be Naturalized," in *Realism and Reason* (Cambridge: Cambridge University Press, 1983), 229–47.

3. In a sense, then, there are mind-independent worlds after all, but the kicker here is that we have no mind- or category-independent access to them. Pluralists—unlike the paradoxicals or the theorists—can go wrong, as well as right, in every world they can be in, and every world has the potential to make "independent" contributions to their beliefs.

4. The view, quite common among—though often unacknowledged by—theorists, that everything reduces to language (or semiotics, tropes, traces, etc.); we are all always and only involved in one language game or another.

5. The view that we have many true beliefs about many things in many worlds is variously expressed in various works by Putnam, Nelson Goodman, Donald Davidson, Jerome Bruner, Daniel C. Dennett, George Lakoff, and David Lewis, among others. For example, on the issue of many true beliefs, Putnam observes that the explanation of our successful behavior "is that certain kinds of beliefs we hold tend to be true." He goes on to note that "most people do have true beliefs about where they live, what the neighborhood looks like, how to get from one place to another, etc." And, at higher levels of complexity, "they have many true beliefs about how other people will react in various circumstances, and many true beliefs about how to do and make certain things" (*Meaning and the Moral Sciences*, 101). For these and similar remarks, see Putnam, *Meaning and the Moral Sciences*, 97–117, and *Realism and Reason*, 184–204, 229–47.

6. Putnam, *Realism and Reason*, 301.

7. A little reflection in passing on all this will reveal why monism, relativism, eclecticism, and skepticism are not the pluralist's cup of tea. The monist has one explanation, not many; all monists (all those theorists who explain each and every thing by reference to a preferred set of categories and terms) are avowed or closet "noumenalists." The anything-goes relativist (Barbara Herrnstein Smith or Stanley Fish, for example) allows many or all explanations but not the absolute truth of any one explanation. The eclectic likes many worlds or versions but cannot find or make just one on any given occasion or one that under the circumstances is just right. And the skeptic can find no real truth anywhere.

8. For example, if it is a contest or conflict we are devising, why not one with high stakes (ten bucks, the family jewels, the family honor)? Why not the highest (life or death)? If the highest stakes are involved, why not go with the most interesting antagonists (brother against brother, father against daughter)? and so on. This kind of "perfectibility" is frequently noted by Kenneth Burke; see, for example, his *Language as Symbolic Action* (Berkeley: University of California Press, 1966), 44–62.

9. In a very different context, one dealing with a variety of dichotomies rendered obsolete by "internal realism" (what I have been calling "pluralism")—such dichotomies as fact and value, "truth-conditional semantics" and "assertibility-conditional semantics," objectivity and subjectivity, and properties of psychic or mental projection and properties of things in themselves—

Putnam makes a companionable point: "What does the world look like without the dichotomies? It looks both familiar and different. It looks familiar, insofar as we no longer try to divide mundane reality into a 'scientific image' and a 'manifest image' (or our evolving doctrine into a 'first-class' and a 'second-class' conceptual system). Tables and chairs (and yes, pink ice cubes) exist just as much as quarks and gravitational fields, and the fact that this pot of water would have boiled if I had put it on the stove and turned on the flame is as much a 'fact' as is the circumstance that the water weighs more than eight ounces. The idea that most of mundane reality is illusion (an idea which has haunted Western philosophy since Plato, in spite of Aristotle's valiant counterattack) is given up once and for all. But mundane reality looks different, in that we are forced to acknowledge that many of our familiar descriptions reflect our interests and choices." For this passage, see *The Many Faces of Realism* (LaSalle, Ill.: Open Court, 1987), 37.

10. See *Ways of Worldmaking* (Indianapolis, Ind.: Hackett, 1978), 35.

11. All interpreters agree, say, that the *chair* of the text *refers to* what we all quite comfortably understand to be a chair; but what we seek to know is in what conceptual scheme or cognitive model it makes the best fit (according to our lights, our shared conception of reasonableness, of plausibility, of coherence, etc.).

12. Goodman, *Ways of Worldmaking*, 21–22.

Chapter 13

1. Perhaps the best-known example of this sort of sensemaking is Stanley Fish's in "How to Recognize a Poem When You See One," in *Is There a Text in This Class? The Authority of Interpretive Communities* (Cambridge, Mass.: Harvard University Press, 1980), 322–37.

2. The allusion here, of course, is to line 7 of Gerard Manley Hopkins's "God's Grandeur," "And wears man's smudge and shares man's smell. . . ."

3. My emphasis on "practices." See *Language as Symbolic Action* (Berkeley: University of California Press, 1966), 33.

4. See *After Virtue: A Study in Moral Theory* (Notre Dame, Ind.: University of Notre Dame Press, 1981), 187–89.

5. For Holland's reliance on new critical "interpretations," see "Literature as Transformation," in *The Dynamics of Literary Response* (New York: Oxford University Press, 1968), 3–30; for relevant passages in Atkins's work, see *Reading Deconstruction/Deconstructive Reading* (Lexington: University Press of Kentucky, 1983), especially chapter 1, "The Sign as a Structure of Difference: Derridean Deconstruction and Some of Its Implications," 15–33.

6. Readers unfamiliar with the details of the interpretive controversies surrounding these works, if there remain such, can gain quick access to them by consulting, for Wordsworth's poem, E. D. Hirsch, *Validity in Interpretation* (New Haven, Conn.: Yale University Press, 1967), 227–30, and for James's story, Wayne Booth, *The Rhetoric of Fiction* (Chicago: University of Chicago Press, 1961), 311–23; also for James, some readers might wish to consult Shoshana Felman, *Literature and Psychoanalysis: The Question of Reading: Otherwise*, ed. Shoshana Felman (Baltimore: Johns Hopkins University Press, 1982), 94–207.

7. Wilson's remarks are taken from Booth, *Rhetoric*, 313.

Chapter 14

1. If this or that work by Picasso or Seurat can alter the way we see, giving us new resources of perceptual understanding, Shakespeare's Othello or Lear can not only engage us deeply in his peculiarly poignant conditions but also enhance our capacity to see and understand human dilemmas in the world beyond the stage, enabling us to see what previously had no functional delineation as an "Othello" attitude or a "Lear" view or as an "Othello-like" or "Lear-like" situation.

2. Nelson Goodman and Catherine Z. Elgin, *Reconceptions in Philosophy and Other Arts and Sciences* (Indianapolis, Ind.: Hackett, 1988), 118–19. Emphases added.

3. On the issue of interpreting new or unfamiliar material, Elgin remarks that "we bring to the task of interpreting an unfamiliar picture or sentence the background of related representations we already understand, along with any additional knowledge and skill we can press into service." See *Reconceptions*, 120.

Select Bibliography

Abrams, M. H. *Doing Things with Texts: Essays in Criticism and Critical Theory*. New York: Norton, 1989.

Alter, Robert. "The Decline and Fall of Literary Criticism." *Commentary*, March 1984, 50–56.

Anscombe, G. E. M. *Intention*. Oxford: Blackwell, 1957.

Arnheim, Rudolf. *Visual Thinking*. Berkeley: University of California Press, 1974.

Arvon, Henri. *Marxist Esthetics*. Trans. Helen Lane. Intro. by Fredric Jameson. Ithaca, N.Y.: Cornell University Press, 1973.

Atkins, G. Douglas. *Reading Deconstruction / Deconstructive Reading*. Lexington: University Press of Kentucky, 1983.

Ayer, A. J. *Probability and Evidence*. New York: Columbia University Press, 1972.

Baker, G. P., and P. M. S. Hacker. *Wittgenstein: Rules, Grammar and Necessity*. Oxford: Blackwell, 1985.

Bakhtin, Mikhail. *The Dialogic Imagination: Four Essays*. Ed. Michael Holquist. Trans. Caryl Emerson and Michael Holquist. Austin: University of Texas Press, 1981.

———. *Speech Genres and Other Late Essays*, Ed. Caryl Emerson and Michael Holquist. Trans. Vern W. McGee. Austin: University of Texas Press, 1986.

Barnes, Annette. *On Interpretation: A Critical Analysis*. Oxford: Blackwell, 1988.

Barsalou, Lawrence W. "Ad-Hoc Categories." *Memory and Cognition* 11 (1983): 211–27.

Barthes, Roland. *Mythologies*. Trans. Annette Lavers. New York: Hill and Wang, 1972.

———. *S/Z: An Essay*. Trans. Richard Miller. New York: Hill and Wang, 1974.

———. *The Pleasure of the Text*. Trans. Richard Miller. New York: Hill and Wang, 1975.

Barwise, Jon. *Situations and Attitudes*. Cambridge, Mass.: MIT Press, 1984.

Battersby, James L., and James Phelan. "Meaning as Concept and Extension." *Critical Inquiry* 12 (1986): 605–15.

Battersby, James L. "The Inevitability of Professing Literature." In *Criticism, History, and Intertextuality. Bucknell Review*, ed. Richard Fleming and Michael Payne, 61–76. Lewisburg, Pa.: Bucknell University Press, 1988.

Bell, Daniel. "The Turn to Interpretation: An Introduction." *Partisan Review* 51 (1984): 215–19.

Bennett, Tony. *Formalism and Marxism*. London: Methuen, 1979.

Berger, Peter L., and Thomas Luckmann. *The Social Construction of Reality: A Treatise in the Sociology of Knowledge*. Garden City, N.Y.: Anchor-Doubleday, 1967.

Bernstein, Richard J. *Beyond Objectivism and Relativism: Science, Hermeneutics, and Praxis*. Philadelphia: University of Pennsylvania Press, 1983.

Bleich, David. *Subjective Criticism*. Baltimore: Johns Hopkins University Press, 1978.

Bloom, Harold. *The Anxiety of Influence: A Theory of Poetry*. New York: Oxford University Press, 1973.

———. *A Map of Misreading*. New York: Oxford University Press, 1975.

———, et al. *Deconstruction and Criticism*. New York: Seabury, 1979.

Boër, Steven E. "Substance and Kind: Reflections on the New Theory of Reference." *College of Humanities Inaugural Lectures*. Columbus: Ohio State University, College of Humanities, 1984–1985: 20–66.

Booth, Wayne C. *Critical Understanding: The Powers and Limits of Pluralism*. Chicago: University of Chicago Press, 1979.

Boruah, Bijoy H. *Fiction and Emotion*. Oxford: Clarendon, 1988.

Bourdieu, Pierre. *Outline of a Theory of Practice*. Trans. Richard Nice. Cambridge: Cambridge University Press, 1977.

Bratman, Michael E. *Intention, Plans, and Practical Reason*. Cambridge: Harvard University Press, 1987.

Brooks, Cleanth. *The Well Wrought Urn: Studies in the Structure of Poetry*. New York: Harcourt Brace, 1947.

Brown, Roger. "How Shall a Thing Be Called?" *Psychological Review* 65 (1958): 14–21.

Bruner, Jerome S. *On Knowing: Essays for the Left Hand*. 1962. Reprint, New York: Atheneum. 1968.

———. *Actual Minds, Possible Worlds*. Cambridge, Mass.: Harvard University Press, 1986.

———, and Carol Fleisher Feldman. "Under Construction." Review of *Of Mind and Other Matters*, by Nelson Goodman. *New York Review of Books*, 27 March 1986, 46–49.

Burge, Tyler. "Belief and Synonymy." *Journal of Philosophy* 75 (1978): 119–38.

Burke, Kenneth. *Counter-Statement*. 2nd ed. Chicago: University of Chicago Press, 1957.

———. *Language as Symbolic Action: Essays on Life, Literature, and Method*. Berkeley: University of California Press, 1966.

Cain, William E. *The Crisis in Criticism: Theory, Literature, and Reform in English Studies*. Baltimore: Johns Hopkins University Press, 1984.

Carruthers, Peter. *Introducing Persons: Theories and Arguments in the Philosophy of Mind*. London: Croom Helm, 1986.

Chapman, Raymond. *Linguistics and Literature: An Introduction to Literary Stylistics*. London: Arnold, 1973.

Chatman, Seymour, ed. *Literary Style: A Symposium*. New York: Oxford University Press, 1971.

———. *Story and Discourse: Narrative Structure in Fiction and Film*. Ithaca, N.Y.: Cornell University Press, 1978.

Cherniak, Christopher. *Minimal Rationality*. Cambridge, Mass.: MIT Press, 1986.

Churchland, Patricia Smith. *Neurophilosophy: Toward a Unified Science of the Mind/Brain*. Cambridge, Mass.: MIT Press, 1986.

Churchland, Paul M. *Matter and Consciousness*. Rev. ed. Cambridge, Mass.: MIT Press, 1988.

Cohen, Avner, and Marcelo Dascal, eds. *The Institution of Philosophy: A Discipline in Crisis*. LaSalle, Ill.: Open Court, 1989.

Crane, R. S., ed. *Critics and Criticism: Ancient and Modern*. Chicago: University of Chicago Press, 1952.

————. *The Languages of Criticism and the Structure of Poetry*. Toronto: University of Toronto Press, 1953.

————. *The Idea of the Humanities and Other Essays Critical and Historical*. 2 vols. Chicago: University of Chicago Press, 1967.

————. *Critical and Historical Principles of Literary History*. Chicago: University of Chicago Press, 1971.

Cresswell, M. J. "The World is Everything that is the Case." *Australasian Journal of Philosophy* 50 (1972): 1–13.

Crews, Frederick. *Skeptical Engagements*. Oxford: Oxford University Press, 1986.

Culler, Jonathan. *Structuralist Poetics: Structuralism, Linguistics, and the Study of Literature*. Ithaca, N.Y.: Cornell University Press, 1975.

————. *Ferdinand de Saussure*. New York: Penguin, 1976.

————. *On Deconstruction: Theory and Criticism after Structuralism*. Ithaca, N.Y.: Cornell University Press, 1982.

Cummins, Robert. *Meaning and Mental Representation*. Cambridge, Mass.: MIT Press, 1989.

Damasio, Antonio R. "Disorders of Complex Visual Processing." In *Principles of Behavioral Neurology*, ed. M. Marsel Mesulam, 45–67. Philadelphia: Davis, 1985.

Dasenbrock, Reed Way, ed. *Redrawing the Lines: Analytic Philosophy, Deconstruction, and Literary Theory*. Minneapolis: University of Minnesota Press, 1989.

Davidson, Donald. "On the Very Idea of a Conceptual Scheme." *Proceedings and Addresses of the American Philosophical Association* 47 (1974): 5–20.

————. *Essays on Action and Events*. Oxford: Clarendon, 1980.

————. *Inquiries into Truth and Interpretation*. Oxford: Clarendon, 1984.

de Man, Paul. *Blindness and Insight: Essays in the Rhetoric of Contemporary Criticism*. New York: Oxford University Press, 1971.

————. *Allegories of Reading: Figural Language in Rousseau, Nietzsche, Rilke, and Proust*. New Haven, Conn.: Yale University Press, 1979.

————. "Dialogue and Dialogism." *Poetics Today* 4 (1983): 99–107.

————. *The Resistance to Theory*. Manchester: Manchester University Press, 1986.

Dennett, Daniel C. *The International Stance*. Cambridge, Mass.: MIT Press, 1987.

Derrida, Jacques. *Of Grammatology*. Trans. Gayatri Chakravorty Spivak. Baltimore: Johns Hopkins University Press, 1974.

————. *Writing and Difference*. Trans. Alan Bass. Chicago: University of Chicago Press, 1978.

————. *Positions*. Trans. Alan Bass. Chicago: University of Chicago Press, 1981.

de Sousa, Ronald. *The Rationality of Emotion*. Cambridge, Mass.: MIT Press, 1987.

Diamond, Cora, and Jenny Teichman, eds. *Intention and Intentionality: Essays in Honour of G. E. M. Anscombe.* Brighton: Harvester, 1979.

Dilthey, Wilhelm. *Selected Works, Volume Five: Poetry and Experience.* Ed. and trans. Rudolf A. Makkreel and Frithjof Rodi. Princeton, N.J.: Princeton University Press, 1985.

Dretske, Fred. *Explaining Behavior: Reasons in a World of Causes.* Cambridge, Mass.: MIT Press, 1988.

Dummett, Michael. *Truth and Other Enigmas.* Cambridge, Mass.: Harvard University Press, 1978.

Eagleton, Terry. *Marxism and Literary Criticism.* Berkeley: University of California Press, 1976.

———. *Literary Theory: An Introduction.* Minneapolis: University of Minnesota Press, 1983.

Eco, Umberto, Marco Santambrogio, and Patrizia Violi, eds. *Meaning and Mental Representation.* Bloomington: Indiana University Press, 1988.

Edelman, Gerald M. *Neural Darwinism: The Theory of Neuronal Group Selection.* New York: Basic Books, 1987.

Elgin, Catherine Z. *With Reference to Reference.* Indianapolis, Ind.: Hackett, 1983.

Ellis, John M. "What Does Deconstruction Contribute to Theory of Criticism? *New Literary History* 19 (1988): 259–79.

Elster, Jon. *Making Sense of Marx.* Cambridge: Cambridge University Press, 1985.

Empson, William. *Seven Types of Ambiguity.* 2nd ed. New York: New Directions, 1947.

Epstein, William H. "Professing the Eighteenth Century." *Profession 85*: 10–15. New York: Modern Language Association of America, 1985.

Fauconnier, Gilles. *Mental Spaces.* Cambridge, Mass.: MIT Press, 1985.

———. "Quantification, Roles and Domains." In *Meaning and Mental Representation,* ed. Umberto Eco, Marco Santambrogio, and Patrizia Violi, 61–80. Bloomington: Indiana University Press, 1988.

Felman, Shoshana, ed. *Literature and Psychoanalysis: The Question of Reading: Otherwise.* Baltimore: Johns Hopkins University Press, 1982.

Feyerabend, Paul. *Against Method: Outline of an Anarchistic Theory of Knowledge.* London: NLB, 1975.

Fillmore, Charles. "The Case for Case." In *Universals in Linguistic Theory,* ed. E. Bach and R. Harms, 1–90. New York: Holt, Rinehart, Winston, 1968.

———. "An Alternative to Checklist Theories of Meaning." *Proceedings of the First Annual Meeting of the Berkeley Linguistics Society,* 123–31. Berkeley: Berkeley Linguistics Society, 1975.

———. "Topics in Lexical Semantics." In *Current Issues in Linguistic Theory,* ed. Peter Cole, 76–138. Bloomington: Indiana University Press, 1976.

———. "The Organization of Semantic Information in the Lexicon." *Papers from the Parasession on the Lexicon,* 1–11. Chicago: Chicago Linguistic Society, 1978.

———. "Towards a Descriptive Framework for Spatial Deixis." In *Speech, Place, and Action,* ed. R. J. Jarrella and W. Klein, 31–59. London: John Wiley, 1982.

———. "Frame Semantics." In *Linguistics in the Morning Calm,* 111–38. Linguistic Society of Korea. Seoul: Hanshin, 1982.

————. "Frames and the Semantics of Understanding." *Quaderni di Semantica* 6 (1985): 222–53.

Fish, Stanley. "Normal Circumstances, Literal Language, Direct Speech Acts, the Ordinary, the Everyday, the Obvious, What Goes without Saying, and Other Special Cases." *Critical Inquiry* 4 (1978): 625–44.

————. *Is There a Text in This Class? The Authority of Interpretive Communities.* Cambridge, Mass.: Harvard University Press, 1980.

————. "Anti-Professionalism." *New Literary History* 17 (1985): 89–108.

————. "Resistance and Independence: A Reply to Gerald Graff." *New Literary History* 17 (1985): 119–27.

Fodor, Jerry A. *Psychosemantics: The Problem of Meaning in the Philosophy of Mind.* Cambridge, Mass.: MIT Press, 1987.

Foucault, Michel. *Madness and Civilization: A History of Insanity in the Age of Reason.* Trans. Richard Howard. New York: Vintage, 1973.

————. *The Archaeology of Knowledge and the Discourse on Language.* Trans. A. M. Sheridan Smith. New York: Harper, 1976.

Gadamer, Hans-Georg. *Philosophical Hermeneutics.* Ed. and trans. David E. Linge. Berkeley: University of California Press, 1976.

Gardner, Howard. *Art, Mind, and Brain: A Cognitive Approach to Creativity.* New York: Basic Books, 1982.

————. *Frames of Mind: The Theory of Multiple Intelligences.* New York: Basic Books, 1983.

Garfinkel, Alan. *Forms of Explanation: Rethinking the Questions in Social Theory.* New Haven, Conn.: Yale University Press, 1981.

Gasché, Rodolphe. *The Tain of the Mirror: Derrida and the Philosophy of Reflection.* Cambridge, Mass.: Harvard University Press, 1986.

Geertz, Clifford. *The Interpretation of Cultures.* New York: Basic Books, 1973.

————. "Blurred Genres: The Refiguration of Social Thought." *American Scholar* 49 (1980): 165–79.

Gellner, Ernest. *Words and Things.* Intro. by Bertrand Russell. Harmondsworth: Penguin, 1968.

Gibson, James J. *The Ecological Approach to Visual Perception.* Boston, Houghton Mifflin, 1979.

Ginet, Carl, and Sydney Shoemaker, eds. *Mind and Knowledge: Essays in Honor of Norman Malcolm.* Oxford: Oxford University Press, 1983.

Gombrich, E. H., Julian Hochberg, and Max Black. *Art, Perception, and Reality.* Baltimore: Johns Hopkins University Press, 1972.

————. " 'They Were All Human Beings—So Much is Plain': Reflections on Cultural Relativism in the Humanities." *Critical Inquiry* 13 (1987): 686–99.

Goodman, Nelson. *The Structure of Appearance.* Cambridge: Harvard University Press, 1951.

————. *Languages of Art: An Approach to a Theory of Symbols.* Indianapolis, Ind.: Hackett, 1976.

————. *Ways of Worldmaking.* Indianapolis, Ind.: Hackett, 1978.

————. *Fact, Fiction and Forecast.* 4th ed. Cambridge, Mass.: Harvard University Press, 1983.

————. "Notes on the Well-Made World." *Partisan Review* 51 (1984): 276–88.

————. *Of Mind and Other Matters.* Cambridge: Harvard University Press, 1984.

————, and Catherine Z. Elgin. *Reconceptions in Philosophy and Other Arts and Sciences.* Indianapolis, Ind.: Hackett, 1988.

Graff, Gerald. " 'Keep off the Grass,' 'Drop Dead,' and Other Indeterminacies: A Response to Sanford Levinson." *Texas Law Review* 60 (1982): 405–13.

———. "Humanism and the Hermeneutics of Power: Reflections on the Post-Structuralist Two-Step and Other Dances." *boundary 2* (1984): 495–505.

———. "Interpretation on Tlön: A Response to Stanley Fish." *New Literary History* 17 (1985): 109–17.

———. *Professing Literature: An Institutional History.* Chicago: University of Chicago Press, 1987.

Grandy, Richard. "Reference, Meaning and Belief." *Journal of Philosophy* 70 (1973): 439–52.

Greenblatt, Stephen. *Renaissance Self-Fashioning.* Chicago: University of Chicago Press, 1980.

Gregory, Richard L., ed. *The Oxford Companion to the Mind.* Oxford: Oxford University Press, 1987.

———. *The Intelligent Eye.* New York: McGraw-Hill, 1970.

Grice, Paul. *Studies in the Way of Words.* Cambridge, Mass.: Harvard University Press, 1989.

Grunbaum, Adolf, and Wesley C. Salmon, eds. *The Limitations of Deconstruction.* Berkeley: University of California Press, 1988.

Gunn, Giles. *The Culture of Criticism and the Criticism of Culture.* Oxford: Oxford University Press, 1987.

Hacking, Ian. *Why Does Language Matter to Philosophy?* Cambridge: Cambridge University Press, 1975.

Hahn, Lewis Edwin, and Paul Arthur Schilpp, eds. *The Philosophy of W. V. Quine.* LaSalle, Ill.: Open Court, 1986.

Hampden-Turner, Charles. *Maps of the Mind.* New York: Collier-Macmillan, 1982.

Harman, Gilbert. *Change in View: Principles of Reasoning.* Cambridge, Mass.: MIT Press, 1986.

Harré, Rom. *Varieties of Realism: A Rationale for the Natural Sciences.* Oxford: Blackwell, 1986.

Harris, Wendell V. *Interpretive Acts: In Search of Meaning.* Oxford: Clarendon, 1988.

Hartman, Geoffrey H. *Criticism in the Wilderness: The Study of Literature Today.* New Haven, Conn.: Yale University Press, 1980.

———. *Saving the Text: Literature / Derrida / Philosophy.* Baltimore: Johns Hopkins University Press, 1981.

Harvey, Irene E. *Derrida and the Economy of Différance.* Bloomington: Indiana University Press, 1986.

Hesse, Mary. "Texts Without Types and Lumps Without Laws." *New Literary History* 17 (1985): 31–48.

Hintikka, Jaakko. *Knowledge and Belief.* Ithaca, N.Y.: Cornell University Press, 1962.

———. *Models for Modalities: Selected Essays.* Dordrecht: Reidel, 1969.

———. *The Intentions of Intentionality and Other New Models for Modalities.* Dordrecht: Reidel, 1975.

Hirsch, E. D., Jr. *Validity in Interpretation.* New Haven, Conn.: Yale University Press, 1967.

———. "Past Intentions and Present Meanings." *Essays in Criticism* 33 (1983): 79–98.

———. "Meaning and Significance Reinterpreted." *Critical Inquiry* 11 (1984): 202–25.

Holland, Norman. *The Dynamics of Literary Response.* New York: Oxford University Press, 1968.

Hollis, Martin, and Steven Lukes, eds. *Rationality and Relativism.* Cambridge, Mass.: MIT Press, 1982.

Howard, Jean E. "The New Historicism in Renaissance Studies." *English Literary Renaissance* 16 (1986): 13–43.

Hunter, I.M.L. *Memory: Facts and Fallacies.* Harmondsworth: Penguin, 1957.

Iser, Wolfgang. *The Act of Reading: A Theory of Aesthetic Response.* Baltimore: Johns Hopkins University Press, 1978.

Jackendoff, Ray. *Semantics and Cognition.* Cambridge, Mass.: MIT Press, 1983.

———. "Conceptual Semantics." In *Meaning and Mental Representation,* ed. Umberto Eco, Marco Santambrogio, and Patrizia Violi, 81–97. Bloomington: Indiana University Press, 1988.

Jameson, Fredric. *Marxism and Form.* Princeton, N.J.: Princeton University Press, 1971.

———. *The Political Unconscious: Narrative as a Socially Symbolic Act.* Ithaca, N.Y.: Cornell University Press, 1981.

Jardine, N. *The Fortunes of Inquiry.* Oxford: Clarendon, 1986.

Johnson, Mark. *The Body in the Mind: The Bodily Basis of Meaning, Imagination, and Reason.* Chicago: University of Chicago Press, 1987.

Johnson, Samuel. *Poems.* Vol. 6 of *The Yale Edition of the Works of Samuel Johnson.* Ed. E. L. McAdam, with George Milne. New Haven, Conn.: Yale University Press, 1964.

———. *Lives of the Poets.* Ed. George Birkbeck Hill. 3 vols. Oxford: Clarendon, 1905.

———. *Johnson: Prose and Poetry.* Ed. Mona Wilson. Cambridge, Mass.: Harvard University Press, 1967.

———. *A Journey to the Western Islands of Scotland.* Vol. 9 of *The Yale Edition of the Works of Samuel Johnson.* Ed. Mary Lascelles. New Haven, Conn.: Yale University Press, 1971.

Johnson-Laird, Philip N., and P. C. Wason, eds. *Thinking: Readings in Cognitive Science.* Cambridge: Cambridge University Press, 1977.

———. *Mental Models: Towards a Cognitive Science of Language, Inference, and Consciousness.* Cambridge: Cambridge University Press, 1983.

———. "How is Meaning Mentally Represented?" In *Meaning and Mental Representation,* ed. Umberto Eco, Marco Santambrogio, and Patrizia Violi, 99–118. Bloomington: Indiana University Press, 1988.

Juhl, P. D. *Interpretation: An Essay in the Philosophy of Literary Criticism.* Princeton, N.J.: Princeton University Press, 1980.

Katz, Jerrold J. *The Underlying Reality of Language and Its Philosophical Import.* New York: Harper and Row, 1971.

Kirk, Robert. *Translation Determined.* Oxford: Oxford University Press, 1986.

Kiser, Lisa J. *Telling Classical Tales.* Ithaca, N.Y.: Cornell University Press, 1983.

Knapp, Steven, and Walter Benn Michaels. "Against Theory." *Critical Inquiry* 8 (1982): 723–42.

———. "Against Theory 2: Hermeneutics and Deconstruction." *Critical Inquiry* 14 (1987): 49–68.

Kolers, Paul A. *Aspects of Motion Perception*. Oxford: Pergamon, 1972.

Kripke, Saul A. *Naming and Necessity*. Cambridge: Harvard University Press, 1972.

————. *Wittgenstein on Rules and Private Language*. Oxford: Blackwell, 1982.

Kuhn, Thomas S. *The Structure of Scientific Revolutions*. Chicago: University of Chicago Press, 1962.

————. *The Essential Tension*. Chicago: University of Chicago Press, 1977.

La Capra, Dominick. *History and Criticism*. Ithaca, N.Y.: Cornell University Press, 1985.

Lakatos, Imre, and Alan Musgrave, eds. *Criticism and the Growth of Knowledge*. Proceedings of the International Colloquium in the Philosophy of Science, London, 1965, vol. 4. Cambridge, Cambridge University Press, 1970.

Lakoff, George, and Mark Johnson. *Metaphors We Live By*. Chicago: University of Chicago Press, 1980.

————. *Women, Fire, and Dangerous Things: What Categories Reveal About the Mind*. Chicago: University of Chicago Press, 1987.

————. "Cognitive Semantics." In *Meaning and Mental Representation*, ed. Umberto Eco, Marco Santambrogio, and Patrizia Violi, 119–54. Bloomington: Indiana University Press, 1988.

Larmore, Charles, E. *Patterns of Moral Complexity*. Cambridge: Cambridge University Press, 1987.

Lawson, Hilary. *Reflexivity: The Post-Modern Predicament*. London: Hutchinson, 1985.

Leitch, Vincent B. *Deconstructive Criticism: An Advanced Introduction*. New York: Columbia University Press, 1983.

Lentricchia, Frank. *After the New Criticism*. Chicago: University of Chicago Press, 1980.

Lerner, Laurence, ed. *Reconstructing Literature*. Oxford: Blackwell, 1983.

Lewis, David. *Counterfactuals*. Oxford: Blackwell, 1973.

————. "Individuation by Acquaintance and by Stipulation." *Philosophical Review* 92 (1983): 3–32.

————. "Putnam's Paradox." *Australasian Journal of Philosophy* 64 (1986): 221–36.

————. *On the Plurality of Worlds*. Oxford: Blackwell, 1986.

Lilla, Mark. "Philosophy: On Goodman, Putnam, and Rorty." *Partisan Review* 51 (1984): 220–35.

Llewelyn, John. *Beyond Meta-Physics? The Hermeneutic Circle in Contemporary Continental Philosophy*. New York: Macmillan, 1984.

————. *Derrida on the Threshold of Sense*. New York: Macmillan, 1986.

Lloyd, Dan. *Simple Minds*. Cambridge, Mass.: MIT Press, 1989.

Longuet-Higgins, Christopher H. *Mental Processes: Studies in Cognitive Science*. Cambridge, Mass.: MIT Press, 1987.

Loux, Michael, ed. *The Possible and the Actual: Readings in the Metaphysics of Modality*. Ithaca, N.Y.: Cornell University Press, 1979.

Lucas, John. "Absence into Presence: Changes in Literary Criticism." *Times Literary Supplement*, 14 November 1986, 1280.

Lyons, John, ed. *New Horizons in Linguistics*. Harmondsworth: Penguin, 1970.

Lyons, William. *The Disappearance of Introspection*. Cambridge, Mass.: MIT Press, 1986.

McCann, J. J. "Retinex Theory and Colour Constancy." *The Oxford Companion to the Mind*. Ed. Richard L. Gregory. Oxford: Oxford University Press, 1987.

McCormick, Peter J. *Fictions, Philosophies, and the Problems of Poetics*. Ithaca, N.Y.: Cornell University Press, 1988.

McFarland, Thomas. *Shapes of Culture*. Iowa City: University of Iowa Press, 1987.

MacIntyre, Alasdair. *After Virtue: A Study in Moral Theory*. 2nd ed. Notre Dame, Ind.: University of Notre Dame Press, 1984.

McKeon, Zahava Karl. *Novels and Arguments: Inventing Rhetorical Criticism*. Chicago: University of Chicago Press, 1982.

Malcolm, Norman. *Knowledge and Certainty: Essays and Lectures*. Ithaca, N.Y.: Cornell University Press, 1963.

Margolis, Joseph. *Pragmatism without Foundations: Reconciling Realism and Relativism*. Oxford: Blackwell, 1986.

———. *Science Without Unity: Reconciling the Human and Natural Sciences*. Oxford: Blackwell, 1987.

Marr, David. *Vision: A Computational Investigation into the Human Representation and Processing of Visual Information*. San Francisco: Freeman, 1982.

Marshall, John C., and Freda Newcombe. "Patterns of Paralexia: A Psycholinguistic Approach." *Journal of Psycholinguistic Research* 2 (1973): 175–99.

Marshall, John C. "Routes and Representations in the Processing of Written Language." In *Motor and Sensory Processes of Language*, ed. Eric Keller and Myrna Gopnik, 237–56. Hillsdale, N.J.: Lawrence Erlbaum, 1987.

Merrill, G. H. "The Model-Theoretic Argument against Realism." *Philosophy of Science* 47 (1980): 69–81.

Miller, George, and Philip Johnson-Laird. *Language and Perception*. Cambridge, Mass.: Harvard University Press, 1976.

Miller, J. Hillis. *The Linguistic Moment: From Wordsworth to Stevens*. Princeton, N.J.: Princeton University Press, 1985.

———. "President's Column: The Obligation to Write." *MLA Newsletter* 18.3 (1986): 4–5.

———. "Presidential Address 1986. The Triumph of Theory, the Resistance to Reading, and the Question of the Material Base." *PMLA* 102 (1987): 281–91.

———. "But are things as we think they are?" *Times Literary Supplement*, 9–15 October 1987, 1104–05.

Millikan, Ruth Garrett. *Language, Thought, and Other Biological Categories: New Foundations for Realism*. Cambridge, Mass.: MIT Press, 1984.

Minsky, Marvin. *The Society of Mind*. New York: Simon, 1986.

Mitchell, W. J. T., ed. *Against Theory: Literary Studies and the New Pragmatism*. Chicago: University of Chicago Press, 1985.

Montefiore, Alan. "Philosophy, Literature and the Restatement of a Few Banalities." *The Monist* 69 (1986): 56–67.

Montrose, Louis. "Renaissance Studies and the Subject of History." *English Literary Renaissance* 16 (1986): 5–12.

Nagel, Thomas. *The View from Nowhere*. Oxford: Oxford University Press, 1986.

Newton-de Molina, David, ed. *On Literary Intention*. Edinburgh: Edinburgh University Press, 1976.

Norris, Christopher. *Deconstruction: Theory and Practice*. London: Methuen, 1982.

Norris, Christopher. *Contest of Faculties: Philosophy and Theory after Deconstruction.* New York: Methuen, 1985.

Novitz, David. "The Rage for Deconstruction." *The Monist* 69 (1986): 39–55.

Olsen, Stein Haugom. *The Structure of Literary Understanding.* Cambridge: Cambridge University Press, 1978.

———. *The End of Literary Theory.* Cambridge: Cambridge University Press, 1987.

Olson, Elder. " 'Sailing to Byzantium': Prolegomena to a Poetics of the Lyric." *University Review* 8 (1942): 209–19.

———. "William Empson, Contemporary Criticism, and Poetic Diction." In *Critics and Criticism: Ancient and Modern,* ed. R. S. Crane, 45–82. Chicago: University of Chicago Press, 1952.

———. "An Outline of Poetic Theory." In *Critics and Criticism: Ancient and Modern,* ed. R. S. Crane, 546–66. Chicago: University of Chicago Press, 1952.

———. *Tragedy and the Theory of Drama.* Detroit: Wayne State University Press, 1961.

———. "The Dialectical Foundations of Critical Pluralism." *Texas Quarterly* 9 (1966): 202–30.

———. *On Value Judgments in the Arts and Other Essays.* Chicago: University of Chicago Press, 1976.

Palmer, F. R. *Semantics.* 2nd ed. Cambridge: Cambridge University Press, 1981.

Parrinder, Patrick. *The Failure of Theory: Essays on Criticism and Contemporary Fiction.* Brighton: Harvester, 1987.

Penrose, Roger. *The Emperor's New Mind: Concerning Computers, Minds, and the Laws of Physics.* Oxford: Oxford University Press, 1989.

Pepper, Stephen C. *The Basis of Criticism in the Arts.* Cambridge, Mass.: Harvard Univesity Press, 1965.

———. *World Hypothesis: A Study in Evidence.* Berkeley: University of California Press, 1966.

Pettit, Philip, and John McDowell, eds. *Subject, Thought and Context.* Oxford: Clarendon, 1986.

Phelan, James. *Worlds from Words: A Theory of Language in Fiction.* Chicago: University of Chicago Press, 1981.

———. "Data, Danda, and Disagreement." *Diacritics* 11 (1983): 39–50.

———. *Reading People, Reading Plots: Character, Progression, and the Interpretation of Narrative.* Chicago: University of Chicago Press, 1989.

Pivcevic, Edo. *The Concept of Reality.* London: Duckworth, 1986.

Plantinga, Alvin. "Actualism and Possible Worlds." *Theoria* 42 (1976): 139–60.

Polanyi, Michael. *Personal Knowledge: Towards a Post-Critical Philosophy.* Chicago: University of Chicago Press, 1958.

———. *The Tacit Dimension.* Garden City, N.Y.: Anchor-Doubleday, 1967.

———. *Knowing and Being.* Ed. Marjorie Grene. Chicago: University of Chicago Press, 1969.

———, and Harry Prosch. *Meaning.* Chicago: University of Chicago Press, 1975.

Popper, Karl R. *The Poverty of Historicism.* New York: Harper and Row, 1964.

———. *Conjectures and Refutations: The Growth of Scientific Knowledge.* New York: Harper and Row, 1968.

————. *Objective Knowledge: An Evolutionary Approach.* Rev. ed. Oxford: Clarendon, 1979.

Poundstone, William. *Labyrinths of Reason: Paradox, Puzzles, and the Frailty of Knowledge.* New York: Doubleday, 1988.

Prickett, Stephen. *Words and "The Word": Language, Poetics and Biblical Interpretation.* Cambridge: Cambridge University Press, 1986.

Putnam, Hilary. *Mind, Language and Reality.* Cambridge: Cambridge University Press, 1975.

————. *Meaning and the Moral Sciences.* London: Routledge and Kegan Paul, 1978.

————. *Reason, Truth and History.* Cambridge: Cambridge University Press, 1981.

————. *Realism and Reason.* Cambridge: Cambridge University Press, 1983.

————. "After Ayer, After Empiricism." *Partisan Review* 51 (1984): 265–75.

————. "The Craving for Objectivity." *New Literary History* 15 (1984): 229–39.

————. "A Comparison of Something with Something Else." *New Literary History* 17 (1985): 61–79.

————. *The Many Faces of Realism.* LaSalle, Ill.: Open Court, 1987.

————. *Representation and Reality.* Cambridge, Mass.: MIT Press, 1988.

————. *Realism with a Human Face.* Ed. James Conant. Cambridge, Mass.: Harvard University Press, 1990.

Putnam, Ruth Anna. "Poets, Scientists, and Critics." *New Literary History* 17 (1985): 17–21.

Quine, Willard Van Orman. *Word and Object.* Cambridge, Mass.: MIT Press, 1960.

————. "On the Reasons for Indeterminacy of Translation." *Journal of Philosophy* 67 (1970): 178–83.

————. "Worlds Away." *Journal of Philosophy* 73 (1976): 859–63.

————. *Theories and Things.* Cambridge, Mass.: Harvard University Press, 1981.

————. *The Time of My Life: An Autobiography.* Cambridge, Mass.: MIT Press, 1985.

————. *Quiddities: An Intermittently Philosophical Dictionary.* Cambridge, Mass.: Harvard University Press, 1987.

————. *Pursuit of Truth.* Cambridge, Mass.: Harvard University Press, 1990.

Rader, Ralph W. "Fact, Theory, and Literary Explanation." *Critical Inquiry* 1 (1974): 245–72.

————. "The Concept of Genre and Eighteenth-Century Studies." In *New Approaches to Eighteenth-Century Literature,* ed. Phillip Harth, 79–115. New York: Columbia University Press, 1974.

Ramberg, Bjørn. *Donald Davidson's Philosophy of Language: An Introduction.* Oxford: Blackwell, 1989.

Raval, Suresh. "Philosophy and the Crisis of Contemporary Literary Theory." *The Monist* 69 (1986): 119–32.

Ray, William. *Literary Meaning: From Phenomenology to Deconstruction.* Oxford: Blackwell, 1984.

Rescher, Nicholas. *Cognitive Systematization: A Systems-Theoretic Approach to a Coherentist Theory of Knowledge.* Totowa, N.J.: Rowman, 1979.

————, and Robert Brandon. *The Logic of Inconsistency: A Study in Non-Standard Possible-World Semantics and Ontology.* Totowa, N.J.: Rowman, 1979.

Restak, Richard M. *The Brain: The Last Frontier.* New York: Doubleday, 1979.

Richards, Tom. "The Worlds of David Lewis." *Australasian Journal of Philosophy* 53 (1975): 105–18.

Rockmore, Tom. *Hegel's Circular Epistemology.* Bloomington: Indiana University Press, 1986.

Roper, Andrew. "Toward an Eliminative Reduction of Possible Worlds." *Philosophical Quarterly* 32 (1982): 45–59.

Rorty, Richard. *Philosophy and the Mirror of Nature.* Princeton, N.J.: Princeton University Press, 1979.

———. *Consequences of Pragmatism.* Minneapolis: University of Minnesota Press, 1982.

———. "Texts and Lumps." *New Literary History* 17 (1985): 1–16.

Rosenfield, Israel. "A Hero of the Brain." Review of *Selected Papers on Language and the Brain,* by Norman Geschwind; *Cerebral Dominance: The Biological Foundations,* ed. Norman Geschwind and Albert M. Galaburda; and *Dyslexia: Current Status and Future Directions,* ed. Frank Hopkins Duffy and Norman Geschwind. *New York Review of Books,* 21 November 1985, 49–55.

———. *The Invention of Memory: A New View of the Brain.* New York: Basic Books, 1988.

———. "Neural Darwinism: A New Approach to Memory and Perception." *New York Review of Books,* 9 October 1986, 21 + .

———. "Seeing Through the Brain." Review of *Vision: A Computational Investigation into the Human Representation and Processing of Visual Information,* by David Marr. *New York Review of Books,* 11 October 1984, 53–56.

Rumelhart, David E., James L. McClelland, and the PDP Research Group. *Parallel Distributed Processing: Explorations in the Microstructure of Cognition.* Vol. 1, *Foundations.* Vol. 2, *Psychological and Biological Models.* Cambridge, Mass.: MIT Press, 1986.

Sacks, Mark. *The World We Found: The Limits of Ontological Talk.* London: Duckworth, 1989.

Salmon, Nathan. "How *Not* to Derive Essentialism from the Theory of Reference." *Journal of Philosophy* 76 (1979): 703–74.

Schaff, Adam. *Language and Cognition.* Ed. Robert S. Cohen. Intro. by Noam Chomsky. New York: McGraw-Hill, 1973.

Schauber, Ellen, and Ellen Spolsky. *The Bounds of Interpretation: Linguistic Theory and Literary Text.* Stanford, Ca.: Stanford University Press, 1986.

Scheffler, Israel. *Science and Subjectivity.* 2nd ed. Indianapolis, Ind.: Hackett, 1982.

Schiffer, Stephen. *Remnants of Meaning.* Cambridge, Mass.: MIT Press, 1987.

Scholes, Robert. *Structuralism in Literature: An Introduction.* New Haven, Conn.: Yale University Press, 1974.

———. *Semiotics and Interpretation.* New Haven, Conn.: Yale University Press, 1982.

———. *Textual Power: Literary Theory and the Teaching of English.* New Haven, Conn.: Yale University Press, 1985.

Scruton, Roger. "Modern Philosophy and the Neglect of Aesthetics." *Times Literary Supplement,* 5 June 1987, 604 + .

Searle, John R. *Expression and Meaning: Studies in the Theory of Speech Acts.* Cambridge: Cambridge University Press, 1979.

———. "The Word Turned Upside Down." Review of *On Deconstruction: Theory and Criticism after Structuralism,* by Jonathan Culler. *New York Review of Books,* 27 October 1983, 74–79.

———. *Intentionality: An Essay in the Philosophy of Mind.* Cambridge: Cambridge University Press, 1983.

———. *Minds, Brains and Science.* Cambridge, Mass.: Harvard University Press, 1984.

Segal, Naomi. *The Unintended Reader: Feminism and* Manon Lescaut. Cambridge: Cambridge Universty Press, 1986.

Selden, Raman. *A Reader's Guide to Contemporary Literary Theory.* Brighton: Harvester, 1985.

Seung, T. K. *Semiotics and Thematics and Hermeneutics.* New York: Columbia University Press, 1982.

Shaw, Peter. *The War Against the Intellect: Episodes in the Decline of Discourse.* Iowa City: University of Iowa Press, 1989.

Shusterman, Richard. "Analytic Aesthetics, Literary Theory, and Deconstruction." *The Monist* 69 (1986): 22–38.

———. "Organic Unity: Analysis and Deconstruction." In *Redrawing the Lines: Analytic Philosophy, Deconstruction, and Literary Theory,* ed. Reed Way Dasenbrock, 92–115. Minneapolis: University of Minnesota Press, 1989.

Skyrms, Brian. "Possible Worlds, Physics and Metaphysics." *Philosophical Studies* 30 (1976): 323–32.

Smith, Barbara Herrnstein. *On the Margins of Discourse: The Relation of Literature to Language.* Chicago: University of Chicago Press, 1978.

———. *Contingencies of Value: Alternative Perspectives for Critical Theory.* Cambridge, Mass.: Harvard University Press, 1988.

Smith, Peter, and O. R. Jones. *The Philosophy of Mind: An Introduction.* Cambridge: Cambridge University Press, 1986.

Sperber, Dan, and Deirdre Wilson. *Relevance: Communication and Cognition.* Oxford: Blackwell, 1986.

Staten, Henry. "The Secret Name of Cats: Deconstruction, Intentional Meaning, and the New Theory of Reference." In *Redrawing the Lines: Analytic Philosophy, Deconstruction, and Literary Theory,* ed. Reed Way Dasenbrock, 27–48. Minneapolis: University of Minnesota Press, 1989.

Steiner, George. "Viewpoint: A New Meaning of Meaning." *Times Literary Supplement,* 8 November 1985, 1262 + .

Stich, Stephen P. *The Fragmentation of Reason: Preface to a Pragmatic Theory of Cognitive Evaluation.* Cambridge, Mass.: MIT Press, 1990.

Stout, Jeffrey. "The Relativity of Interpretation." *The Monist* 69 (1986): 103–18.

Strawson, Galen. *Freedom and Belief.* Oxford: Clarendon, 1986.

Strickland, Geoffrey. *Structuralism or Criticism? Thoughts on How We Read.* Cambridge: Cambridge University Press, 1981.

Sturrock, John, ed. *Structuralism and Since: From Lévi-Strauss to Derrida.* Oxford: Oxford Univesity Press, 1979.

Suleiman, Susan R., and Inge Crosman, eds. *The Reader in the Text: Essays on Audience and Interpretation.* Princeton, N.J.: Princeton University Press, 1980.

Tallis, Raymond. *In Defense of Realism.* London: Arnold, 1988.

Taylor, Mark C. "Descartes, Nietzsche and the Search for the Unsayable." *New York Times Book Review,* 2 February 1987, 3 + .

Todorov, Tzvetan. *Mikhail Bakhtin: The Dialogical Principle.* Trans. Wlad Godzich. Minneapolis: University of Minnesota Press, 1984.

Tompkins, Jane P., ed. *Reader-Response Criticism: From Formalism to Post-Struc-turalism*. Baltimore: Johns Hopkins University Press, 1980.

Trigg, Roger. *Reality at Risk: A Defence of Realism in Philosophy and the Sciences*. Totowa, N.J.: Barnes and Noble, 1980.

Tugendhat, Ernst. *Self-Consciousness and Self-Determination*. Trans. Paul Stern. Cambridge, Mass.: MIT Press, 1986.

Vuillemin, Jules. *What Are Philosophical Systems?* Cambridge: Cambridge University Press, 1986.

Warrington, Elizabeth. "The Selective Impairment of Semantic Memory." *Quarterly Journal of Experimental Psychology* 27 (1975): 635–57.

Watson, Walter. *The Architectonics of Meaning: Foundations of the New Pluralism*. Albany, N.Y.: SUNY Press, 1985.

Weightman, John. "On Not Understanding Michel Foucault." *American Scholar* 58 (1989): 383–406.

Wheeler, Samuel C., III. "The Extension of Deconstruction." *The Monist* 69 (1986): 3–21.

———. "Wittgenstein as Conservative Deconstructor." *New Literary History* 19 (1988): 239–58.

———. "Metaphor According to Davidson and de Man." In *Redrawing the Lines: Analytic Philosophy, Deconstruction, and Literary Theory*, ed. Reed Way Dasenbrock, 116–39. Minneapolis: University of Minnesota Press, 1989.

Whiteside, Anna, and Michael Issacharoff, eds. *On Referring in Literature*. Bloomington: Indiana University Press, 1987.

Wiggins, David. "On Being in the Same Place at the Same Time." *Philosophical Review* 77 (1968): 90–95.

Williams, Bernard. *Ethics and the Limits of Philosophy*. Cambridge, Mass.: Harvard University Press, 1985.

Wittgenstein, Ludwig. *Remarks on Colour*. Berkeley: University of California Press, 1978.

Wollheim, Richard. "Art, Interpretation, and the Creative Process." *New Literary History* 15 (1984): 241–53.

Wright, Crispin. *Realism, Meaning and Truth*. Oxford: Blackwell, 1987.

Zeki, S. "The Construction of Colours by the Cerebral Cortex." *Proceedings of the Royal Institution of Great Britain* 56 (1984): 231–57.

Index

Abrams, M. H., 1, 2
Akenside, Mark, xiv, 31–32; *The Plea-sures of Imagination*, 31–32
Anscombe, G. E. M., 279 n.8
Archive, 6, 9, 12, 15, 22–23, 75, 153, 218–19, 252
Aristotle, 272 n.19, 282 n.9
Atkins, G. Douglas, 241, 283 n.5
Austen, Jane, 203–4; *Emma*, 203; *Pride and Prejudice*, 69, 204
Authors, xii, xiii, xiv, 10, 12, 13, 99, 100–101, 102, 106, 171–72, 182–83, 192–93, 207, 215–16, 227, 228, 240, 248, 251, 263; loss of, xii, 7, 8, 9, 12, 112, 260

Bakhtin, Mikhail, 2, 6, 98–108, 273 nn.14–17, 19, 20
Bakhtinian criticism, xi, 14, 96, 97, 98–108, 116, 250; ideologemes in, 98, 99–101, 102–8
Barnes, Annette, 275 n.12
Barsalou, Lawrence, 183, 185
Bate, Walter Jackson, 1, 2
Battersby, James L., 279 n.10, 280 n.15
Beggar's Opera, The, 52
Beliefs, 22, 28, 29, 43, 44, 90, 96, 98, 119, 120, 122, 123, 124–25, 126, 127, 140, 145, 151, 164–66, 173, 175, 189, 196, 206, 210, 211–13, 220–21, 226, 235, 253, 254; changing, 28, 29, 31–32, 36; unyielding, 23, 24, 80, 218
Benefit of the doubt. *See* Charity
Benham, Harry E., 87, 135, 206
Berra, Yogi, 83
Bloom, Harold, 52, 61–62, 104, 108, 270 n.4

Boër, Steven E., 145, 276 n.7
Booth, Wayne, 2, 52, 58, 267 n.10, 283 nn.6–7
Boruah, Bijoy H., 278 n.5
Boston Red Sox, 111, 188, 243
Boundary conditions, 74–75, 86–88, 90, 93, 95, 104, 204–6, 269 n.8
Boyle, Robert, 226
Brooks, Cleanth, 137, 275 n.13
Bruner, Jerome, 271 n.11, 282 n.5
Burke, Kenneth, 62, 69, 94, 182, 219, 239, 271 n.9, 273 n.13, 279 n.1, 281 n.5, 282 n.8, 283 n.3; "Lexicon Rheto-ricae," 182–83

Cain, William E., 269 n.1
Carnap, Rudolf, 152
Categories, 131, 157, 183–88, 189–90, 194, 195, 253–54; ad hoc, 183–88, 189, 190, 194, 195, 202, 214, 216, 218, 222, 229, 233, 252; always already in place, xii, 4, 7, 8, 9, 10, 14, 81, 109–10; as determinate of objects, 6, 121–22, 131; and fitness, 183, 191, 218; formation of, xiii, 119
Character, 24, 80, 91, 92, 97, 98–99, 101, 105, 106, 107, 108, 229; as ethical ground of behavior, 11, 108, 109, 258–60
Charity, principle of, 31, 134, 136, 142, 157, 176, 211, 218, 226, 246
Chicago Critics, 155–56
Cognitive sameness, 40–46, 60, 129, 132–33, 145–46, 149–50, 175–76; across differences in mental contents, 42–46, 90, 107, 129, 132–33, 145, 175–76

Cohen, Myron, 110
Competence: domain, 201–3; experience, 201–2; linguistic, 201, 203; literary, 203–4
Conceptual schemes, xi, 23–24, 25, 27,
28–30, 31, 32–34, 40–46, 59–60, 90,
129, 133, 134, 136, 156, 179, 182, 188,
197, 206, 212–14, 220, 224, 234, 243,
246, 248, 252; bodily basis of, 197–
201; comparing and judging, 152–56,
205, 215; incommensurability of, xii,
119–31, 153–57; relativity of, 23–24,
212. *See also* Versions; Explanations
Constructionalism, xiii, 2, 265, 267 n.1
Correspondence theory, 7, 12, 13, 25,
27, 71, 149, 185, 206, 247, 253, 254
Crane, R. S., 269 n.6, 277 n.19, 281 nn.
3, 5
Criteria: methodological, 14, 33, 34, 36,
76, 154, 167, 172, 176, 180, 181, 214–
15, 254, 265; shared, 14, 125–26, 127,
128, 129, 130; transcultural, 126, 206;
transparadigmatic, 122–23, 125–26,
130, 161, 179, 206, 211, 215
Culler, Jonathan, 7, 128, 267 n.6, 269
n.1, 272 n.20, 275 n.13
Cultural criticism, xiii, 1, 8–10, 50, 73,
75, 96, 170, 177–78, 179, 184–85, 187,
194, 207, 241

Dante: *The Divine Comedy*, 225
Defeasibility criteria, xii–xiii, 3, 9, 14, 54,
81, 278 n.2
Davidson, Donald, xiii, 43, 173, 180,
213, 278 n.7, 279 n.11, 282 n.5
Deconstruction, xi, xii, 1, 2, 4, 7–8, 11,
12, 14, 16, 21, 22, 33, 34, 58, 60, 71,
85, 91, 96, 98, 104, 113–17, 119, 123,
126, 137, 163, 169, 179, 190–91, 228,
250, 273 n.15, 274 n.26, 275 n.13; and
différance, 58, 112, 114–15, 276 n.9;
and the figural, 8, 12, 96, 116, 117,
229, 250; as mode of reading, 4, 5, 8,
113–14, 169, 240; presence and absence in, 7, 10, 97, 114–15, 117; and
skepticism, 14, 21
De Man, Paul, 96
Dennett, Daniel C., 279 n.8, 282 n.5
Derrida, Jacques, 3, 4, 6, 7–8, 52, 62,
115, 117, 152, 170, 218, 236, 267 n.7,
271 n.14, 274 n.25

De Sousa, Ronald, 278 n.5
De Young, Wayne, 280 n.16
Dickinson, Emily, xiv
Discourse, 1, 4, 21, 34, 71–72, 76, 96, 99,
101, 102, 112, 123, 124, 128, 135, 136,
141, 214, 249; as dialectical, 8–9, 250–
51; historical dimensions of, 8–9;
mind-dependent nature of, 21; privi-
leging of, 9, 10, 189, 252
Donne, John, 262–63
Dostoevsky, Fyodor, 101
Dryden, John, 218
Dummett, Michael, 71, 95, 271 n.16

Eagleton, Terry, 269 n.1
Eclecticism, 14, 21, 25, 57, 58–62, 63, 79,
80–81, 109, 253, 254, 264, 267 n.1,
270 n.1, 275 n.8
Einstein, Albert, 60
Elgin, Catherine Z., 262, 269 n.4, 284
nn.2–3
Eliot, T. S., 45; *Four Quartets*, 52
Emerson, Ralph Waldo, 104
Emotions, 90–92, 107, 108, 130, 150,
171–72, 228, 259, 262, 263; and mental states, 90–94, 98, 107, 117, 188
Empson, William, 278 n.1
Essentialism, xii, 2, 3, 5, 11, 16, 191, 247,
254, 264, 277 n.18
Ethics, 258–60, 264
Explanations, 58, 63, 65, 81–95, 154,
254; higher and lower level, 86–95,
96, 98, 107, 161–62, 205; interesting
and uninteresting, 83, 84–85, 87, 90–
95, 96–97, 106–7, 109, 118, 130, 229;
psychological, 87, 88–94, 97, 98–99,
101, 104, 105–9, 116, 162–63, 216–18,
222–23, 229, 254; reasons for rejection of, 82–83, 84–86, 109; redundant,
83, 109–18; rightness of, relative to interests, 81–87, 91, 92, 94, 97, 109, 207,
216–17. *See also* Versions; Conceptual
schemes

Feldman, Carol Fleischer, 271 n.11
Felman, Shoshana, 62, 270 n.4, 283 n.6
Feminist criticism, 1, 72, 73, 97, 170,
177, 206, 244, 251, 261
Feyerabend, Paul, 120, 274 n.5
Fielding, Henry: *Joseph Andrews*, 155
Fillmore, Charles, xiii, 186, 280 n.7

Fish, Stanley, xii, 9, 52, 64, 120, 125, 126, 140, 154, 170, 172, 218, 267 nn.8–9, 274 nn.4–5, 275 nn. 9, 12, 1, 281 n.2, 282 n.7, 283 n.1

Form, 40–42, 89, 156; indifference of matter, relative to, 40–42, 46, 53, 84–95, 98, 104, 107, 129, 130, 176, 205–6, 268 n.3

Foucauldian criticism, xi, 1, 8–10, 64, 97, 275 n.13

Foucault, Michel, 3, 4, 6, 52, 126, 218

Foundationalism, xii, 2, 4, 5, 6, 7, 11, 12, 13, 15, 121, 153, 189, 191, 228, 247, 252, 254, 260, 264, 267 n.10, 277 n.18

Frege, Gottlob, 133

Freud, Sigmund, 3, 9, 35, 58, 62

Freudian criticism, xi, 5, 59, 61, 74, 80, 97, 104, 112, 272 n.1

Fuctional isomorphism, 42, 89, 129, 268 n.3

Gadamer, Hans-Georg, 47, 58, 64, 71–72, 119, 140, 275 n.13

Garfinkel, Alan, 274 n.2

Genre, 53, 99–100, 131, 239, 258–59, 260–61, 262, 264, 279 n.4

Goldwyn, Samuel, 83

Goodman, Nelson, xiii, 2, 23, 53, 61, 65, 67, 68, 70, 82, 96, 163, 170, 221, 225–26, 227, 267 n.1, 268 nn.2–4, 269 n.4, 270 nn.3, 2–5, 272 nn.2–3, 275 n.7, 276 n.12, 278 n.4, 279 nn. 9, 12, 282 n.5, 283 nn., 10, 12, 284 n.2

Grunbaum, Adolf, 269 n.1

Habitus, 6, 15

Hartman, Geoffrey H., 52, 58

Harvey, William, 226

Hawthorne, Nathaniel, 242; "Young Goodman Brown," 237

Hegelianism, 34, 153

Heilman, Robert, 60

Hermeneutics, xiii, 71–72, 152, 168; hermeneutic circle, 1, 70, 78, 192–93

Hirsch, E. D., 2, 36, 178, 268 n.10, 279 n.10, 283 n.6

Historical criticism, xiii, 1, 8, 48, 54, 79, 106, 152–53, 170, 187, 218, 228, 244, 250, 262, 263, 265

Historicism, 2, 8–9, 16, 34, 54, 73, 79, 100, 101–2, 106, 152–53, 187, 228, 244, 249, 250, 261, 263, 265

History, 9, 48, 51, 72, 100, 101, 111, 112, 178, 184, 206–7, 221, 227, 234, 249; as dialectical, 9

Hobbes, Thomas, 261

Holland, Norman, 104, 240, 250, 283 n.5

Homer, 233

Hopkins, Gerard Manley, 236, 283 n.2

Horace, 218

Humanism, 1, 16, 247, 248, 249, 252, 260

Hume, David, 218, 236, 273 n.18

Ideological criticism, xii, xiii, 1, 8–10, 12, 22, 48, 50, 72, 76, 97, 98–100, 102, 105, 112, 153, 163, 170, 177, 178–79, 181, 194, 206–7, 250, 251–52, 256, 261

Ideology, xiii, xiv, 4, 8–9, 11, 12, 22, 48, 50, 60, 72–73, 78, 85, 98, 99–100, 101, 102, 105, 112, 170, 177, 250, 251–52, 258, 261

Incommensurability, 119–26, 127–31, 149, 153–57, 275 n.12; of conceptual schemes, xii, 12, 15–16, 34, 69, 124–25, 126, 127, 128–30, 134, 152, 156–57; of languages, xii, 124; of theories, xii, 79, 119–24, 130, 149, 153–57

Inference, 163, 167, 171–73, 197; and emotions, 171–72; systems of, 130–31, 154

Intentionality, xiii, xiv, 4, 11–12, 16, 24, 39, 44, 70, 74, 87, 96, 98, 104, 106, 109, 110, 135, 136, 149, 151, 164–66, 173, 174–75, 177, 183, 188–91, 195, 205, 209–10, 214–15, 220–22, 223, 227, 228, 233–34, 243, 244, 246, 248, 255; in relation to beliefs and desires, 151, 164–66, 173, 175, 188–90, 206, 210, 211–12, 220, 235; in relation to interest, 16, 188–89, 191, 209–10, 218, 221–22, 229, 233, 236, 255; and satisfaction conditions, 24, 163, 164, 215, 221

Internal realism, xiii, xv, 2, 246, 254, 265, 267 n.1, 282 n.9

Interpretation, xii, xiii, 4, 8, 11, 13, 14, 24, 25, 31, 41, 43, 47, 49, 57–60, 65, 67, 68, 73, 78, 85, 97, 119, 120, 123,

Interpretation (*cont.*)
125, 127–28, 134–35, 150–52, 153,
161–62, 165–66, 168, 170–73, 181,
191–94, 205, 206–8, 223–29, 234, 236,
238, 240–46, 251, 255–58, 260, 265,
268 n.7; holistic nature of, 150–51,
176, 186–87, 190–91, 193–94, 195–96,
214, 220, 280 n.4; standards of validity
in, xii, 8, 33, 36, 123, 127, 149–50; varieties of, 24, 67, 78, 243; verification
of, xiii, 31, 123
Interpretive communities, 2, 9–10, 14,
15, 34, 54, 64, 72–74, 79, 119, 140,
153, 154, 227, 274 n.2, 275 n.11, 276
n.6
Intersubjectivity, 15, 127, 148, 177–78,
197, 202; across differences in conceptual schemes, 15–16, 148
Intertextuality, 10–12, 48–49, 112, 163,
219, 249, 263

James, Henry, xiv, 241, 242, 283 n.6;
"The Turn of the Screw," 241, 242, 245
Jameson, Fredric, xiv, 8, 9, 267 n.10
Johnson, Mark, xiii, 157, 277 n.20
Johnson, Samuel, xiv, 30–31, 67, 71, 73,
108, 111, 114, 155, 168, 246, 262–63,
271 n.15, 273 n.24; *Preface to Shakespeare,* 155; *Rasselas,* 135; *The Vanity of
Human Wishes,* 30–31, 135, 267 n.10
Johnson-Laird, Philip, 271 n.11
Joyce, James: *Dubliners,* 223–24
Jungian criticism, 61, 80, 272 n.1
Justification, xii, xv, 13, 15, 51, 57, 71,
78, 122, 125, 127, 156, 223, 234, 246,
258; conditions of, 13, 15, 24, 71, 76,
93, 95, 150–51, 152, 161–68, 169–70,
171, 175, 181, 192, 208, 218, 220, 229,
234, 236, 238, 254, 263, 265; systems
of, xiii, 227, 235, 238. *See also* Satisfaction conditions

Kiser, Lisa J., v, 27, 76, 168, 212
Knapp, Steven, 120, 268 n.1, 274 n.3
Knight, G. Wilson, 60
Knowledge, 6, 7, 8, 12, 45, 50, 65, 71,
191, 219; background, 61, 74, 80, 82,
111, 118, 146, 152, 177, 178, 186, 195,
197, 202, 217, 242, 243; objective, 6, 8,
9, 12, 204, 220; in relation to power,
50–51
Kolers, Paul, 67, 70, 270 n.2

Kuhn, Thomas S., 32, 79, 120, 122, 123,
153, 172, 274 n.5, 275 n.12; *The Structure of Scientific Revolutions,* 153

Lacan, Jacques, 9, 58, 62
Lacanian criticism, xi, 9, 154
Lakoff, George, xiii, 157, 183, 186, 187,
197–98, 199, 277 n.20, 279 n.2, 280
nn.6–9, 281 nn. 1, 2, 4, 282 n.5;
Women, Fire and Dangerous Things, 183
Language, xiv, 1, 3, 4, 5, 7, 10–11, 16,
48, 52, 59, 73, 74, 75, 81, 93–95, 96,
97, 102, 107, 112–13, 121, 130, 152,
178, 193, 207, 221, 227, 228, 234, 240,
248, 249–50; and constraints, 76–78;
literary or poetic, 113–14, 136, 137–
40, 150, 250; nature of, *as such,* 4, 8,
13, 114–17, 274 n.6, 277 n.3; rhetorical or tropological dimension of, 4, 8;
as system of differences, 7–8, 74, 114–
17; and translation, xii, 76–77, 96
Leitch, Vincent B., 269 n.1
Lentricchia, Frank, 269 n.1
Lewis, David, 268 n.1, 282 n.5
Literature, 32, 40, 41, 44, 48–49, 50, 53,
59, 82, 91, 98, 101, 104–5, 108–9,
112–13, 120, 134, 136–39, 161, 166,
170–72, 180–81, 199–200, 204, 207,
218–19, 223–29, 240–46, 255, 256–64;
as discourse, 1, 4, 8–9, 112–14, 240,
249–50, 273 n.15. *See also* Texts
Locke, John, 261
Logical positivism. *See* Positivism
Logocentrism, xii, 4, 6–7, 11, 113–14,
115, 116, 117, 137, 152, 179, 249, 250,
271 n.13
Longinus, 263–64
Lyons, Bertha, 89, 213, 265

MacIntyre, Alisdair, 239, 283 n.4
Maps, 25–30, 32, 34, 37–39, 40–41, 46–
53, 131, 173–74; as scheme-dependent, 26, 37–39, 47, 131; social and
cultural biases of, 37–38, 47, 50; as
true versions, 25, 28, 37, 38, 46, 51,
52–54
Marr, David, 169, 183, 213, 277 nn.2–3;
Vision, 162–64, 166
Marxist criticism, xi, xiv, 1, 4, 5, 8–9; 34,
59, 74, 154, 163, 250, 272 n.1; and
historical materiality, 4
Marx, Karl, 3

McCormick, Peter J., 269 n.1
Meaning, xiv, 4, 5, 7, 9, 12–13, 15, 16,
  24, 44–45, 48–49, 51, 70–71, 95, 120,
  132, 134, 137, 138–42, 147–55, 161–
  68, 170–81, 182, 187, 202, 238; assertibility conditions of, 71, 76–78, 95,
  104, 107, 108, 142, 151, 161, 163–66,
  169, 186, 187, 191, 194, 220, 245, 252;
  available possibilities of, 142, 151–52,
  163–64, 168, 169–70, 171, 196, 201,
  214, 221, 251, 254, 259; and conceptual schemes, xii, 7, 13, 14, 15, 24, 27,
  58, 59–61, 67, 69, 96–97, 124–25, 130,
  152, 154, 172, 200; constraints on, 72–
  74, 76–78, 106, 187; context sensitivity
  and interest relativity of, 15, 33, 47–
  49, 57–59, 68–72, 78, 81–82, 83, 87–
  88, 94–96, 99, 102, 105, 108, 121, 131,
  141–42, 147, 152, 165, 174, 186, 191;
  deferral of, xii, 114–15; determinate,
  xi, xii, xiii, 4, 9, 11, 12, 13, 14, 15, 76,
  127, 172, 246, 248, 265; as determined
  by language, xii, 3, 7, 8, 9, 10, 71–72,
  114–15, 133; as determined by use,
  43, 50–51, 71, 77–78, 102, 135, 140,
  141, 143–45, 147, 149, 150–51, 155,
  176, 181; holistic nature of, 150–51,
  167–68, 169, 176–77, 186–87, 189,
  190–91, 193–94, 220; indeterminacy
  of, xii, 12, 74–75, 93, 115, 116, 151,
  153; immanent, xi, 3, 21, 27, 33, 34,
  52, 54, 71–72, 79, 97, 101, 103, 106–7,
  109, 111, 120, 121, 123, 127, 128, 136,
  168, 174, 178–79, 214, 247–48, 260;
  latent and manifest, 12, 86, 177, 178,
  241, 250; in relation to political power,
  8, 9, 10, 15, 50–51, 72, 99; sharing,
  132–33, 134, 141, 142–43, 165, 176,
  195–96; statement, 44–45, 70, 71, 141,
  142, 150, 161; and supplementation,
  xii, 8; utterance, 44–45, 70, 141, 150,
  161. *See also* Reference
Michaels, Walter Benn, 120, 268 n.1, 274
  n.3
Miller, J. Hillis, 4, 5, 14, 267 nn. 2, 5
Milton, John: *Paradise Lost*, 112, 210,
  227, 256
Monism, 3, 14–15, 21, 25, 34, 57, 61,
  80–81, 119, 122–23, 170, 187, 228,
  254, 264, 267 n.1, 269 n.8, 272 n.1,
  282 n.7
Mozart, Wolfgang A.: *Don Giovanni*, 227

New Criticism, 2, 59, 85, 96, 97, 98, 112,
  113–14, 115, 116, 117, 128, 132, 136–
  37, 155, 156, 228, 241, 250, 273 nn.
  15, 18, 275 n.13; as formalists, 155–56
New Historicism, xi, xii, xiv, 1, 5, 6, 8–
  13, 14, 16, 34, 49, 54, 75, 79, 97, 101–
  2, 106, 112, 119, 153, 178, 187, 250,
  262
Newton, Sir Isaac, 60, 226
Nietzsche, Friedrich, 62
Norris, Christopher, 269 n.1

Objectivity, xii, 2, 8, 9, 12, 24, 54, 121,
  170, 172, 191, 204, 233, 248, 253, 254,
  264, 282 n.9; and value judgments, xii,
  214, 221, 222
Oedipus Rex, 75
Olson, Elder, 269 n.6, 271 n.11, 277
  n.19, 278 n.7, 280 n.15, 281 nn. 3, 5–6
Other, the, xii, 9, 12, 115, 234, 250–51

Palmer, F. R., 270 n.7
Paradigm shift, 32, 79, 120, 122–23, 128,
  133
Paradox: kinds of, relative to shared understanding, 120–24, 125–26, 127,
  128–30; and paradoxicals, 121, 123–
  26, 127, 128–30, 140–41, 144, 149,
  150, 153, 172, 205, 282 n.3
Perception (visual): apparent motion in,
  65–68, 78, 161; mistakes in, 64–68
Phelan, James, 279 n.10
Philosophy, 236; Anglo-American, xii,
  xiii, 14, 16, 43, 236; Continental, xii,
  8–9, 71; of mind, xiii, 43
Plot, 11, 60, 91, 92, 97, 98–99, 101, 105,
  106, 107, 108, 153, 199, 229; as system
  of morally determinate actions, 11
Pluralism, xii–xiii, xv, 2, 3, 6, 13–15, 16–
  17, 21–24, 30, 32, 40, 42, 48, 49, 51–
  54, 57–60, 61, 63, 72–73, 74, 76, 79,
  80, 81, 83, 84, 92, 97, 101, 103, 104,
  106, 109, 119, 123–24, 126, 151, 154,
  169, 172, 218, 220, 225, 227–28, 254–
  55, 265, 267 nn. 1, 11, 269 n.8; philosophical, 2, 3, 14, 21, 213, 265, 275
  n.8; and relativism, xii, 14, 54, 79,
  254–55
Poetics, 260–61, 262
Polanyi, Michael, 74, 75, 130, 272 n.17,
  275 n.15
Political unconscious, 4, 6, 9, 10, 75, 152

Pope, Alexander: *Essay on Man*, 225,
227, 256, 257
Priestley, Joseph, 226
Positivism, 2, 3, 5, 10, 23, 34, 84, 137,
153, 187, 248
Poststructuralism, xi–xv, 1–14, 34, 49,
96–97, 112–17, 119, 136, 152–54, 163,
170, 177, 178–79, 184–85, 187, 206,
228, 235, 241, 244, 247, 248–53; and
the *always already*, 4, 7, 8, 109–10, 113,
114, 117–18, 187, 192, 194, 220, 256,
269 n.8, 276 n.9; binary oppositions
in, 5, 9, 96–97, 115, 116, 170, 179,
241, 250–51
Practical reasoning, 16, 76, 194–95, 209–
10, 216, 220, 223–25, 236, 240; moral
nature of, 108–9; problematic method
within, 223–25, 229; as relevant to
making and understanding, 16
Practices, xv, 8, 68, 71, 128–29, 173, 185,
196, 214, 218, 239; as determined by
history or culture, 4, 8–10; discursive,
4, 10, 103, 149; learning, xiv, 4, 71,
238
Pragmatism, xiii, 16–17, 97, 106, 220,
265; and pluralism, xiii, 220
Projectible properties, xiv, 61, 65, 70, 80,
164, 262; ad fittingness, 164
Pruim, Julie, 23, 117, 213
Psychoanalytic criticism, 14, 97, 112,
154, 177, 178, 181, 187, 228, 240, 250,
261
Putnam, Hilary, xiii, xv, 2, 54, 74, 78, 84,
87–88, 89, 90–92, 110, 133, 134, 144,
145, 151, 153, 173, 180, 188, 191–92,
213, 254, 267 n.1, 268 nn. 2, 9, 2, 269
nn.4–5, 270 n.2, 271 n.16, 272 nn. 18,
21, 4, 6–7, 9, 273 n.11, 274 n.2, 275
n.14, 276 nn. 2–3, 7, 277 nn. 15, 17,
21, 278 n.7, 279 n.11, 280 nn. 10, 14,
281 nn.6, 1–2, 282 nn. 5–6, 9

Quine, W. V., 43, 236

Rader, Ralph, 277 n.14, 278 n.4
Ray, William, 269 n.1
Readers, 7, 10–11, 29, 49–52, 64, 66–67,
102, 108, 124, 127, 154, 182–83, 192–
95, 215–16, 227; as determiners of
meaning, 9–12, 49, 126, 170, 172,

173–74, 176; interests of, 49–52; loss
of, 7, 8. *See also* Reading
Reading, 66–67, 96–97, 162–68, 169–73,
192–95, 206–8, 223, 240–41; and misreading, 8, 27, 64–65. *See also* Readers
Realism: naive, xii, 2, 5, 13, 16, 189, 228,
247, 254, 268 n.8. *See also* Internal realism
Reality, xi, 22, 25, 81, 97, 100, 103, 123,
212–13, 254; objective knowledge of,
3, 71, 212, 254; in relation to discourse, xi, xii, 7, 8, 13, 21; in relation
to mind, xi, xii, 7, 8, 13, 27, 136, 151
Reason, 206, 211; bodily bases, in forms
of, 197–201, 240; immanent, 34, 54,
57; transcendent, 34
Recursion, 69–70, 78, 163, 270 n.8
Reference, xiii, xiv, 5, 7, 11–13, 15, 21,
24, 25–26, 31, 32, 48–49, 51, 67, 70–
74, 77, 95, 104, 107, 120, 132–50, 152,
154–55, 161–66, 172, 180, 187, 197,
200, 202, 210; context sensitivity and
interest relativity of, 15, 25, 33, 46–48,
57, 59, 68–69, 70–73, 78, 81–82, 83,
87–88, 93, 94, 95–96, 99, 102, 104,
108, 117–18, 121, 131, 141–42, 147,
152, 174, 186, 191, 253; as determined
by conceptual scheme, 3, 13, 14, 15,
25, 26, 27, 32–33, 39, 42, 43, 47–48,
57, 59–61, 96–97, 123, 124–25, 141–
42, 172; fixing of, by experts, 94, 133–
35, 140, 143–45, 147, 200–201;
grounding of, 12, 13, 25, 26, 31, 34,
94, 104, 116, 119, 133–34; instability,
12; nonce, 147, 148, 149; ordinary, 11,
12, 25, 26, 34, 143–46, 152, 164, 169,
172, 196, 203, 217–18, 223, 226; sharing, 43–44, 60, 76–77, 126, 127, 128–
31, 132–33, 135, 136–37, 141–43,
145–46, 154, 165, 172, 176, 181, 195–
96, 197, 246; stability of, across conceptual differences, xii, xiii, 12–13, 14,
15, 63–64, 132–37, 139, 140–47, 149,
154, 155, 172, 200, 207–8, 215, 226–
27; stipulated, 25, 68, 71, 74, 104, 140,
143–44, 146, 148, 149, 270 n.6. *See
also* Meaning
Regulative ideal. *See* Methodological criteria
Relativism, xii, 3, 6, 14, 21, 23, 24, 34,
54, 58, 79, 81, 119, 120, 122–23, 153,

165, 169, 170, 172, 228, 253, 264, 265, 274 n.2, 282 n.7; in its total or "anything goes" form, 6, 14, 21, 23, 34, 36, 57, 109, 126, 212, 254, 267 n.1, 275 n.8

Representation, 25, 28, 37, 39, 40–41, 46, 197, 199–200, 268 n.7; mental, xiii, 46

Retrospective Construction, 68–70, 74, 77–78, 108, 142, 163–64, 270 n.6

Reynolds, Sir Joshua, 218

Rhetoric, xiii, 12; as a mode of reading, 4, 8, 116. *See also* Rhetorical criticism

Rhetorical criticism, 4, 228, 261, 273 n.15

Rhode Island, xiv, 25, 34, 38, 40, 46–47, 53, 59, 88, 110, 156, 173–74, 175, 181, 212, 273 n.23

Rorty, Richard, 52, 281 n.2

Rosenfield, Israel, 161–62, 277 n.1

Russell, Bertrand, 132–33

Salmon, Wesley C., 269 n.1

Satisfaction conditions, 24, 27, 189, 190, 194, 205, 211, 215, 235, 238; internal, 238–39. *See also* Justification

Saussure, Ferdinand de, 4

Scheffler, Israel, xiii, 121, 146, 274 n.6, 276 n.10

Scholes, Robert, 267 n.3

Scientific method, 23, 54, 74, 137, 153, 249; testability and meaningfulness in, 23

Scott, Sir Walter: *Ivanhoe*, 135; *Waverley*, 132–33, 135

Searle, John, 189, 272 n.8, 273 n.12, 275 n.14, 279 n.8, 280 nn.11–13

Selden, Raman, 269 n.1

Set theory, 10

Shakespeare, William, xiv, 23, 28, 30, 34, 44, 60, 112, 170, 203–4; *Hamlet*, 24, 35, 41, 52, 59, 60, 61, 81–82, 112, 123, 131, 143, 154, 195; *King Lear*, 30, 44–45, 75, 88, 97–98, 224, 225, 227, 256, 284 n.1; *Measure for Measure*, 34–35, 237, 245; *Othello*, 23, 27, 35–36, 41, 75, 88, 108, 204, 222, 229, 256, 257, 284 n.1; "Sonnet 55," 165; "Sonnet 73," 257

Signifier (and signified), xii, 4, 7, 14, 116, 206–7, 236

Signs, xiii, 4, 6, 7, 10, 206–7, 248; and codes, 4; as differential systems, 4, 8, 10, 248; and traces and supplements, 4, 8, 206–7

Skepticism, 14–15, 21, 25, 57, 59, 228, 236, 253, 254, 264, 267 n.1, 282 n.7

Smith, Barbara Herrnstein, xii, 279 n.3, 282 n.7

Solipsism, 120, 122–23; methodological, 23, 123, 126, 274 n.2, 275 n.10

Space-times. *See* Versions

Stereotypes, 143–46, 148, 155, 164, 196, 200–202, 243, 245. *See also* Reference

Structuralism, 1, 2, 4, 5, 7, 10, 183, 248

Subjectivity, 9, 15, 214, 221, 222, 282 n.9

Sutton, Willie, 83–84

Swift, Jonathan, 32, 240, 242; *A Modest Proposal*, 32, 237–38

Synonymy, 40–41, 43, 60, 76–77, 131, 133, 135–36, 137–40, 141–43, 146, 147, 149

Texts, 13–14, 92–93, 120, 161, 170–72, 181, 182–83, 206, 214, 215–16, 223, 226–29, 258–60; as already existing versions, 24, 25, 33, 46, 82–83, 173, 174–75, 180, 218, 222, 233, 255; as intentional objects, 172–75, 190–91, 218, 221, 222, 228; interests of, 13–14, 15, 76, 190–92, 218, 222, 226, 228, 233, 236, 238, 255, 258; internal satisfactions of, 13–14, 238–39, 240, 242–43; mistakes or flaws in, 233–38, 240, 242–46. *See also* Literature

Textuality, 6, 7, 8, 10–12

Transcendental signified, xii, xiii, 3, 11, 12, 13, 211, 253, 265; and the objective order of things, 3

Translation, xii, 41, 63, 76–77, 96, 97, 142, 146, 150–51, 176, 178, 191–92, 202, 233, 275 n.12; and intertranslatability, 41, 76–77, 79, 125, 146, 149, 191–92

Tristram Shandy, 52

Truth, xii, 6, 15, 33, 43, 52, 53, 54, 57–58, 59, 60, 71, 82, 83, 116, 121, 165, 211–12, 235, 246, 249, 254; correspondence theory of, 7, 25, 27, 71, 149, 185, 206, 247, 253; interest relativity of, 23–24, 25, 43, 57, 68–69, 81–

Truth (*cont.*)
82; relative to description, 15, 24, 25, 43; and value, 167–68

Value: default, 143, 202, 203, 204, 215, 216; as determined by conceptual scheme, 3, 32–34; and fact, 167–68, 210, 214–18, 220–22; objective judgment of, xii, xiii, 14, 220, 221, 222; standards of, xii, 33–34, 210, 214–18, 221, 248, 254, 265
Versions, 22–26, 30, 33–34, 36, 39, 46, 52, 58, 63, 66, 80–82, 174–75, 177–80, 189, 211–12, 225, 253–54, 264; adjudication of, 9, 14, 16, 36, 53, 58, 79, 119, 152–53, 215; comparing, 65, 76–77, 79, 109, 119–26, 130–31, 133, 152–57, 205; competing (rival), 16, 36, 41–42, 53, 61, 62, 63, 82, 103, 120–22, 153–57; fitness within, 30–31, 80, 209, 214, 218, 221, 225, 238, 256, 265; plurality of, 13, 36, 52–53, 60, 63, 67, 79, 102, 235; rejection of, 30–32, 36, 53, 58, 79, 80, 83, 109; right and true, 22, 23–24, 25–26, 32, 33, 37, 46, 47–48, 52–54, 65, 76, 79, 81, 82–83, 84, 95, 185, 216–17, 253, 265; self-refuting and incoherent, 23, 25, 30, 33, 53, 63, 79, 80, 124, 129, 206, 235, 262, 265. *See also* Explanations; Conceptual schemes
Vico, Giambattista, 58

Wilson, Edmund, 242, 283 n.7
Wittgenstein, Ludwig, 42
Wordsworth, William, xiv, 112, 225, 241, 262–63, 283 n.6; "Immortality Ode," 225; *The Prelude*, 256; "A Slumber Did My Spirit Seal," 241–43, 245
World-views. *See* Versions

Yeats, W. B., 52, 71

This book was set in Baskerville and Eras typefaces. Baskerville was designed by John Baskerville at his private press in Birmingham, England, in the eighteenth century. The first typeface to depart from oldstyle typeface design, Baskerville has more variation between thick and thin strokes. In an effort to insure that the thick and thin strokes of his typeface reproduced well on paper, John Baskerville developed the first wove paper, the surface of which was much smoother than the laid paper of the time. The development of wove paper was partly responsible for the introduction of typefaces classified as modern, which have even more contrast between thick and thin strokes.

Eras was designed in 1969 by Studio Hollenstein in Paris for the Wagner Typefoundry. A contemporary script-like version of a sans-serif typeface, the letters of Eras have a monotone stroke and are slightly inclined.

Printed on acid-free paper.